CONCEPTS IN SPECIAL EDUCATION

CONCEPTS
IN SPECIAL EDUCATION

Selected Writings
Volume 1

WILLIAM M. CRUICKSHANK

SYRACUSE UNIVERSITY PRESS
1981

Library of Congress Cataloging in Publication Data

Cruickshank, William M
  Concepts in special education.

  Includes bibliographies.
  1. Handicapped children—Education. I. Title.
LC4019.C69   371.9   80-29024
ISBN 0-8156-2238-4

FOREWORD

*I*N THE FIELD OF SPECIAL EDUCATION there are few scholars — people who have thought carefully about the myriad of medical, psychological, social, organizational, and political issues involved in providing appropriate educational services for handicapped children and who have made important, substantial contributions to knowledge in the area.

Historically, few have both commanded respect for the profession and provided leadership of lasting quality in special education. Relatively few individuals have been held in sufficient esteem by their professional colleagues to significantly influence both theory and practice.

Smaller still is the number who have been both scholars and leaders. One of the strongest members of this small cadre of elite special educators is William M. Cruickshank.

In a career spanning four decades, Dr. Cruickshank's scholarly work has been characterized by both breadth and depth. His research on exceptional populations has included children with mental retardation, cerebral palsy, epilepsy, and other forms of brain injury. His research has focused on the learning characteristics of these children as well as on curriculum and organizational arrangements.

Dr. Cruickshank's orientation to the needs of exceptional populations has been interdisciplinary since the beginning of his career. As much as any other individual, Dr. Cruickshank has directly addressed the many complex issues involved in interdisciplinary evaluation, planning, and programming. He has made particularly strong contributions in providing conceptual and substantive bridges between the philosophies, knowledge domains, and technologies of medicine, psychology, and education.

In recognizing the strength and quality of his commitment to scholarship, it is important to realize that much of his research on the learning characteristics of children now called learning disabled was conducted and reported in the professional literature before the Bureau of Education for the Handicapped was established in the United States Office of Education. There were very few training programs in special education, and fewer universities with research commitments in this area. Dr. Cruickshank was busy at work on the difficult research problems in special education before federal funds made this an interesting and inviting area for universities.

In the history of special education, there have been many shifts in emphasis ranging from definitions and labels to the preferred service arrangements for children. Dr. Cruickshank never traveled on popular bandwagons just because they were popular. It is not surprising, therefore, that at times his positions on various issues have been considered too liberal while at other times too conservative, as they have been by some of his colleagues who wished to turn history sharply to the left or to the right.

As a leader, Dr. Cruickshank has provided outstanding service in two major universities, developing one of the first special education training programs in the country at Syracuse University and directing one of the most complex interdisciplinary research and training centers with a focus on developmental disabilities at the University of Michigan. As an indication of the very high regard his colleagues have for him, he has been granted many awards for scholarship and distinguished service by national and private organizations in the United States, Japan, India, Peru, Canada, and the Netherlands, to mention a few. His books have been translated into many foreign languages.

At the international level he has been a consultant to governments and universities in different parts of the world regarding the needs of handicapped children and the development of appropriate services. Most recently he organized and developed the International Academy for Research in Learning Disabilities. He is president of the Academy, whose members now represent more than thirty countries.

Special education did not spring forth out of an explosion of new knowledge about the handicapped. It was not developed because a majority of professional educators recognized that many children were left out of schools, as they were, and approaches to include them had to be developed. Many social, economic, and political forces interacted in complex ways in the development of special services for handicapped children. The nature of these forces and their interactions is an interesting topic debated in college and university classrooms where professional special educators are being trained. However one views the history of the field, the social and economic factors involved in the politics of the coming of age of special education, there is an undeniable common thread. That thread is the caring and commitment of individuals who provided leadership. Most of those who were aware that many children were being left out of educational programs and cared enough to make a personal commitment to do something about it were parents. It was a personal and a moral cause for which they worked. There were very few professionals who joined the ranks of parents and other advocates early in their fight. Fewer still were those who were well-trained, guided by the scholarly tradition, and whose work was governed by a deep personal dissatisfaction with the wrongness of things as they were and a commitment to lead battles for change. William M. Cruickshank was one of the few who provided, and continues to provide, such leadership. Those who know his work best are the children with whom he has worked and their parents. While his scholarly contributions are acknowledged and valued internationally, those who appreciate him most are those who have had the opportunity to observe and learn about this personal commitment and quality of his life and work, his students.

In the papers selected for inclusion in this book the reader will find clear, rational, strongly argued positions; here, too, the reader can review and evaluate important knowledge in special education with the historical perspective provided by the range of topics addressed. William M. Cruickshank's concern for the quality of the lives of our children is obvious in these papers. That concern for his fellow human beings has encouraged hundreds of students, colleagues, and friends — from every walk of life — to build a better world.

Chapel Hill, North Carolina   JAMES L. PAUL, ED.D., Professor
Fall 1980   *School of Education*
                                    Division of Special Education
                                    University of North Carolina

CONTENTS

PART III: **PIONEER STUDIES IN THE FIELD OF LEARNING DISABILITIES**

PREFACE

*I*T IS NOT OFTEN that one has the opportunity during one's lifetime to participate in the publication of one's own selected papers which previously have appeared in journals or as speeches. That this is possible here, partially through the generosity of an anonymous gift, is truly appreciated. Two volumes are planned, the differing natures of which need some explanation.

Volume 1 consists of papers published primarily prior to 1965. Although marked by an early date, these papers have a startling relevancy at the date of this publication, particularly as they relate to current attempts at normalization of education of handicapped children in regular grades of both public and private schools.

Three things need to be pointed out with respect to the papers included in this volume. First, they are selected from a larger number of articles which appeared in journals prior to 1965. In my opinion they represent the best of my writing until that time. Obviously they do not include materials from books which began to appear under my authorship or editorship about a decade earlier.

Second, there is a variety among the selected papers which would probably not characterize the writings of young professionals beginning their careers in the present decade. When I began my professional career in 1937, there were few psychologists or educators specializing in the area of exceptional children. Those who were of necessity had to be concerned with the total field of exceptionality. Hence, my writings prior to 1965 dealt with mental retardation, cerebral palsy, the blind, those with hearing impairments, the physically disabled, epilepsy, and other forms of exceptionality. All are not included here by any means. However, the nature of the professional field in the period of 1935–65 is illustrated by the scope of the subject matter included here.

Finally, many of the articles have co-authors. I stress this because criticism is often leveled at authors who fail to stand on their own as writers of published materials. I do not accept this criticism. It has always been my philosophy and will remain such that university professors who have obtained a reputation in their respective fields have an obligation to share that status and to join with their students in the publication of professional materials. Thus, this action provides the student with an *entry* into the profession, begins his bibliography which is so important if one is to remain in academic life, and in this manner motivates the student to further writing on his own or subsequently with *his* students. I have always done this, and I intend to continue to do so. However, whatever the topic, the idea in each article is mine and the writing is usually much more than 50 percent mine. Often, jointly published articles could have seen print as written solo by me. The joint activity, however, has not only brought me personal satisfaction over the years, but it has solidified deep friendships between me and many of my most capable students. The rewards of teaching are expressed in these jointly prepared articles. Many of the articles selected for this collection will be written by Cruickshank and _____, a fact which brings me satisfaction and which without question was a factor in launching many careers of splendid individuals who at the time were "young." I make no apologies for joint authorship when the motivation is correct and when each author completes at least 51 percent of the work!

This book was made possible by the partial subsidy of an anonymous individual. To this person or persons there is no adequate manner in which to express my thanks. To the journals which hold copyrights of the articles and which have graciously permitted their reprinting here, I also express my deep appreciation.

I do not look upon these volumes as a swan song. I appreciate the generosity of someone who, along with Syracuse University Press, has made them possible. I hope that the appearance of these books will stimulate me to further writing and to further professional contributions in the months and years ahead.

Ann Arbor, Michigan　　　　　　WILLIAM M. CRUICKSHANK, PH.D.
Fall 1980

PART I

MENTAL RETARDATION—
A BASIS FOR MAINSTREAMING

SINCE THE ARTICLES IN THIS SECTION were written before the emphasis on mainstreaming and normalization of instruction was *au currant,* they are included here, because one and all they illustrate at least some of the bases on which decisions regarding mainstreaming must be made. There are differences of unique natures between mentally retarded and intellectually normal children and youth. These studies for the most part were completed with the cooperation of educable mentally retarded boys who were carefully matched with intellectually normal boys on the basis of mental age. This, of course, meant that chronological ages and intelligence quotients varied among the youths in the two groups.

However, unless the mentally retarded pupil has some basis of achieving success on a regular basis, integration of him or her into the regular grade may be one of the worst possible education decisions. There must be a way in which success experiences can be achieved. To accomplish this, the child may be disjointed in other comparisons; that is, if he is equal to the normal children on the basis of mental age, he will be unequal to them on the basis of chronological age and intelligence. However, it would appear that mental age is the best of the three variables on which to consider placement, for if this is done, the mentally retarded youth often has skills which are *in excess* of the intellectually normal child. The first five articles in this section illustrate this on numerous occasions. Obviously, if this is the basis of normalization, issues of mental health must be considered paramount in terms of chronological age, for significant differences will obtain between the retarded and the normal youths. Under the best conditions of integration, however, there will be significant differences on some variables. It appears that the concern for comparability on the basis of mental ages, however, is the most vital in insuring a success experience for the retarded pupil.

2

ARITHMETIC ABILITY OF
MENTALLY RETARDED CHILDREN

I. Ability to Differentiate
Extraneous Materials from Needed Arithmetical Facts

INTRODUCTION

*A*N INVESTIGATION was undertaken to examine the assertion that mentally retarded children of a given mental age are not as successful in arithmetic as are normal children of a similar mental age because the former are not able to select the specific arithmetic elements needed in the solution of the problems. To this end a test, consisting of eight sets of three problems each, was designed to determine whether or not a difference existed in the ability of mentally retarded and normal groups of carefully selected subjects to choose from statements of problems containing various extraneous elements the needed arithmetical facts pertinent to the correct solution of a problem.

Subjects

Two groups of fifteen boys each were tested: one, a group of mentally retarded boys comprising the experimental group with a mean C.A. of 14.29 years, a mean M.A. of 10.06 and a mean I.Q. of 73.33; the other, a group of boys making up the control group who had a mean C.A. of 9.09 years, a mean M.A. of 9.96 years and a mean I.Q. of 110.4. The mean arithmetic age of the experimental group was 9.73 years; of the control group, 9.84 years. The T-score between the mean mental age and the mean arithmetic age of the experimental group is 1.169 at a 5 percent level of significance; for the control group, 1.265 at a 30 percent level of significance. Basic differences do not exist between mental age and arithmetic age. Similarly,

Reprinted from *Journal of Educational Research* (November 1948): 161-70, by permission.

significant differences are not established between the mental ages of the experimental and control groups (T-score 1.195 at 10 percent level of significance) or between the arithmetic ages of the two groups of subjects (T-score 1.120 at 30 percent level of significance). The experimental subjects were pupils at the Wayne County Training School, Northville, Michigan; the control subjects were pupils of the Adams Elementary School, Birmingham, Michigan. Subjects of both groups had arithmetic ability comparable to third grade children as measured by the results of the Stanford Achievement Tests, Form Z, Primary and Advanced. The study was a part of a larger investigation undertaken to investigate other aspects of the same problem.[3]

Sample problems

In order to determine that it was the inability to select the specific arithmetic elements which contributed to faulty problem solution, eight sets of arithmetic problems were developed which would clearly focus attention on this ability. Each set consisted of three problems, *a, b* and *c; problem a* was presented in a form containing a great amount of superfluous material; *problem b* contained only the verbal matter specific to the problem with no extraneous or superfluous material; *problem c* consisted merely of the problem set up in the form of a computation. An example of one of the eight sets of problems is given as follows:

Problem a. A little boy by the name of Billy bought a kite for 8¢. It was a bright red kite and had a long string attached to it. There were many other colored kites in the store, too, but Billy liked the red one the most. Some were 5¢, some were 15¢. The green ones were 20¢, and some white ones with funny faces on them were 25¢. What would three kites like Billy's — one yellow, one pink, and one orange — cost?
Problem b. If one kite costs 8¢, how much will 3 kites cost?
Problem c.   8
                        $\times 3$

Administration of the test

Each of the problems was typed on a large card and presented to the subjects individually. The eight exercises constituting series *a* were administered at one period; forty-eight hours later, the eight exercises in series *b* were given. After another forty-eight hour period, the eight exercises of series *c* were presented to the subjects. The examiner read the problems orally while the subject read silently from the card placed in front of him. One careful, distinct reading was allowed on the part of the examiner, although the subject could re-read the problem as often as he desired.

RESULTS

Comparison of responses of experimental and control groups

Table 1 gives a comparison between the responses of the experimental and those of the control groups in the ability to isolate needed factual material in working arithmetic problems. It is seen that the mentally retarded subjects are inferior to the normal subjects in each series of the presentation. In problem series *a* there is a better than 1 percent level of significance between the results of the two groups, the experimental group having a mean score of correct responses of 3.533 (S. D. 1.499); the control group, 6.800 (S. D. 1.469). Likewise it can be seen from Table 1 that there is a significant difference between the responses of the experimental and control groups on problem series *b*, the T-score between the two means of 6.500 (S. D. 1.655) for the experimental group and 7.266 (S. D. 0.928) for the control group being 4.183, giving a better than 1 percent level of significance.

The difference between the responses of the groups to series *c*, although significant, is not great. Here a 5 percent level of significance is derived from a T-score of 2.219. The great similarity in problem series *c* is to be expected, for elsewhere it will be reported (5) that in problems presented in concrete form there was little significance in the difference of the responses of the two groups. The form of the exercises used in problem series *c* is concrete and thus consistent performance is seen.

Other striking differences between the responses of the experimental and control groups are apparent in Tables 1, 2, and 3. The difference between the mean scores for correctly solved problems in series *a* and *b* for the experimental group is 2.967 points which is significant; for the control group 0.466 points which is *not* significant. The difference in the responses to problem series *a* containing much extraneous material, and series *b*, containing verbal material but no extraneous items, is six times as great for the experimental group as for the control group. The difference between the mean scores of problem series *a* and *c* for the experimental group is 3.600 points for the control group, 1.066 points. Both of these are significant at the 1 percent level, although the difference of the experimental group is more than

TABLE 1

COMPARISON OF THE MEAN NUMBER OF CORRECT RESPONSES IN PROBLEMS SERIES
A, B, AND C OF THE EXPERIMENTAL GROUP WITH THOSE OF THE CONTROL GROUP
AND RESULTING T-SCORES IN TEST OF ABILITY TO DIFFERENTIATE
EXTRANEOUS MATERIALS FROM NEEDED FACTS

Problem Series	Experimental Group		Control Group			Percent Showing Level of Significance of t
	Mean	Standard Deviation	Mean	Standard Deviation	T-Score	
a	3.533	1.499	6.800	1.469	6.274	1
b	6.500	1.665	7.266	.928	4.183	1
c	7.133	1.359	7.866	.339	2.219	5

three times as great as that for the control group. It is apparent from these findings that the presence of extraneous materials does make a real difference in the responses of the two groups of subjects and is responsible for a much greater difference in the responses of the subjects of the experimental group than for those of the subjects of the control group.

The difference in form of the problems between series *b* and *c* is not as great as between series *a* and *b*. In the light of findings already presented, large differences in the responses of the two groups of subjects should not be expected for series *b* and *c*. The difference in mean scores of problem series *b* and *c* for the experimental group is 0.633; for the control group, 0.600. Tables II and III show that these differences are not significant, but the finding is in harmony with statements concerning the solution of problems in concrete form.

Responses of the experimental group

Table 2 shows the results of the experimental group on the test of ability to differentiate extraneous materials from facts needed in the solution of a problem. There is a significant difference between the responses to series *a* and those of series *b*. The mean of the former is 3.533; for the latter, 6.500. The resulting T-score of 5.771 gives better than a 1 percent level of significance. With the experimental group the difference between the means for series *a* and *c* is much greater than that between series *a* and *b* or that between series *b* and *c*. Table 2 shows that the mean score for series *c* is 7.133 as compared to 3.533 for series *a*. The extraordinarily large T-score of 11.506 has far greater than 1 percent level of significance. A 5 percent level of signif-

TABLE 2

COMPARISON OF THE MEAN SCORES FOR PROBLEM SERIES A, B AND C OF THE
EXTRANEOUS MATERIALS TEST AND THE RESULTING T-SCORES
FOR THE EXPERIMENTAL GROUP

Problem Series	Mean Number Correct Responses	Standard Deviation	T-Score	Percent Showing Level of Significance of t
a.....................	3.533	1.499	5.771	1
b	6.500	1.665		
b	6.500	1.665	2.276	5
c.....................	7.133	1.359		
a.....................	3.533	1.499	11.506	1
c.....................	7.133	1.359		

icance, considered as a tendency towards significance, is derived from the means of series *b* and *c*.

Responses of the control group

The results for the control group are quite different from those for the experimental group in the ability to differentiate extraneous materials. Table 3 shows that there is *no* significant difference in the responses of the control group to problems of series *a* and *b*. The mean correct response score for series *a* is 6.800; for series *b*, 7.266. The T-score of 1.704 gives a 10 percent level of significance. The level is not significant. The difference between the means for series *a* and *c* is significant; the mean correct response score for the former being 6.800 and for the latter 7.866. The T-score of 3.191 for this difference represents a 1 percent level of significance.

Clinical differences

It is apparent from statistical analysis that the presence of extraneous materials in a problem situation causes confusion to both normal and mentally retarded boys, but the amount is much greater to the latter group. Analysis of the performance of individual records gives further evidence of the nature of this difference.

The subjects of both groups were permitted to use pencil and paper

TABLE 3

COMPARISON OF THE MEAN SCORES FOR PROBLEM SERIES A, B AND C OF THE
EXTRANEOUS MATERIALS TEST AND THE RESULTING T-SCORES
FOR THE CONTROL GROUP

Problem Series	Mean Number Correct Responses	Standard Deviation	T-Score	Percent Showing Level of Significance of t
a......................	6.800	1.469	1.704	10
b	7.266	.928		
b	7.266	.928	2.197	5
c......................	7.866	.339		
a......................	6.800	1.469	3.191	1
c......................	7.866	.339		

in the solution of the problems if they desired. A total of 120 problems in each series was worked by the fifteen boys of each group. In series *a*, which contained the greatest amount of extraneous material, the experimental subjects use pencil and paper in 58 or 46.4 percent of the problems; the control group subjects, in 98 or 79.4 percent of the problems. The boys who use pencil and paper undoubtedly aid themselves in attaining greater accuracy and provide themselves an opportunity to check with the written problem to insure that they have used the correct elements. All of the boys of the control group make some use of pencil and paper, whereas three boys in the experimental group make no use of it at all.

Problem *a* in the sixth group reads as follows:

> There were 18 boys in Robert's Boy Scout troop. Each boy was to repair four Wooden dogs and animals of all sorts, scooters, bikes, wagons, whistles, kites, and many other kinds of toys. Some had to be painted, others had to be nailed. How many toys did the Boy Scouts have to fix?

Thirteen of the experimental subjects failed to solve this problem correctly. Five of the subjects solved the problem by merely counting the toys listed. One subject remarked, "This is a very long one, isn't it? It's kind of hard." Another mentally retarded boy, after three readings, said, "I can't do it." Still another counted seven toys and then subtracted this figure (7) from 18. Three others showed evidence of embarrassment in not being able to solve the problems and each finally indicated that "You can't work that one." Another boy isolated the correct elements to be multiplied, but made errors in multiplication. In the control group only three boys failed to get the correct answer to this problem; these three isolated the correct elements but made mistakes in computation. Extraneous material had no effect on their performance.

Problem *a* in group 1 is quoted in the initial paragraphs of this article. Eight experimental subjects worked this problem incorrectly; five added every figure in the problem, one made an outright guess, two multiplied incorrectly. One member of the control group failed on this problem by making a mistake in multiplication.

Seven of the experimental group subjects resorted to guessing in the problems of series *a* when they realized that they could not solve the problems and knew that an answer was expected. This tendency to give an answer without recognition of its correctness, because the mentally retarded child believes the social situation demands one, has been commented on previously[4] and is found to be typical of the behavior of the mentally retarded subjects. No guessing was observed among the normal boys.

Problem *a* in group 4 reads:

> Donald's father gave Donald 45¢. Donald goes to the red brick school on the corner. There are 33 children in his room — 10 girls and 23 boys. He is in the fourth grade and wants to be a policeman when he grows up. His father told him to give his brother, Harry, 8¢. He did this and also bought a bar of candy that afternoon. How much money did he have left after he gave the money to Harry?

None of the experimental group were able to solve this problem correctly. Two subjects, after two readings, hurriedly added all the figures mentioned in the problem and quoted answers of "100" and "125" respectively. One boy said, "He wouldn't have any money left because he probably would have lost it 'cause he don't have a pocketbook." Another said, "I can't do it," after three readings and after studying the problem for ninety seconds. One retarded boy realized that subtraction was involved in obtaining the answer and was able to select the correct minuend, but was unable to isolate the correct subtrahend. Four boys made errors in subtraction, although in all cases the correct elements were selected. One member of the control group was unable to determine what the problem demanded and added all the figures mentioned in the problem. Similar evidence of the effect of the presence of extraneous material on the arithmetic performance of the subjects of the two groups is observed in the attempted solutions of the other problems of this series.

SUMMARY

It is evident from the statistical and observational evidence presented that the mentally retarded subjects are not as adept as normal subjects in differentiating unneeded from needed facts in solving arithmetic problems. Evidence is also presented to show that normal children are more successful than mentally retarded children in working problems freed from the extraneous material. The difference in the responses of the two groups in solving problems from which non-essential elements have been eliminated is much greater than that in the responses to the exercises in which the subjects are asked to identify the unneeded elements.

The first conclusion mentioned above, i.e., that mentally retarded subjects are not as capable as normal subjects of the same mental and arithmetic ages in selecting pertinent material in arithmetic problems needed in the correct solution of the problems, is not unexpected in the light of previous research. The problem of inferior language development of the mentally retarded subjects is undoubtedly a factor. Aldrich and Doll,[1] Merrill,[8] and others have shown that mentally retarded children are inferior to normal children of the same mental age in language comprehension and development. Evidence is also available to show that the pupils in the experimental group do not have as great an understanding of arithmetic vocabulary as normal subjects of the same mental and arithmetic ages.[2]

A second factor hindering the experimental subjects in selecting the specific elements from the mass of extraneous material may be inferior reasoning ability. Although no carefully controlled comparative studies are available, it has been assumed that the mentally retarded child is as a rule inferior to the normal child in reasoning. If this is true, the inferior ability in reasoning should account in part for the poorer results of the experimental group in the present test. This fact must be minimized, however, with the subjects of the present investigation.

In the present study the mentally retarded subjects each had *arithmetic* ages within six months of their *reading* ages, a factor considered in the original selection of subjects. A second factor considered was the results of the reasoning test of the Stanford Achievement Test which along with the scores on the computation portion resulted in the arithmetic age. Since, as it has previously been pointed out, the arithmetic ages are highly comparable, it is not surprising to find highly similar results on the reasoning portion of the test. The mean number of reasoning problems correctly solved by the experimental group is 7.25 by the control group, 6.62. A T-score of 1.125 and a 20 percent level of significance exists. The gross mean scores show a slight superiority, in fact, for the experimental group. Merrill[8] found this same similarity of achievement of normal and retarded children in solving reasoning problems of the Stanford Achievement Test when the two groups were matched on the basis of arithmetic ages. She found that retarded pupils of mental ages of eight, nine and ten, when matched with normal pupils of the same mental ages, achieved slightly higher scores on the reasoning test than did the normal pupils. Since the mental ages of the subjects in the present study are all within the eight to ten year period, Merrill's findings are in agreement with those of this investigation. Both studies reveal that mentally retarded pupils of the mental ages of eight to ten year period achieve greater gross scores in the reasoning problems of the Stanford Achievement Test than do normal pupils, but the difference is not statistically significant. It must, therefore, be assumed that insofar as original matching is concerned there is little difference in the ability of the experimental and normal groups in reasoning ability. In the solution of verbal problems, however, where reasoning among other elements is a factor, the experimental group is inferior to the normal group of the present investigation. Note the differences in the means achieved by the two groups on series *a* and *b* of the tests containing extraneous materials.

Fox[6] has shown in a comparative study that mentally retarded children are inferior to normal children of the same mental age in development of insights, ability to form relationships, associations or discriminative judgments. Martinson and Strauss[7] have shown that the retarded child is handicapped in problems involving the "higher mental processes," organization, comprehension, discrimination, and ability to see relationships. These factors mentioned by Fox, Martinson, and Strauss plus the added factor of inferior arithmetic language development noted in the present study are important elements causing the inferior performance of the experimental group in isolating needed arithmetic facts from extraneous material.

BIBLIOGRAPHY

1. Aldrich, C. G., and E. A. Doll, "Comparative Intelligence of Idiots and Normal Infants," *Journal of Genetic Psychology* 38 (1931):227.
2. Cruickshank, W. M., "Arithmetic Vocabulary of Mentally Retarded Boys," *Journal of Exceptional Children* 13 (1946):93.
3. _____, "A Comparative Study of Psychological Factors Involved in the Responses of Mentally Retarded and Normal Boys to Problems in Arithmetic," doctoral dissertation, University of Michigan, 1946.

4. _____, "Qualitative Analysis of Intelligence Test Responses," *Journal of Clinical Psychology* 3 (October 1947):381.

5. _____, "Arithmetic Ability of Mentally Retarded Children: II Understanding Arithmetic Processese," to be published in *Journal of Educational Research*.

6. Fox, E. J., "The Diagnostic Value of Group Tests as Determined by the Qualitative Differences Between Normal and Feebleminded Children," *Journal of Applied Psychology* 9 (1927):127.

7. Martinson, B., and A. A. Strauss, "A Method of Clinical Evaluation of the Responses to the Stanford-Binet Intelligence Test," *American Journal of Mental Deficiency* 46 (1941):88.

8. Merrill, M. A., "On the Relation of Intelligence of Achievement in the Case of Mentally Retarded Children," *Comparative Psychological Monographs* 11 (1924):1–100.

ARITHMETIC ABILITY OF
MENTALLY RETARDED CHILDREN

II. Understanding Arithmetic Processes

INTRODUCTION

*A*N INVESTIGATION WAS UNDERTAKEN to determine the truth or falsity of the assertion that mentally retarded children of a given mental age are not able to understand as well as normal children of the same mental age the processes which should be employed in the solution of simple exercises in arithmetic. A second aspect of the study endeavored to substantiate or deny the observation of teachers of the mentally retarded that, although the child may indicate that problem should be worked in a given way, he, when asked to solve the problem, proceeds along entirely different arithmetical lines from that which he indicated. For example, the mentally retarded child says that he should subtract to find the correct answer in a certain arithmetic problem, but when he is requested to actually solve the problem he has been observed to use a process other than subtraction.

SUBJECTS

Two groups of fifteen boys each were used in the study: the first, a group of mentally retarded boys from the Wayne County Training School, Northville, Michigan, who comprised the experimental group; the second, a group of boys of normal intelligence from the Adams Elementary School, Birmingham, Michigan, who comprised the control group. The experimental subjects had a mean C.A. of 14.29; a mean M.A. of 10.06, and a mean I.Q.

Reprinted from *Journal of Educational Research* (December 1948): 279–88, by permission.

of 73.33; the control subjects, a mean C.A. of 9.09, a mean M.A. of 9.96, and a mean I.Q. of 110.4. The mean arithmetic age of the experimental group was 9.73; of the control group 9.84. The T-score between mean mental and mean arithmetic ages of the experimental group is 1.169 at a 5 percent level of significance; for the control group 1.265 at a 30 percent level of significance, indicating that basic differences do not exist between mental and arithmetic ages. Significant differences do not exist between mental ages of the experimental and control groups (T-score 1.195 at 10 percent level of significance) or between the arithmetic ages of the two groups subjects (T-score 1.120 at 30 percent level of significance). The subjects of both groups had arithmetic ability comparable to third grade achievement. The study is a portion of a much larger investigation undertaken to examine other aspects of the same general problem.[1]

THE TESTS

Part I

This test, consisting of twenty simple verbal problems, was designed to determine difference in the responses of the experimental and control groups in deciding whether to add, subtract, multiply or divide to obtain the answers. Many of the problems were taken verbatim from the arithmetic texts and work books from which the two groups of boys had already studied. Exercises were checked by teachers of the children to determine that they were free of grammatical difficulties and vocabulary which might be beyond the comprehension of the mentally retarded children. Thus an effort was made to confine the difficulty of the test to that of *naming the operations* needed in finding the answers called for.

In order that the reader may see the nature of the test, four problems selected from the list of twenty are reproduced:

1. You know the price of an apple. You know the price of an orange. How do you find the cost of both together?
2. You know how many oranges you had and you know how many of these you have eaten. How do you find the number of oranges you have left?
3. You know the number of pupils there are in each room of your school. How do you find out how many there are in the whole school?
4. John sells boxes of strawberries for 15¢ a box. He sells 37 boxes of strawberries. How do you find out how much money John receives?

Part II

This test, consisting of the twenty problems used in Part I but in slightly different form, was designed to determine whether mentally retarded and normal children would actually solve the problems in the manner they had indicated they would in Part I of the test. The twenty problems used in Part I were put into concrete form for solution. Thus the four examples given above would appear as follows in Part II of the test:

       1. An apple costs 3¢. An orange costs 7¢. What is the cost of both together?

       2. You have twelve oranges. You ate 3. How many do you have left?

       3. There are 35 boys in one room of your school, 24 in another, 17 in another, and 15 in still another room. How many boys are there in the whole school?

       4. John sells boxes of strawberries. He sells 37 boxes for 5¢ a box. How much money does John receive?

Administration of the tests

In administering the test each problem was typed in large letters on a 4 x 6 card. The examiner, sitting across the table from the subject, presented individual cards in a given order. The problems were each read by the examiner at least twice, but no more than three times, while the subject read the problem silently from the card in front of him. Part II was similarly administered twenty-four hours after Part I.

RESULTS

Table 1 shows that there is a statistically significant difference between the ability of the experimental and the control groups to name the process required for the correct solution of a given arithmetic problem and between the ability of the two groups to actually solve the problem as required in Part II of the test.

       Table 1 shows that on Part I of the test, the part requiring the subject merely to indicate what process he would use in solving the problem, the experimental group had a mean score of 11.66 correct responses; the control

TABLE 1

COMPARISON OF THE MEAN SCORES OF THE EXPERIMENTAL GROUP AND THOSE OF
THE CONTROL GROUP WITH RESULTING T-SCORES FOR THE PROCESS
NAMING TEST PARTS I AND II

		Experimental Group		Control Group	
	Process Naming Test	Mean Score	Standard Deviation	Mean Score	Standard Deviation
Line	(1)	(2)	(3)	(4)	(5)
A	Part I (Process Only)	11.66	4.253	18.20	1.275
B	Part II (Worked for Solution)	17.80	2.286	19.46	2.650

T-Scores between:

Line A Columns 2 and 4 ....6.218
Line B Columns 2 and 4 ....2.650
Line A Column 2 and Row B Column 2 ....8.191
Line A Column 4 and Row B Column 4 ....3.676

Percent showing level of signifiance of t between:

Line A Columns 2 and 4 1
Line B Columns 2 and 4 2
Line A Column 2 and Row B Column 2 1
Line A Column 4 and Row B Column 4 1

group 18.20. The resulting T-score is 6.218 which gives a greater than 1 percent level of significance in favor of the control group. A 2 percent level of significance is seen between the results of the experimental group and the control group on Part II which required that the subjects actually solve the exercise. Here a T-score of 2.650 is obtained from the experimental group's mean score of correct responses of 17.80 and the control group's mean score of 19.46. A significant difference is seen between the responses of the groups to Part II in favor of the control group, although this difference is not as great as that observed between the responses of the groups to Part I.

Table 1 also shows a comparison of the mean scores of responses of the experimental and control groups for Part I with those of Part II. The table shows that the experimental group has a T-score of 8.191 between the mean scores of Part I and Part II. The control group also shows a significant difference between the two parts of the test. On the former, the control group has a mean of 18.20 correct responses; on the latter 19.46. A T-score of 3.676 and a 1 percent level of significance is thus obtained. It is therefore possible to conclude that both mentally retarded and normal boys of the mental ages included in this study are prone to indicate that they would solve a problem with a certain operation, but actually solve it by the use of another operation. The size of the T-score for the experimental group is so much larger than that of the control group as to indicate that the changing of operations is much more typical of the former than of the latter. Analysis of the data shows that the number of changes in operation varies from *none* to *thirteen* among the subjects of the experimental group from *one to four* among the subjects of the control group. The average number of operational changes for the experimental group is 6.66; for the control group 1.46.

Clinical differences

Each of the mentally retarded boys was paired with a boy of normal intelligence levels. A comparison of the qualitative results of several of these paired couples proves of value. In one pair the normal pupil indicated a correct method and used the indicated method to solve all of his problems except problem 7. Problem 7 reads: "You know the number of pupils there are in each room of your school. How do you find out how many there are in the whole school?" The normal boy on this problem indicated that he would subtract, but when confronted with the actual problem for which a concrete answer was expected he used the additional operation. His retarded partner, however, changed the operations in problems 1, 2, 4, 7, 9, 10, 12, 13, 15, 16, 17, and 19 — twelve times in the series of twenty exercises. In solving problem 1, which involved addition, this boy responded, "That's easy. I'd *subtract*." In actually solving the problem at a later trial, however, he correctly used the *addition* operation. In problem 2, which called for subtraction, he indicated that he would multiply; but he actually did subtract when asked to work the problem for an answer. This inability to name the correct fundamental but later to correctly solve the problem was observed each time this mentally retarded boy changed operations except in problems 10 and 16. Here the correct operations were initially named, but incorrect processes employed in actual solution. In none of the problems did the subject show any concern for the fact that he was using different operations.

While the difference is greatest between the two above-mentioned subjects, substantial differences are also noted between six other pairs and lesser differences present in all other pairs of subjects.

One normal boy indicated that he would multiply to solve problem 4 which reads: "Jack knows how much he weighed in the spring. He knows how much he weighs in the fall. How does he find out how much he has gained?" This boy correctly subtracted when actually working the problem in Part II. This was his only change of operation in the series of twenty exercises. His partner changed processes eight times in problems 4, 6, 11, 12, 13, 14, 15 and 17. This mentally retarded boy showed a good deal of concern and hesitated noticeably in the first part of the test. It was obvious that he was not sure of himself and numerous readings of the problems were necessary before he gave an answer. The examiner found it necessary to utilize practice problems with this boy in order to familiarize the subject with the type of exercise prior to the beginning of the test. There was a marked difference in the ability of these two subjects to understand what was required of them and to work each individual problem, although their mental ages of 10.33 and 10.00, respectively, are strikingly similar.

In general behavioral manifestations were not dissimilar in the two groups with the exception of the mentally retarded boy noted in the preceding paragraph. It is quite possible that findings noted by Strauss and Werner[6] and Cruickshank[3] are in operation here. These writers have observed a need for mentally retarded children to give a response of some kind in spite of the fact that his response may have no meaning either to himself or to society at large. In addition to the lack of understanding of the essential elements of a problem, the need for maintenance of social position may also be in operation, particularly when it is considered that the correct procedure was employed in the actual solution of the problem. It is evident that the gross differences in the performance of the two groups account for the much larger T-score of the experimental group and permit the conclusion that changing operations are more typical of the experimental group than of the control group.

Analysis of the performance in each fundamental

An analysis of the performance of the experimental and control groups in the four fundamental operations of this test is made in Tables 2 and 3, which show the responses of the two groups of subjects to each item of Part II of the test. Table II shows the results for addition and subtraction; Table 3, multiplication and division.

In the addition items the experimental group performed 55 exercises or 73 percent correctly; the control group, 72 exercises or 96 percent. In subtraction the experimental group solved 63 or 70 percent of the exercises correctly; the control group, 84 or 93 percent. Practically a perfect score of correct responses is obtained by all the subjects of the control group while some rather consistent failures are noted in the responses of the experimental group. It will be observed in Table 2 that subjects 032 and 072 of the ex-

TABLE 2

ADDITION AND SUBTRACTION PROBLEMS CORRECTLY SOLVED BY EXPERIMENTAL AND CONTROL GROUPS IN PART II NAMING PROCESS TEST*

Case Number	Addition Problems					Subtraction Problems						Case Number	Addition Problems					Subtraction Problems					
	1	3	5	7	16	2	4	6	8	9	10		1	3	5	7	16	2	4	6	8	9	10
012....	x	x	x	x	x	x	x	x	x	x	x	011....	x	x	x	x	x	x	x	x	x	x	x
022....		x	x	x	x				x	x	x	021....	x	x	x	x	x	x		x	x	x	x
032....	x						x				x	031....	x	x	x		x	x	x	x	x	x	x
042....	x	x	x	x	x	x			x	x	x	041....	x	x	x	x	x	x		x	x	x	x
052....	x	x	x	x		x	x	x	x	x	x	051....	x	x	x	x	x	x	x	x	x	x	x
062....	x	x	x			x		x	x	x													
061....	x	x	x	x		x		x	x	x	x												
072....	x					x		x	x			071....	x	x	x	x	x	x	x	x	x		x
082....	x	x	x	x		x	x	x	x	x	x	081....	x	x	x	x	x	x	x	x	x	x	x
092....		x	x	x		x		x	x	x	x	091....	x	x	x	x		x		x	x	x	x
102....	x	x	x	x	x	x		x	x		x	101....	x	x	x	x	x	x	x	x	x	x	x
112....	x		x			x			x	x	x	111....	x	x	x	x	x	x	x	x	x	x	x
122....	x	x	x	x	x	x	x	x	x	x	x	121....	x	x	x	x	x	x	x	x	x	x	x
132....	x	x	x	x						x	x	131....	x	x	x	x	x	x		x	x	x	x
142....	x	x	x	x	x	x		x	x	x		141....	x	x	x	x	x	x	x	x	x	x	x
152....	x	x	x	x		x		x	x	x		151....	x	x	x	x	x	x	x	x	x	x	x
Total Correct	12	13	13	11	6	12	5	11	14	12	9		15	15	15	14	13	15	10	15	15	14	15
Process Total ..	55					63							72					84					
Percent Correct	73					70							96					93					

*"x" indicates that the problem was correctly solved.

perimental group show the greatest number of incorrectly solved exercises. Subject 032 has a mental age of only 8.83 and is one of the youngest of the boys in the experimental group—a fact which may account for the great number of failures. However, this subject's matched partner in the control group has a mental age of 8.08 years and received almost a perfect score. Subject 072 of the experimental group has a mental age of 10.33 years, but worked correctly only four of the eleven addition and subtraction exercises.

Table 3 shows that the experimental group solved 19 or 42 percent of the multiplication exercises correctly, whereas the control group solved 38 exercises or 84 percent correctly. The experimental group solved 27 or 47

TABLE 3

MULTIPLICATION AND DIVISION PROBLEMS CORRECTLY SOLVED BY EXPERIMENTAL
AND CONTROL GROUPS IN PART II NAMING PROCESS TEST*

| | Experimental Group | | | | | | | | Control Group | | | | | | |
| | Multiplication Problems | | | Division Problems | | | | | Multiplication Problems | | | Division Problems | | | |
Case Number	12	13	15	11	14	17	19	Case Number	12	13	15	11	14	17	19
012....	x	x	x	x	x	x	x	011....	x	x	x	x	x	x	—
022....	—	x	x	x	x	—	—	021....	x	x	x	x	x	x	x
032....	—	—	—	x	x	—	—	031....	x	x	x	x	x	x	x
042....	—	—	—	—	—	—	—	041....	x	x	x	x	x	x	x
052....	x	x	x	x	x	—	—	051....	x	x	x	x	—	x	x
062....	—	—	—	—	—	—	—	061....	x	x	x	x	x	—	x
072....	x	—	x	x	x	x	—	071....	—	x	x	—	x	x	—
082....	—	—	—	x	—	—	—	081....	x	x	x	x	x	x	x
092....	x	x	x	x	x	—	—	091....	x	x	x	—	x	x	x
102....	x	—	x	x	—	—	—	101....	x	x	x	x	x	x	x
112....	—	—	—	—	x	—	—	111....	—	—	x	x	—	x	x
122....	x	x	x	x	x	x	x	121....	—	—	x	x	—	x	x
132....	—	—	—	x	x	—	—	131....	—	—	x	—	x	x	x
142....	x	—	—	—	—	—	—	141....	x	x	x	x	x	x	x
152....	—	—	—	x	x	x	—	151....	x	x	x	x	x	x	x
Total Correct	7	5	7	11	10	4	2		11	12	15	12	12	14	13
Process Total..	19			27					38			51			
Percent Total..	42			47					84			85			

*"x" indicates that the problem was correctly solved.

percent of the division exercises correctly; the control group solved 51 or 85 percent correctly. The greater percentage of division exercises correctly solved on the part of the experimental group over the multiplication exercises is to be in part explained by the fact that certain of the boys in this group were having division instruction in the academic classrooms of the Training School at the time this part of the experiment was being made.

Tables 2 and 3 show that the percentage of successes attained by the normal pupils of the control group on the exercises involving addition and subtraction is but slightly greater than in the exercises involving multiplication and division, but in all processes substantially greater than the percentage of successes attained by the experimental group. The favorable comparison of the success attained by the control group in each of the four fundamental processes is rather unexpected due to the fact that the pupils of this group have had relatively little experience, particularly with multiplication and division. The mentally retarded children show much less favorable performance in multiplication and division than in addition and subtraction. This finding is also noted elsewhere[4] in connection with an investigation wherein the Busewell-John Diagnostic Chart for Fundaments for Arithmetic was used. In this study it was noted that the mentally retarded boys were less skilled in multiplication and division and evidenced more poor work habits in these two fundamentals than in addition and subtraction. Similarly, in a study which used the Sangren-Reidy Instructional Check Test in Arithmetic, the general inferiority of the mentally retarded in multiplication and division is noted.[1] The fact that the retarded child has had longer experience with all the processes, but particularly with multiplication and division, does not seem to provide him with techniques to allow greater success than that achieved by his chronologically younger matched normal partners as might be expected.

SUMMARY

A group of twenty problems was presented to the experimental and control groups. In the first presentation, the subjects were asked to tell what arithmetic process was to be used in reaching a solution to the problem, i.e., addition, subtraction, multiplication, division; in the second presentation, to actually work the problem and obtain an answer. The test was constructed to determine whether or not there is a difference in the ability of mentally retarded and normal children of the same mental and arithmetic ages to understand arithmetic processes to be used in the solution of problems and whether there is a difference in the ability of the two groups to actually solve the problems.

Mentally retarded children are more likely to indicate that they should solve a problem in one way and actually proceed to solve it in another way than are normal children. Change in operation is not solely limited to mentally retarded pupils but is also found in a significant amount in pupils of normal intelligence. However, in the present investigation T-score showing such tendency to change operations was more than twice as large for the experimental group as that for the control group. Comparison of the T-scores between Parts I and II of the test for the experimental and control groups indicates that the difference in the ability to name processes needed in the solution of problems and the ability to solve the exercises is much greater in the retarded group than in the group of normal pupils.

It is apparent that the pupils of the experimental group have real difficulties in ascertaining the correct arithmetical process to be used in the solution of a given problem which is read silently at the same time as it is being read orally by the examiner. This difficulty is more apparent with multiplication and division, although it is present to some extent in all operations. Results of other studies using the Buswell-John Diagnostic Chart for Fundamentals of Arithmetic and the Sangren-Reidy Instructional Check Test in Arithmetic show that the *inability to understand* is characteristic of the responses of the retarded group and may be due to poor work habits and lack of technical understanding of arithmetic processes, particularly with multiplication and division. An inferior comprehension of arithmetic vocabulary, although it was stated that problems were checked for grammatical and vocabulary difficulties, may account in part for the poor performance of the experimental group in understanding the problems. The results of an arithmetic vocabulary test[3] show that the experimental group is generally inferior to the control group in ability to define arithmetic terms. It is important to note in this instance that the six mentally retarded boys who make the greatest number of operational changes have in another investigation the lowest vocabulary scores.

There is observable from the results of Parts I and II a significant difference between the ability of the two groups to name processes in an abstract presentation and to work the problem when presented in a more concrete fashion, although the difference in favor of the control group is much smaller in this latter comparison. There is a pronounced difference in the ability of the experimental group to solve problems when presented in the concrete rather than abstract form. Both the experimental and control groups show similar abilities to solve concrete rather than abstract problems in a study reported earlier dealing with the ability of mentally retarded children to isolate extraneous materials in arithmetic problems.[5]

Factors of vocabulary and the abstract nature of the presentation are undoubtedly present in the greater inferiority of the experimental group to understand the correct process involved in the solution of arithmetic problems. There is a distinct difference in the performance of both groups when presented with problems for actual concrete solution, although the experimental subjects show a much smaller difference. Factors accounting for the continued inferiority of the experimental group are due to the greater number of poor work habits and general lack of technical skill which have been mentioned above.

BIBLIOGRAPHY

1. Cruickshank, W. M., "A Comparative Study of Psychological Factors Involved in the Responses of Mentally Retarded and Normal Boys to Problems in Arithmetic," doctoral dissertation, University of Michigan, 1946.

2. _____, "Qualitative Analysis of Intelligence Test Responses," *Journal of Clinical Psychology* 3 (October 1947):381.

3. _____, "Arithmetic Vocabulary of Mentally Retarded Boys," *Journal of Exceptional Children* 13 (December 1946):93.

4. _____, "Arithmetic Work Habits of Mentally Retarded Boys," *American Journal of Mental Deficiency* 52 (April 1948):318.

5. _____, "Arithmetic Ability of Mentally Retarded Children. I. Ability to Differentiate Extraneous Materials from Needed Arithmetical Facts," *Journal of Educational Research* 42 (November 1948).

6. Strauss, A. A., and H. Werner, "Qualitative Analysis of the Binet Test," *American Journal of Mental Deficiency* 45 (July 1940):50.

3

ARITHMETIC VOCABULARY
OF MENTALLY RETARDED BOYS

STUDIES OF GENERAL LINGUISTIC DEVELOPMENT show that mentally retarded children are inferior to normal children in their mastery of language.[1] Other studies have also pointed out that mentally retarded children are inferior to normal children in their knowledge and understanding of arithmetic functions and processes.[2] As part of a larger study an investigation was made to determine the importance of vocabulary comprehension to the proficiency of mentally retarded boys in the solution of arithmetic problems.[3]

Two groups of fifteen boys were carefully matched following an examination of the records of 500 individuals: one, the experimental group, mentally retarded boys from the Wayne County Training School, Northville, Michigan, with a mean mental age of 10.06 years, a mean arithmetic age of 9.73 years, and a mean intelligence quotient of 73.33; the other, the control group, normal boys with a mean mental age of 9.96, a mean arithmetic age of 9.84, and a mean intelligence quotient of 110.4. An arithmetic vocabulary test consisting of eighty-five terms was administered individually to the subjects of each group. The terms included in the vocabulary tests were those listed by Guy T. Buswell in his arithmetic vocabulary test, although several additions and deletions were made from the original. The final list appears as follows:

1. add	4. carry	7. difference	10. divide
2. addend	5. check	8. average	11. dividend
3. borrow	6. count	9. digit	12. divisor

Reprinted from *Journal of Exceptional Children* 13 (1946): 65–69, by permission.

13. equal	32. +	50. inch	68. profit
14. estimate	33. −	51. measure	69. rent
15. even	34. ×	52. perimeter	70. sell
16. minuend	35. ÷	53. pound	71. spend
17. minus	36. ⌐	54. quart	72. worth
18. multiplier	37. =	55. square	73. circle
19. multiplicand	38. both	56. weight	74. cube
20. multiply	39. pair	57. allowance	75. rectangle
21. number	40. part	58. bill	76. triangle
22. odd	41. smaller	59. buy	77. column
23. plus	42. twice	60. change	78. per
24. product	43. area	61. charge	79. total
25. prove	44. century	62. cost	80. save
26. quotient	45. acre	63. discount	81. pay
27. remainder	46. dimensions	64. earn	82. debt
28. subtrahend	47. dollar	65. expense	83. balance
29. subtract	48. dozen	66. loan	84. receipt
30. sum	49. hour	67. price	85. oblong
31. times			

COMPARISON OF TWO GROUPS

The gross results of the arithmetic vocabulary test are presented in Table 1. It is evident that the results of the experimental group are inferior to those of the control group. The mentally retarded subjects are superior to the normal subjects on only 7 of the 85 terms of the vocabulary list, i.e., *count, plus, measure, pound, rectangle, pay* and *balance.* The experimental group as a whole defined correctly 626 words; the control group, 803 words — a difference of 177 words. The significance of the difference between the mean number of words correctly defined, i.e., 39.1 for the experimental group and 50.2 for the control group, is at the one percent level of significance (T-score, 3.12) which is significant. The experimental subject is inferior to the control subject in all of the fifteen matched pairs of pupils, the differences being between one to twenty-six words. The experimental group defined 49 percent of the words correctly; the control group, 62 percent.

Analysis of technical terms pertaining to the four fundamental processes

Table 2 has been prepared to show the percentage of correct responses to words specifically pertaining to the four fundamental processes.

TABLE 1

NUMBER OF ARITHMETIC TERMS CORRECTLY DEFINED BY THE EXPERIMENTAL
AND CONTROL GROUPS

Experimental Group		Control Group		Difference in Favor of Control Group
Subject	Number Words Correct	Subject	Number Words Correct	
1	47	1	57	10
2	49	2	54	5
3	40	3	56	16
4	42	4	58	16
5	47	5	48	1
6	37	6	49	12
7	39	7	55	16
8	49	8	53	4
9	41	9	48	7
10	44	10	63	19
11	26	11	52	26
12	44	12	60	16
13	47	13	49	2
14	35	14	48	13
15	39	15	53	14
Total	626		803	177
Mean	39.1		50.2	11.7
Percent Correct	49		60	
T-Score				3.12
Percent level of significance of t				1

Certain differences between the experimental and control groups are immediately apparent. The average percentage of correctly defined words in all four fundamental processes is less for the mentally retarded boys. In *addition* terms the experimental group answered 55.7 percent correctly; the control group, 61.6 percent. The experimental group correctly defined 39.3 percent of the *subtraction* terms; the control group, 59.9 percent. The percentage of correct responses for the experimental group on the *multiplication* terms was 41.1 percent and on the *division* terms, 37.7 percent; for the control group, 49.9 on both multiplication and division terms. The greatest difference between the two groups is in the subtraction process. The average percentage of terms correctly defined for all the technical terms is 43.45 for the experimental group; 55.32 percent for the control group.

TABLE 2

PERCENTAGE OF CORRECT RESPONSES TO THE WORDS PERTAINING
SPECIFICALLY TO THE FOUR FUNDAMENTAL PROCESSES
BY THE EXPERIMENTAL AND CONTROL GROUPS

Word	Percent of Experimental Group Giving Correct Response	Percent of Control Group Giving Correct Response
Addition process		
add	86.6	100.0
addend	−	−
carry*	86.6	100.0
average	6.6	13.3
count	100.0	80.0
plus	33.3	20.0
sum	46.6	80.0
+	86.6	100.0
average percentage	55.7	61.6
Subtraction process		
borrow	66.3	93.3
check*	53.3	86.6
difference	13.3	20.0
minuend	−	6.6
minus	26.6	46.6
prove*	6.6	53.3
remainder*	40.0	80.0
subtract	86.6	100.0
subtrahend	−	13.3
−	100.0	100.0
average percentage	39.3	59.9
Multiplication process		
multiplicand	−	−
multiplier	−	6.6
multiply	73.3	93.3
times	93.3	93.3
×	80.0	100.0
product	−	6.6
average percentage	41.1	49.9

TABLE 2 *continued*

Word	Percent of Experimental Group Giving Correct Response	Percent of Control Group Giving Correct Response
Division process		
divide	86.6	100.0
dividend	—	—
divisor	—	—
quotient	—	13.3
÷	53.3	93.3
⌐	86.6	93.3
average percentage	37.7	49.9
Total average percent	43.45	55.32

*Applicable also to other fundamentals

Type of term showing greatest familiarity

Table 3 shows from the responses of the total list of words made by each group the twenty that were defined correctly by the greatest percentage of the pupils. One notes from this table that 13 words are common to both lists, although the order in which the words appear is different. In the experimental group, 12 of the twenty easiest words relate to commerce and measurement, 7 of the first ten words belong to these same classifications. For the control group, 10 of the easiest words relate to commerce and measurement; 3 in the first list of the ten easiest words and 7 in the ten more difficult words.

Seven of the first ten words which are most familiar to the control group subjects are technical terms relating to the four fundamental operations, and of the first twenty, 9 are of this category. In the first ten easiest terms for the experimental group 3 are technical terms; 7, among the first twenty. Eleven of the twenty terms were defined correctly by all the subjects of the experimental group, 19 by all of the subjects of the control group. It is interesting to note that none of the terms relate to time, space, or quantity, and that only one term relates to spatial figures (*circle*) — all highly abstract terms.

TABLE 3

THE TWENTY EASIEST ARITHMETIC TERMS FOR THE EXPERIMENTAL AND CONTROL GROUPS

	Experimental Group		Control Group	
Rank	Word	Classification	Word	Classification
1	count	Technical	add	Technical
2	+	Technical	divide	Technical
3	dollar	Measurement	number	Technical
4	pound	Measurement	subtract	Technical
5	buy	Commercial	+	Technical
6	change	Commercial	−	Technical
7	rent	Commercial	×	Technical
8	sell	Commercial	dollar	Measurement
9	pay	Commercial	hour	Measurement
10	times	Technical	dozen	Measurement
11	hour	Measurement	allowance	Commercial
12	cost	Commercial	change	Commercial
13	earn	Commercial	price	Commercial
14	price	Commercial	rent	Commercial
15	circle	Spatial fig.	sell	Commercial
16	spend	Commercial	cost	Commercial
17	carry	Technical	spend	Commercial
18	divide	Technical	circle	Spatial fig.
19	subtract	Technical	carry	Technical
20	−	Technical	borrow	Technical

SUMMARY

Studies of general linguistic development show that mentally retarded children are inferior to normal children in their mastery of language. The present study shows that mentally retarded boys, when carefully matched with normal children of the same mental and arithmetic ages, are also significantly inferior in their ability to define, or use properly in a statement, terms specific to the arithmetic processes. This inferior command of arithmetic terms is noted in all four of the fundamental operations. There is no great difference, however, in the knowledge of the easiest arithmetic terms: the experimental group showing slightly greater familiarity with terms relating to commerce; the control group, to technical arithmetic terms. This difference is not enough to be significant, although it points to an important trend, i.e., the stress with the mentally retarded boy should be with the practical application of arithmetic problems and with terms which he will use later as he functions in society. It is possible that the difference noted, however small, is due in part to training and chronological age. The commercial terms with which the mentally retarded group shows greatest familiarity are the more concrete terms closely related to the daily activities of this particular group of children, i.e., *count* money, *count* on fingers, *earn* a *dollar,* how much does the show *cost?* etc.

The lack of ability to use arithmetic vocabulary undoubtedly accounts in large measure for the general inferiority in reading, understanding, and solving problems of various types which has been found to typify the mentally retarded boy.[4] The unsatisfactory achievement of the mentally retarded pupils with verbal problems undoubtedly is closely related to their limited understanding of arithmetical terminology.[5] It is also quite possible that lack of knowledge of vocabulary accounts for the general inferiority of the mentally retarded pupils, which has been noted in their ability to solve correctly concrete exercises in all four of the fundamental processes.[6]

It is thus possible to see that greater emphasis must be placed by teachers of mentally retarded children on the development of vocabulary pertinent to arithmetic. It is of paramount importance that mentally retarded boys and girls be given the tools by which they can achieve some measure of success in their personal community adjustment. The necessity to solve simple arithmetical problems is a daily requirement of the retarded individual, and lack of knowledge of vocabulary basic to this skill is one factor contributing to the maladjustment.

BIBLIOGRAPHY

1. Aldrich, C. G., and E. A. Doll, "Comparative Intelligence of Idiots and Normal Infants," *Journal of Genetic Psychology* 39 (June 1931):227-57. Merrill, Maude, "On the Relation of Intelligence to Achievement in the Case of Mentally Retarded Children," *Comparative Psychology Monographs* 2 (September 1924):1-100.

2. Cruickshank, W. M., "A Comparative Study of the Psychological Factors Involved in the Responses of Mentally Retarded and Normal Boys to Arithmetic Problems," doctoral dissertation, University of Michigan, 1946, 260 pp. Merrill, "On the Relationship."

3. Cruickshank, "A Comparative Study."

4. Ibid., p. 162.

5. Ibid., p. 198.

6. Ibid.

QUALITATIVE ANALYSIS OF INTELLIGENCE TEST RESPONSES

INTRODUCTION

𝒯HE PROBLEM of differentiating mentally retarded children from normal children on the basis of their responses to items in standard intelligence tests has been one of growing interest in recent years.[3,5,6] This has been particularly true in consideration of such instruments of measurement as the Stanford-Binet Intelligence Scale and the Wechsler-Bellevue Intelligence Scale.[4] It has become clear through the research which has been presented that mentally retarded children are often superior to normal children in their responses to certain items while the reverse is also, of course, true in many instances. It has also become clear that behavioral differences in the responses of mentally retarded and normal individuals to the same items may be important in the diagnosis of specific defects.

Little research has been done, however, on the problem of the diagnostic value of responses to items in the intelligence test. Strauss and Werner[5] developed a nine category classification of responses to items in the Binet Test which contributes to the qualitative interpretation of responses to items on that test. The classification which these authors give is as follows: *correct, correct-incomplete, superficial, wrong, egocentric, nonsensical, misunderstanding, inadequate, don't know,* and *ambiguous.* In an analysis of the responses of mentally retarded, normal and delinquent children to the items of the Binet Test it was observed that striking dissimilarities existed in certain types of answers given by the three groups of children. The groups differed most markedly in four categories, namely, *wrong, nonsensical,*

Reprinted from *Journal of Clinical Psychology* 3, no. 4 (October 1947): 381–86, by permission.

don't know, and *ambiguous.* Strauss and Werner found that the percentage of *wrong* answers was higher among the defective group than it was among the normal group and still higher than that noted among the delinquent group. *Nonsensical* answers were noted to be practically absent among the normal and delinquent groups, although 3.7 percent of the answers of the retarded children were of this type. Likewise *ambiguous* answers were typical of the retarded groups in 12.5 percent of the cases while such answers were found much less frequently among the normal and delinquent children. *Don't know* answers characterized the responses of the normal children, but were observed with much less frequency in the responses of the delinquent and retarded groups.

METHOD

As a part of a larger study[1] a test was developed to determine difference in the responses of mentally retarded and normal subjects of the same mental and arithmetic ages to a problem involving logical reasoning in arithmetic but beyond the mental age levels of the children concerned. It was hoped to throw some light on the generalization that mentally retarded children lack a specific mental attitude of autocriticism and also to lend added evidence to the findings of Strauss and Werner relative to the importance of qualitative analysis of intelligence test responses.

Two groups of subjects were selected whose mental age and arithmetic age were similar: One, the experimental group, mentally retarded boys from the Wayne County Training School, Northville, Michigan, with a mean mental age of 10.06 years, a mean arithmetic age of 9.73 years and a mean intelligence quotient of 73.33; the other, normal boys comprising the control group, with a mean mental age of 9.96 years, a mean arithmetic age of 9.84 years and a mean intelligence quotient of 110.4. The range of mental ages of the subjects was from the eight to ten year levels. Fifteen boys carefully selected and matched were included in each group. The level of significance of the difference between the mean mental ages of the experimental and control group was at the five percent level which is not significant (T-score, 1.169); between the mean arithmetic ages, at the thirty percent level which is also not significant (T-score, 1.265). It can thus be concluded that two highly similar groups of children were obtained for the purpose of the study.

In order to obtain a test item known to be above the mental age level of the subjects, the Ingenuity item from the 1937 Revision of the Stanford-

Binet Intelligence Scale Form L of the fourteen year mental level was used. This item is expressed as follows:

> A mother sent her boy to the river to bring back exactly 3 pints of water. She gave him a 7-pint can and a 4-pint can. Show me how the boy can measure out exactly 3 pints of water using nothing but the two cans and not guessing at the amount. You should begin by filling the 7-pint can first. Remember, you have a 7-pint can and a 4-pint can and you must bring back exactly 3 pints of water.

The test item was typed in large 14-point type on a four-by-six inch card and was placed before the subject. The examiner read the item out loud while the subject read it silently from the card before him. After reading the item twice, the examiner inquired whether or not the subject desired further readings. If the subject so requested, the item was reread by the examiner. The examiner recorded the verbatim response given by the subject, all questions which might have been asked by the examiner for clearer understanding of the subject's response, and the subject's answers to these secondary questions.

RESULTS

Utilizing the nine categories of responses developed by Strauss and Werner noted above, the responses of the experimental and control groups were individually considered. The responses of the experimental group are presented in Table 1; of the control group, in Table 2. The responses of the experimental group show the following types of reports: six, *nonsensical* (40 percent); four, *superficial* (26 percent); two, *inadequate* (13 percent); two, *don't know* (13 percent); and one, *correct-incomplete* (6 percent). All of the responses of the control group and subjects fall into two categories: eleven, *don't know* (73 percent); four, *correct* (26 percent).

DISCUSSION

It has been observed in the present study that the child of normal intelligence gives many more answers of the *don't know* variety than does the retarded child of the same mental and arithmetic ages. This finding was also noted by

TABLE 1

ANALYSIS OF THE ANSWERS GIVEN TO THE INGENUITY PROBLEM BY THE EXPERIMENTAL GROUP

Subject	Verbatim answer	Classification
1	"It's be 28." E. "How did you get that?" S. "I multiplied." E. "Is that how you get 3 pints of water?" S. "Yes."................	Nonsensical-wrong
2	"Fill the 3 and the 4, and you have 7 pints." E. Is that the way you get 3 pints of water?" S. "Yes."	Superficial-wrong
3	"You'd add. No, you'd divide by your 7 and 4."	Nonsensical-wrong
4	"Fill the one can full — the 7-pint can." E. "Is that the way you will get 3 pints of water?" S. "Yes."	Nonsensical-wrong
5	"You'd multiply 3 by 7 is 21." E. "How are you going to get 3 pints of water?" S. "4 × 7 is 28." E. "Is that the way you'd get 3 pints of water?" S. "I guess so."	Nonsensical-wrong
6	"14 pints. I added 3 plus 7. That's the answer."	Nonsensical-wrong
7	"I'd put the 3 in the 7-pint can."...........................	Superficial-wrong
8	"Put your 3 pints in and then put your 4 pints in the 7-pint can." ..	Superficial-wrong
9	"21 — I multiplied 3 by 7." E. "Is that how you get 3 pints of water?" S. "Yes."......................................	Superficial-wrong
10	"I'd fill up the four and pour one out. You don't need the 7-pint can at all. I'd guess how much to pour out."	Inadequate-wrong
11	"I don't know."	Don't know
12	"Fill the 3 and the 5 and that makes 7 and that's the answer."	Inadequate-wrong
13	"I don't know how to do that."	Don't know
14	"He had a 7- and a 4-pint can. 7 minus 4 equals 3. He poured 4 pints into the 7-pint can and had 3 pints left."	Correct-incomplete
15	"You'd add. The 4-pint can will hold it."	Nonsensical-wrong

Percent "Don't know" answers		.132
Percent "Correct-incomplete" answers		.066
Percent wrong types of answers......................		.80
Nonsensical	.40	
Superficial	.266	
Inadequate	.133	

Strauss and Werner[5] in the previously mentioned study. These authors, in commenting on the difference noted in their groups, indicate that the presence of many don't know answers among the subjects of normal intelligence is an evidence of a trait of autocriticism. It is a commonly observed fact that children of low intelligence do not possess this autocritical attitude. Evidence of the lack of this capacity for self-appraisal is noted in the types of

TABLE 2

ANALYSIS OF THE ANSWERS GIVEN TO THE INGENUITY PROBLEM
BY THE CONTROL GROUP

Subject	Verbatim response	Classification
1	"I can't do it."	Don't know
2	"I don't think I can do that."	Don't know
3	"I don't think I can do it."	Don't know
4	Subject first tried to work the problem out on paper. "I don't know what this one is all about. It's screwy if you ask me."	Don't know
5	"Fill the 7-pint first. Put four pints into the 4-pint can and you have 3 left."	Correct
6	"You take 4 pints from the 7 and put it in the 4-pint can and you have 3 pints left."	Correct
7	"I don't know how to do it. I can't get it. No. I don't know. It's a funny problem."	Don't know
8	"Fill the 7-pint can first. You could subtract 4 from 7." E. "How are we going to get 3 pints of water?" S. "Fill 4 pints of water. I don't know. I can't do it."	Don't know
9	"I can't do it."	Don't know
10	"Subtract four from seven. You'll have to bring back more than she asked for. I don't know."	Don't know
11	"Put 3 pints into the 7-pint can, but I don't know how he'd get the one in unless there's a measuring cup. He could guess at the other. I don't know."	Don't know
12	"Fill the 7-pint can—that's got me stuck I think. Fill the 7-pint can and dump it in the 4-pint can and you have 3 pints left."	Correct
13	"I don't know."	Don't know
14	"You'd subtract 4 from 7—I'm afraid I don't know."	Don't know
15	"I don't know. I don't see how you do it without guessing. Oh. Fill the 7-pint can up first, and fill the 4-pint from the 7 and you have 3 left in the 7-pint can."	Correct

Percent "Don't know" answers 73.4
Percent "Correct" answers 26.6

answers which the majority of the experimental subjects give, *i.e.,* purely nonsensical, inadequate and superficial. The retarded child, forced by past feelings of inadequacy, makes an answer for the sake of making an answer and feels thereby that he maintains his social equilibrium. The normal child, in contrast, seems to be able to face the reality of the situation and to admit that he does not know the solution to a problem. The normal child can admit to himself and to the examiner who represents the social situation that he is inadequate in answering a specific problem situation. For him the problem situation remains a problem situation *per se,* not, as with the retarded child, another situation in which a felt personal inferiority is again demonstrated and in which it is necessary to fight for the status of the self concept.

The tendency for the retarded children to respond no matter whether correctly or incorrectly was noted several times throughout the course of the larger study.[1] Often the retarded group of boys gave an answer, foreign to the solution of a problem, simply because they knew or felt that an answer was expected and that failure to respond would cause a loss in the examiner's esteem. They gave answers not only to maintain themselves in the sight of the examiner, but also in a larger sense to preserve their status in a social situation in which they realized they should be master but in which, because of their low intelligence, they could not satisfactorily function. In consideration of the results of a test of understanding arithmetic processes, it was noted that the experimental subjects through their verbal responses and patterns of behavior indicated attempts to maintain levels of social acceptance and feelings of personal security in the examination situation whereas this attempt was not to be observed on the part of the normal pupils. A similar observation was made in connection with an analysis of results of a test of the effect of extraneous materials on problem solving ability.

A second factor accounting for the marked difference in response pattern of the two groups of boys should be noted, namely, facility with arithmetic vocabulary. Elsewhere it has been reported[2] that a marked difference in knowledge of arithmetic vocabulary existed between the same experimental and control group subjects as are reported here. It is possible that the retarded group, who were inferior to normal subjects in their use of vocabulary, were impaired in part in their ability to solve the Ingenuity item through a general arithmetic vocabulary inadequacy. It should be pointed out, however, that the two groups were able to define and use the word "measure" equally well in the vocabulary test. This word also appears in the Ingenuity item. Although the word "pint" did not appear in the vocabulary test, the word "quart" did, and on this latter term there was no difference in understanding between the two groups. The inclusion of the terms on both tests reduced somewhat the importance of vocabulary in the difference in response pattern of the groups on the Ingenuity item.

Marked behavioral differences were noted in the responses of the subjects to the Ingenuity item. Several subjects of the experimental group showed embarrassment at not being able to respond immediately. The situation was obviously frustrating to them. Four of the pupils of this group attempted to change the subject, making references to their successes on other portions of the test. Rationalization in various forms was attempted. One subject excused his unsatisfactory response as being due to poor eyesight and to his inability to see the problem. Actually clinical tests showed that his vision could not have been responsible. Two boys asked if they could not be allowed to solve the problem the next day when they would come to the examiner's office. None of these behavioral manifestations were observed in the control subjects.

The behavior which has been noted in relation to verbal responses to the Ingenuity item is comparable to the behavior observed in the feeble-minded individuals on certain performance test items particularly those using form boards and puzzle arrangement. It has long been observed that retarded individuals on these latter type items approach the task blindly. Typical is the child's attempt to force objects into holes of the form board without regard to color or form by pounding and hitting. Similarly, with the verbal item, a blind approach has been observed. Attempts are made to solve the problem by multiplying, subtracting, and useless verbalization which correspond to the random movements observed in the performance items.

SUMMARY

Mentally defective and control subjects show a marked difference in their reactions to the difficult arithmetic problem taken from the Binet Intelligence Test. The mental defectives demonstrate a lack of autocritical attitude and a need for maintaining social integrity. The defectives show no disposition to admit inability to cope with the situation; the control pupils almost universally admit inability to deal with the problem. The defectives proceed blindly in attempting to reason or manipulate numbers; the control subjects respond more realistically to elements pertinent to arriving at a logical answer to the problem.

BIBLIOGRAPHY

1. Cruickshank, W. M., "A Comparative Study of the Psychological Factors Involved in the Responses of Mentally Retarded Children and Normal Children to Problems in Arithmetic," doctoral dissertation, University of Michigan, 1946.
2. Cruickshank, W. M., "Arithmetic vocabulary of mentally retarded boys." *Journal of Exceptional Children* 13 (1946):65.

3. Martinson, B., and A. A. Strauss, "A Method of Clinical Evaluation of the Responses to the Stanford-Binet Intelligence Test." *American Journal of Mental Deficiency* 45 (October 1940).

4. Reichard, S., and R. Schafer, "The Clinical Significance of the Scatter on the Bellevue Scale." *Bulletin of the Menninger Clinic* 7 (1943):93.

5. Strauss, A. A., and H. Werner, "Qualitative Analysis of the Binet Test." *American Journal of Mental Deficiency* 46 (July 1941):52.

6. Werner, H., and A. A. Strauss, "Causal Factors in Low Performance." *American Journal of Mental Deficiency* 45 (October 1940).

5

ARITHMETIC WORK HABITS
OF MENTALLY RETARDED BOYS

INTRODUCTION

*T*HE BUSWELL-JOHN[1] DIAGNOSTIC CHART for Fundamentals of Arithmetic was administered, as a part of a larger study,[2] to two groups of carefully matched subjects: one, a group of mentally retarded boys; the other, a group of boys of normal intelligence levels. It was hoped that through this test it would be possible to determine whether or not there were errors in computation or habits of work which were characteristic of the mentally retarded children and which might contribute to a general inferior performance in arithmetic by this same group.

METHOD

The Diagnostic Chart was administered to determine difference in types of errors made during the solution of simple arithmetic problems. The Chart was originally described in an early publication of Buswell, and was intended to be used as an individual measure of pupil difficulty. Under good educational conditions for which the Diagnostic Chart was intended, a given Chart would be used with a particular child during an entire academic year or longer. For the purpose of this study the entire Chart was administered individually during four successive testing periods.

Reprinted from *American Journal of Mental Deficiency* 52, no. 4 (April 1948): 318–30, by permission.

The Diagnostic Chart itself is divided into four sections corresponding to the four fundamental operations of arithmetic. The addition section contains 46 exercises; subtraction, 44; multiplication, 44; division, 42. The exercises are specially constructed to test specific aspects of the respective arithmetical processes and to provide opportunities for specific habits of work to be shown if those habits are a part of the work procedures of the subject being tested.

The Pupil's Work Sheet for the Diagnostic Chart was placed before the subject who sat at a small table facing the examiner. The examiner recorded on the Examiner's Work Sheet the errors made, the habits of work which slowed the operation under consideration, and other behavior or work habits which were either wrong or poor habits of work procedure. The examiner requested the subject to work all the problems orally in order that the former could be absolutely certain of what was taking place in the subject's reasoning. The child was cautioned to follow the oral procedure continually throughout the course of the examination. The examiner was able to ascertain from this procedure and from the questions which were asked of the subject exactly what work habits had taken place in the solution of the exercise. At a later time the habits which each subject exhibited were grouped together and classified according to headings used by Buswell, although certain additional classifications were also developed.

SUBJECTS

Two groups of fifteen boys each were used: one, a group of mentally retarded subjects comprising the experimental group who had a mean chronological age of 14.29 years, a mean mental age of 10.06 years and a mean intelligence quotient of 73.33; the other, a group of subjects comprising the control group who had a mean chronological age of 9.09 years, a mean mental age of 9.96 years and a mean intelligence quotient of 110.40. The mean arithmetic age of the experimental group was 9.73; of the control group, 9.84. For the experimental group the T-score between mean mental age and mean arithmetic age is 1.169 at a 5 percent level of significance; for the control group, 1.265 at a 30 percent level of significance which is not significant. The difference between M.A. and A.A. for the experimental group while significant at the 5 percent level, was accepted because it was felt that a closer relationship could not be effected with mentally retarded subjects. Neither T-score shows a significant difference between mental age and the arithmetic age. Significant differences do not exist between the mental ages of the experimental and control groups (1.195 at 10 percent level of significance) or between the arithmetic ages of the two groups of subjects (1.120 at 30 percent level of significance). The experimental subjects were pupils at the Wayne County Training School, Northville, Michigan; the control subjects children, pupils of the Adams Elementary School, Birmingham, Michigan. All children of both groups had arithmetic ability comparable to third grade achievement as measured by the results of the Stanford Achievement Tests, Form Z, Primary and Advanced Forms.

RESULTS

Comparison of habits used by experimental and control groups in addition process

The examiner, through analysis of the results of the test and from observations, noted thirty different habits of work dealing with the exercises in addition. Some of these habits were good; others, poor. There are, as is shown in Table 1, statistically significant differences resulting between the means of the experimental and control groups on eight or 27 percent of these habits of work at the 1 or 2 percent level of significance while three additional habits have levels of significance at the 5 percent level.

It is noted that the experimental group make a greater number of errors in the addition combinations than do the control subjects. The experimental pupils count on their fingers and make marks on scratch paper to aid their computations much more often than do normal subjects. Consultation with the teachers of the two groups revealed that these habits (2 and 10)* were permitted almost universally by arithmetic teachers of the retarded boys, whereas it was discouraged by the teachers of the normal boys. The latter fact undoubtedly accounts for the large difference observed between the results of the two groups. It is highly probable that by counting on fingers and by using marks many errors are made which are manifested in the poorer performance of the retarded boys observable in habit 1.

The experimental subjects write down the number to be carried (7) many more times than do the normal boys. The writing of the number to be carried for some of the boys is a distinct aid to accuracy, although, as noted in habit 6, several of the boys write the number irregularly and thereby make additional errors. The fact that the normal boys can retain the number to be

*Numbers in parentheses refer to habits similarly numbered in Table 1 or other related tables.

TABLE 1

WORK HABITS USED IN THE ADDITION PROCESS BY THE EXPERIMENTAL
AND CONTROL GROUPS

Habit	Number of Times Habit Occurred		t Score	Per Cent Level of Significance of t
	Experimental Group	Control Group		
1. Errors in combination	58	41	2.388	5
2. Counting on fingers	171	118	5.998	1
3. Added carried number last	76	56	2.151	5
4. Forgot to add carried number	—	6	3.069	1
5. Repeated work after partly done	17	5	3.309	1
6. Wrote down number to be carried irregularly	19	5	4.114	1
7. Wrote down number to be carried	134	23	16.309	1
8. Omitted one or more digits	—	5	2.659	2
9. Derived unknown combination from known one	3	13	2.659	2
10. Used marks in counting*	12	—	4.020	1
11. Irregular procedure in column	50	53	.328	80
12. Carried wrong number	2	1	.563	60
13. Grouped two or more numbers	19	28	2.374	5
14. Split numbers into parts	3	—	1.811	10
15. Used wrong fundamental operation	2	3	.435	70
16. Lost place in column	3	1	.473	20
17. Disregarded column position	—	1	.515	70
18. Errors in reading numbers	4	2	1.000	40
19. Dropped back one or more tens	—	2	.473	20
20. Disregarded one column	—	1	.515	70
21. Error in writing answer	1	1	0.	99
22. Skipped one or more decades	—	1	.515	70
23. Carried when there was nothing to carry ...	—	1	.515	70
24. Used scratch papers	25	31	.305	30
25. Wrote carried number twice	6	2	1.752	20
26. Multiplied to get addition combination* ...	—	2	1.473	20
27. Added left to right	2	—	1.473	20
28. Wrote carried number in answers*	1	—	.515	70
29. Added digits in two columns together as if in one column*	1	—	.515	70
30. Added same number twice	—	1	.515	70

*Habits not listed in Diagnostic Chart but noted in subjects of present study.

carried and do not need to write it down may be a factor in their superior achievement.

The experimental group tend to add carried numbers last (2), often forgetting them and thereby making errors. The normal group on six occasions forgot to add the carried number (14) and five times forgot to include digits within the problem itself (8) — a tendency suggesting carelessness. The control subjects, however, group numbers in addition more often than the experimental subjects (13). No statistically significant differences are present in the remaining nineteen habits.

The use of marks in counting

Habit 10, the use of marks in calculating, is one which appeared with great regularity with several subjects of the experimental group. The habit is used in all four fundamental processes in a very primitive manner, its use tending to reduce the accuracy and efficiency of the mentally retarded boys in their arithmetic performance. In the addition process groups of marks are placed on the paper which correspond to the digits to be added and each mark is counted to arrive at the answer as in the following problem in which the *sum of eighteen and seven* is required:

IIIIIIIIIIIIIIIIII
IIIIIII   equals 25.

When subtraction is called for, the procedure used by the mentally retarded boys is to write down the marks corresponding to the subtrahend and minuend, cross out those marks which equalize each other, and count the remainder of marks to arrive at the answer. The use of marks causes the greatest error when employed in multiplication operations. One subject of the experimental group was asked to *multiply eight times eight*. His method is illustrated as follows:

IIIIIIII(8)
IIIIIIII(8) IIIIIIIIIIIIIIII(16)
IIIIIIII(8)
IIIIIIII(8) IIIIIIIIIIIIIIII(16) IIIIIIIIIIIIIIIIIIIIIIIIIIIIIIII(32)
IIIIIIII(8)
IIIIIIII(8) IIIIIIIIIIIIIIII(16)
IIIIIIII(8)
IIIIIIII(8) IIIIIIIIIIIIIIII(16) IIIIIIIIIIIIIIIIIIIIIIIIIIIIIIII(32)
                                        equals 64.

This bizarre method is continually used by this subject, and is noted many times throughout the study with other objects of the experimental group. The possibility of error occurring in the use of this primitive procedure is very great and is responsible for many incorrectly solved problems on the part of the experimental subjects. The habit is not typical of any of the control subjects.

Comparison of habits used by experimental and control groups in subtraction process

Twenty-five habits of work were observed in the analysis of the performance of the experimental and control subjects in the subtraction process. Table 2 shows that eleven or 44 percent of these habits have significant differences at the 1 and 2 percent level while three additional habits have levels of significance at 5 percent between the mean scores of the responses of the two groups.

The experimental subjects show a significantly larger number of errors in subtraction combinations (1). Counting (2), as in the addition process, is again a significant factor in the type of habit used in subtraction, and, as in addition, probably accounts for many of the subtraction combination errors. Certain technical aspects of the subtraction process present difficulties to the experimental group. The experimental pupils are significantly inferior to the control pupils in subtraction when there is a zero in the minuend of the problem (3), when a zero appeared in the subtrahend (9), and when the minuend and subtrahend are identical (12). These technical errors denote a specific area which should be emphasized in the arithmetic teaching to mentally retarded children. The experimental pupils make more errors in reading (5) and work from left to right (10) more often than do the control subjects. Closely connected with the habits just mentioned is the habit of completely reversing the problem when it is read. For example, a problem, *two times four,* is read, *four times two.* The experimental pupils are observed to read problems in reverse order (15) a significantly greater number of times than are the subjects of the control group.

The control group subjects continue to make very careless errors by adding instead of subtracting (4). They are also many times observed to write a zero at the left of the answer when it is unnecessary (7). The control group write out the borrowing process many more times than do the experimental group, thereby aiding their accuracy in the subtracting process (9). Observation shows that the control subjects derive an unknown combination from a known one more often than do the experimental subjects (6) thus

TABLE 2

WORK HABITS OBSERVED IN THE SUBTRACTION PROCESS BY THE EXPERIMENTAL
AND CONTROL GROUPS

Habit	Number of Times Habit Occurred		t Score	Per Cent Level of Significance of t
	Experimental Group	Control Group		
1. Errors in combinations	47	19	3.405	1
2. Counting	93	45	4.364	1
3. Errors due to zero in minuend	17	3	4.554	1
4. Added instead of subtracting	2	13	4.050	1
5. Errors in reading	16	6	2.597	5
6. Derived unknown from known combination	1	27	6.177	1
7. Wrote zero in answer when unnecessary* ...	24	58	4.306	1
8. Wrote borrowing process out*	109	162	3.297	1
9. Error due to zero in subtrahend*	10	—	2.804	2
10. Worked from left to right*	6	—	3.069	1
11. Used marks in counting*	4	—	2.271	5
12. Error due to minuend and subtrahend being the same	5	—	2.659	2
13. Increased minuend after borrowing	5	12	2.443	5
14. Used same digit in two columns	3	—	1.879	10
15. Said example backward	24	16	8.787	1
16. Failed to borrow: gave zero as answer	11	6	2.116	10
17. Error in writing answer*	—	1	1.000	40
18. Used scratch paper*	4	3	.586	60
19. Borrowed when unnecessary*	1	—	1.000	40
20. Borrowed from digit in subtrahend*	1	—	1.000	40
21. Did not allow for having borrowed	1	2	.568	60
22. Subtracted minuend from subtrahend	16	15	0	99
23. Omitted a column	1	1	0	99
24. Used trial-and-error method	10	9	.293	80
25. Deducted from minuend when borrowing was unnecessary	4	2	.888	40

*Habits not listed in Diagnostic Chart but noted in performance of subjects of present study.

bringing into a new situation learning and techniques found applicable in other situations.

No significant differences are present between the responses of the two groups of subjects in the eleven remaining habits observed, although certain habits are noted, which, if corrected, should improve the accuracy of both groups of pupils in subtraction. Of these, reversing the subtraction process by subtracting minuend from subtrahend (22) is the most common error and causes the greatest number of errors.

Comparison of habits used by experimental and control groups in the multiplication process

Table 3 illustrates the habits of work used in the multiplication process by the experimental and control groups. Forty-three different habits were observed by the examiner, fourteen or 32 percent of which have t-scores indicating significance. Three additional habits have t-scores at the 5 percent level of significance.

Habit 1 in Table 3 shows that the experimental pupils make a significantly larger number of errors in multiplication combinations than do normal subjects. The experimental pupils evidence more often than do the control subjects multiplication procedures which could be termed *regressive* or typical of immaturity, i.e., counting to get multiplication combinations (5), multiplying by adding numbers together to get a product (6), and repeating part or all of a multiplication table to get a needed digit (13). Errors in reading problems (8), as in addition and subtraction, constitute a habit in which the mentally retarded pupils are significantly inferior to the normal pupils. Certain technical aspects of the multiplication process also produce significant differences between the experimental and control groups. The experimental subjects have difficulty with multiplication problems when a zero appears in the multiplicand (4). It will be recalled that difficulty with combinations involving a zero also constituted a major problem for the experimental group in the subtraction process. The experimental group omits one or more digits in the multiplier (18) and in the multiplicand (19). Counting (16) in order to ascertain the number to be carried, as in the case of the two previous mentioned habits, is noted on sufficient occasions to indicate a trend toward significance. Several times the experimental subjects forgot to carry (11) and forgot to multiply a digit in the multiplicand (12). The experimental group also used scratch paper to assist themselves in the solution of problems more often than did the control group (9).

The performance of the control subjects is characterized by three habits: they write rows of zeros in problems when a zero appears in the multiplier much more often than do the experimental group (2); they write the carried number within the problem in the multiplication operation, the reverse of the procedure they used in the addition process (3); and they make

TABLE 3

Work Habits Used in the Multiplication Process by the Experimental and Control Groups

Habit	Number of Times Habit Occurred		t Score	Per Cent Level of Significance of t
	Experimental Group	Control Group		
1. Errors in combinations	58	25	4.438	1
2. Wrote rows of zeros	12	57	7.556	1
3. Wrote the carried number	97	182	7.377	1
4. Errors due to zero in multiplicand	8	–	3.248	1
5. Counted to get multiplication combination .	53	9	8.010	1
6. Multiplied by adding	26	6	4.685	1
7. Based unknown combination on known one	10	51	5.436	1
8. Errors in reading	7	–	3.526	1
9. Used scratch paper*	19	2	5.298	1
10. Wrote carried number in partial product addition*	6	–	3.069	1
11. Forgot to carry	5	–	2.659	2
12. Did not multiply a digit in multiplicand	8	1	2.659	2
13. Repeated part of a table	22	9	3.402	1
14. Error in position of partial product	1	7	3.069	1
15. Counted in adding partial products*	–	3	1.811	10
16. Counted to carry	27	13	2.299	5
17. Used multiplicand as multiplier	–	1	.515	70
18. Omitted digit in multiplier	4	–	2.271	5
19. Omitted digit in multiplicand	4	–	2.271	5
20. Omitted a digit in product	2	–	1.473	20
21. Illegible figures	–	1	.515	70
22. Forgot to add partial product	1	–	.515	70
23. Wrote wrong digit of multiplier	1	–	.515	70
24. Multiplied from left to right*	–	1	.515	70
25. Added carried number twice*	–	1	.515	70
26. Forgot to add carried number in multiplication portion of problem*	1	–	.515	70
27. Multiplied partial products*	1	–	.515	70
28. Lost place	1	–	.515	70
29. Guessed at product	1	–	.515	70
30. Carried when there was nothing to carry* ..	1	–	.515	70
31. Wrote carried number in answer before carrying to aid memory*	2	–	.515	70
32. Added carried number to multiplicand before multiplying*	3	–	1.473	20
33. Multiplied two digits in multiplicand to get final digit*	1	–	1.811	10
34. Forgot to carry in partial product*	1	–	.515	70
35. Repeated work after partly done*	1	–	.515	70

48   SELECTED WRITINGS

TABLE 3 *continued*

Habit	Number of Times Habit Occurred		t Score	Per Cent Level of Significance of t
	Experimental Group	Control Group		
36. Used marks in multiplying*	2	–	1.473	20
37. Counted to get partial product*	2	–	1.473	20
38. Error in adding carried number	4	6	1.000	40
39. Errors in addition	6	3	1.000	40
40. Used wrong process – added	8	5	.901	40
41. Forgot to add carried number in partial product	3	1	1.000	40
42. Carried a wrong number	2	2	0	99
43. Error in writing product	1	1	0	99

*Habits not listed in Diagnostic Chart but noted in performance of subjects of present study.

more errors than do the experimental group in the position of the partial product (14).

Although the remaining twenty-six habits do not show significant differences, they represent habits which contribute to error and certain facts should be noted. Of the total number of habits used in multiplication, the experimental group uses thirty-five or 81 percent; the control group, twenty-two or 51 percent. In spite of the fact that significant differences do not appear in a large proportion of these observed habits, the experimental group subjects use many habits showing greater lack of familiarity with multiplication procedures than do the control group subjects, e.g., omitting a digit in multiplier (18) and multiplicand (19), multiplying partial products (27), writing the carried number in the answer (31), and adding the carried number to the multiplicand before multiplying (32). Carelessness again typifies many of the non-significant habits which show greater use on the part of the control group subjects. It is observed in this connection that some control group subjects multiply from left to right (24), add a carried number two times (25), make errors in adding partial products (38 and 39), and write illegible figures (21).

Comparison of habits used by experimental and control groups in the division process

Table 4 shows the habits of work observed by the examiner in the performance of the experimental and control groups in exercises employing

TABLE 4

WORK HABITS USED IN THE DIVISION PROCESS BY THE EXPERIMENTAL AND CONTROL SUBJECTS

Habit	Number of Times Habit Occurred		t Score	Per Cent Level of Significance of t
	Experimental Group	Control Group		
1. Found quotient by trial multiplication	17	99	11.811	1
2. Neglected to use remainder within problem .	26	4	5.100	1
3. Omitted digit in dividend	29	5	5.025	1
4. Counted to get quotient	44	2	7.271	1
5. Wrote remainder within problem	—	68	12.870	1
6. Omitted zero resulting from zero in dividend	18	2	4.702	1
7. Said example backwards	15	—	5.076	1
8. Used digits of divisor separately	9	—	3.699	1
9. Omitted final remainder	16	5	2.972	2
10. Used remainder larger than divisor	—	3	1.811	10
11. Error in combinations	44	27	2.554	5
12. Used wrong operation	6	1	2.107	10
13. Grouped too many digits in dividend	3	—	1.811	10
14. Errors in subtraction	1	4	1.386	20
15. Errors in multiplication	—	2	1.473	20
16. Omitted zero resulting from another digit . .	4	1	1.149	30
17. Used short division for long division	4	1	1.386	20
18. Derived unknown combination from known one	—	2	1.473	20
19. Error in reading	4	1	1.811	10
20. Found quotient by adding	4	1	1.811	10
21. Repeated part of multiplication table	9	5	1.170	30
22. Counted in subtraction	1	—	.515	70
23. Used too large a product	1	—	.515	70
24. Used digit in dividend twice	1	2	.563	60
25. Repeated work after partly done*	1	—	.515	70
26. Used too small dividend*	1	—	.515	70
27. Used too large dividend*	1	—	.515	70
28. Omitted digit and carried remainder to second digit*	1	—	.515	70
29. Wrote remainders in quotient*	—	1	.515	70
30. Counted to get remainder*	—	1	.515	70
31. Wrote all of remainders at end of problem .	1	1	0	99

*Habits not included in Diagnostic Chart, but observed in the performance of subjects in present study.

division. Thirty-one different habits were used, of which nine or 29 percent have significant levels of difference between the mean scores of the responses of the two groups. One habit has a level of significance at 5 percent. Twenty-five habits of 80 percent were employed by the experimental group; 22 or 70 percent, by the control group.

The experimental group errors are largely accounted for by habits involving technical aspects of the division process. The mentally retarded boys neglect to use the remainder within the problem (2), omit one or more digits in the dividend (3), say problems backwards (7), use digits of the divisor separately (8), and omit the final remainder (9). It is observed that the mentally retarded pupils omit zeros in the quotient which result from zeros in the dividend (6), a difficulty comparable to that noted in connection with zero combinations in subtraction and multiplication earlier in the test. Counting (4) is employed more often by the experimental group than by the control group subjects. The experimental pupils, as in the other three operations, make a greater number of errors in the division combinations (11).

The control group use the method of finding quotients by trial multiplication (1) much more often than do the experimental subjects. The need for this may be due to the relatively limited experience which the control subjects have had with the division process. The control pupils also write remainders between the digits of the dividend (5), a habit totally ignored by the experimental group. This practice undoubtedly aids normal subjects to achieve greater accuracy. The experimental pupils do not seem to be aware that the technique of writing remainders could be used.

Analysis of the gross results of the Diagnostic Chart

Table 5 shows an analysis of the gross results of the experimental and control groups on the Diagnostic Chart. The table shows that generally the experimental group subjects are able to work fewer problems correctly than are the control pupils. Merely the correctness of the problems was considered here, although in working a problem to get the answer one or more of the habits as shown in Tables 1 to 4, inclusive, might have been employed. In Table 5 the data in the columns with the caption *omitted* indicate the number of problems which the child was unable to work for some reason or another, usually because of lack of previous instruction. The latter accounts for most of the omissions by the control group in multiplication and division.

Table 5 shows that the experimental group solved 535 addition problems correctly; the control group, 577. Table 1, previously mentioned, shows that the mentally retarded subjects have more occurrences of poor addition habits than do normal subjects; Table 5 shows that they are not able to solve as many addition problems correctly. The experimental group worked 78 percent of the problems correctly, have 11 percent wrong and omit 11 percent; the control group, 83 percent correct, 8 percent wrong and omit 7 percent.

In subtraction the experimental subjects work 458 problems or 69 percent correctly, 106 or 16 percent wrong and omit 96 or 14 percent. The control pupils solve 499 problems or 75 percent correctly, 96 problems or 14 percent wrong and omit 65 problems or 9 percent. Of the problems at-

TABLE 5

Analysis of the Gross Results of the Diagnostic Chart Made by the Experimental and Control Groups

Part A. The Experimental Group

Case Number	Addition			Subtraction			Multiplication			Division		
	Correct	Wrong	Omitted	Correct	Wrong	Omitted	Correct	Wrong	Omitted	Correct	Wrong	Omitted
012	41	0	5	38	0	6	37	0	7	27	0	14
022	39	2	5	18	17	9	21	13	10	17	4	21
032	32	9	6	26	7	6	6	8	30	1	3	39
042	26	15	5	35	3	6	10	7	27	10	4	28
052	31	10	5	33	5	6	25	12	7	9	17	16
062	35	6	5	28	10	6	15	12	17	0	0	42
072	40	1	5	36	2	6	28	9	7	13	13	16
082	32	9	5	29	9	6	9	5	20	7	13	22
092	36	5	5	35	3	6	33	5	6	21	7	14
102	41	0	5	37	1	6	35	2	7	22	6	14
112	28	12	6	31	7	6	4	16	24	5	9	28
122	36	4	6	32	6	6	23	8	13	10	13	19
132	40	1	5	29	9	6	13	15	16	5	16	21
142	37	3	6	33	3	8	22	5	17	6	20	15
152	41	0	5	33	5	6	33	8	14	7	10	25
Total	535	76	79	458	106	96	303	135	222	161	135	334
Percent	78	11	11	69	16	14	45	20	33	25	21	52
Percent of those attempted	87	12		81	18		69	30		54	46	

TABLE 5 *continued*

Part B. The Control Group

	Processes											
	Addition			Subtraction			Multiplication			Division		
Case Number	Correct	Wrong	Omitted	Correct	Wrong	Omitted	Correct	Wrong	Omitted	Correct	Wrong	Omitted
011	41	1	4	34	2	8	30	3	11	23	0	19
021	45	1	0	37	1	6	21	1	22	22	0	20
031	37	5	4	22	18	4	20	0	24	17	3	22
041	38	1	7	38	0	6	18	1	25	16	3	23
051	40	2	4	33	9	2	17	2	25	15	6	22
061	33	6	7	24	14	6	17	1	26	14	5	23
071	37	9	0	32	12	0	29	11	4	20	13	9
081	38	2	6	33	5	6	26	4	14	23	4	15
091	38	3	5	29	7	8	19	3	22	9	0	33
101	41	5	0	37	7	0	31	6	7	20	8	14
111	35	3	8	38	0	6	17	1	26	26	0	22
121	33	12	1	40	4	0	39	2	3	20	0	22
131	44	2	0	30	14	0	18	1	25	8	1	33
141	38	3	5	36	1	7	16	3	25	18	2	22
151	39	7	0	36	2	6	30	4	10	19	1	22
Total	577	62	51	499	96	65	348	43	269	263	46	321
Percent	83	08	07	75	14	09	52	06	40	41	07	52
Percent of those attempted ...	90	09		83	16		88	12		85	15	

tempted the experimental group have 81 percent correct; the control group, 83 percent.

The results of the responses to multiplication and division problems show somewhat greater gross differences. In multiplication the mentally retarded subjects solve 303 problems or 45 percent correctly, 135 problems or 20 percent wrong and omit 222 problems or 33 percent; the control group, 348 problems or 52 percent correct, 43 problems or 6 percent wrong and omit 249 or 40 percent. The experimental group have 69 percent of the problems attempted correct; the control group, 88 percent.

In division the experimental group solve 161 or 25 percent correctly, 135 or 21 percent wrong and omit 334 or 52 percent; the control group, 263 or 40 percent correct, 46 or 7 percent wrong and 321 or 52 percent omitted. Of the division problems attempted, the experimental group have 54 percent correct, the control group, 85 percent correct.

It is apparent that as the process becomes more complicated the difference in the performance of the mentally retarded and normal children becomes more marked, the mentally retarded subjects being inferior to the normal subjects in each process.

SUMMARY

Tables 1 to 4, inclusive, have shown some differences in the type of habits used by the experimental and control groups in solving arithmetic problems which involve one of the four fundamental operations. Table 5 has shown that in solving exercises involving all four fundamental operations the mentally retarded boys are inferior to the normal boys, and that in both groups there is greater proficiency in addition and subtraction than in multiplication and division.

In the experimental group the work habits which cause error and difficulty are of four general types. The *first* type of habits includes certain primitive or immature procedures which cause many errors. Counting on fingers and making marks on paper are habits of this category noted in addition, subtraction and multiplication, and are frequently noted in the division process. Multiplying by adding figures together until the required product is obtained is frequently observed. The mentally retarded pupils also find it necessary to repeat part or all of a multiplication table in order to arrive at a specific combination. All these procedures tend to slow up and inhibit the correctness of the operation. Although they may serve as aids in some instances, they provide many opportunities for error and faulty work.

A *second* type of habit which contributes to error is technical in nature. On several occasions the experimental pupils manifest a lack of understanding of basic and crucial procedures in subtraction, multiplication and division. Outstanding among these difficulties is the lack of proficiency in the use and manipulation of combinations involving *zero*. The zero digit is a real hindrance to the mentally retarded pupils in all three processes mentioned above. As the zero is a definitely abstract concept, difficulty with it might properly be expected. Emphasis on the zero should be an important part of classroom instruction with mentally retarded pupils. Other examples of technical difficulties have been pointed out earlier particularly with multiplication and division operations which prove troublesome for the experimental pupils.

Carelessness accounts for a *third* general classification of work habits of the experimental group. Habits such as adding carried numbers irregularly, forgetting to carry, forgetting to multiply, and guessing cause many errors and are important factors in the inefficiency of the experimental group. The factor of guessing is closely associated with the need to maintain social status discussed elsewhere,[3] and thus the mentally retarded boys proffer answers even though they may be incorrect.

Errors in reading constitute the *fourth* type of poor habit. This faulty reading does not result because of a lack of knowledge of arithmetic vocabulary, a factor known to be typical of the experimental group,[4] but because the retarded boys do not know how to read problems written in concrete form. *The problem, 13 − 4, is read, four take away thirteen; 13 ÷ 4, four divided by thirteen.* Not only are reversals common throughout the four operations, but also misreading the problem as printed is often noted, viz., the problem, 2×4, is read *twelve times four*. Similar errors constitute a significant difference between the experimental and control groups.

The primary poor habit demonstrated by the normal pupils is that of carelessness. They hurry, omit digits, forget to add the carried numbers, use the wrong operation by not thinking of what they are doing, and in multiplication make errors in the position of partial products. On the other hand, the normal subjects tend to use aids which facilitate accuracy in their problem solving. They write out the borrowing process in subtraction, write rows of zeros in multiplication, group numbers in addition, and use trial multiplication in division to determine proper quotients. They also write the carried number in multiplication exercises in which the process is more complicated. They show themselves capable of abstract thinking in the addition process by almost universally mentally retaining the carried number to be added.

BIBLIOGRAPHY

1. Buswell, Guy T., *Diagnostic Studies in Arithmetic*. Supplementary Educational Monographs, University of Chicago (July 1926):83–187.

2. Cruickshank, William M., "A Comparative Study of Psychological Factors Involved in the Responses of Mentally Retarded and Normal Boys to Problems in Arithmetic", doctoral dissertation, University of Michigan, 1946.

3. Cruickshank, William M., "Qualitative Analysis of Intelligence Test Responses." *Journal of Clinical Psychology* 3 (October 1947):381.
4. Cruickshank, William M., "The Arithmetic Vocabulary of Mentally Retarded Boys." *Journal of Exceptional Children* 13 (December 1946):93.

6

THE USE OF INTELLIGENCE TESTS WITH CHILDREN OF RETARDED MENTAL DEVELOPMENT

I. Comparison of the 1916 and 1937 Revisions
of the Stanford-Binet Intelligence Scales

(*with Thomas J. Qualtere*)

$\mathcal{S}$INCE THE 1937 Revision of the Stanford-Binet Intelligence Scale has been generally accepted as one of the principal diagnostic instruments in clinical psychology and has superseded the original 1916 Stanford-Binet Scale, many questions have been raised by those using the tests as to their equivalence at different ages and with various ability groups.[1,2,3] In 1947 the New York State Planning Conference for the Exceptional requested that a study be made comparing the 1916 and the 1937 Form L Revisions of the Stanford-Binet Intelligence Scales as instruments utilized in special class placement with children of retarded mental development. It was for this purpose that the present study was undertaken.

THE METHOD AND THE INSTRUMENTS

Method of selection according to educational criteria

One hundred subjects were included in this study among whom were those attending special classes in the public schools of Syracuse, Binghamton, and Yonkers, New York, and some who had already been admitted to the Syracuse State School for high-grade mentally retarded children during the year 1947–48. The subjects of this study were selected in two ways. First, if a teacher in a public school suspected a child to be mentally retarded,

Reprinted from *American Journal of Mental Deficiency* 54, no. 3 (January 1950): 361–69, by permission.

the child was referred to the local board of education. The school psychologist would then examine the child with the 1937 Form L Stanford-Binet Intelligence Scale and if the child received an intelligence quotient score between 50 and 75 he was recommended for placement in one of the special education classes already established in the public school system. All of the students included in the present study had been classified as mentally retarded and were in special classes. Secondly, children who were referred to the Onondaga County Juvenile Court for a number of psycho-social reasons and who were found to be mentally retarded, were admitted to the Syracuse State School. At the time of this study these subjects were already admitted to the school and had been attending special classes there.

Method used in the experiment

The individual tests were administered by an examiner of known competency. Seventy-three subjects were tested by one of the writers; twenty-one, by the school psychologist of Binghamton; six, by the school psychologist of Younkers, New York. Of the seventy-three subjects with whom the writers worked, no child took part except on a voluntary basis.

The subjects had been attending special classes for a period of at least two months when the testing was begun. They had a planned schedule which was different from that of the daily program in the regular classes of the public schools. They arrived at school at the regular time, but instead of having the usual one and a half hours for a lunch period they had only a half hour and were dismissed at 2:30 P.M., an hour before the scheduled time for the remainder of the public school children.

In order to establish the best possible rapport with these children, the examiner visited each school for two days before any testing was begun and sat in on some of the classes which the subjects were attending. The teachers were very cooperative and they, as well as the examiner, told the subjects the purpose of the examiner's presence there. The subjects were told that the examiner would like to work with each one individually and that their cooperation was on a voluntary basis. They were also told that the results of these tests would in no way affect their school grades or their status in the school. Once the testing was begun the subjects themselves made up a list of the order in which they would be examined, and they saw to it that the examiner was not kept waiting for other subjects to be tested.

The time interval between the administration of the two intelligence scales has been eliminated in this study. To eliminate the variable of time the 1916 and the Form L 1937 Scales were administered consecutively. In removing the variable of time, however, a new variable was introduced, for in the administration of the two scales in consecutive order certain changes were made in the 1916 Stanford-Binet Scale. The two tests were administered in the school testing rooms during school hours under the best possible testing conditions. In every case the 1937 Form L was administered first with two minor changes in procedure. Test item five at Year Level IX, "Making Change" was timed. The instructions in the manual[4] do not set any time limit on this item. It was, however, felt by the writers that five minutes for each question of the test item would be sufficient even for mentally retarded subjects. In many instances when the subject did not attempt an answer, but merely made lip movements or counted fingers, the full five minutes were allowed before counting the item as failed. Test item five at Year Level X, "Word Naming," was also timed. Three minutes were allotted with a record of the number of words given at the end of one minute being taken in order that the test item could be scored on both the 1916 and the 1937 Form L scales.

The 1916 scale was administered almost immediately after the 1937 Form L had been completed. A rest period from ten to fifteen minutes was permitted, but many of the subjects were reluctant to leave the testing table unless the examiner suggested such excuses as getting a drink of water, drawing on the blackboard or just standing and stretching a while. The examiner watched carefully for signs of fatigue and in several cases a second testing period was granted.

In the administration of the 1916 scale, no test which could be scored according to the subject's performance on Form L was repeated on the 1916 scale, but credit was given on the basis of his success or failure on Form L. Identical items and similar items which were not identical were scored according to the performance on Form L. Several changes in procedure had to be permitted, however. On the similarities test where the child gives the similarity between two things, credit was given at Year VIII on the original 1916 edition if it had been passed at Year VII on Form L, even though on Form L the question, "How are they the same?" may be used in addition to, "How are they alike?", the only question permitted on the 1916 scale. On the Comprehension Test which is scored at Year VII on Form L, credit was given at Year VIII on the 1916 scale if it had been passed on Form L in spite of the fact that two of the statements are more clearly and simply stated on Form L. On Form L the examiner says, "What's the thing for you to do when you are on your way to school and *see* that you are in danger of being late?" On the 1916 scale the question is worded, "What's the thing for you to do when you are on your way to school and *notice* that you are in danger of being late?" The Ball and Field test was another item where directions were modified on Form L. On Form L the examiner says,

Let's suppose that your purse, with a lot of money in it, has been lost in this big field. Take this pencil and start here (pointing) at the gate, and show me where you would go to hunt for the purse so as to be sure not to miss it.

On the 1916 scale the question is worded,

Let us suppose that your baseball has been lost in this round field. You have no idea what part of the field it is in. You don't know what direction it came from, how it got there, not with what force it came. All you know is that the ball is lost somewhere in this field. Now, take this pencil and mark out a path to show me how you would hunt for the ball so as to be sure not to miss it. Begin at the gate and show me what path you would take.

The Form L instructions are less complex than those on the 1916 scale and hence were the ones used. It should be mentioned that because this test is scored at Year VIII (for an inferior plan or better) and at Year XII on the 1916 scale and once only at Year XIII on Form L, in the majority of cases the test was not administered as part of Form L at the lower age levels into which many of the subjects were found. The change in procedure for the Word naming test at Year X was made in giving Form L as described previously.

In order to keep the score as similar as possible to that which it would have been if each scale had been given alone, the following procedures were adopted. If it was necessary to give a test which appeared on Form L, but which had not been administered, the test was given according to the directions for the 1916 scale. If, in giving the 1916 scale, tests were passed above the level of all failures on Form L, i.e., two successive year level failures, credit was not given on the Form L. It was the practice of the writer, who administered all but twenty-six of the tests personally, to carry out the test to at least two years in which there were all failures. In many cases these two years were in succession. Often after a year level in which all items were failed was reached, the pupil would succeed on an item or items beyond this level. The test was then continued until another year of failures was reached. The writers felt the necessity for a thorough test in the examination of mentally defective children.

RESULTS

It will be recalled from the above that a statistical analysis was to be made between the results obtained by children with retarded mental development on the 1916 Stanford-Binet Scale and the 1937 Form L Revision[5] of the same scale. From the raw data Pearson Product Moment Correlations were computed, and likewise F- and T-tests were made to determine significant differences, if any, which might exist between the difference of the means of the two forms of the scale.

Table 1 shows the dispersion of the one hundred subjects on the 1937 Form L scale according to mental ages and also shows corresponding intelligence quotient ranges. It will be observed from Table 1 that there are six subjects with a mental age between 4-0 and 4-11 whose intelligence quotient range is 62-65, whose mean intelligence quotient, corrected according to McNemar's[6] tables, is 63.34, and whose uncorrected mean intelligence quotient is 64.66. The figures for the remainder of the mental age levels can be read from Table 1 in similar fashion. Mental ages varied from 4-3 to 12-8 within the one hundred subjects.

Table 2 shows the dispersion of the one hundred subjects on the 1916 scale according to mental ages and also shows corresponding intelligence quotient ranges. It will be observed from Table 2 that there are three subjects with a mental age between 4-0 and 4-11 whose intelligence quotient range is 68-73 and whose mean intelligence quotient uncorrected is seventy. The figures for the remainder of the mental age levels can be read from the table in similar fashion. Mental ages varied from 4-6 to 12-8 within the one hundred subjects.

Table 3 shows the results and distributions of intelligence quotients

TABLE 1

STANDARD AND CORRRECTED INTELLIGENCE QUOTIENT RANGE
OF ONE HUNDRED SUBJECTS ON THE 1937 FORM L SCALE

Mental Age	I.Q. Range Corrected	Mean I.Q. Corrected	I.Q. Range Uncorrected	Mean I.Q. Uncorrected	Number of Cases
4-0 to 4-11	62-65	63.34	62-69	64.66	6
5-0 to 5-11	55-89	73.55	55-89	73.55	18
6-0 to 6-11	50-78	67.41	50-78	66.91	22
7-0 to 7-11	51-81	69.41	51-81	68.23	17
8-0 to 8-11	57-83	70.12	57-83	69.00	16
9-0 to 9-11	68-87	72.60	64-87	71.50	10
10-0 to 10-11	68-90	76.80	68-88	75.80	5
11-0 to 11-11	76-82	79.00	76-80	78.00	4
12-0 to 12-11	81-84	82.50	81-84	82.50	2
Total.........					100

TABLE 2

RANGE OF STANDARD INTELLIGENCE QUOTIENT SCORES OF THE
ONE HUNDRED SUBJECTS ON THE 1916 STANFORD-BINET INTELLIGENCE SCALE

Mental Age	Intelligence Quotient Range Uncorrected	Mean Intelligence Quotient Uncorrected	Number of Cases
4-0 to 4-11	68-73	70.00	3
5-0 to 5-11	58-92	74.50	16
6-0 to 6-11	53-101	72.87	24
7-0 to 7-11	48-82	67.35	17
8-0 to 8-11	63-88	73.18	17
9-0 to 9-11	60-86	68.94	16
10-0 to 10-11	72-88	77.67	3
11-0 to 11-11	76-79	77.67	3
12-0 to 12-11	84	84.00	1
Total.........			100

TABLE 3

RESULTS OF THE INTELLIGENCE QUOTIENTS ON THE TWO SCALES USING CORRECTED
AND UNCORRECTED SCORES

Intelligence Quotient Range	1937 Form L		1916
	Uncorrected	Corrected	
45-49..................	0	0	1
50-54..................	2	2	3
55-59..................	12	9	5
60-64..................	16	15	19
65-69..................	16	18	12
70-74..................	22	22	22
75-79..................	16	15	18
80-84..................	10	13	9
85-89..................	6	5	7
90-94..................	0	1	2
95-99..................	0	0	0
100-104..................	0	0	2
Total................... 100		100	100
Mean intelligence quotient 70.19		70.82	71.98
Standard deviation 8.97		9.11	10.05
Mean mental age 7-6		7-6	7-7

of one hundred subjects on the 1916 and 1937 Form L scales. The intelligence quotients ranged from forty-eight to one hundred and one on the 1916 scale; from fifty to ninety on the 1937 Form L scale when the use of McNemar's correction was applied to those scores which came within the age levels to warrant such correction. The intelligence quotients ranged from fifty to eighty-nine when the intelligence quotient scores were left uncorrected. It will be observed from Table 3 that there were no subjects in the intelligence quotient range forty-five to forty-nine on the 1937 Form L scale, both when the scores were corrected or left uncorrected, and that one subject had an intelligence quotient which placed him in the forty-five to forty-nine intelligence quotient range on the 1916 scale. There were two subjects within the intelligence quotient range of fifty to fifty-four on the 1937 Form L when the scores were left uncorrected, two subjects within this range when the intelligence quotient scores were corrected and three subjects within this intelligence quotient range on the 1916 scale. The figures for the remaining number of subjects who scored within the intelligence quotient ranges mentioned in Table 3 can be read from the table in the same manner.

It can further be seen from Table 3 that, according to the distribution of intelligence quotients on the two scales, the 1937 Form L corrected intelligence quotient scores follow the normal curve more closely than do the uncorrected scores of the 1937 Form L or the 1916 scale intelligence quotient scores. Table 3 also shows that the mean intelligence quotient obtained on the 1937 Form L (uncorrected) was 70.19 (S.D. 8.97), and the mean mental age 7–6 years; on the 1937 Form L (corrected), 70.82 (S.D. 9.11), and the mean mental age 7–6 years. On the 1916 scale the mean intelligence quotient was 71.98 (S.D. 10.05); the mean mental age 7–7 years.

The mean distribution for the 1916 Stanford-Binet intelligence quotients is 1.16 points higher compared with the 1937 Form L when the corrected scores on the 1937 Form L are used and 1.79 points higher when the scores are left uncorrected. The difference does not appear to be significant, however, since the critical ratio is only 1.32.

A Pearson Product-Moment Correlation of .899 was found between the intelligence quotients of the 1916 scale and the intelligence quotients from the 1937 Form L scale when uncorrected scores were used. Another correlation was computed between the two scales using corrected scores for the 1937 Form L and a correlation of .88 was found. In light of the two correlations it might be suspected that the two scales are measuring approximately the same factors.

Table 4 presents a comparison of the means of the differences between the intelligence quotients on the 1916 and 1937 Form L scales both when the corrected scores on the 1937 Form L are used and when they are left

TABLE 4

COMPARISON OF THE MEANS OF THE DIFFERENCES BETWEEN THE INTELLIGENCE
QUOTIENTS ON THE TWO SCALES AND THE RESULTING T-SCORES

Scale	Mean	Standard Deviation	Differences Between the Means Compared with 1916 Scale	T-Score	Percent Level of Significance of T
1916...................	71.98	10.05	—	—	—
1937 (Uncorrected)	70.19	8.97	1.79	4.04	1
1937 (Corrected)	70.82	9.11	1.16	2.38	1-2

uncorrected. Table 4 shows that there is a significant difference between the means of the related measures. The mean intelligence quotient score for the 1916 scale is 71.98 (S.D. 10.05); for the 1937 scale uncorrected, 70.19 (S.D. 8.97); for the 1937 scale corrected, 70.82 (S.D. 9.11). A T-score of 4.04 representing a less than one percent level of significance prevails between the difference of the means of the 1916 scale intelligence quotients and the 1937 Form L intelligence quotients when these scores are left uncorrected. A T-score of 2.38, representing a level of significance between one and two percent, prevails between the difference of the means of 1916 intelligence quotients and the 1937 Form L intelligence quotients (corrected). It would appear from this that the means of the two scales did not come from the same population and that perhaps these tests are not measuring the same qualities insofar as mentally retarded subjects are concerned.

Table 5 shows the distribution of the difference between the intelligence quotients when the 1937 Form L intelligence quotient is subtracted from the 1916 Stanford-Binet intelligence quotient. Negative changes indicate instances in which Form L intelligence quotient is higher; positive changes Form L intelligence quotient lower, and zero changes when both intelligence quotients are the same.

Table 6 gives the summary of the changes in intelligence quotients between the 1937 Form L and the 1916 revisions of the Stanford-Binet Intelligence Scale. It can be seen from the table that there was no difference in intelligence quotients between the 1937 and 1916 scales, when the corrected scores on the 1937 scale were used, in twelve percent of the cases; in thirteen percent of the cases, when the uncorrected scores were used. In 35 percent of the one hundred cases there was a difference between the intelligence quotients on the two scales of one to four points when the 1937 corrected scores

TABLE 5

LOSS OR GAIN OF INTELLIGENCE QUOTIENT POINTS ON THE 1937 FORM L SCALE WHEN COMPARED WITH THE 1916 STANFORD-BINET SCALE

Form L Intelligence Quotient Range	Amount and Direction of Change						
	Positive Change				Zero Change	Negative Change	
	20–16	15–11	10–6	5–1	0	1–5	6–10
45–49.................	−	−	−	−	−	−	−
50–54.................	−	−	−	1	−	1	−
55–59.................	−	−	1	8	1	2	−
60–64.................	−	−	3	7	4	0	1
65–69.................	−	1	2	10	0	3	1
70–74.................	−	−	3	9	2	6	2
75–79.................	−	−	2	7	4	2	1
80–84.................	−	−	2	3	1	3	1
85–89.................	1	1	−	2	1	1	−
90–94.................	−	−	−	−	−	−	−
95–99.................	−	−	−	−	−	−	−
100–104.................	−	−	−	−	−	−	−

TABLE 6

AMOUNT OF CHANGE BETWEEN THE 1937 FORM L INTELLIGENGE QUOTIENTS AND THE 1916 STANFORD-BINET INTELLIGENCE QUOTIENTS

Difference	Percent of Cases	
	With Corrected 1937 Scores	With Uncorrected 1937 Scores
No difference.............................	12	13
Differed by 1 to 4 points.....................	35	39
Differed by 5 to 8 points.....................	14	18
Differed by 9 to 12 points	5	4
Differed by 13 to 16 points	2	2
Differed by − 4 to − 1 points................	19	17
Differed by − 8 to − 5 points................	11	7
Differed by − 12 to − 9 points...............	2	0
Total	100	100

were used and a difference of one to four points in 39 percent of the cases when the scores were left uncorrected. Fourteen percent of the cases differed by five to eight points when the corrected scores were used; 18 percent when the scores were left uncorrected. Seven percent of the cases had a difference in intelligence quotient points between nine to sixteen when the corrected scores were used; six percent when the scores were left uncorrected. The above were all cases in which the 1916 scale intelligence quotients were higher than the 1937 scale intelligence quotients. It can also be seen from the table that in 19 percent of the cases there was a difference from one to four points between the two scales in which the 1937 scale was higher when the corrected scores were used; in seventeen percent of the cases when the scores were left uncorrected. Thirteen percent of the cases had differences between the two scales of five to nine points when the corrected scores were used; in seven percent of the cases when the scores were left uncorrected.

Table 6 also shows that when the corrected scores on the 1937 scale were used, fifty-six subjects scored higher in the 1916 scale than on the 1937 Form L scale, thirty-two subjects scored higher on the 1937 scale than on the 1916 scale and twelve subjects scored the same on both scales. When the scores were left uncorrected, sixty-three subjects scored higher on the 1916 scale, twenty-four subjects scored higher on the 1937 scale, and thirteen subjects scored the same on both scales.

SUMMARY

It has been shown in the preceding paragraphs that the mental ages of these subjects ranged from 4–3 to 12–8 on the 1937 Form L and from 4–6 to 12–8 on the 1916 scale. The total intelligence quotient scores ranged from fifty to eighty-nine on the 1937 Form L when the uncorrected scores were used; fifty to ninety on the 1937 Form L when the intelligence quotient scores were left uncorrected and a total range of intelligence quotient scores from forty-eight to one hundred and one on the 1916 scale. The mean intelligence quotient for the uncorrected intelligence quotient scores on the 1937 Form L was 70.19 (S.D. 8.97); for the corrected scores 70.82 (S.D. 9.11). The mean intelligence quotient for the intelligence quotient scores on the 1916 scale was 71.98 (S.D. 10.05). The mean intelligence quotient for the 1916 scale was 1.16 points and 1.79 points higher than the 1937 Form L scale both when the corrected and uncorrected scores were used, respectively. These differences did not appear to be significant statistically since the critical ratio was only 1.32.

The Pearson Product-Moment Correlations obtained between the two scales were .899 and .88 when the uncorrected and corrected scores on the 1937 Form L scale were used, respectively. On the surface, it would thus seem that the two scales were measuring approximately the same qualities. However, when the T-test was applied to see if the two means came from the same population, a T-score of 2.38 was obtained which would tend to show that a statistically significant difference existed between the two scales and that perhaps they were not measuring the same qualities insofar as these mentally retarded subjects are concerned.

BIBLIOGRAPHY

1. H. L. Rheingold and F. C. Pierce, "Comparison of Ratings on the Original and the Revised Stanford-Binet Intelligence Scales at the Borderline and Mental Defective Levels," *Proceedings of the American Association on Mental Deficiency* 41 Part II (1939): 110–19.

2. Eleanor L. Robinson, "A Comparison of Ratings on the 1916 and the 1937 Revisions of the Stanford-Binet Intelligence Scale at the First Grade Level," *Pennsylvania State Bulletin* 2 (1940): 39–51.

3. Morris Krugman, "Some Implications of the Revised Stanford-Binet Scale," *Journal of Educational Psychology* 30 (1936): 504–603.

4. Lewis Terman and Maude Merrill, *Revision of the Stanford-Binet Tests of Intelligence: Directions for Administering.* New York: Houghton-Mifflin Company, 1937.

5. Hereafter the term, 1937 *Form L,* is used consistently in place of the more complete title, "The 1937 Form L Revision of the Stanford-Binet Intelligence Scale." In every case it is this revision that is referred to unless otherwise specified.

6. Quinn McNemar, *The Revision of the Stanford-Binet Scale: An Analysis of the Standardization Data.* Boston: Houghton-Mifflin, 1942.

7

THE USE OF INTELLIGENCE TESTS
WITH CHILDREN
OF RETARDED MENTAL DEVELOPMENT

II. Clinical Considerations

(*with Thomas J. Qualtere*)

A STUDY WAS RECENTLY UNDERTAKEN in which a comparison of results obtained with children of retarded mental development on two forms of the Stanford-Binet Intelligence Scale was made.[1] In this study the 1916 Revision and Form L of the 1937 Revision were used. A problem secondary to the major purpose of the study made itself evident during the collection of data, and it seems pertinent to discuss it fully.

TESTING THE LIMITS

In discussing the customary examination procedure with respect to the desirable range of testing, Terman and Merrill[2] state that:

> It is necessary to go back and give all of the tests of the previous age group, and so on until a level has been reached where all of the tests are passed. This point is the basal age level. In like manner, the examination should be carried up the scale until an age level has been found in which all of the tests are failed. . . . In testing normal children little error will result if we go back no further than the first year in which no failures occurred, and if we stop with the first year in which there was no success. In computing mental age, all successes and failures are taken account of, including any failures that may have occurred below the basal age level, and successes beyond the first year at which all tests have been failed.

Reprinted from *American Journal of Mental Deficiency* 54, no. 3 (January 1950): 370–81, by permission.

The question of how far up the scale the examination must be carried should be considered at this time. Since the number of test items given to the child increases when the test is extended beyond the usual ceiling level, it is imperative that the child respond to items of higher difficulty. The question of fatigue and loss of rapport therefore enter here due to the increasing difficulty of the test items. The number of test items given to each subject will be seen in a later table.

The routine procedure for computation of test items is based on the number of test items administered from the basal year to the last year of complete failure preceded by a success. Table 1 is provided to indicate the range of testing when the suggested normal procedure is used. It was found that over one-fifth (22%) of the subjects were given items from two to five years above their chronological age level and that over three-fourths (76%) of the subjects were given test items two or more years above their present mental age levels.

Table 1 shows the number of test items given to each child from the basal age to the first year level in which all the items were failed. It can be seen from Table 1 that there were two subjects at the mental age level between 4–0 and 4–11 who received eighteen test items from their basal year to their first year of complete failure, two subjects who received twenty-four test items and two subjects who received thirty test items. The average number of test items administered to these subjects at the mental age level 4–0 to

TABLE 1

NUMBER OF ITEMS ADMINISTERED TO EACH CHILD FROM BASAL YEAR
TO THE LAST YEAR OF COMPLETE FAILURE PRECEDED BY A SUCCESS

Mental Age	Number of Items										Average
	18	24	30	36	42	48	50	52	56	60	
4–0 to 4–11	2	2	2	0	0	0	0	0	0	0	24.00
5–0 to 5–11	2	4	4	2	3	1	2	0	0	0	33.22
6–0 to 6–11	1	2	3	5	7	2	2	0	0	0	37.54
7–0 to 7–11	1	2	3	3	4	3	1	0	0	0	36.82
8–0 to 8–11	0	3	4	2	1	2	1	1	1	1	38.75
9–0 to 9–11	0	2	1	3	0	2	1	1	0	0	38.40
10–0 to 10–11	0	0	0	2	1	1	0	1	0	0	42.80
11–0 to 11–11	0	0	1	0	1	1	1	0	0	0	42.50
12–0 to 12–11	0	0	0	1	0	0	0	1	0	0	44.00
Total	6	15	18	18	17	12	8	4	1	1	

4–11 was twenty-four. At the mental age level 5–0 years to 5–11 years, for example, there were two subjects who received eighteen items from their basal year to their first year level of complete failure, four who received twenty-four test items, four who received thirty test items, two who received thirty-six test items, three who received forty-two test items, one who received forty-eight test items, and two who received fifty test items. The average number of test items administered at this age level was 33.22. The figures for the remaining number of test items administered to each of the subjects from the basal year level to the first year level of complete failure can be read from the table in similar fashion. It can also be seen from Table 1 that there was a total of six subjects in the study to whom eighteen test items were administered from the basal year level to the first year level in which all items were failed, fifteen subjects to whom twenty-four test items were administered, eighteen subjects to whom thirty-six test items were administered, seventeen subjects to whom forty-two test items were administered, twelve subjects to whom forty-eight test items were administered, eight subjects to whom fifty test items were administered, one subject to whom fifty-six test items were administered and one subject to whom sixty test items were administered.

The writers feel that in the examination of children with retarded mental development this usual procedure works to the disadvantage of the child. It was the policy, the reader will recall, to extend the upper ceiling limit to two successive year levels in which all the items were failed. The procedure resulted in the acquisition of scores which differed from those which would have been obtained had the usual procedure been followed. Items three or more year levels above the subjects' mental age were administered in almost forty percent of the cases. A study of the actual test items passed by the subjects in this group was made to determine on which particular item or items the subjects had a tendency to succeed on the levels above that which would generally be considered their upper limit.

Table 2 shows the test items passed after the first year of complete failure was reached and the frequency with which they passed the items.

It can be observed from the table that of all the subjects who reached a ceiling at the Year Level IV according to the normal standard procedure, there was one subject who passed one test item beyond this level of failure, and two subjects who passed two test items beyond their normal ceiling level at Year Level IV. It can further be observed that of those subjects who reached a ceiling age at Year Level V, one subject passed one test item beyond that point; one subject, two test items beyond the ceiling at Year Level V; four subjects, three test items beyond that level; two subjects, four test items beyond that ceiling; three subjects, five test items beyond the ceiling

TABLE 2

NUMBER OF SUBJECTS PASSING ITEMS ABOVE THEIR FIRST YEAR OF COMPLETE FAILURE

Number of Items Passed	1	2	3	4	5	6
Failure Level 1937 Form L						
4	1	2	0	0	0	0
5	1	1	4	2	3	3
6	0	7	1	6	4	6
7	2	2	3	1	1	2
8	3	2	0	1	4	0
9	2	0	4	2	3	2
10	0	8	0	0	2	3
11	4	1	1	4	1	1
12	0	2	6	3	1	1
13	2	1	3	0	0	1
14	0	0	1	1	1	0
Average adult	0	0	1	1	0	0
Total.............	15	26	24	21	20	19

level; and three subjects, six test items beyond what would ordinarily have been their ceiling level. The figures for the remaining number of subjects who passed test items beyond the first year level in which there was complete failure and number of test items which they passed beyond each of these levels can be read from the table in the same way. The table also shows that there was a total of fifteen subjects who passed one test item beyond the level where they would have reached a ceiling had the usual normal testing procedure been applied, twenty-six subjects who passed two test items beyond that level; twenty-four subjects, three test items beyond the usually prescribed ceiling level; twenty-one subjects, four test items above this level; twenty subjects, five test items beyond; and nineteen subjects, six test items above the usual ceiling level.

A comparison of the scatter on both the 1937 Form L and the 1916 revisions indicates that a large percentage of children with retarded mental development increase their scores from one to five intelligence quotient points when the tests are extended beyond the year level in which all test items are failed. On the 1937 Form L, thirty-eight percent of the subjects showed increases in scores as compared to thirty-three percent of the subjects on the 1916 scale when the tests were extended beyond what ordinarily would have been their usual ceiling level. The differences in percent of gain seem large but they were not found to be statistically significant since the critical ratio obtained was 2.4. However, there is some indication of a trend in that direction, i.e., towards a significant difference.

Table 3 illustrates the number of subjects who gained intelligence quotient points after having completely failed one whole year level. It will be observed from Table 3 that there were two subjects who gained one intelligence quotient point after having completely failed Year Level V, nine subjects who gained one intelligence quotient point having completely failed Year Level VII, four subjects who gained one intelligence quotient point after having completely failed Year Level IX, three subjects who gained one intelligence quotient point after having completely failed Year Level XII, and one subject who gained one intelligence quotient point after having completely failed Year Level XIII. Twenty subjects gained one intelligence quotient point after having completely failed one whole year level. It can also be observed from the table that there were two subjects who gained two intelligence quotient points after having completely failed Year Level VI, four subjects who gained two intelligence quotient points after having completely failed Year Level VIII, two subjects who gained two intelligence quotient points after having completely failed Year Level X and one subject who gained two intelligence quotient points after having completely failed Year Level XI. There was a total of nine subjects who gained two intelligence quotient points after having completely failed one whole year level. Likewise from the table, there were two subjects who gained three intelligence quotient points after having completely failed Year Level VII, two subjects who gained three intelligence quotient points after completely failing Year Level

TABLE 3

SUBJECTS WHO GAINED INTELLIGENCE QUOTIENT POINTS
AFTER HAVING COMPLETELY FAILED ONE WHOLE YEAR LEVEL

Number of Intelligence Quotient Points Gained	Level at Which First Whole Year Failure Occurred									Total Number of Subjects
	5	6	7	8	9	10	11	12	13	
1	2	–	9	–	4	3	–	1	1	20
2	–	2	–	4	–	2	1	–	–	9
3	–	–	2	–	2	1	–	–	–	5
4	–	–	1	–	1	–	–	–	–	2
5	–	–	–	1	–	1	–	–	–	2
Total.......	2	2	12	5	7	7	1	1	1	38

IX, and one subject who gained three intelligence quotient points after completely failing Year Level X. There was a total of five subjects in this study who gained three intelligence quotient points after having completely failed one whole year level. The table also shows that there was one subject who gained four intelligence quotient points after completely failing Year Level VII and one subject who gained four points after completely failing Year Level IX. A total of two subjects gained four intelligence quotient points after completely failing one whole year level. One subject gained five intelligence quotient points after completely failing Year Level VIII and one subject gained five intelligence quotient points after completely failing Year Level X, making a total of two subjects who gained five intelligence quotient points after failing one whole year level.

Table 3 shows that thirty-eight percent of the subjects in this study gained from one to five intelligence quotient points when the test was extended beyond the first year in which all the items were failed. If, then, an examiner wishes to administer an accurate test, he will need to extend it to at least one whole year level beyond the year in which the child fails all the test items.

Another comparison was made between the mental ages obtained if the test was not continued beyond the first year level in which all the test items were failed and the mental ages obtained when the test was carried beyond that point. Table 4 shows, according to age, the range of increase in mental age, the range of increase in mental age when the test is continued beyond the first year level of complete failure on the 1937 Form L revision.

It will be observed from Table 4 that in all cases located between the age level 4-0 to 4-11 there was a range of increase in months of mental age from zero to two months with the average increase in months of mental age being .5 month. It can also be seen from the table that there was only one subject between the age level 4-0 to 4-11 years who showed any change in intelligence quotient points. In this case there was a range of increase in months of mental age of two months with the average range of increase being the same since only one subject was located in this group. At the age level 5-0 to 5-11, where eighteen subjects were located, the range of increase in months of mental age was zero to six months with an average increase of .7 month. There were three subjects in this age group who showed enough increase in months of mental age to warrant some change in their intelligence quotient rating. The range of increase for these three subjects was from two to six months with an average increase in months of mental age being 3.4 months. The figures for the remainder of the ranges of increase in months of mental age involving all subjects in the study and only those subjects showing enough increase in mental age to warrant some change in their intelli-

TABLE 4

DIFFERENCES IN MENTAL AGE OBTAINED WHEN THE TEST IS EXTENDED
BEYOND THE FIRST YEAR LEVEL OF COMPLETE FAILURE
ON THE 1937 FORM L SCALE

| Mental Age | Number | All Subjects | | Number | Subjects Showing Change in Intelligence Quotient | |
		Range of Increase in Months of Mental Age	Average Increase in Months of Mental Age		Range of Increase in Months of Mental Age	Average Increase in Months of Mental Age
Column 1	2	3	4	5	6	7
4–0 to 4–11	6	0–2	0.5	1	2	2.0
5–0 to 5–11	18	0–6	0.7	3	2–6	3.4
6–0 to 6–11	22	0–8	2.7	2	2–8	4.1
7–0 to 7–11	17	0–4	1.5	5	2–4	2.8
8–0 to 8–11	16	0–8	1.9	14	2–8	3.6
9–0 to 9–11	10	0–4	1.7	8	2–4	3.0
10–0 to 10–11	5	0–6	1.4	3	2–6	3.4
11–0 to 11–11	4	0–2	0.7	2	2	2.0
12–0 to 12–11	2	0	0	0	0	0
Total	100		1.39	38		3.04

gence quotient can be read from the table in similar fashion. Columns 2–4 of the table illustrate the total number of subjects located at each mental age level, the range of increase in months of mental age beyond that level, and the average increase in months of mental age for all those subjects located at that particular age level. Columns 5–7 show the number of subjects at each of the various age levels whose range of increase in months of mental age was large enough to show some change in the intelligence quotient rating. The same columns also show the average amount of increase in months of mental age for these subjects. There were thirty-eight of the total one hundred subjects in this study who showed an average of 3.04 months increase in mental age when the test was extended beyond the first year level in which all test items were failed. The average increase of 3.04 months is not statistically significant; however, it does appear that the change is great enough to warrant the extension of the testing beyond the first year of complete failure. Terman and Merrill indicate, as quoted elsewhere in this paper, that all successes and failures should be taken account of in computing the mental age even though the standardization group was limited to a single basal year and a single ceiling year.

TABLE 5

DIFFERENCES IN MENTAL AGE OBTAINED WHEN THE TEST IS EXTENDED
BEYOND THE FIRST YEAR LEVEL OF COMPLETE FAILURE
ON THE 1916 SCALE

Mental Age	Number	All Subjects		Number	Subjects Showing Change in Intelligence Quotient	
		Range of Increase in Months of Mental Age	Average Increase in Months of Mental Age		Range of Increase in Months of Mental Age	Average Increase in Months of Mental Age
Column 1	2	3	4	5	6	7
4-0 to 4-11	3	0-2	0.7	1	2	2.00
5-0 to 5-11	16	0-4	1.6	4	2-4	3.00
6-0 to 6-11	24	0-10	3.1	9	2-10	4.77
7-0 to 7-11	17	0-6	1.9	5	2-6	3.60
8-0 to 8-11	17	0-8	2.4	10	2-8	3.40
9-0 to 9-11	16	0-4	1.9	3	2-4	3.33
10-0 to 10-11	3	0-2	0.7	1	2	2.00
11-0 to 11-11	3	0	0	0	0	0
12-0 to 12-11	1	0	0	0	0	0
Total	100		1.37	33		3.16

A comparison comparable to the one just described was also done
on the 1916 scale. Table 5 shows, according to age, the range of increase in
months of mental age when the test is continued beyond the first year level
of complete failure on the 1916 revision. It will be observed from Table 5 that
of all the subjects located between the age level of 4-0 to 4-11 there was a
range of increase in months of mental age from zero to two months with an
average increase of .7 month. It will also be noted that of the three subjects
in this age level there was one who showed an average increase in mental age
of two months which was large enough to warrant some change in the intelligence quotient rating. Likewise, it can be seen that with all the subjects at the
5-0 to 5-11 year level there was a range of increase in months of mental age
from zero to four months with an average increase of 1.6 months. There
were four subjects out of this group who showed a range of increase in
months of mental age large enough to show some change in the intelligence
quotient rating. The figures for the remainder of the subjects who showed
increases in months of mental age beyond the first year level in which all
items were failed can be read from the table in similar fashion. Columns 2-4
of the table give the number of subjects located at each of the mental age

levels, the range of increase in months of mental age for all the subjects in the study and the average increase in months of mental age for all those subjects. Columns 5–7 give only the number of subjects at each mental age level who showed enough change in the mental age increase to make some change in their intelligence quotient rating.

It can be noted from the table that, of all the subjects in this study showing some increase in months of mental age, there was a total of thirty-three who showed increases large enough to warrant some change in their intelligence quotient rating. The average increase in months of mental age for these subjects was 3.16 months. Here, too, as on the 1937 scale, the average increase does not appear to be a large change although it does appear that the change is great enough to extend the testing beyond the first year level in which all test items are failed.

In comparing both scales with respect to the average increase in months of mental age, it can be seen that more months of mental age are gained at the upper age levels on the 1937 Form L (from Year Level IX upward) than on the 1916 and *vice versa*. This is due perhaps to the fact that the test items at Year Level XII and above on the 1916 scale are harder than those on the 1937 Form L at the same age levels. Likewise, those items at the lower levels on the 1916 scale are perhaps somewhat easier than those at the corresponding age levels on the 1937 Form L scale.

HARD AND EASY ITEMS

As was mentioned before, some of the subjects seemed to gain in months of mental age after one complete year level had been failed primarily because some items appeared easier than others and also because these items were located at levels beyond that which had already been completely failed. One of the aspects of this study was to investigate the relative difficulty of the test items on both forms of the Binet by means of tabulating the successes and failures on each item for each subject.

Table 6 illustrates the test items which proved to be most difficult and the test items which were easiest for the mentally retarded subjects on Form L; Table 7, the test items which were most difficult and the ones which were easiest on the 1916 scale.

Table 6 shows the hard items for the mentally retarded children on the 1937 Form L scale to be, for example, Copying a Bead Chain, at Year VI; Similarities and Repeating Five Digits at Year VII; and so on. Examples of the easy items are Mutilated Pictures and Maze Tracing, Year VI; Picture

TABLE 6

Comparison of Hard and Easy Items on the 1937 Form L
for Mentally Retarded Children

Easy Items			Hard Items		
Year	Item Number	Item	Year	Item Number	Item
	3	Mutilated pictures			
VI	6	Maze tracing	VI	2	Copying bead chain
				2	Similarities
VII	1	Picture absurdities	VII	6	Repeating five digits
				1	Vocabulary
VIII	2	Wet fall	VIII	3	Verbal absurdities
				2	Verbal absurdities
IX	3	Memory for designs	IX	4	Rhymes
X	5	Word naming	X	6	Repeating six digits
XI	5	Problem situation	XI	3	Abstract words
XII	3	Messenger boy	XII	6	Minkus completion
XIII	4	Problems of fact	XIII	5	Dissected sentences

Absurdities, Year VII; and so on. The remaining items can be read from the table in like manner.

Table 7 shows the hard and easy test items on the 1916 scale for the mentally retarded children and they can be read from the table in the same way as was just described for Table 6. It can be seen from Tables VI and VII that in certain of the items maturity and experience are the factors for the successes of the mentally retarded children while items involving the higher mental processes are the ones which contribute least to the mental age of these children.

It was shown in a study by Merrill[3] that mentally retarded and normal children of a given mental age did not respond equally well to the same test items. Inspection of the items in Tables 6 and 7 shows that the mentally retarded children appear to do very well on those items which seem to depend to a large degree on extended educational or experiential life accompanying increased chronological age. They seemed to do better on the so-called

TABLE 7

COMPARISON OF HARD AND EASY ITEMS ON 1916 SCALE
FOR MENTALLY RETARDED CHILDREN

Easy Items			Hard Items		
Year	Item Number	Item	Year	Item Number	Item
V	1	Weights	V	2 5	Naming colors Patience
VI	5	Naming coins	VI	6	Repeating sentences
VII	1	Number of fingers	VII	5	Differences
VIII	3	Comprehension	VIII	4	Counting 20 to 1
IX	1	Dates	IX	2	Vocabulary
X	3	Designs	X	4	Reading report
XII	7	Picture interpretation	XII	4 5	Dissected sentences Interpretation of tables
XIV	5	Arithmetic reasoning	XIV	1	Vocabulary

educational tests rather than on the power tests merely because of greater exposure during a greater life span to the thing stressed, but seemed to do rather poorly on the power portion of the test largely because of the lack of ability to use effectively the higher mental processes. These children seemed especially weak in areas largely dependent on the ability to reason verbally, to single out significant aspects of a situation and to draw generalizations.

The hard and easy items for the mentally retarded children which were found in the present study are indicative of the general conclusions reached by Merrill and Martinson and Strauss but tend to differ somewhat from those conclusions reached by Doll.[4]

DISCUSSION OF CLINICAL ASPECTS OF TEST ADMINISTRATION

It has been observed in the present study that the children with retarded mental development gave a great many answers which were wrong, ambiguous, or nonsensical in a nature which would seem to indicate a lack of intellectual ability. In relatively few cases were answers such as "I don't know," for example, given if the child did not know the answer to the question. This finding was also noted by Cruickshank[5] and Strauss and Werner.[6]

These authors studied differences between children of normal and subnormal intelligence with respect to responses of test questions. In commenting on the differences noted in their groups, they indicate that the presence of many *don't know* answers among the subjects of normal intelligence is an evidence of a trait of autocriticism. It is a commonly observed fact and one noted in this study that children of low intelligence do not possess this autocritical attitude. Some evidence of the lack of capacity for self-appraisal was noted in the types of answers which the majority of the mentally retarded subjects gave, i.e., wrong, ambiguous, nonsensical, inadequate and superficial. The retarded child gives an answer for the sake of making an answer and feels thereby that he maintains his social status. This is undoubtedly due to the fact that he is pressed by his past feelings of inadequacy. Normal children in contrast, as already mentioned in previous studies, seem to be able to face the reality of the situation and to admit that they do not know a solution to the problem.

The mentally retarded children had a tendency to respond no matter whether correctly or incorrectly. In some cases where they could not think of anything with which to respond they would go through various lip movements and facial expressions in order to show that they were really thinking about a possible answer. Many times an appreciable amount of time was given before the question was marked as failed and the next item administered. Often the retarded children gave an answer, completely foreign to the solution of the problem, simply because they knew or felt that an answer was expected and that failure to do so would cause a loss in the examiner's esteem. They gave answers not only to maintain themselves in the sight of the examiner, but also in a larger sense to preserve their status in a social situation in which they felt they should be master but in which they could not function satisfactorily because of their low intelligence. As an example of this, the examiner gave to fifteen of the subjects as many words of the vocabulary list on the 1916 scale as they could continue to respond to before admitting that they did not know the answer. Twelve of the fifteen subjects gave from ninety-five to one hundred answers out of the possible one hundred words on the list. The other three gave answers to ninety of the one hundred words, but still they did not admit failure to the ones they could not answer. Instead they went on as if thinking very seriously about the question until the examiner proceeded to the next word.

In many instances the mentally retarded subjects remarked that the words or questions on the test were very simple. Several subjects who scored at the higher levels of the scale became very frustrated when they could not think of a definition of a word. Sometimes the children would change the subject if it appeared rather difficult to other questions on the test or to some personal experience which they chose to talk about. Much time was involved between the time a word was given and the response by the child. In many instances responses were given and often the subject forgot the directions for the question either because he would not comprehend all the words, because he had a very short memory span, or because he would undertake conversation entirely foreign to a solution of the problem.

SUMMARY

The results of the comparison on the two scales, when they are extended beyond the first year level in which all the test items are failed, show a range of increase in months of mental age from zero to ten months, with an average increase of 3.16 months, on the 1916 scale and a range of increase in months of mental age from zero to eight months, with an average increase of 3.04 months on the 1937 Form L scale. Thirty-eight percent of all those subjects who showed some increase in mental age on the 1937 scale gained enough months in mental age when the test was extended to warrant some change in their intelligence quotient rating. Thirty-three percent of all those subjects who showed some increase in months of mental age on the 1916 scale gained enough months in mental age to warrant some change in their intelligence quotient rating. The data of this investigation showed that there was a larger number of subjects who gained in months of mental age on the 1937 scale than on the 1916 scale, although the average increase in months of mental age was larger on the 1916 scale. The data also show that it is imperative that the test be extended through two complete year levels in which all items are failed when testing children with retarded mental development. If this is not done, it is working to the disadvantage of the child.

The children with retarded mental development who were used in this study seemed to do well on the educational tests merely because of greater exposure during a greater life span to the thing stressed, but seemed to do rather poorly on the power portion of the test largely because of the lack of ability to use effectively the higher mental processes. The easiest test items for the mentally retarded children were those which had to do with concrete thinking while the most difficult ones were those in which abstract thinking had to be utilized. It seemed very difficult for these children to function in areas largely dependent on the ability to reason verbally, to single out significant aspects of particular situations, and to draw generalizations.

The mentally retarded subjects demonstrate a lack of autocritical attitude and a great need for maintaining social esteem. They showed no disposition to admit inability to cope with the situation, whereas other studies show that normal children admit inability to deal with a situation. The former subjects proceeded blindly in an attempt to arrive at some of the answers to the questions. In many cases where no answer could be found, lip movements and facial expressions were utilized until such time that the examiner found it necessary to proceed to the next question.

BIBLIOGRAPHY

1. W. M. Cruickshank and T. J. Qualtere, "The Use of Intelligence Tests with Children of Retarded Mental Development. I. Comparison of the 1916 and 1937 Revisions of the Stanford-Binet Intelligence Scales," *American Journal of Mental Deficiency.*

2. Lewis Terman and Maude Merrill, *Measuring Intelligence* (New York: Houghton-Mifflin Company, 1937), p. 63.

3. Maud A. Merrill, "On the Relation of Intelligence to Achievement in the Case of Mentally Retarded Children," *Comparative Psychology Monographs* (September 1924): 1–100.

4. Edgar A. Doll, "A Brief Binet-Simon Scale," *The Psychological Clinic* 11 (December 1917; January 1918):197–211; 254–261.

5. William M. Cruickshank, "Qualitative Aspects of Intelligence Test Responses," *Journal of Clinical Psychology* 3 (October 1947):381–86.

6. A. Strauss and H. Werner, "Qualitative Analysis of the Binet Test," *Proceedings, Association of Mental Deficiency* 45 (July 1940): 50–55.

8

THE INTERDISCIPLINARY MODEL
FOR MANPOWER DEVELOPMENT
FOR MENTAL RETARDATION

*J*T IS AN UNFORTUNATE COMMENTARY on the professions that the issue of interdisciplinary models for manpower development in mental retardation or in any other area of human behavior should be a leading topic for a conference program in 1970. This topic should long since have been laid to rest. The concept of interdisciplinary action by now should have become the *modus operandi* of us all. The fact of the case is that while the intention to function from an interdisciplinary base is often present, the reality of such action leaves most everything to be desired. While the goal of interdisciplinary function is verbalized, the selfishness of disciplinary roles often precludes the goal attainment. Although it is recognized that successful interdisciplinary function requires breadth of vision in men of good will, the narrow perspective and the egocentricity of many who profess a belief in multilateral action precludes success and minimizes the truth of the interdisciplinary concept.

It is not this writer's intention here to preach or indeed to assume the role of the great teacher. Better minds are more capable of understanding the interrelationships of people, their roles, and their efforts to attain a common goal. The truth of interdisciplinary action, however, is to be found in many places, and some of these will be examined here in an effort once again to throw light on the approach which we consider fundamental to the development of persons who are capable of combating social ills and of more nearly attaining the sought-after goal of reducing human imperfections. What are the hurdles to interdisciplinary function in the training of people, in the delivery of services, or in the search for fundamental verities through

Reprinted from *Indian Journal of Mental Retardation* 5 (1972): 44–57, by permission.

research? How do these apply to the area of mental retardation and developmental disabilities?

During the past several years many have watched with keen interest the growth and maturation of the young Japanese musician and conductor, Seije Ozawa. Mr. Ozawa, a protegé of Leonard Bernstein and now a conductor of renown with many orchestras, was recently interviewed with respect to his perception of a symphony orchestra. "An orchestra, after all," Ozawa is reported to have said, "is a very unnatural thing. An impossible thing, almost. A musician naturally wants to play alone, or in a group where he can be heard, appreciated, and still express his individuality . . . the musicians must submerge themselves into an orchestra to make the necessary sound and let one musician tell them how to play. Whenever it goes well, I am happy, because it is surprising that it ever works at all" (Robert C. March, "Ozawa in Transit," *Saturday Review,* September 27, 1969, p. 631).

In the sensitive statement of this colorful musician is to be found the nature of some of the problems of interdisciplinary action. If Ozawa's few sentences are considered each alone, a fuller meaning to our problem may be perceived. "An orchestra, after all, is an unnatural thing." This is perhaps more the case in the United States and certain other western countries than it might be in Mr. Ozawa's native Japan. Our cultural heritage has been one of individual initiative and enterprise. The price has been high in the U.S. for people like Sinclair Lewis' Babbitt, his "Main Street," his Dr. Pickerbough in opposition to his Dr. Gottlieb or Arrowsmith. The repeated pleadings of Horace Greeley who urged young men to go west and as individuals to prosper and succeed, characterized and moulded the thought of both young and old in the United States for many years. The aggressiveness of the railroad combines, the mining interests, the oil consortiums, and the Henry Fords have produced a type of individualism which contains few precedents for the cooperative effort required in the interdisciplinary solution of the problems of mankind. That we may now be paying the high costs of individualism in the interdisciplinary challenge to environmental rot may become more evident within the next decade than it now is. Be that as it may, an interdisciplinary partnership like Ozawa's orchestra may indeed be an unnatural expression in the individualistic society and the political and social philosophy of some countries. This in truth may be the reason why so few interdisciplinary models have succeeded. While leaders in the disciplines have urged the interdisciplinary model, their own ingrained experience and long-standing operational model has been that of the homesteader of earlier decades who stakes out his plot and as an individual with his wife and children struggles to achieve. This model has been held before youth and man alike in the United States and Canada for two centuries. It is unrealistic to expect that the individualism of generations in the short span of a few decades could change into a type of allocentrism which would allow one to encompass others as equals in the solution of man's problems.

"A musician naturally wants to play alone." As a psychologist, I am not sure that Ozawa's use of the adverb "naturally" is correct. I suspect that there is no instinct for solo action. I am sure, however, that the training and guidance which children and young people have had in the schools of many countries over the past decades have moved them more in the direction of soloists than as members of a group capable of action in concert. Unilateral action rather than multilateral action has been the order of our individual and collective thinking. The validity of this statement is supported and expounded by Urie Bronfenbrenner in his recent comparison of U.S. and U.S.S.R. children.

As professional persons, irrespective of our area of personal training and concern, we want to play alone or in a small group where each of us can be heard. Witness any discussion group, and note the number of references to "*my* program," "*my* department," "*our* school," "in *my* university," "in *my* experience," "from the point of view of *my* profession," "*my* idea," "*my* efforts," "*my* system," *ad infinitum*. Recently in planning an interdisciplinary conference, it was recommended (and the recommendation was followed) that an extra day be planned at the beginning of the conference so that the individual solos could be given and then permit with greater effectiveness cooperative actions of the group during the second and third days of the sessions.

Group action is not the only way to insure progress; certainly individual efforts in behalf of mankind have historically played a significant role. There is a place for both types of actions and activities. One of the causes of ineffective interdisciplinary action is the failure to realize that there is a place for the soloist and the belief that all things must be solved in concert. The mark of wise leadership is to determine which approach is most appropriate for which activity. An orchestra is sometimes needed, and when this mechanism is demanded to release the beauty of a composer's ideas, then this model of interdisciplinary thrust is called. But on many occasions, the soloist has an equally significant contribution to make and his place in the niche of human history cannot be denied.

When I was a young boy I lived in a suburb of the City of Detroit. An interurban trolley car connected us to the large city and it cost ten cents to ride the sixteen miles which would bring us to the Detroit Art Institute. Diego Rivera was then painting the remarkable murals which adorn the four walls of the beautiful interior court. Huge canvas curtains hung over the doors preventing the general public from disturbing the gigantic Mexican mind which was at work. My mother used to give me a dime, and with another friend or two, I would take the trolley and go to the Museum. I am sure that many knew what we were doing, but we were pleased to think that we were able to sneak in between the canvas drapes and squeeze quietly against the wall and watch the artist at work. He and his assistant, on scaffolded platforms hung many feet above our small heads, would mix colors and then Rivera would apply them in all his artistry to the sketches which he had previously placed on the huge walls. He saw us sitting there, and once in awhile would wave a brush in our direction to acknowledge his awareness. As long as we were quiet, he said nothing nor did anyone else regarding our intrusion. Once he called to us, and said in his very heavy English, "You like?" On another occasion, his assistant pointed out to us the many, many concepts contained in the murals: industry, religion, art, music, life, death, happiness, sadness, and many other fundamental concepts which because of our youth we could not fully appreciate. He once said, in referring to Rivera, "the artist must have many interests and know much and love many things." Rivera's biography and his paintings both in the Detroit Institute of Art, in the Prado Hotel of Mexico City, on the wall of the decaying municipalidad in Cuernevaca, and on the walls of other public places, show him to have been a man intimately interested in and concerned with engineering, military matters, "popular culture", science, surgery, children, social concepts, death, funerals, education, Anglo-Saxon cultures, history, communism and political thought, and many other matters. His was a life of versatility and his remarkable paintings show it. There is here another element in the interdisciplinary mind. The man who functions in the interdisciplinary model must not only be allocentric in his view of life and people, but he must be one who is capable of dealing with many facets in the spectrum of human effort. Closed systems have no place in interdisciplinary work. Open systems and systems which include many subsystems are required.

The system of interdisciplinary attack requires that "the musicians must submerge themselves into an orchestra to make the necessary sound . . ." In its fullest this requires a type of personal discipline and self control of which through the ages philosophers have written. It requires a mentality which can focus on the goal, but simultaneously is appreciative of all which goes on around it. It demands a person who can bring, from all which human development has created, those things which illuminate the issue and clarify its solution. John Romano, the psychiatrist at Strong Memorial Hospital in Rochester, New York, is a remarkable example of this ability. In discussion a schizophrenic patient whose problems were complex, he had the facility and wisdom to draw on Chinese literature for what it could contribute, on the life of Picasso, on Byzantine history, on the Industrial Revolution, on the writings of Bertrand Russell, on the obvious and the illusive, and from each to draw a thread which when woven into a new fabric brought a new insight into a patient's problem. Interdisciplinary function requires a personal depth and understanding of the ways of men and what they have done. Members of an interdisciplinary movement must be of great breadth and must draw on many and often seemingly unrelated fields in their search for solutions. While the Riveras and the Romanos would probably in and of themselves not make good interdisciplinary agents, they represent a mentality which the interdisciplinary participants must use and must seek for themselves. Perhaps as an aside, their breadth of understanding of the ways of people make it unnecessary as well as impossible for them to function as a member of a group. They epitomize the group action in their broad grasp of ideas and things. As an individual each is indeed a group.

To this point, the interdisciplinary model which we seek to build requires individuals willing to submerge themselves into the greater effort of the group. It requires, secondly, individuals of great personal strength and capacity to understand and draw the best from many areas of learning. "The musicians must submerge themselves into an orchestra to make the necessary sound and let one musician tell them how to play." A third characteristic of the interdisciplinary model is the act of sacrifice — personal sacrifice. The model is not without the leader. The model is not necessarily the essence of democracy. The operative model seeks but does not necessarily require that for the moment all disciplines are equals. From the backdrop of understanding in which all disciplines are equals among equals, there must emerge, in an ever changing fashion, one musician to tell them how to play, one disciplinary leader who for the moment is intrusted with the act of coordination, direction, redirection, or if necessary complete restructuring of the model. That leader is one of the most crucial cogs in the entire chain of events. The interdisciplinary leader, the case conference chairman, the team captain, or whatsoever he may be called, must be possessed of a unique blending of egocentricity and allocentricity. He must be a respector of other personalities, and yet firm in his unyielding effort to achieve the goal. He must be able to draw out the best from the minds of his colleagues without stunting the creativeness of any one. He must be the catalytic agent to group action and to group decision without stultifying the imagination and vitality of any member of his group. He is indeed a paragon of virtue, but not to such an extent that he is unobtainable. Were he as a paragon unobtainable, the issue to which we address ourselves might better be left as wishful thinking. I am of the mind to believe that man, more often than not, can be conditioned to the type of leadership of which we here speak to the end that the reservoir of interdisciplinary captains, orchestral or choir conductors, leading actors and actresses of the theater, political shoguns, and university deans and presidents—each both a soloist and a member of a team if he is effective—can be available to tackle the complex issues of our society, mental retardation and developmental disabilities among them.

The team leader of which Ozawa speaks must have traits of compassion and understanding as well as a firm resolve to unite his group into a common action. To this end, the goal to be attained is the first priority, not the fact that he is a pianist, a cellist, a psychologist, a physician, a lawyer, or an educator. To the end of concerted action, far greater in its implications than the contribution of a single discipline, will be drawing the best from each whatever may be its contribution. Under this concept, historical roles of medicine, for example, cease to be important. The historical roles of education, psychology, law, and other significant disciplines of our time change. Legal responsibilities of a given profession can be accepted or may need redefinition and modification. The concept of paramedical is soon understood to be no more fundamental or important than any other disciplinary term. Sometimes education is paramedical; but equally as often if not more so, medicine is paraeducational. When this is learned and understood, interdisciplinary power is ready to be released in the appropriate solution of human problems. The leader of the interdisciplinary team understands this delicate balance and deals with it. The team members know that the disciplinary leader of today's attack group may not be the appropriate person for the same role for tomorrow's problem by the same group of people. Leadership flows from discipline to discipline and falls when and where it is appropriate on a given discipline. Leadership never remains fixed, nor is it the property of a given discipline. In the interdisciplinary team, medicine may one day be the focal point of the team; occupational therapy, nutrition, nursing, speech pathology, education or other, the core profession of the next day. Position in the interdisciplinary structure is of little import; each discipline uses its skills of the moment in the best possible way to seek solution to the problem before it. The leadership role is not defined by historical prerogatives, regulation or law, by length of academic preparation, salary schedule, or chronological age, but by the pertinence of the discipline to the agenda before the team and by the capacity of the individual representing that discipline to weld the other members into a force for the problem's solution, whatever it may be.

Ozawa represents in his final comment what is so necessary in every disciplinary situation, a sense of humor. "When it goes well, I am happy, because it is surprising that it ever works well at all." Often a Rube Goldberg construct, never a smoothly operating mechanism, it is surprising when the interdisciplinary team works well at all. It works better if the individuals on the team do not become either too serious about what they are doing or too enamoured of the roles they play. Each must be devoted to the goal he seeks, but each member must also maintain a perspective. In a tense professional operation, the wheels grind more smoothly when there is also a court fool at work. The individual who can bring high academic purpose and lofty pronouncement to the level of the mundane and instill into the minds of those who struggle with ideas a smile — that person is worth his weight in gold.

As a student at the University of Chicago in 1937, I was privileged to experience a seminar on governments in crisis led by the great Eduard Beneš, then until recently the President of Czechoslovakia. In the face of the personal and political tragedies of himself, his family and his country, Beneš used to caution us as we listened to him quietly speaking at the end of a long oval table, "Never lose your sense of the enjoyment of things. Never forget that at the basis of the good life there must be humor." Humor in the interdisciplinary model is an ingredient the absence of which will quickly bring the house down.

The thoughts which have been expressed thus far constitute the background of our thinking to the solution of manpower development problems in the broad area of mental retardation. Since 1830, and before that date in some European countries, individuals in the United States have been seeking solutions to the diverse problems of mental retardation. The efforts in this country have been largely unilateral, however. Little evidence is at hand until the last few years which demonstrates any serious approach to the problem of retardation via cooperative efforts among disciplines. Medicine early carved out its role with the mentally retarded, and particularly in residential care facilities. The medical model, even though quite inappropriate for many if not most of the residents served, has over many years been the dominant approach. The public schools undertook the responsibility for mentally retarded children several decades later, but few mechanisms existed which brought special educators and medical personnel together to solve a common problem. As a matter of fact history indicates a tendency to draw further apart rather than to cooperate because it appeared to the medical superintendents that an intrusion in their sphere of influence was underway by educators.

There are areas of legitimate medical concern in mental retardation; likewise there are areas of legitimate concern which are predominately educational. Although today there are residuals of earlier attitudes still to be observed, the situation is considerably changed. There is no necessity here to trace the evolution of these changes, save to note that the definition of mental retardation — even the more limited one of the American Association for Mental Deficiency — requires shift in emphasis and a modification of disciplinary roles to combat mental retardation. Figure 8.1 illustrates the complexities of the definition of mental retardation which is held by us and recognized as a valid basis for programmatic development by many others. In the first instance one will notice that the traditional concept of mental retardation based upon the intellectual differential is still included. What is not included on the schema is the total spectrum of clinical problems, e.g., hydrocephalus, cretinism, mongolism, and others. It is assumed that the presence of these clinical problems will be understood to be found as appropriate at whatever level of intelligence.

On even this dimension of intelligence, however, we have stretched the definition to bring it to term with contemporary socioeconomic, educational, and medical concepts. The traditional definition of mental retardation does not include individuals with measured intelligence above 90 I.Q. The slow learner, except in the state of Ohio where slow learner is synony-

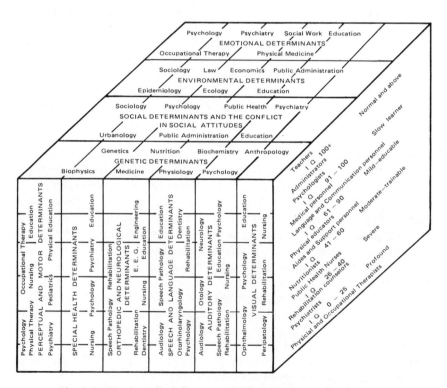

Fig. 8.1. The interdisciplinary model for manpower development.

mous with the term, educable, is not generally included in a concept of mental retardation. If, however, we consider that anything which may have an impact in intellectual development or function results in mental retardation insofar as the potential of that individual is concerned, then the traditional limitations must be quickly expanded. Individuals with measured intelligence in the normal or higher ranges may be considered mentally retarded if other factors are brought into consideration.

With the expanded concept before us, we must look to the other factors which are immediately related — etiological factors which are inherent in a definition of retardation. Mental deficit or mental retardation may be the result of emotional determinants, environmental determinants, social determinants (and particularly as a result of the conflict in social attitudes which all too often exists between groups within the community), and the result of genetic determinants or imperfections. Throughout any one of these factors there may also be the nutritional determinants which more and more are becoming known as factors in the production of mental deficit.

Other human problems which may play a significant role in the way an individual can use or utilize his intelligence include the total spectrum of physical disabilities and illnesses. The impact of perceptual determinants on intellectual function has been illustrated during the past thirty years. Perceptual and motor handicaps, separately or in relationship to one another, will almost universally result in a reduction of the intellectual level of function. Special health problems, epilepsy, cardiac problems, asthma, and other long-term physical problems, have been observed to result in lowered school achievement. Orthopedic and neurological determinants, speech and language problems, auditory and visual disabilities have each in their own perverse ways been found to contribute to mental retardation. Studies show the tremendous impact of cerebral palsy, for example, on intellectual function. A study in New York State showed 30 percent of the blind children under twenty-one years of age also to be retarded intellectually. The deaf are generally down-graded in school achievement between two and three years. Other examples are readily at hand.

Mental retardation is something more than has been traditionally considered for many decades. If the problem is as complex as we have depicted it here to be, and it is, how then can it be attacked? It is obviously not the domain of a single discipline. It bothers me even to hear someone trying to justify their position by stating that mental retardation is 90 percent nonmedical, or others who write that mental retardation is 75 percent educational. These figures are worthless. Indeed every individual with mental retardation may be the responsibility of the discipline of medicine; they may also all be the responsibility of a dozen other professions. Hopefully we can soon reach the point in professional development where the disciplinary instruments of the orchestra need not play alone, but can blend with one another to make music. No one discipline can solve the problems of the retarded, educators, physicians, psychologists, or social workers notwithstanding. If ever there were a problem which demanded interdisciplinary attack, it is this one.

Figure 8.1 is much over-simplified. It is over-simplified in large measure because of limitations of space. However, the limitations of a structured paradigm are inherent here too. What one can see from this additional schema is that, if one believes at all that the issue of mental retardation, broadly defined, can in our time be reduced in gross amount and proportion, then the interdisciplinary model must be applied. Each dimension in the paradigm requires a somewhat different alignment of the professions. Professions not indicated may also have a significant role to play, but are omitted here for reasons already stated. The multi-educational personnel noted to the right of the schema are intended to all function at any or all levels of measured intelligence. It is not being said or here implied that the disciplinary interrelationships are new or have never before been tried. Oftentimes creative unions have been effected. Only in the past few years, however, have geneticists, nutritionists, biochemists, anthropologists, neurophysiologists, psychologists, educators, biophysicists, and medical personnel joined to try multilateral attacks on genetic determinants of retardation. That it may be successful is seen in the writings of Cravioto, Birch and their colleagues, among others who could be mentioned. Occupational therapy, psychology, and education must cease their separate ways and unite in a concerted attack on perceptual-motor disabilities. There are too few persons in any one of these disciplines who understand the problem to be able to afford unilateral action.

We wish again to point out that there is a role for the individual discipline in combating mental retardation and related disabilities. Not all problems of human life, prenatal, perinatal, or postnatal, require or lend themselves to interdisciplinary study. The economy of time would in and of itself preclude such action. In this century, however, techniques have been developed which often go beyond the normal parameters of a single discipline and which require the cooperation of numerous disciplines in the economy of both time and function. The perinatal studies of the National Institutes of Health are examples of this, wherein at all stages of human growth and development, following conception and through the twelfth chronological year of postnatal development, many disciplines are blending their skills in an attempt to understand both normative growth and those factors which impede normal growth. Already, with nearly sixty thousand mothers and their offspring included in the study, data have begun to be released which have great significance for all those concerned with disabled children. These significant bits of information, could not alone have been accumulated or understood through the mechanisms of single disciplines. They have become significant only as two or more disciplinary thrusts have in union combined to bring multi-dimensional techniques, skills, information, and bases of interpretation of data into a focus.

Join me for a moment in consideration of another dimension of this problem, one which is too often overlooked. In an examination of Figure 8.1 aide-support personnel are noted as significant persons in the solution of some problems related to mental retardation. If one follows the paradigm it is quickly observed that aide and support personnel may have contact with every cell in the structure. The preparation of support personnel has been overlooked and oftentimes supposed to be completely unnecessary except on the job itself.

In the paradigm, law as a profession is noted to have a role, and it too is, or can be reflected in, every cell of the structure, in greater or lesser degree. Yet lawyers generally have little exposure to those issues of mental retardation which until of late have been considered the province of medicine, education, psychology, and social work. There must also be provided programs of interdisciplinary continuing education program for all court judges. To the judicial profession will be brought some of their legal colleagues along with psychologists, educators, physicians, nutritionists, social workers, and others in an in-depth program of understanding the multifaceted issue of retardation and the alternatives within the law regarding the mentally retarded defendant and often his family before the court.

Limitations of time preclude an examination of the total spectrum of retardation and multidisciplinary exposure. The paradigm of Figure 8.1 is oversimplified and is incomplete. The possible combinations are much greater than suggested. That the combinations which are suggested be effected for purposeful attack on a major social and economic issue is mandated. Combinations which are not here illustrated, but which are significant to the solution of the problem in some large or small way, must be brought to light and implemented. The focus of single disciplines where appropriate must be encouraged and bridges must be constructed from them to others in order that full measure of profit from their findings can be quickly translated into action programs.

These heroic and significant attempts at the solution of one uniquely significant human problem demand the best of every discipline. The outcome will be successful only insofar as individuals alone and professional disciplines representing many of the same mind, mature and demonstrate a willingness to work together in Ozawa's "unnatural thing", to cease playing alone except where solo action is truly appropriate, to be content to express individuality through the harmony of action in concert, to submerge themselves into an orchestral team to make the necessary sound out of which will emerge a new concept often larger than any of its parts. In this manner professions can take on a new dimension as servants of mankind. The pieces of the human mosaic receive the attention of the total skills of science and the puzzle is constructed with accuracy and permanence in a way no other attack can accomplish.

PART II

PSYCHOLOGICAL STUDIES OF CRIPPLED CHILDREN

*J*N 1955, CONSIDERABLY BEFORE THE CONTROVERSY took place regarding mainstreaming, integration, or normalization, I wrote ". . . There appears to be no difference in the rate of acceptance or rejection between crippled and non-crippled children . . . as demonstrated by the children's own choices. The factor of visible disability alone, in other words, is apparently not a basis on which acceptance or rejection of crippled children is made in a classroom situation." We advocated the normalization of crippled children into the regular grade, although on a more adequate basis and with better community planning than is currently apparent on a national scale.

The studies included in this section deal with crippled children, a miscellaneous group to which there has been a minimal amount of attention paid during the past few years. When studies have been done, they have been directed toward the younger elementary school-aged child. In this section the reader will find a considerable amount of data concerned with adolescent and secondary school-aged youth, a group which only in the past few years has attracted the attention of professional persons. Included in this section also are a number of articles directed at studies of measurement of certain psychological characteristics of groups of crippled children in general and studies of the psychological and adjustment characteristics of adolescent physically handicapped children.

9

THE IMPACT OF PHYSICAL DISABILITY
ON SOCIAL ADJUSTMENT

*P*HYSICALLY HANDICAPPED CHILDREN are essentially the same as their physically normal counterparts. It is the thesis of this paper that the adjustive problems of the handicapped child in the home and community are no different than those of the normal child except (1) in instances where the handicap itself is organically irremovable, (2) when the handicap cannot be compensated for by the child, or (3) when the handicap functionally stands for something irreparable to the child.

Approaching the problem from a phenomenological frame of reference it is seen that the physically handicapped child in his social relationships is, as are all children, attempting to insure not his physical organic self, but his phenomenal self, the concept of himself of which he is cognizant. Two types of problems are to be observed in the handicapped child from this point of view, (1) adjustive problems which might occur in the normal developmental progress of any individual who is simultaneously striving for expansion of self and for the maintenance of the self concept already developed, and (2) adjustive problems which are solely resultant from the fact that a physical handicap is inserted between the goal and the self desire to achieve such a goal. Such a dichotomy is, of course, highly artificial, for no such neatly conceived division ever exists in a given personality. However, the failure to recognize the duality of the problem accounts for much of the current misunderstanding with reference to the handicapped. Frequently all the problems of the handicapped child are conceived of by his parents and the community to stem solely from the presence of a handicap. Rarely are parents or other adults who have occasion to work with the disabled child

Reprinted from *Journal of Social Issues* 4, no. 4 (1948): 78–83, by permission.

observed to distinguish between emotional maldevelopment which is potential in all children and emotional disturbance which is the direct result of
frustration due to a physical disability.

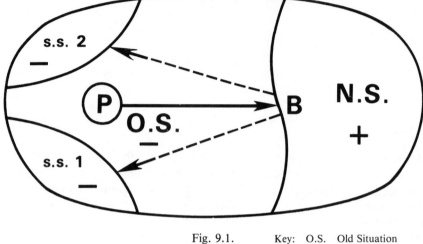

Fig. 9.1.   Key: O.S.   Old Situation
                          N.S.   New Situation
                          B   Barrier
                          P   Personality
                          s.s.1 Substitute satisfac-
                                 tion of n number

   Figures 9.1 and 9.2 will serve to illustrate the point under consideration. Figure 9.1 shows a non-physically handicapped person (P) attempting
to move out of an old situation (O.S.) which no longer holds value (−) to
him into a new situation (N.S.) of social relationship in the family or community sphere which has been interpreted in terms of his self concept to have
meaning and value (+). In the course of this movement to a new life region
an insurmountable barrier (B) is developed between the striving personality
and the new situation. Three possibilities are now open to the child: (1) He
may retreat away from the barrier and possibly develop a wall of protection
around himself which will permit his self concept to remain unchallenged.
(2) He may escape entirely from the life space into a region of unreality, or
(3) he may, as Figure 9.1 shows, disregard the barrier and develop substitute
satisfactions of n-number (s.s.1, 2, n) which bring to the personality as much
or almost as much value (+) as the originally desired goal region.

THE HANDICAP IS THE BARRIER

These avenues are not equally open to the handicapped person. In the first place the barrier to achievement for the non-handicapped child rarely remains the same in the attempts of the personality to adjust in different situations. For the non-disabled person the barrier may change as the situation and the self concept are subject to or have experienced modification. The barrier for the handicapped child always remains the same. *The handicap is the barrier* and as such either organically or functionally is always present no matter what type of adjustment is demanded or desired. The handicap likewise constitutes a barrier regardless of whether or not the environment or the self concept have been subject to modification from situation to situation. This is illustrated in Figure 9.2.

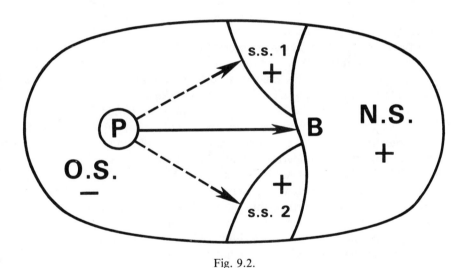

Fig. 9.2.

Figure 9.2 shows a physically handicapped child attempting to move from an old situation (O.S.) which at the moment of movement holds no value to the self (−) into a new life space (N.S.) which does hold value (+). The barrier (B) to successful adjustment is the physical handicap — cerebral palsy, impaired vision, impaired hearing, progresive muscular distrophy, epilepsy, or any other condition — which is irremediable in actuality or which the child *feels* is irremediable. When the *normal* personality was confronted by the barrier in Figure 9.1, one of his avenues for successful adjustment was that of developing substitute satisfactions which contained nearly the same positive value as the originally desired new situation. Substitute satisfactions comparable to the original goal region are rarely possible to the handicapped child, because the same barrier to the original goal region is also a barrier to the development of substitute satisfactions of a value (+) equal in any respect to that contained in the originally desired new situation. Thus the handicapped individual's personality, in addition to the possibilities of escaping the life space into unreality or retreating to protect the self, has the added *negative* possibility of developing substitute satisfactions *within* the old situation life space. All of these avenues have little value (−) to the personality as the behaver conceives his needs. Thus a condition of continued frustration frequently is to be observed in the handicapped person.

Syngg and Combs[1] point out that the "causes of behavior lie completely within the phenomenal field of the behaver." They further state that "this field is not open to the direct observation of any outside observer and is not open to the introspection of the behaver without a resultant modification of the field. . . ." If the individual "changes his purpose he changes his field." While the present writer agrees with these statements wholeheartedly, it must be pointed out that a dynamic dilemma is presented to the handicapped person. The handicapped child, because of the presence of a disability, frequently cannot effect a modification of the phenomenal field even when introspection is undertaken and when change is desired by the behaver. The handicap thus not only constitutes a physical reality ever to be coped with, but also a perennial psychological threat to the self as the child attempts to satisfy his needs within the family and the community spheres. The dilemma may be understood from two points of view: (1) the point of view of the physically handicapped child's self concept and (2) from the point of the social situation in which the handicapped child lives and is observed.

With regard to the former frame of reference, little basic research is available. Barker, Wright, and Gonick,[2] in a summary of "Attitudes of the Disabled" indicate that the self-concept of the crippled is usually negative. This feeling may be traced to unsuccessful attempts on the part of the handicapped individual to cross the barrier between old and new life regions.

INFLUENCE OF SOCIAL FORCES

Lowman and Seidenfeld[3] in studying the effects of poliomyelitis on the social adjustments of 437 persons found that 39.5 percent of the individuals of an employed group and 52.0 percent of the individuals of an unemployed group reported between only a "fairly normal" social life and no social life at all. Of the same unemployed subjects 46.2 percent indicated that problems relating to social popularity, family relationships, health, and fear of lack of future security were the most perplexing problems which faced them. Forty-three percent indicated that getting a job was their most perplexing problem. Among the group of employed poliomyelitis subjects 68.4 percent expressed problems of health, social and family adjustments, and inferiority feelings to be among the outstanding barriers to satisfactory personal adjustment. Insofar as children are concerned it has been demonstrated[4] in a preliminary study that physically handicapped children do not accept or reject other disabled children because of the obviousness of the defect. A sociometric study of this aspect of the problem of social relationships among physically handicapped children shows that social acceptance and degree of obviousness of the disability have a coefficient correlation of only .36 ± .13. The physically handicapped child many times apparently functionally feels that his social adjustment and acceptability is frustrated by the obviousness of his defect, but this study shows his self concept may be unnecessarily restricted.

The studies referred to here point quite clearly to the basic assumption that both functionally and organically the handicap frequently constitutes a barrier to satisfactory movement of the personality into new life regions. This situation is further demonstrated from the protocol of a counseling situation with an adolescent boy, a sixteen year old quadriplegic cerebral palsy client.[5]

> Subject: I just don't know why the doctors let me live when I was born. I'm no use to any one the way I am.
> Counselor: You feel that you are of no value to society and that discourages you.
> Subject: Yes, I know what I want to do and I can talk O.K., but every time I try to do anything I'm stymied. I can't walk or even eat without some help.
> Counselor: You feel, because of your physical condition that you can't do many of the things you want to do and you feel frustrated when this happens.
> Subject: It's worse than that. When I can't succeed in something and when I know I could succeed if I weren't a C.P. (cerebral palsy), I get more than discouraged because I'm so helpless. You're stuck and you hate yourself for being stuck.

This client represents the problem demonstrated by many handicapped persons in their attempt to seek self-satisfactions. The handicap sets into operation a vicious circle: the handicap is a barrier to success; frustration results; attempts are made to substitute satisfactions for the original activity; the handicap is again a barrier; greater frustration results; more activity; more blocking *ad infinitum* until "you hate yourself for being stuck." One of the most important characteristics of human activity is the continuous attempt to find new understandings and new meanings which will assist the personality to live more efficiently in achieving its goals. It is little wonder that study after study reports greater personal maladjustment among handicapped groups of children than among other groups when the efforts of the disabled child to find new understanding and new meaning in his environment is continually met with frustration resulting from an integral part of his self concept, yet a part over which he has no control.

The results of a current study, now in preparation, are pertinent with relation to the point under consideration and to the larger topic of this paper, i.e., the impact of physical disability on the adjustment of the handicapped in the social group. Snygg and Combs have observed that "since the purpose of an individual's behavior is the satisfaction of his own need the phenomenal field is usually organized with reference to the behaver's own phenomenal self." In order to determine the emotional and personal needs of crippled children from this point of view the Rath's Self Portrait-N Test was administered to a large group of crippled children between the school grades of four and twelve.[6] The test gives a measure of need in eight different areas: to beong, to achieve, to have a feeling of economic security, to be free from feelings of fear, to love and be loved, to be free from intense feelings of guilt, to share in decision making, and to understand the world. It is interesting to note from the preliminary treatment of the data that throughout the different age groups there is an expressed need to be free from feelings of fear and a need to be free from feelings of guilt. It is also observed that among these crippled children, concomitant with increasing age, there is an increasing need, unfulfilled, to share in decision making and for an understanding of the world.

In this latter situation again can be seen the impact of disability on the child's potential for healthy social adjustment and for satisfactory interpersonal relationships. The study further shows that throughout the several age groups the physically handicapped children express the feeling that their need for love and affection is being *over met*. It will be recalled above it was stated that the dilemma of the handicapped child could be understood from the point of view of the child's self concept and from the point of view of the social situation in which the child lives. The finding just noted to the effect that society is giving too much love and affection to the disabled child, i.e., too much protection, is significant in considering the importance of the attitude which society brings to the handicapped child. A second vicious circle envelops the child: he is handicapped, society sympathizes, over-protection results, the child feels over-protected in terms of what he sees society doing for his non-handicapped friends, he feels frustrated.

The child's self concept and society's approach to the handicapped child thus frequently are unknowingly in opposition. The importance of this is particularly evident, if as has been stated, "all behavior, without exception, is completely determined by and pertinent to the phenomenal field of the behaving organism." With basic human needs remaining unsatisfied, these unsatisfied needs become dynamic factors in the phenomenal field of the physically handicapped child and thus become factors which force the child into adjustments which are unsatisfactory from his point of view and maladjustive from the point of view of society.

BIBLIOGRAPHY

1. Snygg, D., and Combs, A. W., *Individual Behavior: A New Frame of Reference for Psychology* (New York: Harper, accepted for publication).

2. Barker, R. G., Wright, Beatrice A., and Gonick, Mollie R., *Adjustment to Physical Handicap and Illness* (New York: Social Science Research Council, Bulletin 55, 1946).

3. Lowman, C. L. and Seidenfeld, M. A., "Psychosocial Effects of Poliomyelitis," *Journal of Consulting Psychology* 11 (1947): 30.

4. Cruickshank, W. M., and Medvé, J., "Social Relationships of Physically Handicapped Children," *Journal of Exceptional Children* 14 (1948): 100.

5. Taken from the files of the Laboratory for the Handicapped, Psychological Services Center, Syracuse University, Syracuse, New York.

6. Cruickshank, W. M. and Dolphin, J., "A Study of the Emotional Needs of Crippled Children," *Journal of Educational Psychology* 40 (1949):295–305.

10

RESPONSES OF HANDICAPPED AND NORMAL CHILDREN TO THE ROSENZWEIG P-F STUDY

(with Charles Smock)

INTRODUCTORY STATEMENT

*T*HE HANDICAPPED CHILD is confronted with a permanent barrier to the satisfaction of his needs in certain areas. He is restricted in the number of ac- tivities through which most children derive need-satisfaction. The impact of the handicap on the level of adjustment of a particular child depends upon the "functional significance" of the handicap to the total personality struc- ture. Cruickshank[3] has taken the position that the problem of the functional significance of the handicap becomes clearer if one is cognizant of the fact that the handicapped child is faced with two types of adjustive problems: (a) those which occur in the normal developmental process, and (b) those arising out of and from the handicap itself. This dichotomy, admittedly arti- ficial, is none the less useful for a better understanding of the handicapped child, since the importance of the handicap to the level of adjustment will vary with each individual. At the same time this point of view places the handicap in the proper perspective regarding all factors influencing the total personality development and structure.

The recognition of the varying significance of the handicap to ad- justment does not lessen an interest in the location of instruments which are sensitive to this problem area and which can be used to assess both general reaction patterns and those specific mechanisms of adjustment which seem to be typical of the handicapped as a group. Most comparative studies have found that handicapped and non-handicapped children are very similar in terms of level of adjustment.

Reprinted from *The Quarterly Journal of Child Behavior* 4, no. 2 (April 1952): 156–64.

One such study[7] compared the responses of crippled and non-crippled children on a test of emotional needs. The two groups proved quite similar in all areas, including the areas involving fears and guilt feelings. As the authors point out, however, it is important to remember that the dynamics underlying the feelings of fear may be different for the one group even though the quantitative scores obtained on an objective test showed them to be similar. Broida[2] and his associates examined this problem further and completed a study designed to clarify the dynamics of the fear reactions characteristic of thirty of the children used as subjects in the earlier study. "Of major importance is the finding that the presence of feelings of fear (*in crippled children*) is coupled with an evidenced desire to experience social participation. It is also observed that crippled children who participate in group social activities experience significant guilt feelings." Thus, it would seem that many of the problems of the crippled children result from inadequate ability, or opportunity, to experience social interaction and interpersonal relationships. The absence of feelings of guilt among some of the children also seems closely related to this same problem.

PROCEDURE

The study reported herein is an attempt to assess the fruitfulness of the Rosenzweig P-F Study in evaluating important areas of frustration with crippled children and to determine if, on this Study, crippled children differ from normal children in the type of responses which are given. The P-F Study is particularly applicable to this situation because of the test structure and the nature of the individual stimulus pictures. A series of 24 cartoons are presented to the subject in which frustrating circumstances are portrayed. The subject is to fill in the comments of the frustrated person in terms of what the subject thinks the latter would say in that situation. The items are constructed to present about an equal number of *ego* and *super-ego-blocking* items. The ego-blocking situation is one wherein an obstacle interrupts, disappoints, or deprives the person. Super-ego-blocking situations, on the other hand, are those wherein the person is incriminated by others or is accused of some offense. It is assumed that the test items involving the frustration of some physical activity will also be particularly useful in a study involving physically handicapped children.

The Rosenzweig Picture Frustration Study (Children's Form)[9] was administered to a matched group of thirty handicapped and thirty non-handicapped children. The handicapped children were enrolled in a school for exceptional children in Syracuse. The groups were matched on the basis of age, sex, and intelligence. The handicapped children had a mean chronological age of 157.8 months (S.D. 12.22) and a mean intelligence quotient of 93.73 (S.D. 11.02); the normal children, a mean chronological age of 157.3 (S.D. 11.39), a mean intelligence quotient of 95.57 (S.D. 11.49). No statistically significant differences were obtained between the two groups on the matching criteria. The sample included fourteen males and sixteen females in each group. The handicapped group consisted of fifteen orthopedically handicapped, ten cardiacs, two partially sighted, and two hard of hearing children.

The test was administered to groups of six subjects each in a classroom at their respective schools. Directions were read aloud by the examiner as the subjects followed the directions silently.

RESULTS

An over-all comparison of the two groups is presented in Tables 1 and 2. Inspection of the data in Table 1 indicates no significant differences between the two groups in respect to either the reaction to frustration or the direction of aggression. This similarity of behavior is consistent with other studies in the assessment of differential reaction patterns of handicapped and normal groups. Although the results indicate a gross similarity of the two groups, Table 2 suggests that there are basic differences underlying the gross responses and provides specific clues as to the dynamics of these differences.

TABLE 1

COMPARISON OF HANDICAPPED AND NORMAL CHILDREN'S RESPONSES
DIRECTION OF AGGRESSION AND REACTION TO FRUSTRATION

	Percent of Responses						
	Extra-punitive	Intro-punitive	Im-punitive	Obst. Dominance	Ego Defensive	Need Persistive	General Conformity Rating
Normal	41.2	30.2	28.5	16.6	50.1	33.4	60.5
Handicapped	42.6	28.8	28.6	17.7	51.7	30.1	60.8
Critical Ratio	.54	.58	.51	.56	.61	1.35	.52
p-value[a]	.29	.27	.30	.29	.27	.09	.30

[a]p-values of less than .01 are considered significant for the purposes of this study.

TABLE 2

COMPARISON OF HANDICAPPED AND NORMAL CHILDREN'S RESPONSES
ON THE TEST FACTORS[a]

	Percent of Responses								
	E'	E	e	I'	I	i	M'	M	m
Normal	5.7	18.8	16.6	5.7	19.2	6.9	6.9	12.0	9.7
Handicapped	5.5	21.9	14.7	4.3	18.2	6.4	8.0	11.7	8.9
Critical Ratio	.42	1.46	1.20	1.22	.49	.43	.80	.18	.52
p-value	.34	.06	.12	.10	.31	.33	.21	.43	.30

[a]See Rosenzweig, Flemming, and Clarke in the Bibliography for information regarding scoring symbols.

Thus, as observed in Table 1, both groups manifest a similar degree of extrapunitiveness, but as noted in Table 2, the handicapped groups tend toward more ego-defensive-extrapunitive responses and tend toward significantly fewer need-persistent responses which, as noted above, is reflected only in this category. The handicapped children respond intropunitively less often throughout the test and tend to deemphasize the frustrating nature of the external barrier to need-satisfaction (I') or to ignore the external barrier altogether (M').

The super-ego factors and patterns are derived from those ego-defensive reactions where the person aggressively denies the offense with which he is charged (E̲), or admits the guilt but denies any essential fault (I̲). Table 3 presents the data from a comparison of the handicapped and normal children on these factors.

TABLE 3

COMPARISON OF HANDICAPPED AND NORMAL CHILDREN'S RESPONSES
SUPER-EGO PATTERNS AND FACTORS[a]

	Percent of Responses					
	E̲	I̲	E̲ + I̲	E – E̲	I – I̲	M +I̲
Normal	5.4	10.4	15.8	13.0	9.0	39.1
Handicapped	5.3	8.6	13.9	16.5	9.6	37.2
Critical Ratio	.84	1.17	1.02	1.34	.73	.74
p-value	.20	.12	.15	.09	.23	.23

[a]Underlined letters are qualified ego-defensive reactions. See Rosenzweig, Flemming, and Clarke for further information.

The handicapped children are less likely to admit their guilt in any situation ($\underline{I}$), are less likely to deny responsibility for an offense, ($\underline{E}$), but tend to direct their hostility toward the environment and at the same time to ignore the accusation (E − $\underline{E}$). Likewise, this group manifests less inclination to excuse themselves or others for instigating a frustrating situation (M + $\underline{I}$). As other studies have shown, the handicapped child herein is prone to protect and maintain the *status quo*.[4,5,6] The aggressiveness noted in their responses is a manifestation of this tendency and at the same time, the unwillingness to accept responsibility for their own behavior indicates a factor or factors hindering the handicapped child from developing techniques which might improve upon the *status quo*.

The results thus far suggest the handicapped children's responses are more often motivated by fear in that they show a larger amount of ego-defensive reactions. Fewer need-persistive responses further suggest that the handicapped child is more likely to protect his ego rather than to concentrate on the resolution of a problem. These findings and the analysis of the super-ego factors and patterns warranted further investigation. Consequently, an item analysis, grouping (a) ego-blocking items, and (b) super-ego blocking items was completed. It is significant to note that the analysis of the ego-blocking items, which involve an external interference with an activity, yielded no differences between the two groups. However, Tables 4 and 5 present a comparison of the obtained scores on the super-ego items for the two groups wherein differences were obtained.

The normal child is generally less extrapunitive and significantly more intropunitive. The factor comparison reveals, however, an even more basic difference underlying these two obvious ones. The handicapped chil-

TABLE 4

COMPARISON OF HANDICAPPED AND NORMAL CHILDREN'S RESPONSES
DIRECTION OF AGGRESSION AND REACTION TO FRUSTRATION
SUPER-EGO ITEMS

	Percent of Responses					
	Extra-punitive	Intro-punitive	Im-punitive	Obst. Dominance	Ego Defensive	Need Persistive
Normal	29.3	59.1	11.6	14.7	62.9	22.4
Handicapped	34.3	52.0	13.8	14.7	66.4	18.9
Critical Ratio	1.23	1.65	.74	.00	.84	.99
p-value	.10	.05	.23	.50	.20	.16

TABLE 5

COMPARISON OF HANDICAPPED AND NORMAL CHILDREN'S RESPONSES
ON THE TEST FACTORS
SUPER-EGO ITEMS

	E'	E	e	I'	I	i	M'	M	m
	\multicolumn{9}{c}{Percent of Responses}								
Normal	2.3	19.3	7.7	3.1	42.5	13.5	9.3	1.2	1.2
Handicapped	1.5	28.7	4.1	1.9	37.3	12.8	11.3	.4	1.9
Critical Ratio	.68	2.54	1.76	.88	1.22	.24	.75	.78	.65
p-value	.23	.005	.04	.19	.10	.41	.22	.21	.25

dren react ego-defensively to more situations, and it is in connection with these reactions that the greatest differences are observed. The handicapped children seem to rely upon one defense mechanism to protect their ego-structure. Whereas the normal child utilizes and even requests aid from the environment, the handicapped child is most likely to project all the blame and hostility on the environment. The normal child accepts some blame and responsibility, while the handicapped child characteristically refuses to do so, even where their responsibility seems unquestionable.

Items of the test in which some physical activity is depicted, and for which it might be hypothesized that the handicapped child would feel more frustration than the normal child, were also analyzed. The data from this breakdown is presented in Tables 6 and 7.

TABLE 6

COMPARISON OF HANDICAPPED AND NORMAL CHILDREN'S RESPONSES
DIRECTION OF AGGRESSION AND REACTION TO FRUSTRATION
MOVEMENT ITEMS

	Extra-punitive	Intro-punitive	Im-punitive	Obst. Dominance	Ego Defensive	Need Persistive
	\multicolumn{6}{c}{Percent of Responses}					
Normal	46.9	34.4	18.6	13.8	56.5	29.6
Handicapped	50.5	32.5	17.0	14.3	59.5	26.3
Critical Ratio	1.02	.60	.59	.20	.86	1.04
p-value	.15	.27	.27	.42	.20	.15

TABLE 7

COMPARISON OF HANDICAPPED AND NORMAL CHILDREN'S RESPONSES
ON THE TEST FACTORS
MOVEMENT ITEMS

	Percent of Responses								
	E′	E	e	I′	I	i	M′	M	m
Normal	6.0	26.1	14.8	5.0	20.6	8.8	2.8	9.8	6.0
Handicapped	5.0	32.0	13.5	5.5	19.0	8.0	3.8	8.5	4.8
Critical Ratio	.62	1.84	.53	.32	.57	.41	.79	.64	.75
p-value	.26	.03	.30	.38	.28	.34	.21	.26	.23

Although these twelve items consist of one-half of the ego-blocking and one-half of the super-ego blocking items, the data suggest very similar trends to that of the previous analysis of super-ego items. The handicapped children are more extrapunitive and less of their attention is given to the solution of the frustrating situation, the greatest difference being in those ego-defensive reactions to frustration. The handicapped children again project their hostility toward the environment while the normal children are more likely to seek aid from the environment in resolving the difficult situation.

An analysis of the data reveals no differences between the sexes in their responses on the test. Although the handicapped male group tended to be more extrapunitive than any other group, this did not prove to be a statistically significant difference.

DISCUSSION

Patterns of reaction to frustration and direction of aggression as measured by the Rosenzweig Picture-Frustration Study indicate a general similarity of adjustment mechanisms in handicapped and normal children. This similarity is somewhat superficial, however, as further analysis of the groups' responses reveal significant differential response patterns to frustrating situations.

One such consistent difference between the groups is that the handicapped group responds to frustration in terms of its ego-threat value, whereas the normal children's responses were more in terms of reaction to the frustration of a specific need or interference with immediate goal activity. The level of frustration tolerance of the handicapped child is apparently much lower than that of the normal child. Consequently, frustrating situations are likely to be perceived by handicapped children as a threat to the total personality structure. This is not only true where the frustrating circumstances elicit a characteristic ego-defensive response from both groups, but is also the only area wherein a differential reaction is noted in the over-all comparison of the groups. Thus, the handicapped child is likely to ignore the barrier to need-satisfaction and/or project blame and hostility upon the agent of frustration. The normal child is able to concentrate more of his attention upon the resolution of the problem with which he is immediately confronted.

Evidence presented in a study by Broida and his co-workers suggested that a desire for and a fear of participation in social relationships constituted one source of anxiety and fear reactions in the handicapped child. In line with this, one of the purposes of this study was to discover if social relationships did constitute an area of frustration which seemed more central to the personality structure of the handicapped than of the normal children. Data from the present study confirm the findings of the study of Broida *et al.*, and, furthermore, indicate that the handicapped child simply cannot tolerate any situation wherein personal inadequacy is either explicitly or implicitly implied in the relationship. The lack of any difference between the groups' reaction to ego-blocking situations indicates that interference with goal activity alone is not significant enough to elicit characteristic group reactions. It is when an individual is accused of some offense by another person that the greatest differences between the groups are noted. In such situations the handicapped child manifests significantly more ego-defensive-extrapunitive responses. There seems to be no question but that the handicapped child is basically insecure in his relationships with others and that he feels quite inadequate in dealing realistically with external appraisal or criticism by others.[4,5,6] The result seems to be that in these situations the handicapped child utilizes a characteristic defense mechanism, *i.e.,* the projection of blame and hostility upon the interpersonal environment.

The low level of frustration tolerance and the sensitivity to the possible threat stemming from interpersonal relationships are limiting factors in the learning of new, and more adequate, mechanisms of adjustment. For example, the handicapped child in this study is observed to be less likely to blame himself or to accept responsibility for the frustration of others, less likely to experience feelings of guilt, and is also less likely to excuse himself or others when confronted with frustrating circumstances. The most prominent characteristic is the attempt to defend and maintain the present ego-structure.

Of course, all individuals are confronted with blocks or barriers to need-satisfaction, but for the handicapped child it seems possible to delin-

110 SELECTED WRITINGS

eate the two most significant barriers or threats to adequate need-satisfaction. One, the continual internal threat resulting from the handicap and, two, the external threat of social disapproval which the child feels. The factors which differentiate the significance of the latter barrier in terms of adjustment of the handicapped child as compared to the normal child are: (a) fear of disapproval may be a result of feelings of inadequacy revolving around the handicap, (b) the handicap is irremovable, and (c) society's attitude toward the handicap. Thus, it is important to be cognizant of the fact that the fear of social disapproval may be a consequence of the child's inadequate resolution of the problem of the handicap during an earlier developmental period and/or the complications introduced by society's attitudes toward the handicapped child. The low level of frustration tolerance, especially in interpersonal relationships, inadequate mechanisms of adjustment, and the negative approach to the resolution of frustrating situations which are characteristic of the handicapped child result not only from the impact of the handicap, but from society's and the child's own attitudes regarding the disability.

The Rosenzweig Picture-Frustration Study has proven fruitful as a method for accruing additional and corroborative information concerning the adjustment mechanisms of the handicapped child. The test has demonstrated that frustrating situations involving interpersonal relationships, especially of an aggressive nature, are particularly revealing of the handicapped child's sensitivity to and fear of the reactions of others toward him. Analysis of the items involving motor activity or suggestions of physical activity and the super-ego items suggests that a fruitful area of investigation might be to compare handicapped and normal children on a projective instrument designed to portray physical activity or highly structured social-interaction situations. It is assumed that such a test might well elicit significantly different responses from the handicapped children and normal children. Further study is also needed to determine the significance of different types of disabilities upon the mechanisms and level of adjustment. A study of handicapped children under stress conditions, utilizing the P-F Study or other instruments, is as yet another unexplored area of research.

BIBLIOGRAPHY

1. Bernard, J., "Rosenzweig Picture-Frustration Study: I. Norms, Reliability and Statistical Evaluation., II. Interpretation," *Journal of Psychology* 28 (1949):325–43.

2. Broida, D. C., Izard, C. E., and Cruickshank, W. M., "Thematic Apperception Reactions of Crippled Children," *Journal of Clinical Psychology* 6 (July 1950):243-48.

3. Cruickshank, W. M., "The Impact of Physical Disability on Social Adjustment," *Journal of Social Issues* 4 (1948):78-83.

4. Cruickshank, W. M., "A Study of the Relation of Physical Disability to Social Adjustment," *American Journal of Occupational Therapy* 6 (March-April 1952).

5. Cruickshank, W. M., "Relation of Physical Disability to Fear and Guilt Feelings," *Child Development* 22 (December 1951):291-98.

6. Cruickshank, W. M., "Effect of Physical Disability on Personal Aspiration," *Quarterly Journal of Child Behavior* 3 (July 1952):323-33.

7. Cruickshank, W. M. and Dolphin, J.E., "The Emotional Needs of Crippled and Non-Crippled Children," *Journal of Exceptional Child* 16 (November 1949): 33-40.

8. Rosenzweig, S., Flemming, E. E., and Clarke, H. J., "Revised Scoring Manual for the Rosenzweig P-F Study," *Journal of Psychology* 24 (1947):165-218.

9. Rosenzweig, S., Flemming, E. E., and Rosenzweig, L., "The Children's Form of the Rosenzweig P-F Study," *Journal of Psychology* 26 (1948):141-91.

11

THEMATIC APPERCEPTION REACTIONS OF CRIPPLED CHILDREN

(with Daniel C. Broida and Carroll E. Izard)

PROBLEM

*T*HOROUGH UNDERSTANDING of the needs, problems, and attitudes of children who are distinguished by the fact of physical disability is greatly needed. Understanding of this question may be gained through the projective techniques. Research utilizing projective devices in the examination of crippled children is exceedingly scarce. It is our opinion that the employment of such techniques in research will considerably aid in the development of insight into the psychology of crippled children.

This study represents a preliminary attempt to utilize a modified form of a new thematic projective test, the Symonds Picture-Story Test,[8] in the investigation of the fantasy productions of a group of crippled children. The Symonds Picture-Story Test was designed for use with children of adolescent age thus lending itself more readily to the projections of subjects at the younger age levels than the more widely used Murray Thematic Apperception Test.[3] The present study was originally planned as an extension of a specific problem area noted for crippled children. Two earlier studies by Cruickshank and Dolphin [1,2] indicated that crippled children demonstrated, in contrast to several other areas of emotional adjustment, a need to be free from intense feelings of fear. Although the crippled and non-crippled children were similar in this regard, it is desirable, in order to adequately plan for the former group, to ascertain the nature of the feelings of fear which have been indicated.

The data of this study, however, went somewhat beyond the specific

Reprinted from *Journal of Clinical Psychology* 6, no. 3 (July 1950): 243–48, by permission.

aim enumerated above and did not lend itself entirely to interpretation in terms of the Cruickshank and Dolphin studies. Although the authors structured this present investigation in terms of the framework of the previous studies, they attempted to utilize the obtained data to the fullest in delineating factors in personality dynamics other than the one stated in the original purpose.

PROCEDURE

The subjects utilized in this study were thirty children enrolled in a public school for exceptional children. There were fifteen girls and fifteen boys ranging in age from ten to twenty. The average age was fourteen. They were included in grades from five to twelve, inclusive, the average grade being the eighth. The group was composed of children with cerebral palsy, arthritis, rheumatic fever, and poliomyelitis. These thirty subjects were selected from the sample of crippled children used by Cruickshank and Dolphin. They were divided into three groups: A, B, and C. Group A included seven children; B, thirteen; C, ten children. The three groups were developed on the basis of the child's expressed need to be free from intense feelings of fear as determined through the use of the Raths Self-Portrait N Test.[6] Group A is defined as the group where the need to be free from feelings of fear was overmet; Group B, normal with respect to this need; Group C, where the need was not being met.

Ten of the twenty pictures from the Symonds Picture Story Test were utilized. Ten competent judges cooperated in the selection of the final series of pictures, namely those pictures which would best give insight into the nature of anxiety and fear in the crippled children. The final selection included pictures numbered: B7, B6, A6, B9, B5, B3, A4, B1, B10, and A3.

After a preliminary interview aimed at establishing maximum rapport and interest the instructions embodied in the Symonds' manual were given. The subjects were individually tested and their stories were transcribed in long hand as nearly verbatim as possible.

Method of analysis

After the tests had been administered each of the three hundred stories was carefully studied. An attempt was made to find the significant and meaningful themas. For quantitative analysis the themas were identified

TABLE 1

SIGNIFICANCE OF THE DIFFERENCE IN THE NUMBER OF THEMAS PRODUCED
BY THE THREE GROUPS OF CRIPPLED CHILDREN

Themas	Total frequencies for three groups			Mean frequencies			t A&B	t B&C	P A&B	P B&C
	A N=7	B N=13	C N=10	A	B	C				
Family..........	21	30	20	3.0	2.3	2.0	–	–	–	–
Aggression	31	61	39	4.4	4.6	3.9	–	–	–	–
Economic concern	8	20	16	1.1	1.5	1.6	–	–	–	–
Punishment	10	18	13	1.4	1.4	1.3	–	–	–	–
Separation	–	3	6	–	.2	.6	–	–	–	–
Eroticism	8	11	7	1.1	.8	.7	–	–	–	–
Style	1	15	6	.1	1.1	.6	–	–	–	–
Anxiety..........	17	22	22	2.4	1.6	2.2	–	–	–	–
Altruism	–	2	2	–	.2	.2	–	–	–	–
Depression	9	12	6	1.3	.9	.6	–	–	–	–
Success	1	7	6	.1	.5	.6	–	–	–	–
School..........	1	2	2	.1	.2	.2	–	–	–	–
Positive emotion ..	1	6	2	.1	.5	.2	–	–	–	–
Repentance.......	6	24	7	.9	1.8	.7	–	–	–	–
Accident	1	9	6	.1	.7	.6	–	–	–	–
Social	10	6	23	1.4	.5	2.3	2.3	2.9	.05	.01
Thinking........	–	1	–	–	.1	–	–	–	–	–
Escape..........	2	2	3	.3	.2	.3	–	–	–	–
Morality	2	5	1	.3	.4	.1	–	7.3	–	.001
Strange	1	8	3	.1	.6	.3	–	–	–	–
Appearance	1	–	3	.1	–	.3	–	–	–	–
Evil	5	9	9	.7	.7	.9	–	–	–	–
Jealousy	2	1	–	.3	.1	–	–	–	–	–
Guilt	3	14	6	.4	1.8	.6	3.2	3.4	.01	.01
Oedipal	5	3	–	.7	.2	–	–	–	–	–
Rejection	1	4	1	.1	.3	.1	–	–	–	–
Inadequacy.......	2	7	2	.3	.5	.2	–	–	–	–
Independence.....	1	2	1	.1	.2	.1	–	–	–	–

according to Symonds' categories. At the time of this study there was no information which specifically defined these categories. The present authors agreed on criteria which were used to determine the category of a given thema, according to the criteria implied in Symonds' categories. However, there were certain of his categories which were meaningless to the writers, *e.g.,* "age," "excitement," thinking," "concealment," "place of residence." Also it was felt necessary to add categories to the list in order to cover certain observed themes. Those added were "oedipal," "rejection," feelings of inadequacy," and "need for independence."

In addition to analyzing the individual stories on a quantitative basis the authors wrote an interpretative summary for each subject. An individual's summary was based on the total ten stories which he told. This part of the qualitative analysis was done to surmount the limitations of the Symonds' categories mentioned above. The attempt more specifically was to obtain a brief integrated picture of the particular individual's personality dynamics.

RESULTS

Quantitative analysis

Symonds' twenty-four categories, plus four added by the present authors, were used to describe the themes. The frequency of each theme was determined for each individual. For each theme an analysis of variance was calculated to test whether the mean frequencies of the three groups differed significantly. The F for the social theme was 4.38 which is significant at the .025 level of probability. The t test for the difference between group means was used to compare Group A with Group B and Group B with Group C. The t value comparing A with B on the social theme yielded a P less than .05. This t was not considered significant because in computing fifty-six t ratios the chance occurrence of one significant t in five is probable. The t value for C and B was 2.9 which was significant at the .01 level of probability. There were no other significant F's. Although not customary, the t's, as described above, were calculated for all themas regardless of the non-significant F's. Table 1 gives the names of the themas, the group frequency, and the mean frequency for each thema. Only the significant t's and their respective P values other than the one noted above, are to be found in the extreme right hand columns. The t for the difference between the means of Groups B and C showed that Group B had a significantly higher number of morality themas. The value in this instance was 7.3 which was significant at the one percent level of probability. Group B also had a significantly larger number of guilt themas than did Groups A or C. The t's were 3.2 and 3.4 respectively, and both of these values are significant at the one percent level of probability.

DISCUSSION

It is interesting that the children in Group C whose results on the Self-Portrait N. Test indicated that their need to be free from feelings of fear was being under-met, produce the greatest number of social themas. Frequently these children expressed the desire in their stories for social acceptance and social participation. On the other hand the children in Group A whose need to be free from fears is grossly over-met also produce a large number of social themas. The significance of this is undoubtedly the same for Group A as for Group C. The earlier study of these children[1] showed that the children of Group A were also those whose need for love and protection was, as with the fear factor, over-met. These crippled children who are over-protected and sheltered to an extreme show in their themas hesitancy and insecurity about entering into social activities. The wish for social participation is nevertheless present. Conversely, children in Group C whose fears were not alleviated also expressed caution concerning social situations. The children of Group C produced almost four times as many social themas as did the children of Group B.

For further corroboration the authors studied the thirty protocols and noted those which clearly and predominantly exemplified a need for social participation. This analysis was made without cognizance to which group (A, B, or C) the individual belonged. It was found that thirteen, or forty-three percent, of the summaries were characterized by this need. Of the thirteen, it was found that twelve were produced by members of either Group A or Group C. Careful analysis of the individual stories tends to support the conclusion reached in the paragraph above, namely, that in those crippled children whose adjustment is impeded by the presence of intense feelings of fear, there ensues a need for greater social acceptance by the peer group and for social activities among those peers.

A second area in which significant differences prevail concerns the themas dealing with guilt. Children of Group B, whose need to be free from feelings of fear is within normal limits, produce almost five times as many guilt themas as Group A and more than twice as many as the children of Group C. Children of Group B also produce more morality themas than did children in Groups A and C. The difference in this latter comparison with Group A, however, is not statistically significant. Although it is speculative, the following hypothesis is offered as a tentative explanation of these observed facts. Morality is developed, at least in part, through social interaction both in and out of the family. It was found that Groups A and C had a significantly greater number of social themas and the qualitative analysis showed these themas to be expressive of a need for social acceptance and social participation. Thus the fact that children of Groups A and C produce fewer morality and guilt themas may reflect on their lack of social judgment, social experience, and social maturity. Group B children, perhaps because of a lack of fear which serves as an inhibiting force, experience social activities to a greater degree. Out of such activities experiences may occur which produce feelings of guilt on the part of this group of crippled children.

The hypothesis stated in the preceding paragraphs is further substantiated when the anxiety themas are considered. It is of note that the mean number of themas which reflect anxiety, while not significantly different, was greater for Groups A and C than for B. This finding is closely related to the original basis on which the groups were selected. Fear and anxiety are closely related. It is to be observed that the children who deviate insofar as feelings of fear is concerned also produce more themas demonstrating anxiety. Those children who relate stories showing anxiety are those who evidence need for social acceptance and social participation.

Qualitative analysis

Due to the general difficulties involved in attempting to quantify projective material and due to the specific inadequacies of the quantitative breakdown employed in this study, an attempt was made to cull from the interpretations and protocol material trends and characteristics which seemed to appear in a number of productions. Of significance in the themas is the lack of overt mention of physical disability in the characters (heroes) with whom the subjects identified. Although there is an occasional mention of illness, it is not frequent and there is a complete lack of stories which involve crippled or handicapped individuals.

Several hypotheses may be advanced to explain this rather interesting phenomenon. First, it may be that the test employed is a good enough instrument to pick up the subtleties of these children's preoccupation with their handicap without directly tapping it in manifest form. Secondly, it also may be that in this group of thirty children none perceived their handicap as a realistic barrier and thus have no concern or preoccupation with it. Finally, it could be argued that these children are consciously repressing recognition of their handicap.

The first hypothesis can be meaningful in the strictest sense only if a careful control group is used and such was not available in the current study. However, it has been shown elsewhere that the children who were tested in the current study when a part of a larger group of crippled children and when compared with a like group of non-crippled children were strikingly similar to non-handicapped children. No statistically significant differences appeared between crippled and non-crippled children on any one of eight emotional needs evaluated.[2] It can be assumed generally that the crippled children herein tested are similar in the aspects of adjustment studied in the current investigation to non-crippled children. The possibility that these children are consciously repressing the recognition of their handicap has not been investigated. However, as yet unpublished data involving responses of nearly three hundred crippled children to a projective sentence completion test, would tend to adequately support the findings of the current study and to confirm the validity of the lack of overt reference to a physical disability or illness. Although the grounds are admittedly tenuous, it would appear that the first mentioned hypothesis is more valid.

It will be noted in analysis of the themas that a large number revealed anxiety and difficulties in the home situation. In addition, there appears to be a constant reference to economic matters. A need to be economically independent is expressed frequently and resentment of economic dependence is voiced by the crippled children.

Of interest also were the frequent misperceptions which occurred on Card B3, a picture portraying two rather young males. Nine of the subjects or thirty-three percent, perceived one of the figures (the right-hand figure) as a female. Of the nine subjects, five were females and four males. Although the figures were constructed to be equivocal in terms of sex, the significance of such misperceptions do not readily lend themselves to interpretation with this population. Rapaport[5] and Stein[7] have suggested that misrecognition of the sex of the figure on certain ambiguous cards of the Thematic Apperception Test may be related to homoerotic or strong feminine tendencies in adult males. The possibility of such tendencies of the part of the four males was not investigated here and the meaning of the female subjects' misrecognition cannot be demonstrated at this time. However, it may be postulated that, broadly speaking, perceptions which deviate from agreed-upon reality are suggestive of psychopathology. One of the subjects, a girl, not only misperceived the figure on Card B3 but also misrecognized the sex of the figure in Card A4. She was the only subject who did so. In view of the above postulate it is interesting to note that this subject presented a rather serious picture of maladjustment. The themas which she produced portrayed, very vividly, an oppressive and demoralizing home situation wherein she was having to assume responsibilities not equal to her social and emotional maturity. In addition, there is evidence of delinquent ideation. This interpretation has been corroborated by material gathered about the subject from the school records. In conclusion, it may be stated that the problem of misrecognition of the sex of the figures on the cards is one which warrants further careful investigations before very definitive statements regarding its significance may be made.

Another apparent group feature which may warrant some discussion was the marked paucity of some of the protocols. The average length of most of the stories was approximately thirty to forty words. They frequently were also devoid of what might be termed rich imagination. What conclusions were drawn from these particular protocols were done so reluctantly because of the above fact. Murray writes concerning the Thematic Apperception Test that, "Stories from a sane adult averaging less than 140 words per story usually indicate lack of rapport and cooperation, lack of self-involvement. As a rule they are not worth scoring."[4] There is no data at this writing on the average length of stories necessary to deal validly with those elicited by the Symonds Picture-Story Test. The authors feel that lack of self-involvement may be functioning here. The authors also question the suitability of the test for pre-adolescent children. The subjects who had at least chronologically reached fourteen years of age or above tended to produce protocols of a more self-involved and more complex nature. Another hypothesis may be advanced that the paucity of the stories may be qualitatively significant of a generally constricted and non-committal attitude or feelings of inadequacy in the situation.

SUMMARY

A modified form of the Symonds Picture-Story Test was administered to thirty crippled children in a preliminary investigation of the usefulness of the instrument in psychological diagnosis of orthopedically handicapped children. The study was also undertaken to ascertain the psychodynamics involved in three groups of crippled children which deviated from one another insofar as the presence of feelings of fear is concerned.

There is evidence that the sample used in this study consists of children deeply in need of and striving for social acceptance particularly among their peers. Of major importance is the finding that the presence of feelings of fear is coupled with an evidenced desire to experience social participation. It is also to be observed that crippled children who participate in group social activities experience significant guilt feelings. The need for thoughtfully planned guidance and counseling services for crippled children and their families, and for realistic education of handicapped children is indicated herein once again.

The study also shows that misperceptions, as regards the sex of the figure on a certain equivocal card of the Symonds Test (Card B3), occurred with approximately one-third of the subjects and may be indicative of maladjustment. The evidence here is very meagre but is tentatively corroborated by school records in one case and indirectly by investigations with the TAT elsewhere.

Qualitatively, it appears that the Symonds Picture-Story Test is an efficacious device in revealing those, from among a group of handicapped children, who are extremely maladjusted. It may be concluded that the Symonds Test can be gainfully used with handicapped children to uncover significant dynamics of behavior and adjustment.

Consistent with the original intent of the Test, the obtained data seem to indicate that the most fruitful application of the technique is with pubescent and post-pubescent subjects. It is suggested that further verification and exploration of the obtained data may be made through the use of a control group, which is planned for future research.

BIBLIOGRAPHY

1. Cruickshank, W. M. and Dolphin, J. E., "A Study of the Emotional Needs of Crippled Children." *J. educ. Psychol.* 40 (1949):295–305.

2. Cruickshank, W. M. and Dolphin, J. E., "The Emotional Needs of Crippled and Non-Crippled Children." *J. Except. Child.* 16 (1949):33–40.

3. Morgan, C. D. and Murray, H. A., "A Method of Investigating Phantasies: The Thematic Apperception Test." *Arch. Neurol. Psychiat.* 34 (1935):289–306.

4. Murray, H. A., *Thematic Apperception Test* (Cambridge: Harvard University Press, 1943).

5. Rapaport, D., Gill, M., and Schafer, R., *Diagnostic Psychological Testing,* Vol. II (Chicago: Yearbook Publishing, 1946).

6. Raths, L., "A Test of Emotional Needs." *Educ. Res. Bull.* 26 (1947):14–16.

7. Stein, M. L., *The Thematic Apperception Test* (Cambridge: Addition-Wesley, 1948).

8. Symonds, P. L., *Manual for the Symonds Picture-Story Test* (New York: Bureau of Publications, Teachers College, Columbia University, 1948).

12

EVALUATION OF A MODIFICATION OF THE THEMATIC APPERCEPTION TEST FOR USE WITH PHYSICALLY HANDICAPPED CHILDREN

(with Marvin Greenbaum, Thomas Qualtere, and Bruce Carruth)

PROBLEM

*T*HIS STUDY WAS DESIGNED TO EVALUATE the Bachrach and Thompson[1] modification of the Murray Thematic Apperception Test[5] for use with physically handicapped children. The new series consists of twenty-three cards: fourteen new cards, seven TAT cards including the blank card, and two modifications of TAT cards. The authors of the new series state their rationale for designing the modification was similar to that used by Thompson in the development of a modified form of the TAT for a Negro group.[6] This rationale is based upon the assumption that identification should be greatest when there exists "the greatest number of symbolic elements common to the perceiver." The expectation is that if representations of handicapped persons are substituted for those of physically normal persons, the identification will then be increased for handicapped subjects.

If this identification is facilitated, one should expect the handicapped child to be more productive on the new cards than he would on the original TAT cards. In addition, one might reasonably feel that the cards would promote the production of specific reactions to the peculiar conditions and situations which the handicap imposes upon the child in contrast to physically normal children. In other words, to make this test of particular value for use with physically handicapped children one would expect it to produce more abundant interpretative material and also to provide material which would allow the psychologist to appreciate the specific problems which the individual faces because of his handicap. The present study is an

Reprinted from *Journal of Clinical Psychology* 9, no. 1 (January 1953): 40–44, by permission.

attempt to determine the extent to which this new test[1] can be utilized in terms of the above mentioned criteria.

PROCEDURE

The subjects used in this study consisted of two groups of thirty-one children each who were obtained from a public school for exceptional children in Syracuse, New York. The children were all classified as orthopedically handicapped. The two groups were matched on the basis of age, sex, grade, intelligence, and type of handicap.

In control Group I there were seventeen boys and fourteen girls. The C. A. range was between 8-1 years and 18-9 years; the average age, 12-6 years. The subjects were included in grades from two to twelve, the average grade being the sixth. The range in IQ, based on the California Test of Mental Maturity, was from 65 to 126, with a mean of 96.

The experimental Group II consisted of sixteen boys and fifteen girls who ranged in C. A. from 7-0 years to 18-4 years; the average age, 12-3 years. They ranged from grade two to grade twelve, the average grade being the sixth. The IQ range was between 64 and 130 with a mean of 95.

The groups were also well matched in terms of their handicap. They were composed of children with spinal tuberculosis, spina bifida, cerebral palsy, poliomyelitis, Perthe's Disease, muscular atrophy, arthritis, congenital dislocated hip, deformed chest, and club foot.

Three of the twenty-three pictures of the new modification were utilized in the testing procedure. Two pictures were chosen because of their exact similarity to two pictures of the original TAT series except that the new cards depicted a person with a handicap. For example, Card 5 of the Murray TAT series shows a figure sitting on the floor leaning against what appears to be a cot; Card 5 in the Bachrach version shows the figure in the same position with a brace on the left leg. The second card chosen, 7GF from the Murray series, shows a young girl and a woman; the new one, Card 12 from Bachrach, adds a crutch which is leaning against the wall next to the girl.

The third card of the new modification which was used did not have a close duplicate in the original series. It shows a boy sitting in a wheelchair gazing out of a window. The authors, therefore, had an artist prepare a wash drawing of this card similar in all respects except that the boy is sitting in an ordinary arm chair. For objective purposes the delineation of the handicap in all of the new cards was extremely obvious.

The children in Group II were administered the pictures with handicapped persons on them after they had been shown a trial picture (boy with violin from original TAT). Both the males and the females in this group were asked to respond to the picture of the person with the brace who is sitting on the floor. If the subject was a male he was next shown the boy sitting in a wheelchair and if it was a female she was shown the picture of the woman and girl with the crutch standing nearby. The children in the other group, Group I, were also shown two cards following the same initial sample card, except that in their case they were presented with the cards from the original TAT series in which pictorial representation of the handicap was absent from the picture. The sample card was not used in the evaluation of the results. Thus, for each child, the responses from two pictures provided the data for the experiment. The two groups varied only in terms of the kind of picture to which they were asked to respond, i.e., either a person with a handicap of one without a handicap.

The testing was done by three clinicians experienced in the administration of the TAT. The subjects were individually tested and their stories were transcribed in long hand as nearly verbatim as possible. If the child did not produce a story complete with a beginning, middle, and end, he was not urged to finish it. Thus, in all instances the examiners obtained only the spontaneous productions of the children.

Method of analysis

After the tests had been administered, each of the stories was carefully studied. Gerver's method of scoring, as reported by Coleman,[3] was used in analyzing the data for the productivity level of the responses. Certain revisions and additions in the productivity criteria were made by the authors where it was felt that the criteria were unsuitable for the purposes of the study. In using this revised method each story is given a rating ranging from one to six, corresponding to the level of productivity criteria. The criteria and their scores are shown outlined in Table 1.

The stories were rated independently by three judges. There was agreement among the judges in 92 percent of the stories rated. Two of the three judges agreed in the remaining eight percent of the ratings. No instances were noted in which all three judges disagreed. This compares favorably with the degree of reliability reported by Coleman in his study.

Stories produced by the children in Group II were then broken down into categories in order (a) to see what extent and in what manner the stories relate to the effects of the handicap and (b) to determine the child's reaction to the handicap. Four categories were devised to evaluate the above factors.

Category one includes stories which deal *directly* with the effect of

TABLE 1

LEVEL OF PRODUCTIVITY CRITERIA AND SCORE FOR EACH LEVEL

Level	Description	Score
1st Level	Rejection	1
2nd Level	Static Enumeration	2
3rd Level	Description of Action	3
4th Level	Interpretation I	4
5th Level	Interpretation II	5
6th Level	Interpretation III	6

the handicap and the child's reaction to it. Examples: "This boy is crying because his braces hurt," or, "This boy is in a wheelchair thinking of giving and receiving presents because of his handicap." Stories in response to Card 5 (Bachrach) which deal with a person who had fallen, but which do not attribute the fall directly to the handicap, are also included in this category. Category two includes stories in which there is recognition of a handicap but where the effect is not mentioned and no reaction is made to it. Examples: "This girl has crutches. She is playing house." or, "This boy is in a wheelchair. He's looking out a broken window. He's puzzled." Category three includes stories in which there is no direct recognition of a handicap. Example: "This boy is crying because he was spanked and because he can't get a toy that he wants." Category four includes stories where the handicap is attributed to someone other than the "hero" or "heroine." Example: "The mother of the girl in this picture is crippled and the girl is trying to help the mother." A further analysis of the first category was then made to determine the variety of effects of the handicap upon the person and the kind of reactions which are made to the handicap.

RESULTS

The mean productivity level of Group I, as computed from the judges' ratings of each story, was 3.87 (S. D. 1.02); Group II, 4.31 (S. D. 1.30). The critical ratio for the difference between means was 2.07 which is significant at the .04 level of probability. These results indicate that the cards from the original TAT series encouraged a greater level of productivity than did the modified series if one accepts the .04 level of significance as indicative of a real difference.

The analysis of all the stories produced by the children in Group II revealed that twenty-nine of the sixty-two stories dealt directly with the effect of the handicap and the child's reaction to it; fifteen dealt with a recognition of a handicap, but without effect or reaction. There were sixteen stories in which there was no direct recognition of a handicap; two stories in which the handicap was attributed to someone other than the hero or heroine. It may be mentioned in passing that the children in Group I produced only one story which would fall in the first category, i.e., one which deals specifically and directly with a handicap.

The twenty-nine stories which dealt with a direct response to a handicap were then further analyzed for the effect which the handicap had on the person in the story. This analysis is shown in Table 2. It is seen that in approximately seventy-six percent of the cases the chief effect was concerned with falling, not being able to play, or not being able to walk. The twenty-nine stories with a direct response to a handicap were also examined for the reaction to the handicap. In eighty-six percent of these stories the reaction fell into the following categories: (a) *Crying* about the effect of the handicap, (b) *Wishing* not to be effected by the handicap, and (c) *Thinking* about the effect of the handicap.

SUMMARY AND CONCLUSIONS

Our results indicate that the introduction of a handicap into the TAT pictures does not stimulate a greater productivity on the part of the handicapped subjects than do the cards from the Murray TAT series. Moreover,

TABLE 2

CLASSIFICATION OF THE EFFECT OF THE HANDICAP IN THE TWENTY-NINE STORIES
OF GROUP II WHICH DEAL DIRECTLY WITH THE PRESENCE OF A HANDICAP

Hurting	3
Falling	9
Unable to play	9
Unhappiness about braces or crutches	4
Unable to work	1
Deserves presents	1
Unable to walk	2
	29

there is some evidence that the Bachrach cards stimulated even less productivity than the original series since the mean level of productivity of Group I was greater than that of Group II with the difference being significant at the .04 level of probability.

Only fifty percent of the stories produced in response to the new modification dealt with the specific influence of a handicap upon the hero. Further, even though the children in Group I produced only one story of this nature there is some reason to feel that the additional information about the child obtained by these specific reactions to the handicap does not add materially to an understanding of these children.

The authors find that the most significant effects of the handicap are barriers against playing, walking, and getting around without falling. It is also discovered that the method of handling the barriers as revealed by these stories is restricted predominantly to such mechanisms as crying, wishing they weren't there, and just thinking about them. This lack of variability in response to a barrier makes it very difficult to see how each child is individually reacting to his handicap. It may be that there is a commonality of response to being handicapped but the authors feel that even if this were so, each individual would embellish this reaction in his own peculiar fashion. It is precisely these embellishments which the pictures of handicapped children do not seem to promote.

As was mentioned above, only one child in Group I made an overt reference in his story to a physical disability or illness. The fact that a child will tend to deny the presence of a handicap if he is not forced to perceive it has been borne out in studies by Broida, Izard, and Cruickshank[2] and in further data gathered by Cruickshank[4] involving responses of nearly three hundred crippled children to a projective sentence completion test. This present study would lend support to the hypothesis that the disability is denied by the handicapped individual.

Since the Murray TAT is known to be an effective instrument in obtaining information about the individual's interpersonal relationships, the authors thought it would be worthwhile to compare the Murray series and the Bachrach version on this basis. A tabulation was made of the number of stories in each group which offered some idea as to how the person relates to specific others in the environment such as, mother, father, siblings, aunts, and uncles. There were twenty-one of these stories in Group I out of a total of sixty-two whereas there were only seven out of a total of sixty-two in Group II. A critical ratio of the difference between proportions was computed and was 7.2. This results in a difference significant at the .001 level of probability. In conjunction with the other data gathered in this study, one could hypothesize that in pictures where the child is forced to perceive a handicap his main preoccupation is with this barrier and he only cursorily treats the nature of the goal region from which the handicap is barring him. On the other hand, pictures which do not force a response to a handicap seem to encourage the production of fantasy material in which the child tells about the nature of his wishes in regard to interpersonal goals.

It is recognized by the authors that the Bachrach version also contains seven original TAT cards from which such material could be elicited, but the investigators feel it is important to evaluate the kind of material which is obtained when the individual's attention is focused upon his handicap. Further verification and exploration of this last point calls for a control group of physically normal children who would be administered the pictures of the Bachrach version and whose responses would be compared to those of our two original groups. Such a study is now in progress and will be reported in the near future.

BIBLIOGRAPHY

1. Bachrach, A. J. and Thompson, C. E., *Manual for Experimental Set Thematic Apperception Test, Modification for the Handicapped. Series A: Child,* 1949.

2. Broida, D. C., Izard, C. E., and Cruickshank, W. M., "Thematic Apperception Reactions of Crippled Children." *J. clin. Psychol.* 6 (1950): 243–248.

3. Coleman, W., The Thematic Apperception Test. I. Effect of Recent Experience. II. Some Quantitative Observations. *J. clin. Psychol.,* 1947, 3, 257–263.

4. Cruickshank, W. M., The Relation of Physical Disability of Personal Aspiration. *Quart. J. Child Behavior,* 1951, 3, 323–333.

5. Murray, H. A., *Thematic Apperception Test.* Cambridge: Harvard University Press, 1943.

6. Thompson, C. E., *Manual for Thematic Apperception Test,* Thompson *Modification.* Cambridge: Harvard University Press, 1949.

13

A STUDY OF THE EMOTIONAL NEEDS
OF CRIPPLED CHILDREN

(*with Jane E. Dolphin*)

INTRODUCTION

*M*ANY FACTORS OPERATE SIMULTANEOUSLY in affecting the total personality adjustment in children who are handicapped by orthopedic or neurological defects. It is recognized by thoughtful educators that the same factors which influence personal adjustment may also in many instances account for fluctuations in school achievement and academic or vocational success. Thus, the importance of emotional adjustment on the learning situation is recognized as paramount, and is a particularly vital consideration with the crippled child who, while subject to all the adjustment problems of children who are physically normal, has the added factor of an atypical physical organism as a basic influence in his attempt to attain wholesome self concepts and relationships with the social situation. The problem is a complex one as determined both by observation and the reports of several studies which have been completed. It is seemingly apparent that, as a group, crippled children show personal socio-emotional adjustments which deviate from those which are considered healthy.

Seidenfeld,[1] reporting a partially completed study, points out that the results of the California Test of Personality administered to one hundred ten boys and girls in chronic phases of poliomyelitis demonstrated "a number of interesting patterns of response which are related to deviations resulting directly from illness or indirectly induced by prolonged confinement to bed, altered structural functional relations, alterations in parent-child relations and from the school-child-family relationship." The author feels that

Reprinted from *The Journal of Educational Psychology* (May 1949): 295–305, by permission.

poliomyelitis is a disease which exerts a psychological as well as physical influence on the child and that it is of sufficient importance to justify further investigation. Gates[2] has noted that crippled children on several tests of personality adjustment obtained scores which compared to those obtained by non-handicapped individuals at inferior adjustment levels. Rosenbaum[3] has shown that crippled girls between the ages of sixteen and twenty-five on the 1929 edition of the Thurstone Personality Schedule obtained scores which, if compared with the norms for non-handicapped freshmen women, placed the handicapped, as a group, in the 'emotionally maladjusted' category. Similarly, other authors[4,5] have commented on the adjustment problems of the orthopedically handicapped child, and have stressed the importance of psychological problems resulting from the handicap as an integral part of the total problem.

METHOD

In order to combat the devious psychological changes which have taken place in physically handicapped children, it is necessary to understand more fully the nature of the psychological adjustments which such children make. To this end a study was undertaken. The Raths' Self Portrait-N Test was administered to eighty-seven children who had orthopedic or neurological defects. The group consisted of seventeen children with cardiac conditions; nineteen, cerebral palsy; and twenty-one, post-poliomyelitis. The remaining thirty children were handicapped by such defects and diseases as Perthe's Disease, post-encephalitis, club foot, progressive muscular dystrophy, spina bifida, tuberculosis of the spine or joints, arthritis, osteomyelitis, etc. The children were all in grades IV through XII, inclusive: eleven in the fourth grade; seventeen in the fifth; fifteen in the sixth; twelve in the seventh; thirteen in the eighth; and nineteen in grades IX through XII, inclusive. The children had chronological ages between nine years three months and nineteen years two months and included forty-two boys and forty-five girls. All the children were pupils in a public day school for physically handicapped children.

The Self Portrait-N Test is a test of emotional needs. The test, developed by Raths and still in its preliminary form, is concerned with eight basic human needs[6]: to belong, to achieve, to have a feeling of economic security, to be free from fears, to love and be loved, to be free from intense feelings of guilt, to share in decision-making, and to understand the world. The items which are included in the test are arranged in sets of four. There are thirty-six sets, totaling one hundred forty-four statements. The pupil, in his selection of statements, is afforded the opportunity to indicate his reaction to each of the eight needs mentioned above on eighteen different occasions. The Self Portrait-N Test is constructed in such a way that statements representing a specific need appear in combination with statements representing other needs at least five times throughout the test. To each of the thirty-six sets of statements the child reacts by noting which of the statements is 'most' or 'least' typical of himself. Two statements in each of the sets are omitted. At the present writing the test is not fully standardized nor have norms been accurately established. Raths, however, states that, if a pupil has carefully followed the directions provided him, he should have revealed thirty-six needs, should have shown thirty-six met, and should have omitted a total of seventy-two items. A child responding with a truly average adjustment pattern should show four or five needs in each of the eight categories and eight or nine omitted. It is recognized that rarely will a child follow this normal pattern. From inspection, however, it is apparent that children who have checked seven or more statements in one need category are identifying a need which deserves attention by qualified persons, and that between five and seven needs checked in one area is indicative of a tendency toward an emotional need which has the potential to be dynamic in the over-all healthy adjustment of the child. It is within this frame of reference that the results noted below will be considered.

The fact that standardized scores are unobtainable necessitated administering the test to a control group of non-handicapped children. A comparative study of the two groups of children will be reported elsewhere; the present study deals solely with the children who are handicapped. The tests were administered to the children in groups of approximately ten. The children were urged to complete the test in one sitting, but frequently it was necessary to continue the test over to a second or third sitting. Time limitations were avoided.

RESULTS

A null hypothesis was established to the effect that the mean scores obtained by the subjects for the presence of a need and the fulfillment of a need would not vary within the grade group or within the groups of children as a whole. To establish the validity of the null hypothesis an analysis of variance of the children's scores was computed.[7] Table 1 shows that the null hypothesis, insofar as the presence of needs is concerned, is rejected in two instances, *viz,*

TABLE 1

ANALYSIS OF VARIANCE IN SCORES OF CRIPPLED CHILDREN
INDICATING THE PRESENCE OF A NEED

Need	Source of Variation	d.f[a]	Sum of Squares	Mean Square	F[b]	Null Hypothesis
Belonging	Between grades	5	28.67	5.73		
	Within grades	81	436.94	5.39	1.06	Accept
Achievement	Between grades	5	14.71	2.94		
	Within grades	81	318.81	3.94	.75	Accept
Economic Security	Between grades	5	15.03	3.01		
	Within grades	81	399.04	4.93	.61	Accept
Free from Fear	Between grades	5	39.47	7.89		
	Within grades	81	588.76	6.90	1.14	Accept
Love and Affection	Between grades	5	46.16	9.23		
	Within grades	81	287.24	3.55	2.60	Reject between 5% and 1% levels
Free from Guilt	Between grades	5	39.56	7.91		
	Within grades	81	492.67	6.08	1.30	Accept
Share in Decision-making	Between grades	5	71.79	14.36		
	Within grades	81	341.47	4.22	3.40	Reject at 1% level
Understand world	Between grades	5	30.78	6.16		
	Within grades	81	374.21	4.62	1.33	Accept

[a]Degrees of freedom used in F table were 6 and 80; actual degrees of freedom 5 and 81.

[b]F for 5 and 80: 2.33 at 5% level; 3.25 at 1% level.

the need for love and affection and the need to share in decision-making, and is accepted for the remaining six needs. It will be recalled it was stated above that in answering the questions a child normally might show four or five needs in each of the eight categories. The raw data show that the mean score for the presence of a need to share in decision-making for the fourth-grade pupils was 3.5; for the fifth-, 4.2; for the sixth-, 5.7; for the seventh-, 5.0; the eighth-, 5.8; and for the upper grades, 3.5. It is apparent from the above scores and from Table 1 that while a need for greater participation in decision-making is present during the sixth-, seventh- and eighth-grade groups of crippled children this need is being over-met with the fourth-grade and high-school pupils. While this may not be so significant with the younger fourth-grade pupils, it is extremely significant insofar as the older crippled children are concerned.

132   SELECTED WRITINGS

Of even more importance are the findings concerning the need for love and affection. The mean scores for the grade groups concerning this need are as follows: fourth-grade children, 4.1; fifth grade, 2.7; sixth grade, 2.9; seventh grade, 1.9; eighth grade, 2.0; high-school children, 1.1. With the exception of the fourth-grade children, throughout the grade levels the crippled children in the present study indicate that their need for love and affection is being over-met, *i.e.,* that they are experiencing too much parental solicitude and parental protection. This is most pronounced during the seventh-grade and the high-school years.

While Table 1 shows that there are no significant variations in the scores of the children insofar as the need to be free from feelings of fear is concerned, the mean scores of the crippled children's responses are illuminating in this regard. The raw data show that the mean score for the presence of a need to be free from feelings of fear for the fourth grade is 6.5; for the fifth, 7.0; for the sixth, 6.1; for the seventh, 5.2; for the eighth, 7.6; for the high-school grades, 6.3. In each of the grades, with the possible exception of the seventh, the mean score is greater than that supposed by Raths to be typical of the child of average adjustment. The nature of the fears present in these children has not been determined, but the fact is significant that throughout the several chronological ages included in this investigation fears of one sort or another typify the groups. The mean score of 6.4 for the need for the group as a whole is the largest mean score of any of the eight needs sampled in the Self Portrait-N Test. Insofar as fulfillment of needs is concerned the analysis of variance indicates that the null hypothesis is rejected between the one percent and five percent levels of significance in the case of feelings of freedom from fear. In all other areas the null hypothesis is accepted and no significant variation is indicated.

A test was made to determine the significance of difference between the mean score of a given need and the mean score of the remaining seven needs sampled by the Test.[8] Although the data are too voluminous to include *in toto,* Table 2 is provided as a summary table and shows the number of times each need has a statistically significant t-score when compared individually with each of the other seven needs. It will be observed from this table that the mean score achieved by the crippled children for the need to be free from feelings of fear resulted in statistically significant t-scores on twenty-five occasions as compared with the mean scores achieved on the other seven needs. Fourteen t-scores were significant at the one percent level or better, nine at the two percent level, and two at the five percent level of significance. Evidence is thus again present to indicate the impact of the fear factor in the adjustment of the crippled children. It is likewise to be observed from Table 2 that the mean scores achieved by the children on the need for love and af-

TABLE 2

NUMBER OF TIMES EACH NEED RECEIVED A SIGNIFICANT DIFFERENCE
WHEN COMPARED WITH THE SEVEN REMAINING NEEDS BY GRADE

Need	Number of Significant t-scores by Grade						
	IV	V	VI	VII	VIII	IX-XII	Total
Belonging	1	2	5	0	3	4	15
Achievement	0	3	4	1	4	2	14
Economic security	1	2	3	1	3	3	13
Free from fear	6	5	4	1	5	4	25
Love and affection	1	5	3	6	5	7	27
Free from guilt	1	1	4	1	4	5	16
Decision-making	1	3	4	1	4	4	17
Understanding world	1	5	1	1	2	3	13

fection are statistically significant in twenty-seven instances as compared with the mean scores of the other needs. Twenty-one of these scores are significant at the one percent level or better; four, at the two percent level; and two at the five percent level. Table 2 indicates that the mean scores of the remaining six needs are statistically significant as compared with one another between thirteen and seventeen times and, as noted elsewhere above, are probably within the limits which would be obtained by an unselected group of physically normal children. This assumption will be tested when analysis of the results of the control group is completed.

EMOTIONAL NEEDS EVIDENCED BY DIFFERENT CLINICAL GROUPS

It will be recalled that among the group of eighty-seven children there were several who had the same general medical diagnosis. Comparison of the mean scores achieved on the test were made where such clinical groups were large enough to warrant statistical analysis to determine whether or not children with a particular affliction showed characteristic needs. Table 3 shows that for the most part no differences are to be observed among cerebral palsy, cardiac, and poliomyelitis children. Insofar as the presence of needs is concerned only one need showed a statistically significant difference among the three groups. Both cardiac and poliomyelitis children showed greater presence of feeling of fear than do the cerebral palsy children. The mean

TABLE 3

T-SCORES OF THREE CLINICAL GROUPS OF CRIPPLED CHILDREN*

Need	Cardiac Group Compared with Cerebral Palsy Group		Cardiac Group Compared with Poliomyelitis Group		Cerebral Palsy Group Compared with Poliomyelitis Group	
	t-score	Percent Level of Significance of t	t-score	Percent Level of Significance of t	t-score	Percent Level of Significance of t
Part A: Presence of Needs						
Belonging	.491		.939		1.307	
Achievement	1.413		1.103		.225	
Economic security	1.034		.337		.574	
Free from fear	3.326	1	.374		2.914	1
Love and affection	.895		.805		.054	
Free from guilt	1.046		.929		.349	
Decision-making	.203		.362		.528	
Understanding world	.029		1.676		.894	
Part B: Fulfillment of Needs						
Belonging	1.652		.528		1.080	
Achievement	.559		1.243		.631	
Economic security	.297		.761		.482	
Free from fear	1.339		.820		.628	
Love and affection	.398		.153		.634	
Free from guilt	.577		1.617		2.38	2-5
Understanding world	.755		1.308		.647	

*Unless indicated t-scores are significant at less than the 5 percent level of significance.

score of the cardiac children in this instance is 7.32; of the poliomyelitis children, 7.00. The mean score achieved by the cerebral palsy children is 4.72. The latter is within the normal range, whereas the mean scores for the cardiac and poliomyelitis children indicates need of careful professional evaluation. The t-score resulting from a comparison of the above mean scores between the cardiac and cerebral palsy subjects and between the poliomyelitis and cerebral palsy subjects are significant at the one percent level.

Part B of Table 3 shows that only one pair of mean scores resulted in a statistically significant t-score insofar as the fulfillment of needs is concerned, viz., a comparison of the scores of the cerebral palsy and poliomyelitis children on the need to share in decision-making. The difference in the two means, 5.11 and 3.71, respectively, is significant between the 2 and 5 percent levels. The difference is probably due to chance in view of the lack of any difference on any of the other needs. It can thus be concluded that, within the exception of the difference insofar as fear is concerned, no statistically significant differences exist among the three clinical groups in the presence or fulfillment of emotional needs.

EMOTIONAL NEEDS EVIDENCED BY CRIPPLED BOYS AND CRIPPLED GIRLS

Table 4 constitutes a comparison of the mean scores achieved by the group of forty-two boys and the group of forty-five girls. There is no statistically significant difference between the means of the two groups on that portion

TABLE 4

COMPARISON OF THE MEAN SCORES OF CRIPPLED BOYS AND GIRLS*

Need	Mean Scores		t-score	Percent Level of Significance of t
	Boys	Girls		
Part A: Presence of Needs				
Belonging	3.40	3.52	.239	
Achievement	4.76	4.12	1.526	
Economic security	3.64	4.17	1.127	
Free from fear	6.09	6.67	1.025	
Love and affection	2.62	2.50	.283	
Free from guilt	5.53	5.74	.391	
Decision-making	4.89	4.24	1.411	
Understanding world	5.00	4.98	.043	
Part B: Fulfillment of Needs				
Belonging	5.84	6.00	.288	
Achievement	4.60	5.52	2.074	2–5
Economic security	4.36	4.12	.463	
Free from fear	4.26	3.81	1.144	
Love and affection	5.13	5.57	.814	
Free from guilt	3.71	3.26	1.277	
Decision-making	3.98	4.52	1.35	
Understanding world	3.73	3.07	1.287	

*Unless t-scores are indicated the percent level of significance is less than five.

of the test which deals with the presence of a need. Similarly regarding the fulfillment of needs, a statistically significant difference is obtained in only one area. On the need for satisfactory achievement a difference between the mean scores is present within the two and five percent levels of significance. The need to achieve is more satisfactorily fulfilled in girls than in boys.

SUMMARY

A test of emotional needs was administered to eighty-seven crippled children. No statistically significant differences were found between the scores achieved by the boys and girls, and, with few exceptions, no differences were observed between three clinical groups of children; namely, children with cerebral palsy, cardiac conditions, and poliomyelitis. In this connection statistically significant differences were obtained between the means of scores achieved by the three groups showing that cereral palsy and poliomyelitis children had more feelings of fear than did the cardiac group of children.

In considering the group of eighty-seven children as a whole it was observed that the need to share in decision-making and the need for love and affection were being over-met by parents, teachers, and other adults in the children's environment. These two needs are closely related. The adult who showers a child with an over-abundance of affection and a demonstration of love is very likely to be one who makes frequent decisions for the child in the interest of protecting the child. Crippled children, even more than non-handicapped children, need the security of well-tempered affection, and also need the greater security which can be gained through the knowledge that they can be independent in their thoughts and actions as to as great or nearly as great a degree as their non-handicapped friends.

The extent to which fear modifies successful adjustment has been recognized for a long while. The current study shows that at all ages the crippled child expresses a need to be free from feelings of fear. The exact nature of such fears is unknown at this writing, but the mere presence of feelings of fear demonstrated in significant amount by crippled children of this study should warrant serious consideration by parents, school personnel, and medical consultants who work with such children. Healthy normal adjustment cannot be obtained by a child when fear predominates the frame of reference within which the self concept is developing.

Within the tentative norms for the Self Portrait-N Test the scores achieved by crippled children on items dealing with a need to belong, to achieve, to have economic security, to be free from feelings of guilt, and to understand the world are within the range of scores attributed by the author to those which would be achieved by the average child population. Confirmation of this assumption will rest in comparison of scores achieved by crippled children and by a control group of non-handicapped children.

BIBLIOGRAPHY

1. M. A. Seidenfeld, "Behavior of Post-Polio School Children on the California Test of Personality," Abstract, *American Psychologist* 2 (1947): 274.

2. M. F. Gates, "A Comparative Study of Some Problems of Social and Emotional Adjustment of Crippled and Non-Crippled Boys and Girls," *Journal of Genetic Psychology,* 68: 219, 1946.

3. B. R. Rosenbaum, "Neurotic Tendencies in Crippled Girls," *Journal of Abnormal and Social Psychology,* 31: 423, 1937.

4. R. Barker, *et al, Adjustment to Physical Handicap and Illness,* Social Science Research Council: New York, Bulletin 55, 1946.

5. W. M. Cruickshank, "The Impact of Physical Disability on Social Adjustment," *Journal of Social Issues,* 4: 78, 1948.

6. L. Raths, "A Test of Emotional Needs," *Educational Research Bulletin,* 26: 14, January 15, 1947.

7. $$F \text{ equals } \cfrac{\dfrac{S_{ts}(\overline{Y}_{s.} - \overline{Y}_{11})^2}{K - 1}}{\dfrac{S(Y_{st} - \overline{Y}_{s.})^2}{N - K}}$$

   discussed by G. W. Snedecor in *Statistical Methods,* Iowa State College Press, 4th Ed., 1946 together with notation by R. W. B. Jackson, *Application of Analysis of Variance and Co-Variance Methods to Educational Research,* Department of Educational Research, University of Toronto.

8. $$T \text{ equals } \cfrac{\overline{Y}_1 - \overline{Y}_2}{\sqrt{\dfrac{[N\Sigma Y_1{}^2 - (\Sigma Y_1)^2] + [N\Sigma Y_2{}^2 - (\Sigma Y_2)^2]}{N^2(N - 1)}}}$$

   from E. F. Lindquist, *Statistical Analysis in Educational Research,* Boston: Houghton-Mifflin, 1940.

14

THE EMOTIONAL NEEDS OF
CRIPPLED AND NON-CRIPPLED CHILDREN

(with Jane E. Dolphin)

*A*CCURATE KNOWLEDGE of the degree to which physically handicapped children approximate their non-handicapped playmates insofar as emotional and social characteristics are concerned is not available. The picture is a confused one. Studies are available which, on the one hand, demonstrate that crippled children are less well adjusted than non-crippled children.[1,2,3] Similarly, each of these studies can be matched by one which shows that crippled children as a group are equally as well adjusted or better adjusted than their non-crippled contemporaries.[4,5] The problem needs clarification because so much depends upon accurate knowledge and understanding. Crippled children are segregated or non-segregated, are accepted or not accepted, are pitied or not pitied, are understood or not understood in terms of the particular group of studies which fall into the hands of psychologists, teachers, and administrators.

The present writers do not proport to answer the problem *in toto* in the report of a current study. They do, however, hope to throw some light on one phase of the problem through a study employing adequate numbers of children in its samples and through the application of careful statistical analysis of the results. These two factors have been absent in all too many of the earlier studies.

Selecting the emotional phase of childhood adjustment, the writers earlier reported findings pertaining to the crippled children alone, and projected certain questions which of necessity remained unanswered until adequate data regarding non-crippled children were available.[6] The latter data has been collected, and thus comparative statements can be made.

Reprinted from *Journal of Exceptional Children* 16, no. 2 (November 1949): 33–40, by permission.

METHOD

The Raths Self-Portrait N Test, adequately described elsewhere,[7] was administered to two groups of children: one, a group of eighty-seven crippled children; the other, a group of 193 non-crippled children. The group of crippled children consisted of forty-two boys and forty-five girls; the group of non-crippled children, ninety-seven boys and ninety-six girls. The former group included children handicapped by cardiac conditions, cerebral palsy, poliomyelitis, Perthe's Disease, progressive muscular dystrophy, spina bifida, and other orthopedic or neurological impairments. The children of the crippled group were enrolled in a public day school for exceptional children and included pupils in grades four through twelve, inclusive. The non-crippled children were from a comparable socio-economic background, enrolled in a public school, and included pupils in grades four through nine, inclusive. Non-cripped children of high school age were not included in the current study due to the very small number of such children found in the crippled group.

While the details of the test used are adequately described elsewhere, it is necessary to state that the Raths Self-Portrait N, a test of emotional needs, is concerned with eight basic human needs, *viz.*, to belong, to achieve, to have a feeling of economic security, to be free from fear, to love and be loved, to be free from intense feelings of guilt, to share in decision-making, and to understand the world. Children obtaining scores of four or five on any one of the above needs are within the tentative norms of normal adjustment thus far established for the test. Scores between five and seven are indicative of a tendency towards an emotional need; scores above seven, demonstrate the need for assistance of qualified persons in the child's adjustment problems.

The tests were administered to the crippled children in small groups of ten or less during one or more testing periods. A similar procedure was followed with the non-crippled children. Time limits were avoided.

RESULTS

Table 1 shows the mean scores achieved by both groups of children on two portions of the test, *i.e.*, the presence of needs and the fulfillment of needs. To determine the significance of the difference between the means of each group, t-scores were computed.[8] It can be observed from Table 1 that no significant differences exist between the mean scores achieved by the non-crippled children and the crippled children on any of the eight needs in either

TABLE 1

SIGNIFICANCE OF THE DIFFERENCES IN MEANS OBTAINED BY CRIPPLED
AND NON-CRIPPLED CHILDREN

	Means			
	Crippled Group	Non-Crippled Group		Percent level of significance
Need	n 87	n 193	t-scores	of t
Part A: Presence of Needs				
Belonging	3.46	2.88	1.4367	10–20
Achievement	4.45	3.81	1.4286	10–20
Economic Security	3.90	3.97	.0147	90
Freedom from Fear	6.37	6.07	.4517	60–70
Love and Affection	2.56	2.28	.8505	30–40
Freedom from Guilt	5.63	7.12	1.9487	5–10
Decision Making	4.57	3.77	1.7010	5–10
Understanding World	4.99	5.99	1.5242	10–20
Part B: Fulfillment of Needs				
Belonging	5.92	5.82	.1558	80–90
Achievement	5.05	5.02	.0532	90
Economic Security	4.24	3.83	.8888	30–40
Freedom from Fear	4.09	4.43	.6730	50–60
Love and Affection	5.34	6.19	1.2513	20–30
Freedom from Guilt	3.49	3.47	.0488	90
Decision Making	4.24	4.35	.2171	80–90
Understanding World	3.41	3.02	.9934	30–40

presence of needs or fulfillment of needs. Inspection of the table shows surprisingly similar scores and trends for both groups of children. In the report of the earlier study with crippled children, the writers found that throughout the span of grade groups included, *i.e.,* the fourth through the twelfth, the scores achieved in the area of feelings of fear were higher than those obtained in the other areas. Earlier it was felt that this phenomenon probably stemmed from certain inherent fears associated with or pertaining to the child's handicap. It is now observed that, although the dynamics may be different (a fact not yet determined), non-crippled children show the same trend as do crippled children. It should also be pointed out that whereas earlier it was thought that the low score achieved by the crippled children in the area of need for love and affection indicated that the need was being over-met by protective parents and teachers, it is now observed that the non-crippled children achieve similarly low scores in this area and that no significant difference obtains. In this latter instance the t-score obtained is .8505 and the percent level of significance of *t* falls between thirty and forty.

Although significant differences do not prevail, it should be noted that the non-crippled children achieved a mean score of 7.12 in the presence of the need to be free from feelings of guilt. This score places the group of non-crippled children in the more seriously deviate category while the crippled children's score remains more nearly within the normal limits.

Tables 2 and 3 compare the results achieved by the boys and the girls as separate groups. Table 2 specifically illustrates a comparison between the mean scores achieved by the crippled and non-crippled boys. It will be observed in this and the following paragraphs that when comparisons by sex are made, certain relatively minor differences are apparent. Table 2 shows

TABLE 2

Significance of the Differences in Means Obtained by Crippled
Boys and Non-Crippled Boys

| | Means | | | |
| | Crippled Boys n 42 | Non-Crippled Boys n 97 | t-scores | Percent level of significance of t |
Need				
Part A: Presence of Needs				
Belonging	3.40	2.79	1.4541	10–20
Achievement	4.76	3.89	2.2615	2–5
Economic Security	3.64	3.85	.5939	50–60
Freedom from Fear	6.09	5.71	.9043	30–40
Love and Affection	2.62	2.46	.5086	60–70
Freedom from Guilt	5.53	7.26	3.4380	1
Decision Making	4.89	4.10	1.8698	5–10
Understanding World	5.00	5.86	1.9103	5–10
Part B: Fulfillment of Needs				
Belonging	5.84	6.06	.4653	60–70
Achievement	4.60	4.77	.4693	60–70
Economic Security	4.36	3.98	.9170	30–40
Freedom from Fear	4.36	4.67	.8688	30–40
Love and Affection	5.13	5.57	1.0351	30–40
Freedom from Guilt	3.71	3.48	.7156	40–50
Decision Making	3.98	4.43	1.0976	20–30
Understanding World	3.73	3.13	1.7761	5–10

that the need to achieve is more adequately met with the non-crippled boys than it is with the crippled boys. The former obtain a mean score of 3.89; the latter, 4.76. This results in a t-score of 2.2615 which falls between the two and five percent levels of significance indicating fair significance between the two means. Likewise a greater than one percent level of significance is noted between the means of the two groups of boys in the need to be free from feelings of guilt. The non-crippled boys demonstrate this latter need much more intensively than the crippled boys. In all other areas of need presence or need fulfillment, similar scores are achieved by the two groups and the resulting t-score does not prove to be significant.

Table 3 shows the results achieved by the two groups of girls. These results are similar to those obtained by the boys in the greater number of instances. The area of guilt feelings, as with boys, shows a significant difference and the mean scores indicate that greater guilt feelings exist within the

TABLE 3

SIGNIFICANCE OF THE DIFFERENCES IN MEANS OBTAINED BY CRIPPLED
GIRLS AND NON-CRIPPLED GIRLS

	Means			
Need	Crippled Girls n 45	Non-Crippled Girls n 96	t-scores	Percent level of significance of t
Part A: Presence of Needs				
Belonging	3.52	2.97	1.3648	10–20
Achievement	4.12	3.74	1.1137	20–30
Economic Security	4.17	4.10	.1605	80–90
Freedom from Fear	6.67	6.43	.5370	50–60
Love and Affection	2.50	2.17	.8876	30–40
Freedom from Guilt	5.74	6.99	2.7068	1
Decision Making	4.24	3.43	2.0230	2–5
Understanding World	4.98	6.14	2.5333	1–2
Part B: Fulfillment of Needs				
Belonging	6.00	5.59	.9240	30–40
Achievement	5.52	5.29	.5628	50–60
Economic Security	4.12	3.66	1.2623	20–30
Freedom from Fear	3.81	3.83	.0608	90
Love and Affection	5.57	6.88	2.7292	1
Freedom from Guilt	3.26	3.46	.5867	50–60
Decision Making	4.52	4.27	.6212	50–60
Understanding World	3.07	2.90	.4522	60–70

group of non-crippled girls than among the crippled girls. Likewise the non-crippled girls show a greater need to understand the world than do the crippled girls.

The scores also show that the need to share in decision making is being over-met in the lives of the non-crippled girls. Part B of Table 3 also shows that the need for love and affection, while over-met with both groups of girls, is more adequately fulfilled for the non-crippled girls than for the crippled girls. In this instance the mean score for the non-crippled girls is 5.57 for the non-crippled girls; 6.88 for the crippled girls. This results in a t-score of 2.7292 and a greater than one percent level of significance.

Table 4 deals only with the non-crippled children. It contains a comparison of the non-crippled boys and non-crippled girls. Similar findings will not be presented for the crippled children due to the fact that they have been published elsewhere.[9] The reader will note from Table 4 that little dis-

TABLE 4

Significance of the Differences in Means Obtained by Non-Crippled
Boys and Non-Crippled Girls

	Means			
	Crippled Boys	Non-Crippled Girls		Percent level of significance
Need	n 97	n 96	t-scores	of t
Part A: Presence of Needs				
Belonging	2.79	2.97	.5629	50–60
Achievement	3.89	3.74	.5156	50–60
Economic Security	3.85	4.10	.8044	40–50
Freedom from Fear	5.71	6.43	2.2209	2–5
Love and Affection	2.46	2.17	1.0969	20–30
Freedom from Guilt	7.26	6.99	.6893	40–50
Decision Making	4.10	3.43	2.0272	2–5
Understanding World	5.86	6.14	.7433	40–50
Part B: Fulfillment of Needs				
Belonging	6.06	5.59	1.3125	10–20
Achievement	4.77	5.29	1.6194	10–20
Economic Security	3.98	3.66	1.1042	20–30
Freedom from Fear	4.67	3.83	3.2382	1
Love and Affection	5.57	6.88	3.6922	1
Freedom from Guilt	3.48	3.46	.0736	90
Decision Making	4.43	4.29	.4680	60–70
Understanding World	3.13	2.90	.8388	40–50

similarity exists between normal boys and girls. Boys are shown to have slightly less intense feelings of fear than do girls. The per cent level of significance for the need falls between two and five. A difference at the two to five percent level of significance also prevails in the need to share in decision making. The reader will recall that when the earlier comparison was made between the scores of the crippled boys and girls, no significant t-scores were obtained. However, the degree of significance between the non-crippled groups, namely, between two and five percent, is such as to bring the results of these groups into close agreement with those of the crippled children.

The difference between the mean of two needs does show significance insofar as fulfillment is concerned. This, however, serves primarily to confirm results noted in previous tables. Part B of Table 4 shows that the need to be free of feelings of fear is less fulfilled for non-crippled girls than for non-crippled boys. Likewise, the need for love and affection is shown to be more completely fulfilled, i.e., overly fulfilled, among non-crippled girls than among non-crippled boys.

DISCUSSION

It has been stated previously that physically handicapped children are in essence similar to their physically normal contemporaries insofar as adjustment problems are concerned. It has been stated by these writers and others that adjustment problems of the crippled children are little if any different from those of non-handicapped children.[10] Certain exceptions to this statement can be made in terms of the attitudes which the handicapped child holds toward his physical disability. At the present writing the authors feel that the adjustment of handicapped and non-handicapped children is undoubtedly similar save in those instances wherein the handicap functionally represents something irreparable to the child or constitutes a factor to which acceptance is impossible. Earlier it was felt by one of the authors that when the physical handicap was irremovable adjustment problems would be greater for the handicapped child. In the light of the current findings and those of other studies which are in the process of completion, it is felt that this latter factor does not necessarily constitute a hazard to the healthy adjustment of crippled children. The above assumptions which these and other writers have made without the support of objective data have been corroborated by the findings of the present study.

In the current study a test of emotional needs showed that in eight basic human needs no statistically significant differences prevailed between the crippled children and the non-crippled children. In all areas they were strikingly similar. That the crippled children are similar to all children is attested to by the fact that in those areas where the non-crippled children show deviations in adjustment the crippled children show the same general deviations. This is neither good nor bad. The point which is being made is that of the similarity of the two groups of children. Where the non-crippled children show an intense need to be free from feelings of fear, the crippled boys and girls show a like trend. Where feelings of guilt constitute a barrier to healthy adjustment for the handicapped children, they likewise produce blocks to the crippled children. Both the crippled and the non-crippled children express a need to love and be loved, but in the present test situation they indicate through their answers that they are experiencing an over-abundance of love, protection, and affection.

A fruitful investigation should be made to further understand the nature of the fears and feelings of guilt which are represented in the children of this study and undoubtedly, if these children are typical in any respect to other children of the same ages, of most children. Fear alone, to say nothing of guilt, constitutes one of the most serious hindrances to healthy adjustments. As an emotion it has broad ramifications not only in relation to specific objects, but to generalized ideas, events and things. These two areas of adjustment stand out from the other six needs on the current test to such an extent as to warrant concern. The interrelationship between fear and guilt is close, and to see both of these factors so outstandingly deviant in comparison to the other emotional needs which can be expressed by children causes thoughtful educators and psychologists to be rightly concerned.

It must not be thought that without exception all crippled children in the present study compare exactly to the normal children. Generally speaking, the figures of this study can be considered valid. However, it is known that adjustment depends upon the degree to which the individual is able to accept his environment, to develop an understanding of the meaning of his behavior and that of others, and to be able to be accepted by others. Individual crippled children, as did individual non-crippled children, deviated markedly from that which could be considered healthy in terms of the Rath's Self-Portrait N Test. In most of these cases of atypical adjustment it can be observed that the children concerned are ones who are unable to accept their handicap primarily because they are not able to understand the meaning of the handicap for them. Maladjustment occurs when the meanings which an individual has for a situation differ markedly from those which are held by others in the same situation. If a child has a false understanding of his physical handicap, if he does not accurately comprehend the implications of the handicap or both the positive and negative limitations imposed by the handicap, maladjustment is likely to develop. When the individual comes into a situation, regardless of its nature, in which misunderstanding or different understanding from his own is current, feelings of insecurity, anxiety, fear and guilt are the frequent concomitants. The nature of this development together with the gross findings of this study warrant serious consideration by psychologists, mental hygienists, parents, and teachers.

Closely related to the factors of fear and guilt is a third and perhaps seemingly unrelated aspect of adjustment, namely, the need to love and to be loved. In the current study this aspect of childhood adjustment is shown to be over-met. In other words, children are stating unconsciously that in their contact with adults they are experiencing an over-abundance of attention, love, sympathy, and solicitation. One of the authors in counseling a high-school-aged girl recorded the child's remarks to the following effect:

> Mother and Dad have always showered me with love and attention. I suppose perhaps more than other parents because of my legs. I didn't used to think much about it. In fact, I guess I liked it. But, now that I'm a little older and I realize that I'm not too much different from other children I feel guilty at all the time my parents devote to me.

A freshman college student who had contracted poliomyelitis at the age of five and who still used crutches reported during a counseling interview:

> The one thing I can remember as an outstanding feeling of mine all during my life was the feeling of aggression I had to aunt, uncles, my grandmother, friends, and at times even to my mother for the never-ending stream of sweet-sounding things that were said to me when I entered a room. You know you can give kids too much love.

The close interrelationship between activities of affection, love, guilt, and aggression is brought out beyond question in the excerpts from these two counseling protocols. It is quite possible that the findings of the current study can be interpreted in the same rationale. If such is true even in partial degree, the need for parent counseling and family counseling is indicated in order that all parts of the family constellation can be brought into harmonious and understanding relationship. The need to approach adjustment from a wholistic point of view rather than from the point of view of any of the segments of adjustment is stressed in these findings.

BIBLIOGRAPHY

1. K. Nilson, "Certain Intelligence Aspects of a Group of Physically Disabled Pupils in the Minnesota Public Schools," *Journal of Educational Research* 26 (1933):344-53.
2. F. Strauss, "The Initiative of the Crippled Child," *The Crippled Child* 13 (1936): 164.
3. A. Brockway, "The Problems of the Spastic Child," *Journal of the American Medical Association* 116 (1936):1635-38.
4. M. F. Gates, "A Comparative Study of Some Problems of Social Emotional Adjustment of Crippled and Non-Crippled Girls and Boys," *Journal of Genetic Psychology,* 68 (1946):219-44.
5. E. J. Westenberger, "A Study of the Influence of Physical Defects Upon Intelligence and Achievement," Catholic University of America, 1937.
6. W. M. Cruickshank and J. E. Dolphin, "A Study of the Emotional Needs of Crippled Children," *Journal of Educational Psychology* 40 (May 1949): 295-305.
7. L. Raths, "A Test of Emotional Needs," *Educational Research Bulletin* 26 (January 1947):14.
8. E. F. Lindquist, *Statistical Analysis in Educational Research* (Boston: Houghton-Mifflin, 1940).
9. Cruickshank and Dolphin, "A Study of the Emotional Needs of Crippled Children," *Journal of Educational Psychology* 40 (1949):303.
10. W. M. Cruickshank, "The Impact of Physical Disability on Social Adjustment," *Journal of Social Issues* 4 (1948):78-83.

15

ADJUSTMENT OF PHYSICALLY
HANDICAPPED ADOLESCENT YOUTH

(with Howard J. Norris)

*I*T IS RECOGNIZED that the adolescent years present problems which are largely peculiar to this period of life, or at least are encountered at this period in greater intensity for the first time. Enhanced strivings for independence combined with the fear of being alone, the unknown consequences of increased self-reliance, heightened sexual drive in the face of recently learned social taboos, half truths, and pure fiction, and a fuller realization of the desirable activities permitted adults which are beyond the range of acceptable adolescent behavior despite rapidly maturing physical development, are only a few examples of such problems. Meeting these and other conflicts and successfully dealing with them is a necessary prerequisite for satisfactory adjustment during both this period and adulthood.

Further consideration, however, must be given to those individuals who are physically handicapped, for not only are they faced with the general problems of adolescence, but their disabilities per se, present increased and/ or additional barriers to be overcome. Gauging the extensiveness and ramifications of these barriers has been an extremely difficult undertaking, for differentiating general adolescent problems from special problems of the handicapped adolescent is often, for practical purposes, almost impossible because of the close inter-relatedness and interdependence of the two. The paucity of sound research in this area can at least partially be interpreted as a testimonial of such difficulty. Despite the restriction imposed by the quality of the research, Barker and others[1] point out that handicapped children often make good adjustments to both their disability and the environment. At the same time the literature illustrates that many times the presence of a physical disability affects healthy adolescent growth and development.

Reprinted from *Exceptional Children* 21, no. 8 (May 1955): 282–88, by permission.

REVIEW OF THE LITERATURE

Today, virtually all professional people in the social sciences, regardless of their theoretical orientation, recognize that experience is a primary molding agent of personality and thus of the total adjustment of the individual to his society. Since the range of possible experiences is practically infinite and varies from person to person, it is not surprising that the behavior of two individuals is never exactly alike. Nevertheless, it has been implicitly assumed, if not explicitly stated, that within broad limits groups of people will show general similarities in their behavioral characteristics, i.e., similarities which are at least in part a function of a more or less homogeneous background. If such an assumption were not made, many of the "controls," such as socio-economic history, length of institutionalization, type of school attended, and other commonly accepted bases used in psychological research would be meaningless. An extension of this hypothesis can be found when examining some of the better research done with physically handicapped children and youth. It is held that, because of the general restrictions imposed by a disability upon the activity potential and upon social interaction, homogeneity of experience will result in certain adjustive likenesses which can be compared with and differentiated from the adjustment of similar, but nonhandicapped groups.

Relation of physical disability to social and emotional adjustment

One of the earlier studies intimating the acceptance of such a position is that done by Nagge and Saylor.[16] They attempted to determine whether or not there was a difference in introversion-extroversion, using the Neymann-Kohlstedt Test, between 144 physically handicapped adolescents and a group of nonhandicapped children who were matched for sex, age, and race. The results produced no significant correlation between the two groups nor was any relationship discovered between length of time of crippling experience and introversion-extroversion.

A relatively large number of studies has been published on social and emotional adjustment, such as that mentioned above, in which no measurable significant differences between handicapped and normal children were found. For example, Levi and Michelson[14] completed an intensive psychological examination of 10 disabled adolescent boys which for the most part disclosed negligible differences between this group and the expected hypothetical findings of a similar, nonhandicapped group of adolescents. The pattern of scores on the Wechsler-Bellevue Intelligence Scale did not differ from that of a normal population nor did an analysis of the administered test battery reveal any intellectual or emotional pattern which seemed peculiar to those under consideration. Analysis of group discussions revealed there was no particular variance in perceived problems. Two factors, however, were found to be important in contributing to success in a rehabilitation program. These were "sound personality structure" and "ability to relate to people."

Gates[10] administered an extensive battery, including tests of intelligence, personality, achievement, interest, and mechanical aptitude, to a group of crippled adolescents and to their control subjects. No significant differences between the two groups were found on any of the measures used. A study of autobiographies, however, suggested that cultural background and personal-social relations in the home may affect adjustment more than crippling does. Generally in support of Gates' findings were those of Kammerer[12] whose intertest comparisons between experimental and control groups were highly similar.

In contrast to the above research, a number of studies have been published which indicate differences in personality variables and adjustment between handicapped and nonhandicapped children. Cruickshank[5] had a sentence completion test administered to 264 physically disabled children and to a like number of control subjects in junior and senior high schools in six large centers in the United States. The test was constructed so as to evaluate the individual's self-concept in five different situations, two of which were: "(a) family, including father and mother, (b) society, including peer group." By categorizing and analyzing responses it was found that the handicapped group demonstrated better relations with their mothers than with their fathers. The normal group of children, on the other hand, showed better relationships and greater identification with the father than did the handicapped children. In line with this the handicapped children appear to have a tendency to withdraw from social contacts and were not as able to evaluate interpersonal relationships as were nonhandicapped children. In lieu of such contacts, fewer normal adolescent interests were revealed while substitute satisfactions seemed to be sought through phantasy by the crippled children. It then might follow from the findings of this study, that the adjustment of the handicapped group is less mature than that of a comparative normal group, and that despite this relatively unsatisfactory adjustment the disabled group of children appears to be satisfied with the "status quo." The desire to maintain this framework was noted by other researchers[20] when they observed the handicapped children's attempts to preserve their ego-structure rather than to adjust it to a new situation.

The data gathered by Broida, Izard, and Cruickshank[2] suggested that the area of social relationships is indeed one of conflict for physically incapacitated children. There was reason to believe that the existence of both a desire for and a fear of joining in such relationships resulted in feelings of anxiety. Added confirmative evidence for these findings was gathered by Smock and Cruickshank[20] who report that social interaction is a region of frustration to the handicapped. They employed the Rosenzweig Picture-Frustration Study and administered it to 30 disabled children and an equal number of normal peers who were matched for age, sex, and intelligence. An over all similarity was noted between the two groups of children to frustration and to the direction of aggression. Further analysis, however, demonstrated that there was a consistent difference between these. Response to frustration by the handicapped group was in terms of its threat to the ego while responses by the normal children were "more in terms of reaction to the frustration of a specific need or interference with immediate goal activity." This being the case, the former child "is likely to ignore the barrier to need satisfaction and/or project blame and hospitality upon the agent of frustration," while the latter is more able to attend to some solution of the immediate problem. Thus, the normal child is better able to judge and appraise and therefore deal more successfully and permanently with a frustrating situation than is his handicapped counterpart. Of interest, too, and related to ego threat, is the indication that the disabled child cannot tolerate negative insinuations concerning his adequacy.

Using material gathered earlier, but emphasizing personal aspiration, Cruickshank[4] found that the handicapped child seems to have greater need for acceptance, although such is of a minimal type. In many areas the normal child feels that he is accepted and so strives for more than this minimal level. He is not satisfied with the status quo which he already has achieved. Possibly of greatest import in terms of planning a mental hygiene program for handicapped children is the finding that these children often use the physical factor as a basis of making their comparisons of self with peers. The author hypothesizes that, as a result of this type of comparison, a "vicious circle" might be created such that the disabled child, having a need to feel on a par with those of normal physical ability and employing his handicap as a standard, never is able to feel up to par. Thus, when faced with this dilemma and forced to recognize reality, his only possible conclusion is that he is inferior. Some evidence in support of such reasoning can be found in the research of Greenbaum and others.[11] Their findings seem to indicate that a child will deny his handicap if no pressure is exerted upon him to perceive it. The study by Broida and his associates[2] further upholds this viewpoint. An explanation of handicap denial can be found in the phenomenological theory of behavior, as outlined by Snygg and Combs.[21] They hold that individuals tend not to perceive or else distort those aspects of themselves which do not enhance or at least maintain an existing self-concept. The crippled child, then, whose basis for comparison is often a physical one, would repudiate the existence of a handicap thus making the incorporation of that aspect of self virtually impossible and to that degree denying an important segment of reality. Consequently, recognition of the handicap would not occur unless external pressure made its denial no longer tenable.

Some interesting information was obtained by Cruickshank and Medve[7] which sheds a bit of light on four factors determining the degree of acceptance of physically handicapped children by a group of essentially normal peers. It was determined on the basis of teachers' ratings on a five-point scale, a "Guess Who" Test, and the Elementary Series, Form A, of the Mental Health Analysis, that the two most significant of these four factors are intelligence and extent of disability necessitated by the handicap. The two other factors, i.e., degree of obviousness of the defect and the scores on personality tests, were found to have no significance in the acceptability of the child in the social group.

Considerable literature appears which deals with the social and emotional adjustment of those individuals who have experienced poliomyelitis. Few, however, will be mentioned here, since the majority do not deal with the adolescent group. For example, Phillips, Berman, and Hanson[17] worked with a large number of school-aged children who had had poliomyelitis and an equally large number of control subjects. They administered a carefully selected battery of tests of intelligence and personality and also of brain damage. Of the subjects examined, however, only a few had even a moderate residual handicap, one of the criteria being considered herein. Consequently, the results cannot be considered as pertinent information leading to a better understanding of the adjustment of crippled adolescents. Lowman and Seidenfeld's well-known article[15] must be passed over too, for the age-range of subjects used was between 16 and 42 years and exceeds the adolescent limit herein considered. No separate statistics are provided by these authors for their younger adolescent group of handicapped which was contained within the total population. More acceptable in terms of the arbitrary criteria established for this paper is the work done by Seidenfeld.[19] His subjects, all characterized by poliomyelitis, completed the California Test of Personality. It was found that they demonstrated consistently better adjustment in the various areas covered by this instrument than did the groups on which it was standardized. The scores suggested greater self-reliance, freedom from nervous symptoms, freedom from withdrawal tendencies, greater sense of personal worth and a feeling of belongingness.

Levi[13] obtained information on 100 children who were receiving rehabilitation services after having had poliomyelitis. Two groups were employed, one consisted of people for whom rehabilitation was working well; the other consisted of eight individuals who were doing little more than "vegetating" and who responded negatively to the rehabilitation experiences. It was found that the postpoliomyelitis rehabilitation seemed to be related to prepoliomyelitis adjustment. In addition, all of the latter group were "of the egocentric or narcissistic type of individual." Rubenstein[18], noting the free discussion of seven boys hospitalized with poliomyelitis, believes that the onset of polio and the trauma associated with it reactivates fears and anxieties which are latent within the individual. He found that among the most common anxieties were the concern over success in heterosexual relationships and in vocational adjustment. From these findings, it would seem that the resolution of prepolio fears and anxieties might be related to the potential success of postpolio rehabilitation programs since the anxieties and fears with which the child has successfully dealt will not be reactivated. Thus, it appears that adjustment before the onset of the disease is positively related to adjustment subsequent to the acute phase of the illness.

Relation of physical disability to fears and guilt

Cruickshank and Dolphin[6] administered the Raths Self-Portrait N Test to a group of orthopedically and cardiologically handicapped children and to a matched group of normal subjects. Although not statistically significant, there seems to be a trend showing that the nonhandicapped children have a greater need to be free from feelings of guilt. When the group was broken down according to sex and then compared, such feelings were found to be statistically significant at the one percent level—the normal members of each sex having the greater need.

In a later publication Cruickshank[3] noted that handicapped children "see themselves as having more fears and more feelings of guilt than do (adolescent) children of normal physical characteristics." These fears are directly related to the children's handicaps. The most significant differentiating feature separating the disabled from the normal, in terms of the scope of the paper under consideration, is the former's fear of their disabilities. The conclusions of these two articles—on the one hand that normal children have greater need to be free from feelings of guilt and on the other that handicapped children perceive themselves as having more feelings of fear and guilt—seem irreconcilable at first glance. A possible explanation might be forthcoming in that the latter group has been found to be less mature and more overprotected than the former. This being the case, it is conceivable that such a group might find it to their advantage not to feel the need to rid themselves of guilt feelings since the suffering thus engendered can be used as a wedge or lever to control or punish overindulgent parents who themselves often feel guilty for the incapacities suffered by their children.

Broida and his associates[2] used the Raths Test to separate physically handicapped children into three groups. Group A had the need to be free from feelings of fear overmet (that is, a large proportion of fear-provoking areas were anticipated by significant persons in the child's life and were therefore, avoided. The children in this group were described as being "overprotected and sheltered to an extreme"). Group B was normal with respect to this need. The children in Group C had no such overprotection as those in Group A and showed more than normal reactions of fear.

An analysis was then made of Symonds Picture story protocols. The results disclosed that among those children who suffered from intense feelings of fear, there is a need for greater acceptance by the peer group and also a need "for social activities among these peers." It was further found that members of Group B perceived significantly more situations that indicated guilt feelings than did Groups A or C. The authors offered a possible hypothesis for this finding. Since the children of Groups A and C demonstrated a greater need for social participation and produce fewer morality and guilt perceptions, it "may reflect on their lack of social judgment, social experience, and social maturity." The group that has only a "normal" amount of fear, experiences social activities to a greater degree, some such experiences possibly producing feelings of guilt.

Employing some of the data gathered at an earlier date,[9] but limiting it to cardiacs and normal adolescent controls, Freed and Cruickshank analyzed the completions of open-ended sentences. One of the most important differences found between the cardiacs and a matched group was the former's fear of their handicap. Aside from this, however, the situations feared by both groups could be characterized as being "essentially similar" rather than different. It was further noted that the nonhandicapped children evidence a greater fear of interpersonal relations. A possible explanation was offered that since cardiac children have had less experience in social situations, they fear them less. Quite generally, the common reaction of both groups to feelings of fear was withdrawal and internalization, although this was significantly more so for the nonhandicapped group.

A comparison of the adjustment of visibly and non-visibly handicapped adolescents

It was stated earlier that one effective method of doing research on the adjustment of the physically handicapped adolescent is to gather material on such a group and compare it with data obtained from nonhandicapped children equated on the basis of any one or a number of several different variables. A greater refinement of this method is made when the former group is further broken down into various subclassifications, such as clinical (poliomyelitis, arthritis, rheumatic fever), location of disability (arm, leg, back) or degree of disability (slight, moderate, severe). Another approach although grosser than those just mentioned, can be made relative to the apparency of the disability. Thus, one may compare those who are visibly handicapped with those whose handicaps are not readily observable, contrasting both with a normal population. The rationale for any obtained variance may be found in the explanation mentioned previously which suggested that intergroup differences are largely a function of consistent variations in some of the experiences of the separate groups as a result of, or due to the absence of, handicaps.

Very little research has been done contrasting the adjustment of these three categories and, since this paper is primarily concerned with crippled children who are visibly disabled, only two studies will be mentioned. Both were done on a rather select sample and therefore the generalities which might otherwise be made, are limited. Freed and Cruickshank[8] employed cardiac children as their nonvisibly handicapped subjects and a more heterogeneous group as their visibly handicapped subjects. All the information gathered on them and on equated normal groups was originally obtained from a previous study.[5] The emphasis here, however, was placed on family and parent relationships. It was found that both cardiacs and normal adolescent youth demonstrated good adjustment to fathers. Cardiac children, however, showed poorer adjustment to their mothers while the opposite was true of the normal group. The authors believe that this is due largely to the many restrictions mothers must place on the activities of their cardiac offspring. It was further noted that the "cardiac group was more similar to its control group than the whole handicapped group was to its control group." Such factors as more ambivalence and inability to evaluate interpersonal relations on the part of the handicapped child, found in an earlier study[5] did not hold for the cardiac in evaluating his parental and family adjustment. In a later publication based upon data obtained from the same subjects,[8] it was noted that cardiacs also seemed to have less difficulty in evaluating their adjustment than do a more heterogeneous group of physically handicapped. Upon further analysis, no indication was observed that the adjustment of the cardiac child was regressive and immature, a finding which was made when the entire disabled group was compared with normal controls.

DISCUSSION

One of the primary aims of research in any field is the establishment of a reliable body of information which may either test existing theory or point the way to the creation of higher level, more encompassing generalizations capable of explaining wider ranges of observable phenomena consistently, accurately and without exception. A cursory examination of the material reviewed in this paper reveals that such a goal has yet to be achieved when dealing with the psychological adjustment of the physically handicapped adolescent. The few generalizations which may be drawn are narrow in their applicability and are often tenuous. One of the many reasons for this condition is the relative infancy of interest in the field by any sizable number of people. As a result, a great deal of the research has been exploratory in nature, both in terms of results and methodology. Such factors as representativeness of samples, adequate differentiation between problems arising from physical handicaps per se and those commonly found among the adolescent population as a whole, reliability of many of the test materials, variables used as a basis for the selection of controls, and statistical techniques have all, in varying degrees, been open to questions of adequacy and appropriateness.

Another reason can be found in the dearth of theoretically oriented research. While empirical investigations are extremely important in the essential work of gathering scientific data, overemphasis on this procedure often leads to sterility of concept formation and to an acceptance of data as isolated fact rather than as merely a cog in a greater behavioral scheme. Thus, there has been a tendency in this field to gather "facts" rather than to relate these bits of information to broader, explanatory constructs which permit generalities.

Some of the research reported herein appears to be contradictory, especially when results are categorized into (a) no essential differences found between adjustment of physically handicapped and normal adolescents and (b) significant differences found between these two groups. This variance, at least in part, probably can be explained if note is taken of the factors mentioned above, such as representativeness of samples, selection of controls, and the like. Above and beyond these methodological inequalities, however, a rather consistent pattern can be discerned when the two categories are compared. It seems as if those workers who discovered no essential differences employed standardized paper and pencil tests of adjustment and/or personality, while differences were found in those cases where less structured tests were used. Thus, dissimilarities have been located when the rigidity of the test structure has been relaxed and freer expression permitted, allowing more intensive and extensive examination of needs and emotions.

The question, therefore, may logically be raised whether or not paper and pencil tests are sufficiently sensitive to differentiate between handicapped and nonhandicapped children on the basis of various personality variables.

SUMMARY

This paper is introduced by a brief statement asserting that the physically handicapped adolescent is faced with the general problems common to those of his age as well as the more specific problems arising from his particular disability. It is followed by a short explanation of the rationale underlying the method used in most of the more acceptable investigations concerned with the crippled child's adjustment. Emphasis is placed on the common experiences of this group and those of a normal group, thus permitting intergroup comparisons. The main body of the present article reviews research which has been separated into three broad categories: (a) the relation of physical disability to social and emotional adjustment, (b) relation of physical disability to fear and guilt, (c) a comparison of the adjustment of visibly and nonvisibly handicapped adolescents.

The studies reviewed in category (a) are somewhat arbitrarily divided into those which reveal no significant differences between crippled and normal groups and those which do reveal significant differences. The more reliable findings obtained from research on social and emotional adjustment follow:

1. For the most part, negligible differences between handicapped and nonhandicapped groups are observed when the instruments used to obtain information are of the standardized paper and pencil variety.

2. Handicapped adolescent children demonstrate better relationships with their mothers than with their fathers.

3. Normal adolescent children show "better relationships and greater identification with the father than do handicapped children."

4. The adjustment of the handicapped adolescent is less mature than that of the normal.

5. The handicapped adolescent would rather maintain his existing ego structure than adjust it to new situations.

6. The handicapped adolescent child often denies his handicap.

7. Social relationship is an area of conflict for the crippled child.

8. The degree of acceptance of the handicapped by their normal peers seems to be partially related to intelligence and extent of disability caused by the handicap.

9. Postpolio rehabilitation seems to be related to prepolio adjustment.

The following are the most significant findings when physical disability is related to fear and guilt:

1. Normal members of each sex have a greater need to be free from guilt feelings than do crippled members.

2. Handicapped children believe they have more fears and guilt feelings than do normal children and these fears are directly related to their handicaps.

3. An important feature differentiating the crippled child from his normal counterpart is the fear of his disability.

The following findings are considered important when the adjustment of visibly and nonvisibly handicapped adolescents are compared, the latter group being limited to those with a cardiac disability.

1. Cardiacs and normal adolescent children demonstrate good adjustment to their fathers.

2. Cardiac children demonstrate poorer adjustment to their mothers while the opposite is found among normal children.

3. Cardiac adolescents are generally more similar to normal adolescents than are a heterogeneous handicapped group.

4. The adjustment of cardiacs is not regressive and immature.

The authors conclude this paper by discussing some reasons for the caution they feel must be placed on generalizations arising from research thus far completed in the field of adolescent adjustment to physical handicap. The opinion is also expressed that a primary reason for some researchers not finding any significant differences between groups of handicapped and normal children while others do find such a difference is the variance in the sensitivity of the instruments used.

BIBLIOGRAPHY

1. Barker, Roger G.; Wright, Beatrice A.; Meyerson, Lee; and Gonick, Mollie R., *Adjustment to Physical Handicap and Illness: A Survey of the Social Psychology of Physique and Disability* (New York: Social Science Research Council).

2. Broida, Daniel C.; Izard, Carroll E.; and Cruickshank, William M., "Thematic Apperception Reaction of Crippled Children," *Journal of Clinical Psychology* 3 (1950):243–48.

3. Cruickshank, William M., "The Relation of Physical Disability to Fear and Guilt Feelings," *Child Development* 22 (1951): 291–98.

4. Cruickshank, William M., "The Effect of Physical Disability on Personal Aspiration," *Quarterly Journal of Child Behavior* 3 (1951):323–33.

5. Cruickshank, William M., "A Study of the Relation of Physical Disability to Social Adjustment," *American Journal of Occupational Therapy* 3 (1952).

6. Cruickshank, William M., and Dolphin, Jane E., "Emotional Needs of Crippled and Non-Crippled Children," *Journal of Exceptional Children* 33 (1949).

7. Cruickshank, William M., and Medve, J., "Social Relations of Physically Handicapped Children," *Journal of Exceptional Children* 14 (1948):100–106.

8. Freed, Earl X., and Cruickshank, William M., "The Effect of Cardiac Disability on Adjustment to Parents and Family," *Quarterly Journal of Child Behavior* 4 (1952):299–309.

9. Freed, Earl X., and Cruickshank, William M., "The Relation of Cardiac Disease to Feelings of Fear," *Journal Pediatrics* 43 (1953):483–88.

10. Gates, Mary F., "A Comparative Study of Some Problems of Social and Emotional Adjustment of Crippled and Non-Crippled Girls and Boys," *Journal Genetic Psychology* 68 (1946):219–44.

11. Greenbaum, Marvin; Qualtere, Thomas; Carruth, Bruce; and Cruickshank, William M., "Evaluation of a Modification of the Thematic Apperception Test for Use with Physically Handicapped Children," *Journal Clinical Psychology* 1 (1953):40–44.

12. Kammerer, Robert C., "An Exploratory Study of Crippled Children," *Psychological Record* 4 (1940):47–100.

13. Levi, Joseph, "Personality Makeup in Relation to Rehabilitation of Handicapped Children," *Cerebral Palsy Review* 14 (1953):7–8.

14. Levi, Joseph, and Mickelson, Barbara, "Emotional Problems of Physically Handicapped Adolescents — A Study of Ten Adolescent Boys," *Journal of Exceptional Children* 18 (1952):200–206.

15. Lowman, C. L., and Seidenfeld, Morton A., "A Preliminary Report of the Psychosocial Effects of Poliomyelitis," *Journal Consulting Psychology* 11 (1947):30–37.

16. Nagge, Joseph W., and Saylor, R. H., "Physical Deficiency and Extroversion — Introversion," *Journal of Social Psychology* 4 (1933):239–44.

17. Phillips, E. L.; Berman, Isabel R.,; and Hanson, H. B., "Intelligence and Personality Factors Associated with Poliomyelitis Among School Age Children," *Monograph of the Society for Research in Child Development* 12 (1948):1–60.

18. Rubenstein, Beatrice, "Therapeutic Use of Groups in an Orthopedic Hospital School," *American Journal of Orthopsychiatry* 15 (1945):662–74.

19. Seidenfeld, Morton, A., "The Psychological Sequelae of Poliomyelitis in Children," *Nervous Child* 7 (1948):14–28.

20. Smock, Charles, and Cruickshank, William M., "Responses of Handicapped and Normal Children to the Rosenzweig P-F Study," *The Quarterly Journal of Child Behavior* 2 (1952):156–64.

21. Snygg, Donald, and Combs, Arthur W., *Individual Behavior,* (New York: Harper Brothers, 1949).

16

THE RELATION OF PHYSICAL DISABILITY
TO FEAR AND GUILT FEELINGS

𝒯HE DEGREE TO WHICH FEAR AND ANXIETY SERVE as motivating and inhibiting factors to achievement or adjustment has been recognized for some time. Fear and anxiety are emotions which in themselves are extraordinarily complex and whose impact on the adjustment of the individual is great. Studies are available which indicate that the emotional characteristics of children who have physical impairments do not differ greatly on a quantitative basis from children who are physically normal and of the same age and general socio-economic background.[3] On the other hand, it has been observed that of eight aspects of affect which were evaluated in a recent study, the factor of fear stood out from the others as an area in which statistically significant differences were obtained. Fear, or the presence of a need to be free from feelings of fear, was noticed as an important barrier to the successful adjustment of the children included in the study, both crippled and non-crippled children. Similar observations have been made by other authors.[1,6,7] The study recently completed by Henri indicates that the anxiety demonstrated by crippled children in opposition to that shown by non-crippled children was one of the outstanding characteristics in an evaluation of the adjustment of the two groups of subjects. There was a statistically significant difference in the number of responses to projective test materials which indicated basic anxieties on the part of crippled children as opposed to non-crippled children. Findings of a generally similar nature have likewise been observed by other research workers in the field.[8,9]

While the presence of fear as a factor in the adjustment of children has been established, the similarity or dissimilarity of the fears of crippled children to those of non-handicapped children is unknown. Further, the de-

Reprinted from *Child Development* 22, no. 4 (December 1951): 291–98, by permission.

162   SELECTED WRITINGS

gree to which the handicap itself constitutes the basis for fears and anxieties on the part of handicapped children, and the degree to which the handicap is a factor in the process of reaching goals and satisfying wishes is unknown.

THE METHOD

The present study is a part of a larger investigation, some results of which have been presented earlier.[2] The method used was previously elaborated extensively and will herein only briefly be outlined.

A Projective Sentence Completion Test, developed by the author, was administered to 264 physically handicapped children in six centers in the United States and to a similar group of non-handicapped adolescent children who resided in communities whose social and economic background was in large measure comparable to the former group.[2] The Projective Sentence Completion Test consisted of forty-five sentences geared to evaluate the self-concepts of adolescent children in several areas of life adjustment, i.e., (a) family, (b) society, (c) goals and wishes, including attitudes toward thwarting situations, (d) fear and guilt situations, and (e) other persons with physical defects. Analysis of the first two areas mentioned above has already been made;[2] the present paper will deal with section (d) of the Projective Sentence Completion Test.

The responses to the uncompleted sentences were assigned to categories dependent upon the significant feelings expressed by the children. A reliability check of the distribution was made by competent judges, and a high reliability for the procedure was obtained. Following the categorization of responses, standard errors,[4] critical ratios, and associated probability values[5] for the differences between percentages were computed.

The physically handicapped children were characterized by twenty-four different medical diagnoses. The largest number of children was handicapped by three physical disabilities, i.e., cardiac conditions, poliomyelitis, and cerebral palsy. No deaf, hard of hearing, known mentally retarded, or visually impaired children were included in the groups. Each of the subjects in the group of physically handicapped children was matched according to age and sex with a child who was physically normal.

RESULTS

The Projective Sentence Completion Test included a number of sentences which were sufficiently structured to cause the children to think in terms of their fears, yet at the same time permitting sufficient latitude to exploit the essential elements and advantages of the projective technique. The four sentences which particularly sampled fears were:

> I'm afraid of . . .
> I wish I could stop being afraid of . . .
> My fears sometimes make me . . .
> I am worried about . . .

Through the above open-end sentences the author has tried to obtain a statement of the children's fears, their wishes concerning their fears, and their reactions to feared objects.

As there is a wide range of responses to the items concerned with fear and guilt, and since the majority of the responses are essentially one-word answers, it has appeared more practical to tabulate the data than to state the results for individual categories. This has been done in the data which follow by imposing certain breakdowns upon the data.

In Table 1 the reader will find a comparison of the responses to the

TABLE 1

Analysis of Responses of Handicapped and Non-Handicapped Adolescents
to Sentences Eliciting Specific Fear Situations

	UNCOMPLETED SENTENCES					
	I'm afraid of . . .			I wish I could stop being afraid of . . .		
	Experimental Group	Control Group		Experimental Group	Control Group	
Response	Percent Response	Percent Response	p	Percent Response	Percent Response	p
my handicap..........	7.3	—	.00001	5.1	—	.001
vocation	0.7	0.7	—	0.3	—	.61
education	9.0	11.5	.34	6.2	8.8	.24
recreation	0.7	—	.25	1.0	—	.09
hospitals	5.0	—	.001	3.4	—	.001
family	4.0	1.8	.14	5.8	3.3	.14
animals	22.6	19.4	.36	5.1	13.3	.53
people	6.6	9.7	.19	15.7	24.0	.01
accidents.............	2.0	1.8	.88	0.7	1.1	.96
vehicles	1.0	—	.09	2.0	—	.01
water...............	2.3	1.8	.68	1.0	1.4	.96
high places	2.3	1.8	.68	2.0	0.7	.89

TABLE 1 *continued*

	UNCOMPLETED SENTENCES					
	I'm afraid of . . .			*I wish I could stop being afraid of . . .*		
	Experi- mental Group	Control Group		Experi- mental Group	Control Group	
Response	Percent Response	Percent Response	p	Percent Response	Percent Response	p
neutral	6.0	4.7	.51	5.7	5.5	.92
nothing	7.6	10.0	.34	2.4	2.5	.93
storm................	1.3	2.1	.48	1.0	2.2	.27
being alone in dark	6.0	10.8	.04	5.8	11.3	.02
fire..................	2.0	1.4	.61	1.0	1.1	.90
aggression............	1.6	1.4	.84	1.3	1.7	.71
omission	2.0	–	.02	7.5	6.2	.54
dreams	0.7	–	.25	0.7	–	.24
being talked about or looked at...........	0.7	–	.25	1.7	0.3	.16
deep places	0.7	–	.25	–	–	–
war	1.0	2.8	.14	–	1.1	.07
disease...............	0.7	0.3	.68	0.7	–	.24
the unknown	1.6	–	.07	0.3	–	.62
speaking before others .	–	2.9	.008	1.7	4.4	.06
the future	–	0.7	.31	1.7	0.3	.16
not being a success.....	–	0.7	.31	–	–	–
trains................	–	1.0	.14	–	–	–
misbehaving..........	–	2.8	.01	–	–	–
myself...............	–	–	–	0.3	1.1	.24
death................	.	.	.	0.7	2.2	.06
superstitions..........	–	–	–	–	1.1	.07
my behavior	–	–	–	–	1.8	.04
everything............	–	–	–	–	1.1	.07

uncompleted sentences, *I am afraid of . . .* and *I wish I could stop being afraid of. . . .* The first striking fact to be observed from this data is the strong fear of the handicapped group of their handicap. This is seen in the responses ". . . handicap," ". . . hospital," and ". . . disease." Other responses which are probably relevant to these in terms of fear of getting hurt are: "recreation," "accident," "vehicle," "aggression." The response of "being looked at" or "talked about" is likewise directly related to the handicap.

The strong need for conformity and accord with the demands of society is seen in the responses of the non-handicapped children, i.e., *I am afraid of* "family," "people," "being alone in the dark," "war," "speaking before others," and "misbehaving." Although many of these responses appear in the handicapped children's completions, a greater percentage is found in those of the non-handicapped group.

Further evidence of the immature and withdrawing type of adjustment which is made by the handicapped group is afforded by the responses, "dreams," the "unknown." The regressive type of adjustment characterizing the handicapped children is substantiated by the fact that the handicapped group gives larger percentages of those responses which we would expect from younger children. These include "animals," "water," high places," and "fire." On the other hand, there is a restatement of the concern of the non-handicapped children which was seen in other aspects of this study with "education," the "future," and "success."

It is most interesting to examine the possible dynamic differences produced by the different wording and interpretation of the two sentences. In one sentence there exists a plain statement of fact; in the other a wish is involved, a wish to stop a definite threat. We would expect that responses threatening to the self would be suppressed when the individual was confronted with the statement item. However, when the individual is given the task of completing the wish sentence, it is less threatening to him to state that of which he is afraid because partial relief is afforded him by the wish which, in a sense, reduced the threat.

If we accept this theoretical formulation, then, it is interesting to note that in 15 out of 23 categories of responses which are common to both of the items, percentages given per response by the handicapped group to the wish item are less than those given to the fear statement item. In two categories the percentages remain the same; in six, the percentages increase in response to the wish item. We can explain the decrease in percentage in the fifteen responses as due to the increase in the six responses which necessitated a reduction in other responses. Of the six items, one refers to recreation, and the decrease is only .3 percent. Others are "omission" and "vehicles." However, the remaining three show greater increases and refer to interpersonal relationships. These are "being looked at" or "talked about," "people," and "family." What we may conclude, therefore, is that the handicapped group has a great fear of their position in interpersonal relationships, perhaps as a result of their lack of social techniques.[1] Consequently, they entertain a wish to correct this situation.

With reference to the wish, it is interesting to note five responses which do not appear as statements but only as a wish. The greater percentages of these responses appear in the non-handicapped protocols. The responses are "death," "superstition," "myself," "my behavior," and "everything." It is not too difficult to see that these are responses which, if given in a statement, would be most threatening to the individual.

In Table 2 there is listed the responses and statistical data derived from the sentences: *I feel most concerned about* . . . and *I am worried about.* . . . The great concern of the handicapped group with their handicap is seen in the responses, "handicap," "disease," "health," "hospital," and "handicapped people." In contradistinction to the fear responses, the major areas of concern and worry are "family" and "education." Interpersonal relations are also important but do not constitute as large a percentage of the total responses as they did in the fear items. Responses included here are "people," "my behavior," "the world." There seems to be a great concern with the self as evidenced by the responses, "my appearance," "myself," "my personality." Emotional maturity is indicated by such categories as "vocation" and "being a success."

The close relationship between guilt and fear has been recognized for some time and has been observed in crippled children.[1] Four sentences were structured to sample the feelings of guilt which might be held by the two groups of children. The first of these reads: *At times I have felt ashamed of.* . . . "At times I have felt ashamed of my handicap" is found in 7.7 percent of the responses of the handicapped; in 0.3 percent of the non-handicapped (p, .00006). It is interesting to note that in addition to other responses which can be traced to the handicap, there also results the feeling of guilt at having a handicap.

The self seems to be that to which the most guilt is attached with both groups of children. "At times I have felt ashamed of myself" appears in 23.9 percent of the completions of the handicapped, in 36.6 percent of the non-handicapped (p, .001); ". . . ashamed of my behavior" is found stated by 22.8 percent of the handicapped, 26.7 percent of the nonhandicapped (p, .30); ". . . ashamed of my personality" in 5.6 percent of the handicapped, and in 1.0 percent of the non-handicapped (p, .004); and "ashamed of my appearance" is found in 7.5 percent of the handicapped and in 10.2 percent of the non-handicapped (p, .08). It should be noted that the responses referring to being ashamed of the handicap are essentially similar to these responses indicating shame of the self.

Again, interpersonal relations seem to be an important area for both groups. For the handicapped group, the feeling concerning behavior toward members of the family, and especially the parents, is very strong. "At times I have felt ashamed of my ill treatment of my family" is found in 6.3 percent of the completions of the handicapped and 1.8 percent of the non-

TABLE 2

ANALYSIS OF RESPONSES OF HANDICAPPED AND NON-HANDICAPPED ADOLESCENTS
TO SENTENCES ELICITING GUILT FEELINGS

	UNCOMPLETED SENTENCES					
	I feel most concerned about . . .			*I am worried about . . .*		
	Experimental Group	Control Group		Experimental Group	Control Group	
Response	Percent Response	Percent Response	p	Percent Response	Percent Response	p
family	24.4	26.5	.56	14.8	13.9	.76
omission	4.8	2.3	.10	5.5	4.0	.41
neutral	3.7	6.7	.11	5.1	4.0	.10
handicapped people . . .	1.7	0.6	.27	—	—	—
my handicap.	5.5	0.0	less than .0001	8.7	0.0	.0000001
people	12.6	8.7	.13	3.5	5.1	.35
education	20.1	22.8	.42	24.9	39.1	.0001
my health	2.4	1.0	.16	0.0	1.4	.02
the future	5.5	7.0	.46	7.4	7.3	.96
my appearance.	2.4	3.0	.64	1.3	1.4	.90
recreation	4.8	6.0	.53	2.2	0.7	.16
vocation	2.0	2.0	.00	0.0	2.9	.003
animals	2.0	1.0	.31	1.3	0.7	.48
my home.	1.3	0.0	.03	0.0	0.7	.24
myself	3.1	3.7	.58	0.6	0.3	.72
the world	0.0	1.3	.03	0.6	2.5	.10
music.	0.0	2.3	.003	—	—	—
my behavior	2.0	1.6	.72	—	—	—
being a success	0.0	1.0	.09	0.6	1.4	.34
money	0.0	0.6	.31	0.6	1.8	.27
disease.	—	—	—	0.6	0.0	.32
hospitals	—	—	—	1.3	0.0	.03
nothing	—	—	—	4.8	2.9	.22
many things	—	—	—	0.0	1.9	.05
my personality	—	—	—	0.0	1.1	.07

handicapped (*p*, .008); ". . . ashamed of my family" appears in 4.5 percent of the handicapped and 5.8 percent of the non-handicapped (*p*, .50); and ". . . ashamed of people" occurs in 3.6 percent of the handicapped and 7.6 percent of the non-handicapped (*p*, .04). In the sentence, *I would do anything to forget the time I . . .*, the author is trying to ascertain what events in the children's lives they considered to be real traumas. The responses of the handicapped group are predominantly concerned with handicaps and general state of health. Their handicap has produced tunnel vision in their perceptions.

Direct references to the handicap appear in 7.5 percent of the responses of the handicapped and in none of the non-handicapped (*p*, .00001); references to an injury constitute 13.2 percent of the handicapped responses and 9.3 percent of the non-handicapped (*p*, .15); allusions to being sick are found in 8.7 percent of the handicapped and 3.7 percent of the non-handicapped (*p*, .02); responses referring to time spent in the hospital are found in 7.1 percent of the handicapped and in 1.5 percent of the non-handicapped (*p*, .002); references to accidents constitute 6.8 percent of the handicapped and 20.4 percent of the non-handicapped (*p*, less than .00001).

There are no outstanding differences between the two groups to the sentence, *My fears sometimes make me. . . .* Rather we see that they are essentially similar in that the general response to fear is primarily one of withdrawal into the self. Such responses as "afraid," "nervous," "cry," "worry," "unhappy," "ashamed," "feel bad," "regress," "sick," "sad," "dream," "stay home," "depress," "irritable," "upset," and "shy," all seem to indicate an attempted suppression of the fear response. The response emerges overtly in a few cases as seen in the responses of "angry" and "do things."

The last sentence in this group began, *When I do or think something which I know is wrong, I. . . .* These responses are essentially the reactions to feelings of guilt. The outstanding characteristic of the differential responses observed here is that the handicapped group appear very anxious to conform to society. This may well be a result of their fear of losing the love of those about them. Substantiation of the need for conformity is seen in the responses, "I correct for what I've done," "I don't do it," "I stop and think," "I am worried," "I undo it," "I do it right," "I do it better next time," "I'm ashamed," "I change it," "I make up for it," "I think of an alternative," "I don't do it again," "I make it right," and "I do what's best."

Thus, it is seen that the children of the handicapped group try not to do things which they know are wrong, or if they do them, they try to atone for what they have done in terms of a counteraction activity. The non-handicapped group, on the other hand, shows fewer such responses and also gives responses which indicate that once they have done the deed, they may feel self-critical and guilty about it, but they do not take as much positive action as the handicapped children do to make up for what they have done. This is observed in such responses as "I get angry," "I'm afraid," "I'm ashamed," "I feel guilty," "I feel bad," "I try to forget it," "I turn to religion," "I feel sorry," "I withdraw," "I confess," "I don't feel bad," "I can't forget it," "I make excuses," and "I become nervous."

In general, then, the non-handicapped child feels that he may do such things and reproach himself and still not fear a loss of love whereas the handicapped child, being insecure in his interpersonal relations, has to make every effort to make up for what he has done so that his already shaky status will not be further disturbed.

SUMMARY

It has been noted earlier that fear and anxiety serve as motivating and inhibiting factors to healthy social, emotional, and academic adjustment and achievement. The results of the portion of a study which have been reported here illustrate well the fact that children with various types of orthopedic, cardiac, and neurological handicaps see themselves as having more fears and more feelings of guilt than do children of normal physical characteristics. There is little question but that the presence of such emotions and feelings has direct impact on the less satisfactory social adjustment which the handicapped children feel that they are making and which has been reported elsewhere.[2]

BIBLIOGRAPHY

1. Broida, D.; Izard, C.; and Cruickshank, W. M., "Thematic Apperception Reactions of Crippled Children." *J. clin. Psychol.* 6 (1950):243–48.

2. Cruickshank, W. M., "A study of the relation of physical disability to social adjustment." *Quart. J. Child. Behavior.* 3 (1951):323–33.

3. Cruickshank, W. M., and Dolphin, J. E., The emotional needs of crippled and non-crippled children. *J. except. Child.* 16 (1949):33–40.

4. Edgerton, H. A. and Paterson, D. G., Table of standard errors and probable errors of percentages for varying numbers of cases. *J. appl. Psychol.* 10 (1926):378–91.

5. Fisher, R. A., and Yates, F., *Statistical Tables for Biological, Agricultural, and Medical Research.* Edinburgh: Oliver & Boyd, Ltd., 1943.

6. Henri, E. A., The emotional reactions of crippled children towards their physical defects. Unpublished Master's thesis, Catholic Univ. America, 1949.

7. Ladieu, G., Hanfman, E., and Dembo, T., Studies in adjustment of visual injury: evaluation of help by the injured. *J. abnorm. soc. Psychol.* 42 (1947): 169–92.

8. Minski, L., Psychological reactions to injury. *Proc. Royal Soc. Med.* (1942):130, 195–99.

9. Temple, R., and Amen, E. W., A study of anxiety in children by means of a projective technique. *Genet. Psychol. Monogr.* 30 (1944):59–114.

17

THE EFFECT OF PHYSICAL DISABILITY ON PERSONAL ASPIRATION

*J*T HAS BEEN POSTULATED that the potential for healthy adjustment is not equal for handicapped persons as compared to non-handicapped individuals because of the presence of the handicap itself.[2] It is felt that the handicap exerts a marked influence on all aspects of personal adjustment in spite of what may superficially appear to be good adjustment.[5] Such has been shown to be true in terms of the self concepts of handicapped adolescents with respect to social adjustment within the family, with their peers, and society[3] and also in terms of fears and feelings of guilt which motivate the handicapped child.[1,4] Further examination of this problem has been undertaken with respect to the impact of the physical disability on the child's aspiration level, i.e., his goals, his wishes, and his ambitions.

METHOD

The method used in the current investigation has been adequately described elsewhere,[3] and thus only a brief statement will be made here. A Projective Sentence Completion Test consisting of forty-five incompleted sentences was administered to 265 handicapped adolescent boys and girls in six major cities of the United States. Several of these sentences were so structured as to direct the thinking of the children towards their personal aspirations and yet sufficiently unstructured so as to give relatively complete freedom for the expression of personalized self concepts. The incompleted sentences which

Reprinted from *The Quarterly Journal of Child Behavior* 3, no. 3 (July 1951): 323–33.

were used in this portion of the study are as follows: a. Most of all I want
to . . .; b. I could be happy if . . .; c. I can . . .; d. Compared with others,
I . . .; e. I know I could succeed if . . .; f. I try . . .; g. If I weren't blocked
by. . . .

Each of the handicapped children was matched with a non-
handicapped child who had also completed the test on the basis of sex and
chronological age. The responses given by the 528 children were categorized
using judges to get a reliable agreement as to which category each response
should be placed. Following the categorization of responses standard errors,
critical ratios, and associated probability values for the differences between
percentages were computed.

The physically handicapped children were characterized by twenty-
four different medical diagnoses, the largest groups of which were children
with cardiac disturbances, poliomyelitis, and cerebral palsy.[3] All children
could be grouped under the headings of orthopedic, neurological, or cardiac
defects.

RESULTS

The impact of the disability on the handicapped group is clearly indicated in
analysing the responses of the children to incompleted sentences dealing
with wishes, goals, and ambitions. This has already been observed with regard to the children's feelings about their relationship to adult society and to
a lesser extent in relation to a society of peers,[3] but the magnitude of the impact in the present adjustment area far outweighs that in previously discussed aspects of adjustment. Large differences obtain between the two
groups in this response as a result of the great number of responses referring
to the handicapped which appear in the protocols of the handicapped group
and the minimal number which appear in the protocols of the non-
handicapped children. Due to the fact that a sizeable portion of the handicapped group's responses are utilized for this *handicap* category, it follows
that differences in other categories will, of necessity, have to occur wherein
the handicapped children give a lower percentage of responses than the normal children. The handicapped children have, so to speak, used up their
available quota of responses in the handicap category. Thus, the physical
disability has a direct effect in producing marked differences in the responses of the two groups of children in several response categories.

The responses of the first incompleted sentence, *Most of all I want
to . . .,* clearly indicate the impact of the disability on the handicapped

group. Responses of the type, "Most of all I want to get over my handicap" occur in 10.5% of the protocols of the handicapped group; in 0.6% of the non-handicapped group (p being less than .000,001). A desire to excel in athletics, a common characteristic of adolescents appears in 2.5% of the protocols of the handicapped; in 6.2%, non-handicapped (p. .03). References to more overt forms of recreation are noted by 7.6% of the handicapped; by 3.1% of the non-handicapped (p. 02). This may indicate a wish to compensate for the limited scope of behavior imposed upon the former group by virtue of their physical disability. Thus, for example, a large number of such responses would be expected from cardiac children for whom there exists a large number of external restraints. A wish for recreation in the form of travel appears in 4.7% of the responses of the handicapped; in none of the non-handicapped (p less than .001). This is possibly explained in terms of the withdrawing tendencies of the handicapped children and also by the fact that travel is essentially passive form of recreation requiring little overt physical activity.

A good comparison of the emotional needs of both groups of children in terms of relationships with other people is afforded by the responses to this item, *i.e.*, a need for acceptance is found in 1.1% of the protocols of the handicapped (p .12), a need for identification in 1.4% of the protocols (p .12), a drive for independence in 1.4% of the protocols (p .12), and a need for recognition by others appears in 2.9% of the handicapped protocols (p .008). The foregoing account for 6.8% of the responses of the handicapped children. None of these above mentioned responses appear in any of the protocols of the normal group.

On the other hand, no responses of the type, "Most of all I want to be popular," appear in the protocols of the handicapped children, whereas such responses occur in 5.0% of the non-handicapped group (p less than .001). Thus, there is a recurrence of the clinical picture observed elsewhere, *i.e.*, the handicapped group is striving for acceptance while the non-handicapped group, having already achieved acceptance, has need for even better interpersonal relations.

There is additional evidence of the strong interest of the normal children in education. "Most of all I want an education" is a response found in 14.1% of the handicapped children's protocols; in 21.1% of the non-handicapped children's responses (p. 02). This may be closely related to the strong drive of the non-handicapped group for success. Many of their responses indicate they feel that education is a necessary prerequisite for success. "Most of all I want to be successful" is stated by 1.1% of the handicapped and by 13.4% of the non-handicapped (p less than .000,000,1).

Responses indicative of a desire for improvement of family relations appear in 0.4% of the handicapped protocols and in 0.6% of the non-handicapped protocols (p. 84). This would tend to indicate that in a total overview, the children in both groups feel they have equally good home environments in terms of the contributions provided by the parents. In terms of a purely "physical" home environment, 2.9% of the handicapped children and none of the non-handicapped children expressed a desire for improvement (p. 008). This may be due to the fact that many of the former children have been confined to hospital rooms for rather long periods of time.

Vocation, specific or general, is indicated as a goal in 34.6% of the protocols of the handicapped and in 30.0% of those of the non-handicapped children (p .23). Medicine as a specific vocation is indicated by an additional 7.6% of the handicapped children and by 5.6% of the non-handicapped (p. 36). The medical area was delimited specifically to see whether or not the handicapped group would show a significant difference from the non-handicapped group as a result of the former's most frequent association with medical personnel as a result of their physical handicap.

"Most of all I want to be married" occurs in 5.0% of the responses of the handicapped; in 5.3% of the non-handicapped (p .88). This response together with the one on vocational goals is indicative of rather mature adjustment for both groups. Neutral responses constitute 0.7% of the handicapped children's responses and 3.9% of the non-handicapped (p .014). The small number of neutral responses, especially for the handicapped group, coupled with the complete absence of omissions in the protocols of both groups, indicates that in terms of the wording of this item, both groups know what they want.

To the second sentence, *I could be happy if . . . ,* further interesting responses are made. "I could be happy if I weren't handicapped" is a response appearing in 17.9% of the handicapped children's protocols and in none of the non-handicapped (p less than .000,000,000,1). Other signs of insecurity among the disabled children are seen in the response, "I could be happy if I were secure," noted by 0.4% of the handicapped and none of the non-handicapped (.50); in the response, "I could be happy if I were sure of the future", found in 1.7% of the handicapped and none of the non-handicapped (p .03). "I could be happy if I were a success" appears in 0.4% of the handicapped protocols and in 1.0% of the non-handicapped protocols (p .47). The total percent of the above responses is large (20.4%) and points up the problem of the disability *per se* for the child.

The need of the handicapped group to engage in normal recreational activities and thus emulate their non-handicapped peers is seen in the response, "I could be happy if I could play." This response appears in 12.1% of the handicapped children's protocols and in 10.0% of the non-handicapped children's responses (p .42). It likewise appears in responses referring to overt recreation which are made by 4.6% of the handicapped and none of the non-handicapped (p less than .001).

The desire for travel is found in 2.1% of the handicapped protocols and in none of the non-handicapped protocols (p .009). The non-handicapped group, on the other hand, seems to be more outgoing and gives 7.8% of the following type response, "I could be happy if I had friends." The handicapped group gives 6.4% to this category (p .50). Feelings that happiness is dependent upon proper family relations appear in 12.5% of the handicapped protocols and in 13.6% of the non-handicapped protocols (p. 70). It is now clear why the non-handicapped responses fall into a wider content range than the handicapped group's responses. Forty-seven percent of the handicapped group's responses appear in the categories referring to handicap, recreation, and family, while only 23% of the non-handicapped group's responses appear in these categories. A large number of further categories were reported by both groups. The number of responses included in each category was far too few to be meaningful, thus discussion of them will be omitted.

The sentence, *I can . . . ,* probes the area of wishes, goals, and drives which the subjects feel have been realized. However, as shall be seen upon examination of the data, many of the responses to this particular question appear to be rationalization and compensatory statements when viewed in the light of data which has been previously analyzed.[2,3]

References to handicap appear in 5.4% of the handicapped protocols and in 0.3% of the non-handicapped protocols (p less than .001). Recreational activity is given as a response by 6.2% of the handicapped; by 9.5% of the non-handicapped (p. 17). "I can study" or ". . . get good grades in school" appears in 4.2% of the handicapped children's protocols and in 5.5% of those of the non-handicapped children (p .50). "I can travel" is found in 0.7% of the handicapped response total and none of the non-handicapped (p .24). References to specific talents and abilities (e.g., musical instruments and hobbies) constitute the largest number of the responses for both groups to this item and appear in 35.3% of the responses of the handicapped and in 36.1% of those of the non-handicapped (p .59).

An interesting comparison of the two groups results from an analysis of their responses which imply some sort of an evaluation of their interaction with others. "I can be dependent" occurs with 1.1% of the handicapped children and with 0.8% of the non-handicapped children (p .72); while "I can be independent" is found in 7.3% of the handicapped and in 2.9% of the non-handicapped (p .02). This last percentage for the former group in all probability is a wish for independence rather than an actual achievement of it. The word "can", may be interpreted as a wish, and it is doubtful if such differences would have been obtained had the item been worded, "I am".

To the sentence, *Compared with others I . . . ,* 8.3% of the handicapped group answer with "handicap" or give responses implying handicap (p .000,1). No such responses occur in any of the protocols of the normal subjects. "I am physically poorer" is the response by 5.4% of the handicapped and by 3.0% of the non-handicapped (p .16). "I am physically better" appears for 0.4% of the handicapped and for 2.6% of the non-handicapped (p .000,1). Thus, for a large percentage of the handicapped children, the basis for comparison with others is a physical one and one in which they give themselves a poor evaluation.

Responses indicating *equality* in terms of a comparison with others constitute 22.3% of the responses of the handicapped and 18.0% of the non-handicapped (p .22). The insistence on the part of the handicapped children that they are equal to others has been consistently seen throughout the study.[3,4] "Compared with others, I am O.K." appears in 6.1% of the responses of the handicapped, in 4.5% of the non-handicapped (p .42); "I am average", in 2.6% of the handicapped and 9.3% of the non-handicapped (p .001); "I am middle", in 0.7% of the handicapped, in 0.4% of the non-handicapped (p .72); and ". . . I am normal", in 0.4% of the handicapped and 3.3% of the non-handicapped (p .17). These responses stress the need of the disabled children to conceive of themselves as equal to their normal peers.

In terms of the responses, ". . . I am O.K.", and ". . . I am lucky", which appears with 1.9% of the handicapped and with 3.3% of the non-handicapped (p .12), it would seem that some of the handicapped children perceived this item as, "compared with other children who have more serious handicaps than I have, I:". Further evidence of the impact of the handicap in producing differential evaluations appear in the responses, "Compared with others, I am different" or "unusual", reported by 5.4% of the handicapped pupils and by 1.8% of the normal pupils (p .05). Again, the over-critical self-evaluation made by the non-handicapped group is seen in this item. ". . . I am poorer" is reported by 12.7% of the handicapped and by 18.7% of the non-handicapped (p .06); and ". . . I am better" by 16.1% of the handicapped and by 15.8% of the non-handicapped (p .93).

"Compared with others, I am rejected" occurs in 0.7% of the handicapped protocols and in none of the non-handicapped protocols (p .24). ". . . I don't know" is the response in 0.4% of the protocols of each group. Omissions occur in 8.1% of the protocols of the crippled children and in 5.2% of those of the non-handicapped subjects (p less .01); and neutral responses constitute 6.9% of the responses of the handicapped and 12.0% of the non-handicapped (p .05). This last response is not in accord with previously obtained data in which it was found that the non-handicapped children were more capable of evaluating themselves with others than the handicapped group. However, if the handicapped group *has*, in fact, interpreted the item to mean a comparison with other handicapped people, then the results on the present item are understandable since this group of children has had more contact with handicapped people.

Another sentence began with the phrase, *I know I could succeed if.* . . . In a broad overview of this item, it is found that the response of the normal pupils more than those of the handicapped group indicate they feel their success is dependent on themselves, on what they can do, or on what changes they can effect. The normal children place more stress on the feeling that success is dependent on others. Both groups, however, place a great deal of emphasis on factors external to themselves (society, money, family) as important determinants of success. The one response in which the handicapped children implicate themselves a great deal is the response dealing with the handicap. The response, "I know I could succeed if I weren't handicapped", is made by 7.3% of the handicapped pupils and by none of the non-handicapped (p. 000,001).

Other significant responses in terms of personality dynamics are "I know I could succeed if I had a chance", occurring in 7.3% of the handicapped and in 7.8% of the non-handicapped (p .82); ". . . if I try", found in 40.1% of the handicapped and in 46.4% of the non-handicapped (p .13); ". . . if I put my mind to it", in 2.9% of handicapped and in 4.6% of the non-handicapped (p .30); ". . . if I had the skill", in 1.4% of the handicapped and 1.7% of the non-handicapped (p .76); ". . . if I were smarter", in 1.0% of the handicapped and 2.5% of the non-handicapped (p .20); ". . . if I could change my personality", in 0.7% of the handicapped, 4.6% of the non-handicapped (p .006). An analysis of this data reveals that the non-handicapped more consistently assumes responsibility for whether or not they will succeed than does the handicapped group. There is a greater stress by the former group on intelligence and this is related to the responses, "I know I could succeed if I had an education", found in 4.4% of the handicapped children's response and in 8.2% of the non-handicapped (p .06).

There is also a picture of success being, for some of the subjects, dependent upon interpersonal relations. One response already considered, ". . . if I had a chance", falls into this category. Other related responses are, ". . . if I were left alone", ". . . if people weren't in some way involved", ". . . if my family weren't in some way involved", ". . . if I received help", and ". . . if I received encouragement". In terms of the above mentioned responses which imply that success is, in part, dependent upon others and relationships with them, the groups respond in essentially similar fashion.

An interesting response for several reasons is "I know I could succeed if I were determined", occurring in 3.2% of the handicapped pupils' responses and in 0.7% of those of the non-handicapped children (p .03). As this is a response similar to those which took the view that success must be self-initiated, it is surprising in the light of other data, to find that the handicapped group gives a significantly high percentage of such responses than does the non-handicapped group. A plausible explanation for this seems to be that some of the handicapped children have interpreted this item as if it read: "I could succeed *in overcoming my handicap* if:". Therefore, their responses may well be lip-service for what many of them have been taught, namely, that they can overcome their handicap if they are determined to do so.

Neutral responses constitute 11.2% of those of the handicapped and 6.9% of the non-handicapped (p .08) while omissions appear on 2.9% of the handicapped protocols and on 0.3% of those of the non-handicapped (p .03). These last two categories would tend to indicate that the handicapped group has difficulty in evaluating this item.

A further sentence started with the words, *I try.* . . . "I try to overcome my handicap" or "I try, but I'm handicapped" appears in 1.5% of the disabled children's protocols and in none of the non-handicapped protocols (p .09). This is a relatively small percentage of such responses when compared to the large percentage contributing to the handicapped category on previous items. It will be evident, in examining the remaining categories of responses to this item, that the handicapped group is less concerned with their handicaps than with "aiming to please" in one way or another. Such apparently is their technique for establishing social rapport.

Thus, responses indicating an attempt for improvement in interpersonal relationships appear in 20.5% of the handicapped protocols and in 24.9% of the non-handicapped protocols (p .23). It would be expected, on the basis of previous responses, that the non-handicapped group would show a greater striving in the area of interpersonal relations than the handicapped group.

The handicapped group presents the picture of a stronger need to conform than that of the non-handicapped group. Responses referring to family relations appear in 7.1% of the handicapped protocols and in 4.3% of the non-handicapped protocols (p .16). "I try to behave" appears in 23.3% of the handicapped protocols; in 14.4% of those of the non-handicapped pupils (p less than .000,000,001). Finally, "I try to do as others do" is found in 1.9% of the handicapped children's responses and 0.3% of those of the non-handicapped (p .14). The importance of education to the non-handicapped group is again in the responses, "I try in school" or "I try to learn", which constitute 16.5% of the handicapped responses and 25.0% of the non-handicapped (p .02). The continual striving of the non-handicapped group for an improvement of the *status quo* is again apparent. "I try my best" appears in 10.2% of the protocols of the handicapped group and in 15.5% of the protocols of the non-handicapped group (p .07).

The handicapped group is also trying to change the *status quo*, but the children of this group are faced with a different *status quo* than are the children of the normal group. The handicapped child has a need for independence and a need to be treated on equal footing with others. This may, in part, account for the stress they place on conformity. Conformity to the disabled child may be a technique of identification with normal society and, through conformity, acceptance by society. Their need for independence is seen in the responses, "I try to earn money" (money being a symbol of independence) which is found in 1.1% of the responses of the handicapped and in none of the non-handicapped group (p .07). Similarly, "I try to help myself" constitutes 1.1% of the responses of the handicapped and none of the non-handicapped (p .07).

The sentence, *if I weren't blocked by . . . ,* was designed as an attempt to obtain information about the things which the children felt were the frustrating agents influencing their behavior. Two striking facts emerge as a result of a general overview of the data. The first of these is that the impact of the physical disability makes itself most clearly evident on this item. "If I weren't blocked by my handicap" occurs in 27.3% of the handicapped children's protocols, and in 3.0% of those of the non-handicapped pupils (p much less than .000,000,001). Thus, it is obvious that the handicapped children are aware of their physical disabilities as hurdles and as major deterrents to healthy adjustment.

The second important conclusion to be drawn from the data on this item is that a large proportion of the subjects confronted with this item do not know how to deal with it. Reality may be too ominous to face. Thus, neutral responses are obtained from 17.4% of the handicapped protocols and 23.3% of the non-handicapped protocols (p .09) while omissions are found in 22.7% of the responses of the handicapped and 19.1% of those of the non-handicapped (p .31).

Blocking due to personal factors is seen in the responses, ". . . personality", ". . . fear, ". . . my age", and ". . . my appearance". The normal children in each category attributed a greater percentage of their responses. In general, then, as these above factors are considered, a larger percentage of non-handicapped children feel that the blocking is very much a personal thing. This parallels the data on the responses to "I know I could succeed if", wherein it was seen that the normal group felt much more strongly than the handicapped group that success was dependent on some personal, individual factors. However, the fact that a handicap is also an individual, personal factor must not be overlooked.

CONCLUSIONS

It can be generally concluded from the self-expressions given by the two groups of children to the items of the Projective Sentence Completion Test herein discussed that there is an important influence exerted on motivation of children by the occurrence of a physical disability. Numerous findings have been mentioned in the body of the discussion. Only outstanding conclusions which seem to permeate the responses of the children to all of the sentences will be considered here. These major conclusions demonstrate that (a) the handicapped children express a wish to compensate for the limited scope of behavior imposed upon them by reason of a physical disability. (b) The handicapped children show a marked drive for acceptance. This factor has been observed in the self concepts of the handicapped children which referred to their adjustment to social situations involving peers, family, society generally[3] and again in those situations which examined their feelings concerning fears and guilt.[4] The handicapped children are striving for acceptance of a minimal nature. The normal children also desire to be accepted, but they are striving for something better than minimal acceptance. The normal child is not satisfied with the status which he now has which is already one of acceptance in many areas. He strives for something better. The handicapped child on the other hand, not feeling that he has gained acceptance, strives for a feeling of minimal acceptance by society.

(c) Happiness, or a lack of personal happiness, is seen to depend directly upon a presence or absence of a handicap in a large number of instances. (d) The handicapped children evidence a need to engage in normal recreational activities. (e) Forty-seven percent of the responses to one sentence by the handicapped children dealt with the handicap *per se,* recreational needs, and family adjustment as opposed to 23% of the responses of the normal children which were concerned with these categories.

(f) It is observed that the basis for comparison with others is a physical one, although there is a continuous insistence by the handicapped children that they are equal to others. Herein may be a vicious circle causing maladjustment in some handicapped children. There is a basic need to conceive of themselves as equal to their normal peers. The basis of comparison is physical. Upon being realistic, the handicapped child realized his physical inadequacies. The reality of the situation coupled with his concept of comparison on a physical basis serves in combination to create an unsolvable conflict situation. This fact is stressed moreover by the (g) finding that the handicap is recognized by the disabled children as a significant barrier *per se,* to their success on whatsoever basis of evaluation.

BIBLIOGRAPHY

1. Broida, Daniel; Izard, Carroll; and Cruickshank, William, "Thematic Apperception Relations of Crippled Children," *J. Clin. Psycho.* 6 (1950):243.

2. Cruickshank, William, "The Impact of Physical Disability on Social Adjustment," *J. of Social Issues* 4 (1948):78.

3. _____, "A Study of the Relation of Physical Disability to Social Adjustment," *Am. J. Occ. Therapy* 6 (1952):100–109.

4. _____, "The Relation of Physical Disability to Fear and Guilt Feelings," *Child Development.* 22 (1951):292–98.

5. Cruickshank, William M. and Dolphin, Jane E., "The Emotional Needs of Crippled and Non-Crippled Children," *J. Exceptional Children* 16 (1949):33.

18

A STUDY OF THE RELATION OF PHYSICAL DISABILITY TO SOCIAL ADJUSTMENT

INTRODUCTION

*P*HYSICALLY HANDICAPPED CHILDREN have been observed to be similar to non-physically handicapped children insofar as emotional adjustment is concerned.[3] If, however, it is agreed that the body image is an important factor in the phenomenal field of an individual, then the impact of the physical handicap on personal adjustment of disabled individuals may be significant, although the over-all adjustment as depicted on objective tests shows similarity to that of non-handicapped persons. Schilder[6] and Bender[1] have stressed the importance of the body image on adjustment. Recently Snygg and Combs[7] have pointed out that with human beings the attempt at adjustment is not toward the insurance of the physical self, but the phenomenal self, *i.e.,* the self of which the individual is cognizant. As such, the impact of the physical disability on the body image and the feeling which the individual has about his handicap as it relates to factors in his life environment become important in understanding the dynamics basic to the adjustment of physically handicapped persons.

METHOD

A study, using a projective sentence completion test, was undertaken to determine the impact of physical disability on adjustment of handicapped ado-

Reprinted from *The American Journal of Occupational Therapy* 6, no. 3 (May–June 1952): 100–109, by permission.

lescent children. The sentence completion type test was selected as the instrument by which the data would be gathered, because it could be administered in groups and still retain the essential elements of a projective situation. The sentence completion test could also be roughly structured in such a way as to stimulate the child's thinking in certain directions and yet permit latitude for personalized self-expressions. A projective sentence completion test was developed consisting of forty-five uncompleted sentences. This test together with a set of simple instructions was provided to administrative personnel directing programs for the education of handicapped children in six large centers in the United States. A total of 264 handicapped children in junior and senior high school grades of these six centers cooperated in completing the test. All tests were returned to the author for analysis. The group of children was characterized by a wide variety of physical disabilities as noted in Table 1. The largest number of children was handicapped by three physical disabilities, i.e., cardiac conditions, poliomyelitis, and cerebral palsy. No effort was made to differentiate the children by sex.

The projective sentence completion test was also administered to more than four hundred non-handicapped children. From this large group 264 non-handicapped children were selected who could be matched according to age and sex with children in the handicapped group.

The forty-five sentences included in the projective sentence completion test were devised in such a way as to evaluate the children's self-concepts in a number of situations, i.e., (a) family, including father and mother; (b) society, including peer group; (c) other persons with physical disabilities; (d) goals and wishes, including attitudes toward thwarting situations; and (e) fear and guilt situations. The first two of the above-mentioned areas will be discussed in the present paper.

The sentences were analyzed by placing the responses into categories representative of the significant feelings expressed. A reliability check was made wherein judges were asked to classify responses and a high reliability for the procedure was obtained. Following classification of the responses, data for the various categories were tabulated and percentages of responses, using the total number of responses per sentence as one hundred percent calculated. Standard errors were figured,[4] critical ratios computed, and associated probability values determined.[5]

Father—To obtain feelings toward the father, four incomplete sentences were presented to the subjects. The analysis of the responses by categories which were selected to typify the general intent of the completions is shown in Table 2.

Good adjustment to the father by the handicapped children is indicated in the first category, "My father hardly ever is nice." Of the handi-

TABLE 1

PHYSICAL DISABILITIES WHICH CHARACTERIZE THE CHILDREN
OF THE EXPERIMENTAL GROUP

Disability	Number
Cardiac	75
Poliomyelitis	63
Cerebral Palsy	40
Congenital deformity	13
Accident	13
Tuberculosis of joint, spine	10
Epiphysitis	10
Scoliosis	6
Muscular distrophy	6
Osteomyelitis	5
Spina bifida	4
Perthe's disease	3
Arthritis	3
Hemophelia	2
Epilepsy	2
Potts disease	1
Club foot	1
Dorsal kyphosis	1
Hyperthyroidism	1
Hypothyroidism	1
Diabetes	1
Fredericks ataxia	1
Hypercalcium	1
Hypocalcium	1

capped group, 19.0% give this response while 24.3% of the non-handicapped group make this completion (p value .13). In the sentence, *My father and I . . .* , which was included in the hope that some clue as to the phantasy wishes might be revealed, the handicapped group also gives more responses of the type, "My father and I get along well together" than does the normal group, the difference being associated with a *p* value of 0.25. In the third sentence the evidence of this good adjustment seems to be borne out by the response, "If my father would only be nicer," which was reported less often by the handicapped group (34.9%) than by the normal group who gave

TABLE 2

PERCENTAGE OF RESPONSES GIVEN BY SUBJECTS TO SENTENCES DEALING WITH
ADJUSTMENT TO FATHER*

Sentence and Response Category	% response Handicapped Group	% response Normal Group	Critical Ratio	P Value
My father hardly ever . . .				
is bad or mean	40.8	50.5	2.25	.02
is nice	19.0	24.3	1.50	.13
ambivalence	1.1	3.0	1.21	.22
neutral responses	34.2	19.7	3.80	.0001
omitted response to item	1.5	3.8	1.53	.13
no answer	3.0	1.9	.77	.44
My father and I . . .				
get along well together	48.6	43.7	1.14	.25
don't get along well	9.8	11.1	.50	.62
response omitted	3.4	1.1	1.98	.05
do things together	17.7	28.8	3.02	.002
neutral responses	14.2	4.8	3.82	.0001
no answer	3.4	2.9	.35	.72
ambivalence	.4	.3	.12	.90
are alike	1.8	3.7	1.27	.20
don't do things together	—	2.2	2.44	.02
do things together sometimes	—	.3	.50	.62
differ	—	.7	1.17	.24
handicap is an adjustment factor	.4	—	.67	.50
If my father would only . . .				
be nicer	34.9	52.6	4.17	.0001
no father	7.2	1.5	3.11	.003
stay as nice as he is	2.2	.7	1.39	.16
neutral responses	43.7	36.5	1.67	.09
no answer	1.0	8.3	4.06	.0001
handicap is an adjustment factor	.4	—	.60	.50
My father . . .				
would be nicer	52.1	51.5	.14	.89
stay as nice as he is	9.3	7.9	.57	.57
responses omitted	5.0	1.5	2.11	.03
neutral responses	24.1	33.7	2.42	.02
no answer	8.5	4.1	2.04	.04
ambivalence	.7	1.1	.48	.63

*Actual terms used by the subjects differed from those noted in this column and in similar columns in the succeeding tables of this study. Terms used have been selected by the author as those typical of the general sense of the responses grouped within the category.

52.6% such responses (p, .0001). In this same sentence the response category, "If my father would only stay as nice as he is," the handicapped group
gives evidence of being content with the present adjustment to the father in
more cases than does the non-handicapped group, though the percent of
such responses is small, being 2.2% for the handicapped and 0.7% for the
normal group.

The analysis of the completions to these sentences, however, does
not show consistent evidence of superior relationships with the father for the
handicapped group. A further inspection of the first sentence shows that
40.8% of the handicapped give the response, "My father is hardly ever bad
or mean," while 50.5% of the normal group give this response. The difference between the two groups is significant at the .02 level of probability. In
the sentence beginning, *My father and I . . .* , there is again a contradiction
to the picture of good adjustment to the father for the handicapped in that
the normal group gives more responses of the type, "My father and I do
things together," more frequently than does the handicapped group; the difference between the two groups being significant at the .002 level of significance. It does not seem unwarranted to assume that the feeling underlying
this response of "togetherness" is essentially a positive one and that it therefore is permissible to add these responses to those expressing positive feelings. If this is done, a significant difference is obtained, the non-handicapped
giving the greater percent of responses showing positive feelings toward the
father.

It appears, then, that there is evidence showing good relationship
with the father for the handicapped group, and at the same time an indication of the reverse. Looking at the categories of the first two sentences which
express neutral responses, it is seen that in both instances the handicapped
group give many more such responses than does the normal group, the difference being significant at the .0001 level. A clearer picture may emerge if
we note that the normal group is reporting more positive and more negative
feelings toward the father while the handicapped group tends to give more
neutral responses. This indicates that the handicapped group is less able to
evaluate their relationship with the father than is the normal group.

They have less tendency to express real feeling toward the father,
seeming rather to be more content with the status quo. The normal group,
on the other hand, is more anxious for even better relationships with the
father. This conclusion is also seen with respect to the trend observed in
another response category. "My father and I are alike," a response of identification is given by 1.8% of the handicapped and 3.7% of the non-
handicapped. In the response of differentiation, "My father and I are different," none of the handicapped so indicate this while 0.7% of the normal

group give this response. In neither of these categories are the differences significant, but they give evidence that the non-handicapped are better able to evaluate their relationship with the fathers. On the other hand, the significance of the greater number of neutral responses given by the handicapped is evidence of their inability to evaluate their relationship with others possibly since they lack the greater opportunity for social relationships.

Mother — A group of four sentences were used to sample feelings toward the mother. The tabulation of these data is seen in Table 3.

To the sentence, "My mother and I get along well," both groups gave a higher percent of positive responses than in the same sentence dealing with the father. However, while the handicapped group gave nearly the same number of positive responses to this sentence as with father, the normal group gave many more such responses indicating better relationship to the mother, the difference being significant at the .005 level. To the sentence, "My mother hardly ever is not nice," and "My mother hardly ever is nice" the non-handicapped group again shows better adjustment to the mother, in both cases a difference exists which is significant at the .002 level. However, these two responses do not present unequivocal evidence of less satisfactory adjustment for the handicapped children, since it can be noted that there is no significant difference in the ambivalent responses in completing the above sentences. This would tend to indicate that in the case of the mother, the handicapped child feels sufficiently secure in his relationship with his mother to view her in a more critical light.

To the sentence, "My mother and I don't get along well," there is a significant difference (p, .009) in favor of the handicapped children which is somewhat contradictory to the first response category in which a better relationship is noted for the normal group. It is felt that again we are seeing the effect of the non-handicapped children's striving for a better relationship. This is indicated in the response to the sentence beginning, *If my mother would only*, to which 52.9% of the non-handicapped children completed it by saying: "If my mother would only be nicer;" 44.7% of the handicapped children gave this response (p, .06). However, in dealing with the father, the non-handicapped gave nearly the same number of responses to this item while the handicapped gave ten percent more such responses and sixteen percent fewer neutral responses to this sentence dealing with the mother. This again is an indication that the handicapped child is being more accurate and more mature in his evaluation of his feeling toward his mother rather than an indication of better father adjustment for him.

In general, while both groups show better relationship with the mother than with the father, the handicapped children show an adjustment to the mother which is superior to that of the normal group. They are better

TABLE 3

PERCENTAGE OF RESPONSES GIVEN BY SUBJECTS TO SENTENCES DEALING WITH
ADJUSTMENT TO MOTHER

Sentence and Response Category	% response Handicapped Group	% response Normal Group	Critical Ratio	P Value
My mother and I . . .				
get along well	49.0	61.1	2.81	.005
do things together	21.4	19.0	0.69	.49
are alike	4.6	2.1	1.64	.10
don't get along well	4.2	9.8	2.59	.009
don't do things together	0.4	0.4	0.00	—
ambivalence	3.0	1.8	0.88	.37
miscellaneous..................	12.8	4.7	3.37	.0007
no mother.....................	1.1	1.1	0.00	—
no answer	3.0	1.4	1.28	.20
My mother hardly ever . . .				
gets along well	45.6	58.3	2.95	.002
doesn't get along well	18.8	10.0	2.93	.002
ambivalence	1.5	1.8	0.24	.81
miscellaneous..................	13.3	11.8	0.52	.60
takes time to relax	15.3	13.0	0.76	.44
no answer	5.3	4.4	0.51	.61
no mother.....................	00.0	0.3	0.50	.61
My mother . . .				
gets along well	60.9	67.0	1.46	.14
doesn't get along well	4.5	4.1	0.23	.82
miscellaneous..................	26.28	22.2	1.25	.21
no mother.....................	1.5	1.1	0.37	.71
no answer	6.0	3.7	1.20	.23
ambivalence	1.1	1.5	0.37	.71
If my mother would only . . .				
not get along so well	3.5	2.2	0.87	.38
get along better	44.7	52.9	1.87	.06
miscellaneous..................	27.5	29.0	0.38	.70
take time to relax	5.9	3.3	1.40	.16
no answer	17.0	11.4	1.83	.07
no mother.....................	00.0	1.1	1.83	.07

able to define their feelings toward her and are secure enough in the relationship to be more critical in the evaluation of the parent-child relationship.

Family—On the whole as seen in Table 4 both groups show that they derive a good deal of satisfaction when they are at home with their families. Approximately 70 percent of both groups give a positive response to the sentence, *When I am at home with my family.* . . . On this sentence, however, the handicapped group shows more negative feelings (p, .11) as well as more ambivalent feelings (p, .09). Again, on the completion of the sentence beginning *When my family.* . . . , the trend toward better relationships for the normal group is seen. While both groups show that they enjoy being with the family, the handicapped group shows less responses indicating positive feelings (p, .02) and they also give fewer responses indicating that they value being at home more than they value getting together with the family. The reverse is true for the normal group. This latter difference may reflect the handicapped child's feeling of the home as a place of security while the prospect of getting together with the family tends to bring interpersonal relationships into focus and this, as has been noted previously, is a situation in which he has more concern about his role. Again, on this second sentence there are more negative responses (p, .01) by the disabled children as well as more omissions (p, .02). There is also an indication that the handicapped child has partially withdrawn from social contacts (p, .31).

The sentence beginning *When there is a quarrel in my family* . . . depicts both groups tending to avoid participation in this situation. Approximately 45 percent of each group gives this avoidance response, though a greater number of the non-handicapped group indicate participation in such family altercations (p, .11). While only a small number of the handicapped children group gives an ambivalent response (3.8 percent), there are no responses of this nature from the normal group (p, .001). This uncertain feeling about family quarrels is again characteristic of the general uncertainty which the handicapped child has with regard to his attitude toward others. The remainder of the data indicates approximately equal participation in family quarrels since if all the participation responses are added, it is found that the total for the handicapped is 29.5 percent, for the non-handicapped, 30.2 percent.

The adjustment problems of children are often different in social situations with peer groups and with society generally than when considering adjustment within the relatively limited boundaries of the home. The present study, therefore, was extended to include the child's self-evaluation of adjustment to situations which are beyond the limits of relationships with the parents and in the family. Adjustment to girls, boys, and society generally will be considered.

TABLE 4

PERCENTAGE OF RESPONSES GIVEN BY SUBJECTS TO SENTENCES DEALING WITH
ADJUSTMENT TO FAMILY

Sentence and Response Category	% response Handicapped Group	% response Normal Group	Critical Ratio	P Value
When there is a quarrel in my family . . .				
I like it	0.7	00.0	1.17	.24
ambivalence	3.8	00.0	3.17	.001
I don't like it	11.0	9.2	0.71	.48
I stay out of it	45.8	47.7	0.44	.66
no answer	2.2	0.7	1.39	.17
miscellaneous	1.8	3.2	1.04	.30
I get in it	6.8	10.7	1.57	.11
I try to solve it	19.4	16.6	0.84	.40
there aren't any quarrels	1.9	2.5	0.45	.65
I'm to blame	1.9	4.0	1.40	.16
I take sides	2.2	1.8	0.31	.75
I take both sides	1.1	1.1	0.00	—
I get the worst of it	0.7	1.8	1.02	.30
When I am at home with my family . . .				
we get along well	71.7	70.3	0.35	.72
ambivalence	1.5	00.0	1.67	.09
we don't get along well	9.9	6.2	1.57	.11
no answer	2.6	2.9	0.20	.84
miscellaneous	8.3	8.0	0.13	.89
we don't get together	0.4	0.7	0.36	.72
I behave	2.2	3.2	0.75	.45
I work	3.0	5.1	1.24	.21
I study	00.0	3.2	3.20	.001
When my family gets together, . . .				
they do	67.1	76.5	2.42	.02
ambivalence	2.2	00.0	2.44	.02
they don't	12.4	9.0	2.53	.01
no answer	9.1	4.2	2.27	.02
miscellaneous	7.5	4.5	1.40	.16
I don't get together with them	0.7	0.4	0.36	.72
I behave	0.7	0.7	—	—
I stay by myself	2.2	1.1	1.02	.31
I help around the house	00.0	1.5	1.67	.09
I am social	00.0	1.1	1.83	.07

Boys — In evaluating the adjustment of the handicapped child to boys, four incomplete sentences were presented as are shown in Table 5. The response to the first incomplete sentence, *Boys think I . . . ,* shows approximately 40% of each group who attribute positive feelings toward themselves. There is, however, a great disparity between this and the percent of responses to the completion, "Boys think I am not nice," (p, .0001). In this case the handicapped group show themselves less willing to be the recipient of negative feelings than are the normal group. Instead, they

TABLE 5

PERCENTAGE OF RESPONSES GIVEN BY SUBJECTS TO SENTENCES DEALING WITH ADJUSTMENT TO BOYS PEERS

Sentence and Response Category	% response Handicapped Group	% response Normal Group	Critical Ratio	P Value
Boys think I . . .				
am nice	46.6	40.1	1.53	.12
am not nice	28.4	45.4	4.14	.0001
ambivalence	4.0	0.4	2.69	.007
miscellaneous	10.2	5.6	1.97	.05
no answer	7.0	7.1	0.04	.96
handicap noted as adjustment factor	3.3	00.0	3.30	.001
don't know	00.0	1.1	1.83	.07
Most boys like . . .				
miscellaneous	6.5	4.5	1.04	.29
no answer	1.1	0.9	0.24	.81
fun	2.2	0.3	1.90	.06
a hobby	1.4	00.0	2.33	.02
handicap noted as adjustment factor	0.4	00.0	0.67	.50
to tease me	1.8	0.9	0.90	.36
recreation	45.2	49.0	0.93	.35
girls	25.8	25.8	0.00	—
don't like girls	1.1	00.0	1.83	.07
school	0.4	0.3	0.12	.90
me	12.5	11.2	0.50	.62
friends	0.4	00.0	0.67	.50
marriage	0.7	00.0	1.17	.24
work	0.4	00.0	0.67	.50
food	00.0	2.5	2.50	.01
money	00.0	2.6	1.00	.31
animals	00.0	.9	1.50	.13
people	00.0	.9	1.50	.13

TABLE 5 *continued*

Sentence and Response Category	% response Handicapped Group	% response Normal Group	Critical Ratio	P Value
When I am with boys . . .				
I'm nice	54.2	59.3	1.18	.24
I'm not nice	18.4	17.6	0.24	.81
ambivalence	0.4	2.2	1.67	.09
miscellaneous	6.7	5.0	0.83	.41
no answer	6.4	2.6	2.04	.04
handicap noted as adjustment factor	0.4	00.0	0.67	.50
I'm sociable	9.0	6.2	1.20	.23
I'm not	0.7	2.2	1.39	.16
I conform	1.8	1.5	0.24	.81
I misbehave	1.5	1.8	0.24	.81
I try to be liked	00.0	1.1	1.83	.07
I think boys . . .				
are nice	53.3	51.1	0.50	.62
are not nice	19.1	24.6	1.52	.13
ambivalence	5.3	6.4	0.56	.57
no answer	13.0	3.7	3.86	.0002
miscellaneous	7.6	12.1	1.72	.08
like girls	0.7	0.3	0.48	.63
vary	0.4	0.4	–	–
like me	0.4	0.4	–	–
don't like me	00.0	0.7	1.17	.24

respond with more ambivalent completions (p, .007) or with neutral completions (p, .001). In addition 3.3 percent see the handicap as an adjustment factor. This expression of insecurity in the face of possible recognition of negative feelings toward himself is clearly brought out.

To the sentence beginning *I think boys . . . ,* just over 50 percent of both groups show positive attitudes toward boys. Although the difference is not significant, more of the normal group are willing to express negative feelings in the completion, "I think boys are not nice" (p, 13). The major difference between the two groups in completing this sentence is seen in the unwillingness of the handicapped group to complete the sentence (p, .0002).

In the sentence directed toward the behavior when with the peer group, the same trend is seen. The biggest difference again occurs in the frequency with which the handicapped children omit an answer (p, .04). Slightly more of the normal group gives the response, "When I am with boys, I am nice" (p, .24). However, with this sentence and with the sentence dealing with interests of this peer group (*Most boys like . . .*), there are no outstanding differences or trends.

These latter areas are apparently sufficiently distant so that the threat in making such a judgement is less. Judgements by both groups tend to be similar, and it is probable that the male peer group is less devious in showing their feelings than are the adult groups in showing their attitudes toward the handicapped child. Thus, he is comparatively better able to evaluate his feelings toward boys. Identification with boys would seem to be better judging from the similarity of interests and attitudes. Apparently, the most sensitive area is incurred in facing possible negative feelings directed toward him from the male peer group.

Girls — Four incomplete sentences were constructed which concerned girls. Two dealt with the individual's feelings toward girls; one attemped to get an estimate of the subject's evaluation of girls' attitudes toward him, and one attempted to obtain some indication of the child's view of his behavior in such a relationship.

With regard to the evaluation of the attitude toward him, the handicapped child as seen in Table 6 again shows himself to be less certain of his relationships. While nearly 50 percent of each group report that girls see them in a favorable light, many more non-handicapped children are willing to attribute unfavorable attitudes toward themselves (p, .003). The handicapped child evades making such an evaluation by giving more miscellaneous completions (p, .001) and more ambivalent responses (p, .14).

The sentence beginning, *Most girls like . . . ,* tends to show also a less mature attitude on the part of the handicapped inasmuch as fewer of this group give the response, "Most girls like boys." (p, .06) and more give the completion, "Most girls don't like boys" (p, .04). Such a suggestion of immaturity is seen to be at least partially due to a lack of experience in social contacts (3). As would be expected, more of the control groups respond with the completion, "Most girls like me" (p, .21).

The interests attributed to the adolescent girls by the handicapped, while they are not significant, are seen to reflect some of the values that are important to them. For example, handicapped children see girls as valuing (a) the home (p, .5), (b) helping the family (p, .31), and (c) household interests (p, .16).

To the sentence beginning *When I am with girls . . . ,* we see a greater percentage of the non-handicapped group giving the completion, "When I am with girls, I am nice" (p, .04). However, a few more of the normal group respond with negative completions to this sentence (p, .45) as well as showing more ambivalence about their behavior with girls (p, .66), which,

TABLE 6

PERCENTAGE OF RESPONSES GIVEN BY SUBJECTS TO SENTENCES DEALING WITH
ADJUSTMENT TO GIRLS PEERS

Sentence and Response Category	% response Handicapped Group	% response Normal Group	Critical Ratio	P Value
Girls think I . . .				
am nice	46.8	50.7	0.89	.37
am not nice	21.9	33.2	2.90	.003
ambivalence	4.6	2.2	1.45	.14
miscellaneous	12.7	4.9	3.17	.001
no answer	8.8	6.4	1.03	.30
don't know	3.4	2.2	0.85	.39
Most girls like . . .				
don't like me	1.3	0.6	0.83	.40
miscellaneous	5.8	4.0	1.01	.31
no answer	2.9	2.0	0.70	.48
don't know	0.4	0.3	0.12	.90
like boys	29.1	36.2	1.86	.06
don't like boys	1.6	00.0	2.00	.04
appearances	2.3	0.6	1.70	.09
clothes	12.2	10.7	0.57	.57
school	0.6	1.7	1.10	.27
household interests	6.9	4.3	1.40	.16
movie stars	1.3	00.0	2.17	.03
me	8.6	11.7	1.25	.21
friends	2.6	2.6	0.00	—
don't like me	0.6	0.6	0.00	—
to help family	0.6	00.0	1.00	.31
their home	1.0	0.6	0.67	.50
material things	2.3	0.6	1.70	.09
recreation	19.2	18.7	0.15	.88
food	00.0	1.6	2.00	.04
other girls	00.0	0.6	1.00	.31
to be popular	00.0	2.3	2.88	.003
When I am with girls . . .				
I'm nice	43.2	52.4	2.10	.04
I'm not nice	20.4	23.1	0.75	.45
ambivalence	1.5	10.7	0.44	.66
miscellaneous	6.9	5.7	0.55	.58
no answer	8.5	2.2	3.13	.001
I enjoy myself	7.3	2.2	2.79	.01
don't know	0.7	00.0	1.17	.24
I don't like girls	0.4	00.0	0.67	.50
I'm not	1.9	1.9	—	—
I act the same	0.7	0.7	—	—

TABLE 6 *continued*

Sentence and Response Category	% response Handicapped Group	% response Normal Group	Critical Ratio	P Value
I think girls . . .				
are nice	52.9	41.4	2.71	.007
are not nice	20.7	42.2	5.51	.0000001
miscellaneous	11.6	8.3	1.26	.21
no answer	7.9	2.6	2.69	.007
ambivalence	4.9	2.6	1.40	.16
like me	00.0	0.3	0.50	.62
like boys	1.8	1.9	0.08	.93
vary	0.3	0.3	–	–
don't like boys	0.4	00.0	0.67	.50

though only a slight difference, is in contrast to previous responses. These data seem to indicate that here the non-handicapped child is concerned with an evaluation of his behavior with girls in much the same way that the handicapped child is generally concerned with his uncertainty concerning such relationships.

The difference between the groups comes out most clearly with the incomplete sentence, *I think girls. . . .* The handicapped groups give more responses of the type, "I think girls are nice" (p, .007), but they cannot afford to show the large number of negative completions toward this peer group that characterizes the normal group's responses (p, .0000001). The normal group again can be critical in their judgement of others, and, as such, these two reports by them tend to depict adolescent attitudes. The expected ambivalence concerning their feelings is shown by the disabled group in contrast to the definite expression of feelings by the normal group (p, .007).

Society — A number of sentences were developed to evaluate the adjustment of the children to broad social situations in which adults play an important role. Table 7 presents this data. One of the sentences reads *If people would only. . . .* In examining the responses to this sentence, it is found that 7.5 percent of the handicapped children's responses contain some reference to the child's handicap. As no such responses were given by the normal group, the *p* value associated with such a difference is less than .00001. As this sentence represents a wish and a wish with particular reference to adult society in contradistinction to society as represented by peers, the results point conclusively to the fact that adults are impressing upon the child an increased awareness of his physical disability. One may speculate by saying

that perhaps a reason for the poor social adjustment of the handicapped
child is the fact that members of adult society define the child in terms of his
handicap. Another response to this sentence, "If people would only be nice,"
is given by 38.3 percent of the handicapped children; by 52.3 percent of the

TABLE 7

PERCENTAGE OF RESPONSES GIVEN BY SUBJECTS TO SENTENCES DEALING WITH
ADJUSTMENT TO SOCIETY

Sentence and Response Category	% response Handicapped Group	% response Normal Group	Critical Ratio	P Value
If people would only . . .				
handicap noted as an adjustment factor	7.5	00.0	4.69	.00001
miscellaneous....................	25.3	24.7	0.16	.88
no answer.......................	2.8	1.5	0.97	.33
like me	38.3	52.3	3.30	.001
not pity me......................	1.7	00.0	2.13	.03
be more careful	3.9	8.5	2.13	.03
treat me equally..................	1.4	0.3	1.31	.19
mind their own business	18.6	12.5	1.96	.05
People who watch me . . .				
handicap noted as an adjustment factor	7.4	00.0	4.63	.00001
are nice	6.0	0.7	3.29	.001
are not nice.....................	17.5	14.6	0.91	.36
make me feel bad..................	26.1	32.9	1.72	.08
pity me	2.6	0.3	1.98	.05
think I'm nice....................	11.9	13.8	0.66	.50
ambivalent in attitude toward me	0.4	0.3	0.12	.90
don't think I'm nice................	5.5	10.8	2.19	.03
no answer.......................	6.0	3.3	1.50	.13
ambivalence.....................	0.7	00.0	1.17	.24
miscellaneous....................	16.4	18.7	0.71	.48
judge me........................	00.0	4.1	3.42	.001
People who do things for others . . .				
are nice	74.8	78.0	0.81	.42
aren't nice......................	1.9	1.1	0.74	.46
ambivalence.....................	1.1	00.0	1.83	.07
no answer.......................	4.6	2.2	1.45	.15
miscellaneous....................	6.1	8.3	0.97	.33
expect reward....................	11.1	8.3	1.10	.27
feel good........................	00.0	1.8	2.00	.05

TABLE 7 *continued*

Sentence and Response Category	% response Handicapped Group	% response Normal Group	Critical Ratio	P Value
I like to be treated . . .				
handicap noted as an adjustment factor	1.9	00.0	2.11	.04
nice	32.5	37.6	1.22	.22
no answer	4.9	1.1	2.66	.008
miscellaneous	7.6	5.2	1.12	.26
normal	2.6	1.1	1.20	.23
like others	34.9	26.1	2.18	.03
my age	5.7	1.9	2.18	.03
human	2.6	4.1	0.93	.35
fairly	1.1	7.0	3.47	.0004
equal	4.2	3.7	0.30	.76
like a boy	1.5	0.7	0.74	.46
as an adult	00.0	6.3	4.20	.00001
as a friend	00.0	2.6	2.60	.01
bossily	00.0	0.7	1.17	.24
badly	00.0	1.4	2.33	.02

non-handicapped children (p, less than .001). Here both groups express rather strong dissatisfaction with adult society and a wish for improvement in relations with adults. One would probably expect, as a result of the relationship described in terms of the handicap above, that the handicapped group's responses would yield a larger percentage of such responses. However, there is apparently here a recurrence of the pattern observed so often in this study wherein the handicapped children, although showing currently poorer relationships with adults than do the non-handicapped children, seem to be satisfied with the *status quo*. The non-handicapped group, on the other hand, although seemingly better off in terms of adjustment with adults, is constantly striving for even better relationships.

The responses which indicate a wish for people to be nicer should, in reality, be added to other responses given to this uncompleted sentence which is similarly representative of a wish for better treatment on the part of adults and society. One such response, "If people would only treat me equally," is given by more of the handicapped children than non-handicapped children and is associated with a probability of .19. Here again there is evidence for the fact that adults are treating the handicapped child differently than the non-handicapped and that such treatment can be attributed to the fact that a handicap exists. "If people would only not pity me" is found in 1.7 percent of the responses of the disabled children and in none of the responses of the normal subjects (p, .03). The response, "If people would only mind their own business," is observed in 18.6 percent of the handicapped children's responses; in 12.5 percent, non-handicapped (p, .05). Thus, it would seem in terms of this last response that a good proportion of the children of both groups, and especially the children in the handicapped group, feel that there is too much adult interference in their lives. Perhaps this is a further reason for the many negative feelings expressed by the children of both groups toward their individual parents and toward their families as a whole. In terms of this, the motivation can be understood for the last quoted responses on the part of the handicapped child, most of whose needs are taken care of by the parent. It will later be seen that these children have a strong need for independence and that this response, which is indicative of negative feelings toward adult interference, may well be a result of the fact that many handicapped children are not allowed to do things for themselves and may be overprotected by the parent.

Although both groups of children indicate a great deal of disfavor with adult society, in large measure a normal adolescent characteristic, the types of responses given by both groups seem to be basically different. Thus the responses indicating a wish for better relationships on the part of the handicapped group are responses directly connected with the handicap. In other words, the handicapped child is seeking better relations in terms of a hope that adult society will forget his handicap, ignore it.

In general, the remaining material in Table 6 serves to expand the concept discussed in the above paragraphs. One further aspect concerning social relationships warrants discussion however. One of the sentences in this section began *I like to be treated.* . . . "I like to be treated nicely," is found in 32.5 percent of the responses of the handicapped subjects; in 37.6 percent, normal subjects (p, .22). Thus, one sees from this response and from others below a strong wish to be treated somehow better and differently than they now are being treated. However, the reader shall see in the types of responses given by each group that the handicapped child wants to be treated *like others*, whereas the non-handicapped child wants to be treated *more than like others* and also in a positive manner. The non-handicapped children, having already attained the position of equality, are striving for something better. Evidence of these facts is seen immediately below.

The response, "I like to be treated not as a handicapped person," is seen in 1.9 percent of the responses of the handicapped group and, as might be expected, in none of the responses of the normal group (p, .04). The handicapped group gives responses, such as, "I like to be treated normally,"

(p, .23); ". . . like others," (p, .03); ". . . equally," (p, .76); ". . . my age,"
(p, .03); and ". . . like a boy" or ". . . a girl" (p, .46). The handicapped child
is here observed asking to be treated as he is, namely as a boy or a girl, and
equally, as an individual of a certain age. He wants to be treated as others
are treated. The non-handicapped children, however, give a different type of
response, i.e., "I like to be treated as a human" (p, .35); ". . . treated fairly"
(p, .0004); ". . . as an adult" (p, .00001); ". . . as a friend" (p, .01); and
". . . as the boss" (p, .24).

Examination of these latter responses given by the normal group
subjects is evidence of the fact that these children are not seeking treatment
in terms of the way others are treated as is seen in the case of the handicapped subjects. Rather, they are seeking treatment in terms of specialized
self-concepts, e.g., "adult," "friend," "boss," or "human." What the reader
sees then is an expressed desire to be treated as special individuals rather
than to be treated as others are treated. In addition, the non-handicapped
children reveal their pre-occupation with interpersonal relations in their desire to be treated as a friend or in other of the above categories. This latter is
further emphasized by the fact that the disabled children once more produce
more responses of omission (p, .008) and more neutral responses (p, .26).

SUMMARY

From the detailed material presented above, a number of conclusions can be
made. With respect to the handicapped children, both positive and negative
findings are observed.

1. The adolescent children who have physical impairments demonstrate better relations with the mother person than with the father person.

2. The handicapped children show a real interest in comparing themselves with others in an effort to determine their standings with others. This
is considered a somewhat positive characteristic since it indicates that the
children are maintaining a relatively aggressive attitude in social situations,
but at the same time it indicates insecurity and anxiety in social situations.

3. The handicapped children indicate greater dissatisfaction with
adults and adult society than do non-handicapped children.

4. The handicapped children frequently indicate a desire to be
treated like other children rather than as children with handicaps.

A number of conclusions point to the fact that the handicapped
adolescent group has difficulty in effecting happy social and emotional adjustment.

1. The handicapped children seem less able to evaluate interpersonal relations, and thus they produce many ambivalent and neutral responses and also omit many responses.

2. The responses of the handicapped group indicate a definite tendency to withdraw from social contacts and relations. The group is apparently satisfied with current adjustments despite the fact that the *status quo* is unsatisfactory in the area of social relations.

3. The handicapped children show fewer normal adolescent interests than the non-handicapped children, and they indicate that they are seeking substitute gratifications in phantasy.

4. The adjustment of the handicapped children appears to be on a more immature level than that observed among normal children of the same age and sex.

5. The impact of the physical handicap is impressed on the disabled adolescents more by adults than by their peer group.

The normal group is almost universally characterized by factors which are essentially positive in nature.

1. The normal children show better relationships and greater identification with the father than do the handicapped children. The group of normal children, while showing less positive relationships with the mother than with the father, nevertheless shows greater and more positive relations with the mother than does the handicapped group of children. More children of both groups show good relationships both with parents and with peers than show poor relationships. The normal group, however, shows greater positive adjustments to parents and peers than do the handicapped subjects.

2. The normal group subjects seem better able to evaluate relationships with other people, both with adults and with peers. There seems to be a better *status quo* arrangement for the normal subjects, but in spite of this they are continuing to strive for even better relationships. Their adjustment is characterized by allocentricity rather than self-interest as is seen with the disabled children. A critical evaluation of relationships is seen on the part of the non-disabled children as a part of a continuing drive for self-improvement and a change in the *status quo*. Such a critical evaluation of social relations is observed to be absent with handicapped children.

BIBLIOGRAPHY

1. Bender, L., "Body Image Problems of the Brain Damaged Child," *Journal of Social Issues* 4 (Fall 1948):84.

2. Broida, D., Izard C., and Cruickshank, W. M., "Thematic Apperception Reactions of Crippled Children," *Journal of Clinical Psychology* 6 (July 1950): 243.

3. Cruickshank, W. M., and Dolphin, J. E., "Emotional Needs of Crippled and Non-Crippled Children," *Journal of Exceptional Children* 16 (November 1949): 33.

4. Edgerton, H. A., and Paterson, O. G., "Table of Standard Errors and Probable Errors of Percentage for Varying Numbers of Cases," *Journal of Applied Psychology* 10 (September 1926):378.

5. Fisher, R. A., and Yates, F., *Statistical Tables for Biological, Agricultural, and Medical Research* (Edinburgh: Oliver and Boyd, Ltd., 1943).

6. Schilder, P., *Image and Appearance of the Human Body* (London: Kegan Paul, 1935).

7. Snygg, D., and Combs, A. W., *Individual Behavior: A New Frame of Reference for Psychology* (New York: Harper, 1949).

19

THE RELATION OF CARDIAC DISEASE
TO FEELINGS OF FEAR

(with Earl X. Freed)

CRUICKSHANK[2] HAS STATED that "fear and anxiety serve as motivating and inhibiting factors to healthy social, emotional, and academic adjustment and achievement." In recognition of the importance of fears in striving for healthy adjustment, much work has been done on their nature and etiology. For the most part, it has been difficult to establish causal relationships between fears and other factors. However, such relationships have been demonstrated in some cases as, for example, between children's fears and those of their parents.

Recently, Cruickshank[2] contributed evidence on another of these relationships. He found that children handicapped by a variety of physical disabilities, principally cardiac conditions, poliomyelitis, and cerebral palsy, perceived themselves as having more fears than nonhandicapped children and that the fears were directly related to their being handicapped. That which most significantly differentiated these children from matched non-handicapped children were their fears of their handicaps.

A more recent study[5] has indirectly questioned the practice of studying the problems of handicapped children as a whole. It was found that cardiac children adjusted to members of their families differently from children handicapped by a number of other physical disabilities. One of the pertinent conclusions drawn from this study was that the "cardiac group was more similar to its control (non-handicapped) group than the whole handicapped group was to its control group." It was possible to differentiate between a cardiac handicap and other handicaps, such as blindness or poliomyelitis, on three counts: a cardiac dysfunction (a) less severely inhibited the

Reprinted from *The Journal of Pediatrics* 43, no. 4 (October 1953): 483–88, by permission.

establishment of good intrafamily relationships, (b) was less externally evident, and (c) did not necessarily directly limit the behavior of the child. The present paper is a further investigation, in the area of fear and anxiety, of the similarities and differences between a group of cardiac children, a mixed handicapped group, and a group of physically normal children.

THE METHOD

The method used in the present study has been described in an earlier publication[1] and will be reviewed briefly. A Projective Sentence Completion Test was compiled by Cruickshank[1] to investigate various areas of adjustment, one of which was fear, the subject of the present paper. Following administration of the test to 264 handicapped children in six centers of the United States and to 400 nonhandicapped adolescents, 264 of the latter group were matched with the handicapped children with respect to age and sex. Seventy-five of the handicapped children had a cardiac disability but the tests of four of these were not scored due to total illegibility of responses. The subjects of the present study were, therefore, the seventy-one cardiac children and their matched, nonhandicapped, controls.

Responses to the sentences were classified in terms of the feelings expressed in the completions. Two additional categories were included, (a) "omission," where no response was given, and (b) "unclassified," where the response could not be conveniently classified or was illegible. Utilizing judges, a high reliability was obtained for this procedure. The sum of the responses for each sentence was regarded as 100 percent and the statistical treatment of the data consisted of the conversion of the frequencies in each category into percentages, the calculation of standard errors and critical ratios[3] and the determination of the associated probability values.[4]

RESULTS

For the purposes of clarity and brevity, data on the responses to two of the projective sentences have been brought together into one- or two-word categories expressing the essential feeling of the completion. Table 1 contains data on two sentences investigating fear situations, "I'm afraid of . . ." and "I wish I could stop being afraid of . . ."

From the first of these sentences, "I'm afraid of . . . ," it was hoped

TABLE 1

RESPONSES OF CARDIAC AND NONHANDICAPPED CHILDREN TO SENTENCES
INVESTIGATING FEAR SITUATIONS

| | UNCOMPLETED SENTENCES | | | | | |
| | *I'm afraid of . . .* | | | *I wish I could stop being afraid of . . .* | | |
Response	Control Group % Response	Non-handicapped Group % Response	P	Control Group % Response	Non-handicapped Group % Response	P
Interpersonal relations	5.0	18.0	.001	16.5	42.9	.001
My handicap	8.9	–	.005	4.1	–	.07
Death	3.8	–	.08	2.7	–	.17
High places	6.4	1.3	.08	5.5	1.3	.16
Storms	–	2.7	.17	2.7	1.3	.55
Not being successful	–	2.7	.17	–	–	–
Vehicles	2.5	–	.19	2.7	–	.17
War	2.5	–	.19	–	–	–
Accidents	2.5	–	.19	–	–	–
Misbehaving	2.5	6.9	.21	–	–	–
Education (school)	8.9	15.2	.23	9.7	6.9	.55
Animals	25.6	18.0	.25	18.0	16.6	.84
Hospitals	1.2	–	.27	2.7	–	.17
Family	6.4	2.7	.27	2.7	–	.17
Illness	–	1.3	.27	–	1.3	.27
Many things	–	1.3	.27	–	–	–
Nothing	5.1	8.3	.42	1.3	2.7	.55
Darkness	5.1	8.3	.42	6.9	9.7	.55
Fire	3.8	2.7	.72	2.7	–	.17
Unclassified	7.6	8.3	.88	6.9	4.1	.45
Omission	1.3	1.3	–	6.9	4.1	.45
Water	–	–	–	–	2.7	.17
My personality	–	–	–	4.1	4.1	–
Aggression	–	–	–	1.3	1.3	–
Vocation	–	–	–	1.3	–	.27

that a purely descriptive statement of feared situations would be obtained.
Two categories of responses to this sentence especially distinguished between the cardiac children and the nonhandicapped children, (1) "inter-

personal relations," and (2) "my handicap." Significantly more of the non-handicapped children evidenced a fear of interpersonal relationships than cardiac children. This fear was also demonstrated in related areas such as "not being successful," "misbehaving," and "education," which are all related to social conformity and to all of which, a greater (though not significant) percentage of nonhandicapped than cardiac children responded. The one area in which more cardiac children than nonhandicapped children evidenced social anxiety was "family" and was probably related to the difficulty in adjustment with the mother experienced by the cardiac child and also his inability to participate in family activities.[5]

Probably the reason fewer cardiac children feared social contacts was that they had been excluded from such experiences by their handicaps. If this is true, then it would appear that the different responses of the cardiac children were directly attributable to their handicap. This follows from the fact that the other significant differences which were found were in the categories of "handicap" and "death." It is not too difficult to relate responses of "high places," "vehicles," "war," "accidents," and "hospital," more of which were given by cardiac children, to instances wherein injury and possible handicap could occur.

Cruickshank[2] stated that "the regressive type of adjustment characterizing the handicapped children is substantiated by the fact that the handicapped group gives larger percentages of those responses which we would expect from younger children." According to data presented here such a statement does not seem warranted for cardiac children. It is true that more cardiac children than their controls gave responses indicating fear of "animals," "fire," and "high places." On the other hand, responses indicating fear of "darkness," "storms," "many things," and "nothing" were found in more of the records of the nonhandicapped children. Also, on the "wish" sentence, more of the control children than the cardiac children evidenced fear of "water." The objection may be raised that completions of "nothing" and "many things" are not related to immaturity and, largely, the decision as to whether these responses should be so classified is one of individual choice. It would seem to the authors that "I am afraid of nothing," *is* a vague, immature response, expressing an infantile, undifferentiated feeling. If this is true, then Cruickshank's conclusion, based on his total handicapped group, does not seem applicable to the cardiac children in this study. The cardiac children do *not* give "larger percentages of those responses which we would expect from younger children."

An earlier finding[1] that more handicapped than nonhandicapped children are unable to evaluate their adjustment — as measured by responses of "omission" and "unclassified" — was not borne out in the case of cardiac children. These two responses were the least significant of the differences in the responses to "I'm afraid of . . ."

In general, then, the cardiac children and their normal controls are more alike than different in their respective responses to this test. The outstanding differences were in the area of interpersonal relationships and in the reaction to the cardiac handicap. As previously mentioned, it is likely that differences in the latter response (cardiac handicap) were responsible for differences in the former response (interpersonal relations). Prohibited by cardiac dysfunction and/or his mother's perception of his handicap[5] from participating in social relationships, the cardiac child is not subject to the classical conflicts and turmoils occasioned by the adolescent's social adjustment and, consequently, he has less reason to fear them than the nonhandicapped child. In addition, those who react to the cardiac child may do so with deference and special attention. Thus, the cardiac child, having had less traumatic experience in interpersonal situations than the nonhandicapped child, has less reason than the latter to fear them.

The essential similarity between the cardiac and the nonhandicapped children in the area of feared situations is more evident in the responses to the sentence, "I wish I could stop being afraid of . . ." Only the category of interpersonal relations" was significant at the 1 percent level of confidence or better, with the control children producing more such responses. The only other response significant at the 10 percent level or better was "my handicap." The nature of this incomplete sentence is different from the statement of "I'm afraid of . . ." The task of completing such a descriptive statement can be perceived as a most threatening one to the self.[2] As such, it is possible that prevalent fear situations may be suppressed. On the other hand, the sentence containing "I wish . . ." in a sense renders the threat one step removed from the self and, furthermore, by associating the fear with the fantasy of a wish, may make it less real for the individual. Therefore, it would seem that less guarded projection could be anticipated on the "wish" sentence. Furthermore, the wording of "stop being afraid of" would partially assure us that the completions refer to relatively long-term feelings which are high in the hierarchy of feared situations.

To return to the data, completions of "not being successful," "war," "accidents," "misbehaving," and "many things" were totally absent. Both groups showed percentage increases in the categories of "interpersonal relations," "darkness," and "omission," and both showed decreases in the completions of "animals," "family," "nothing," "fire," and "unclassified." Four new completions are to be noted, significant among which were "my personality" and "aggression." The former were similar to the category of "misbehaving" but sufficiently different (in terms of insight) to warrant separate categorization.

Again, the greatest shift occurred in the categories of "interpersonal relations" and "handicap." It is noteworthy that differences in only two categories were associated with significance levels of 10 percent or better. In Cruickshank's study[2] of the group with a variety of handicaps, a much larger proportion of categories showed significant differences between the handicapped and nonhandicapped groups (see Table 2). For both sentences a higher percentage of categories was found significant at almost all levels between Cruickshank's total handicapped group and their controls than between the cardiac group and their controls.

One further uncompleted sentence, designed to investigate the reaction to fear, was included. This sentence was "My fears sometimes make me . . ." Equal percentages of the responses of both groups were found in the classifications of "nervous," "ashamed," "I have no fears," "sick," and "withdraw."

Only four categories were significant at the 10 percent level or better. Responses of "afraid" were found in 25.0 percent of the protocols of the nonhandicapped and in 7.0 percent of the handicapped (p = .002); responses of "worry" constituted 5.6 percent of the responses of the control group, and 0.0 percent of the cardiac group (p = .04); and "unclassified" completions were found in 9.8 percent of the records of the nonhandicapped and 1.4 percent of the handicapped (p = .02). Only one response of the four significant ones was found more frequently in the protocols of the cardiac children. The completion, "do things" or "misbehave," occurred in 12.6 percent of their records and in 1.4 percent of those of the control group, the

TABLE 2

COMPARISON OF PERCENT OF TOTAL NUMBER OF CATEGORIES WHICH WERE
SIGNIFICANTLY DIFFERENT FOR CARDIAC CHILDREN AND TOTAL HANDICAPPED GROUP

| | | UNCOMPLETED SENTENCES | | | |
| | | I'm afraid of . . . | | I wish I could stop being afraid of . . . | |
Group		Cardiac (%)	Total Handicapped (%)	Cardiac (%	Total Handicapped (%)
Percent level of confidence	1	9.5	13.3	5.0	12.9
at which difference	5	0.0	6.6	0.0	6.4
was significant	10	9.5	6.6	5.0	19.3
Total percent		19.0	26.6	10.0	38.7

probability value being .006. It seems, therefore, that the normal children react to their fears by internalizing the feelings provoked by their fears while the cardiac children act out their fears. However, it is interesting that 5.6 percent of the responses of the handicapped and 1.4 percent of the responses of the nonhandicapped were "dream" (p = .16). Reference to the cardiac handicap was found in only 1.4 percent of the cardiac children's responses (p = .25).

CONCLUSIONS

1. A fear of their handicap significantly differentiated the cardiac group from their matched, physically normal controls.

2. A greater fear of interpersonal relations outstandingly characterized the nonhandicapped group. This difference is probably related to the handicap in that the cardiac children, having had less experience in social situations owing to their handicap, did not fear them as much as normal children who had experienced more conflicts.

3. The data did not indicate that the adjustment of the cardiac child was regressive and immature.

4. Essential similarity, rather than difference, characterized the specific situations feared by both the handicapped and nonhandicapped groups.

5. As noted previously, in the adjustment to parents and family, the cardiac children were more similar to their control group than the total handicapped group was to its control group in the area of feared situations.

6. Grossly, the reaction of both groups to feelings of fear was one of withdrawal or internalization of the feelings. However, this was significantly more often the case in the nonhandicapped group than in the cardiac group. The evidence indicated that cardiac children may act out their feelings extratensively.

7. The cardiac children did not show the same degree of difficulty in evaluating their adjustment as do a group of children with miscellaneous handicaps.

BIBLIOGRAPHY

1. Cruickshank, W. M., "A Study of the Relation of Physical Disability to Social Adjustment," *Am. J. Occ. Therapy,* 6 (1952):100–109.

2. Cruickshank, W. M., "The Relation of Physical Disability to Fear and Guilt Feelings," *Child Dev.* 22 (1951):291.

3. Edgerton, H. A., and Paterson, D. G., "Table of Standard Errors and Probable Errors of Percentages for Varying Numbers of Cases," *J. Appl. Psychol.* 10 (1926):378.

4. Fisher, R. A., and Yates, F., *Statistical Tables for Biological, Agricultural and Medical Research.* Edinburgh, Oliver and Boyd, Ltd. 1943.

5. Freed, E. X., and Cruickshank, W. M., "The Effect of Cardiac Disability on Adjustment to Parents and Family," *Quart. J. Child Behav.* 4 (1952):299.

20

THE EFFECT OF CARDIAC DISABILITY
ON ADJUSTMENT TO PARENTS AND FAMILY

(with Earl X. Freed)

*T*HE PRESENCE OF A PHYSICAL HANDICAP in an individual has been viewed as an impediment to his strivings for a healthy adjustment comparable to that of a non-handicapped individual. It has been felt that the impact of the handicap is an all-pervading one, influencing every aspect of adjustment.[2] Cruickshank[2] has substantiated this hypothesis in his investigation of the self-concepts of adolescents handicapped by a variety of physical disabilities. He has demonstrated that the social adjustment of these adolescents is strongly influenced by their perceptions of their handicaps. It has also been shown that the differences in personal aspiration[3] and feelings of fear and guilt[4] which exist between handicapped and non-handicapped children are attributable to the very presence of the handicap in the former group.

In these studies, children handicapped by a variety of physical disabilities have been treated as composing one large group. It was the purpose of the present investigation to examine the adjustment to parents and family of one major sub-group of handicapped children, those with a cardiac disability. The question was raised as to whether or not the adjustment described for the total handicapped group would be characteristic of these cardiac children.

PROCEDURE

The same technique referred to by Cruickshank[3] was employed in this study. A Projective Sentence Completion Test which he devised was administered

Reprinted from *The Quarterly Journal of Child Behavior* 4, no. 3 (July 1952): 299–309.

to 264 handicapped children in six large centers in the United States. These children were enrolled in junior and senior high school grades. The test was also administered to more than 400 non-handicapped children from among whom, 264 were randomly selected to be matched with the handicapped children in terms of age and sex. The majority of the exceptional children were handicapped by cardiac disability (75), poliomyelitis (63), and cerebral palsy (40).

Although relatively "open-ended" in terms of the responses they evoked, the 45 incompleted sentences were structured to investigate five areas of adjustment: (a) family, (b) society, (c) other persons with physical disabilities, (d) goals and wishes, including attitudes toward thwarting situations, and (e) fear and guilt situations. The present report is concerned with the first of these areas, family and parental adjustment.

SUBJECTS

Of the responses of the 264 handicapped children used in Cruickshank's study, those of 71 cardiac children were selected for analysis. Four of the original 75 cardiac children were not included in this study because of illegibility of their responses. The 71 cardiac children were matched with 71 children from the group of non-handicapped children in terms of the factors of age and sex referred to previously.

METHOD OF ANALYSIS

Inspection of the raw data indicated that the best method of analysis would be to determine the feeling expressed by the subject in his completion of the sentence. For a number of the responses to several incomplete sentences, therefore, the authors attempted to list the feelings expressed. In the case of most of the responses to any particular sentence, it was found that they could be grouped into a minimum number of categories. This made statistical analysis more feasible than with a large number of categories of responses with minimal frequencies. For each sentence there were also included two categories, (a) "omission", if the subject failed to respond; and (b) "unclassified", where the response was illegible or could not conveniently be placed in any of the existing categories. A check was made on the reliability of such a method of classifying responses. Judges were asked to categorize a large number of responses and a high reliability was obtained for the procedure.

The initial statistical analysis of the data consisted of converting the frequencies in each category into percentages and using the total number of responses per sentence as 100%. Standard errors and critical ratios were then calculated.[5] The "two-tail" probability values associated with the calculated critical ratios were next determined.[6]

RESULTS

Father adjustment

The feelings of children toward their fathers were investigated by four incomplete sentences. The responses and statistical data associated with these responses are presented in Table 1.

With respect to the first sentence in this group, "My father hardly ever . . .", the two groups of children seemed to have few differences in their responses. The only major difference was in the category indicating "no father", and this difference was found throughout the other three sentences. In all four sentences, the probability associated with the differences in response to this item were below the 10% level of confidence. The responses to the first sentence in the area of father adjustment indicated twice as many positive responses as negative ones for both the cardiac and non-handicapped children. Twice as much ambivalence toward the father was evidenced by the non-handicapped children, but this difference was not a significant one. The unclassified responses included such completions as "My father hardly ever cuts his hair" and "My father hardly ever eats ice cream", etc. The completions included in the unclassified area were unclassified in terms of showing positive or negative feelings toward the father.

The generally positive attitude toward the father was substantiated by the responses to the second sentence in this area, "My father and I . . .". Approximately 50% of each group gave positive responses toward the father and more specifically, toward relations with him. Only 4% of the cardiac group and 1% of the control group expressed negative reactions. Slightly more non-handicapped children than cardiac children gave evidence of direct identification with the father, but the difference was not a significant one. If one might make the assumption that responses indicating companionship were also expressive of positive feelings, then the addition of these responses to the positive ones resulted in between 70% and 80% positive

TABLE 1

ADJUSTMENT TO FATHER

Response	Percent of Subjects Who Produced Response		Level of Significance
	Cardiac	Non-Handicapped	
My father hardly ever . . .			
he is nice	47.9	50.0	.80
he is not nice	23.2	25.0	.80
I have no father	5.4	0.0	.04**
unclassified	20.5	18.3	.72
ambivalence	2.7	5.6	.39
omission	0.0	1.4	.25
My father and I . . .			
get along well	49.2	52.1	.72
don't get along well	4.2	1.4	.27
ambivalence	2.8	2.8	—
do things together	22.5	29.5	.34
are alike	1.4	4.2	.27
unclassified	11.2	5.6	.23
I have no father	4.2	0.0	.07***
omission	4.2	4.2	—
If my father would only . . .			
he is nice	1.4	1.4	—
be nicer	49.2	50.7	.88
unclassified	26.7	40.8	.07***
I have no father	12.6	0.0	.002*
omission	9.8	7.0	.55
My father . . .			
is nice	49.2	57.7	.31
is not nice	8.4	2.8	.13
ambivalence	1.4	4.2	.27
unclassified	21.1	0.0	.008*
I have no father	8.4	30.9	.17
omission	11.2	4.2	.10***

Level of Confidence: *1%; **5%; ***10%.

feeling responses of the total feelings expressed by both groups toward the father.

The third sentence, "If my father would only . . .", was included in the Projective Sentence Completion Test to aid in examining phantasy and wish activity in the area of father adjustment. As would be expected by the nature of such an item, a large percentage of each group (approximately 50%) reacted with wishes for better father adjustment, while only approximately 1% of each group reported positive feelings toward the father. It was interesting to note that the percentage of cardiac children reporting no father varied with each of the sentences and that this percentage was highest and the difference between the groups was most significant in relation to the sentence keyed to investigate phantasy.

The fourth sentence included in the area of father adjustment, "My father . . .", was included for the purpose of obtaining purely descriptive statements about the father. A report of the qualitative examination of the responses to this incomplete sentence would be of extreme value but space limitations prevent publication of this data at this time. In terms of a statistical analysis, however, approximately 50% of the responses of each group were positive in feeling expressed toward the father, with 8% of the responses of the cardiac children and 2.8% of the responses of the non-handicapped children being negative. This last difference was not statistically significant.

A general overview with respect to father adjustment would have to stress as the outstanding factor in this data the similarities rather than the differences which were found between the responses of the two groups. The cardiac and the non-handicapped children both showed many more positive feelings toward their fathers than negative feelings. Generally, more ambivalence was shown by the non-handicapped children.

One of the main reasons for selecting the cardiac children for this study was to explore the question of whether or not they could be considered to be representative of handicapped children as a group as reported by Cruickshank. Table 2 presents data pertinent to this issue. This data was calculated by computing the percentage of total categories which were significant at each of the three confidence levels for the two groups. There was clear cut evidence that the cardiac children, as a group, differed significantly from the rest of the handicapped children, as a group, with respect to the father adjustment. The data derived from the study with the handicapped children indicated rather definite trends in which the adjustment of the non-handicapped children toward their fathers was superior to that of the handicapped children. One of the major differences was with respect to the category of responses dealing with father and child doing things together. The hypothesis was advanced that handicapped children, because of their handicap, were unable to participate as much in activities with their fathers as the non-handicapped children were. This hypothesis would seem to be contradictory to the data of the present study unless it seems feasible to make a dis-

TABLE 2

COMPARISON OF PERCENT OF TOTAL NUMBER OF CATEGORIES
WHICH WERE SIGNIFICANTLY DIFFERENT FOR CARDIAC CHILDREN
AND TOTAL HANDICAPPED GROUP IN AREA OF FATHER ADJUSTMENT

Group	Percent Level of Confidence at Which Difference Was Significant			Total Percent
	1	5	10	
Cardiac	8.0%	4.0%	12.0%	24.0%
Total Handicapped	20.0%	20.0%	3.3%	43.3%

tinction between the type of handicap which burdens the child. This, in fact, was one of the purposes of the present study. Apparently, the handicap of cardiac dysfunction is not as great a block toward father adjustment, in terms of such factors as participation with the father in various activities, as are such handicaps as poliomyelitis and cerebral palsy. It will be necessary to further investigate the validity of this hypothesis in terms of other data in this study. It is also possible to hypothesize, on the basis of data already reviewed, that cardiac children are more like non-handicapped children than they are like the handicapped group. Seven of the thirteen categories of the handicapped children which were found significant at one of the three confidence levels and *all six* of the six categories of the cardiac group were concerned with responses classified as "omission", "no father", or "unclassified". Thus, none of the differences found between the cardiac children and their controls were in categories expressing feelings of great positive or negative significance.

Mother adjustment

The second of the twelve major areas investigated was the area of mother adjustment. Results of the four sentences probing this area are presented in Table 3. The first sentence, "My mother hardly ever . . .", gives clear cut evidence of the difficulty in adjustment with the mother experienced by the cardiac children. The cardiac children gave more negative and fewer positive responses than the control group. In addition, the greater number of unclassified responses for the cardiac children plus their greater number of omitted responses would indicate that the cardiac children had difficulty

TABLE 3

ADJUSTMENT TO MOTHER

| | Percent of Subjects Who Produced Response | | |
| | --- | --- | --- |
Response	Cardiac	Non-Handicapped	Level of Significance
My mother hardly ever . . .			
she is nice	32.3	65.2	.00006*
she is not nice	22.5	6.9	.008*
ambivalence	0.0	5.5	**.05**
unclassified	38.0	19.4	.012**
omission	5.7	2.7	.39
I have no mother	1.4	0.0	.25
My mother and I . . .			
get along well	40.0	61.9	.008*
don't get along well	4.2	4.2	−
ambivalence	5.7	1.4	.16
do things together	17.1	21.1	.55
unclassified	22.7	4.2	.001*
are alike	7.1	2.8	.23
I have no mother	1.4	2.8	.55
omission	1.4	1.4	−
If my mother would only . . .			
she is nice	16.9	15.4	.80
she is not nice	46.4	53.5	.39
omission	19.7	11.2	.01*
unclassified	15.4	19.7	.48
I have no mother	1.4	0.0	.25
My mother . . .			
is nice	53.5	70.4	.03**
is not nice	4.2	2.8	.65
ambivalence	2.8	4.2	.65
unclassified	29.5	16.9	.07***
I have no mother	1.4	1.4	−
omission	8.4	4.2	.25

Level of Confidence: *1%; **5%; ***10%.

in evaluating just how they stood in relation to their mothers. This increased number of omissions for the cardiac group was a somewhat general trend seen throughout the remainder of the sentences probing the area of mother adjustment.

The same picture of the cardiac children reported more negative feelings and fewer positive feelings than the control group with regard to the mother appeared in the responses of both groups to two other sentences in this area, "My mother and I . . ." and "My mother . . .". It was interesting to note that on the sentence keyed to investigate phantasy and wish activity, "If my mother would only . . .", the two groups were fairly similar in feelings expressed toward the mother.

Since the sentence completions were used with respect to both the father and mother, it was interesting to compare results in these two areas. In every one of these sentences, the control group gave a larger percentage of positive responses to the mother than to the father. This would be predicted to some degree by various studies in child and adolescent psychology.

The cardiac children, on the other hand, showed a trend toward maintenance of better relations with the father than the mother. When the handicapped children used by Cruickshank were compared as a whole with their controls, the picture of better relationship with the mother than with the father appeared throughout the responses on the test for both groups of children. It would appear, therefore, that the nature of a cardiac handicap is detrimental to the maintenance of good relationships with the mother. This may well be due to the fact that the cardiac child is forced into a closer, more dependent relationship with his mother, a relationship which, from the child's frame of reference, is one characterized by limitations, censures, etc. This is especially true of the cardiac child because the nature of his handicap is not externally obvious and, furthermore, is not necessarily one which limits him directly as in the case of poliomyelitis or blindness, for example. It is necessary for the mother of a cardiac child to remind him of his many limitations and, from the child's point of view, it is the mother, not the cardiac handicap, who is blocking him from many enjoyable activities and from participation as an equal with his peers.

The fact that in the area of mother adjustment, the cardiac group was much more similar to the handicapped group than in the area of father adjustment, is borne out by the data in Table 4. The table shows a slight trend for the cardiac children to have been even poorer in the area of mother adjustment than the total handicapped group.

Family adjustment

Three sentences were used to investigate the area of general family adjustment, differentiated from the two previously discussed areas in that no specific parent or family member was included in the wording of the sentences. Data on the responses to these sentences are presented in Table 5.

TABLE 4

COMPARISON OF PERCENT OF TOTAL NUMBER OF CATEGORIES
WHICH WERE SIGNIFICANTLY DIFFERENT FOR CARDIAC CHILDREN
AND TOTAL HANDICAPPED GROUP IN AREA OF MOTHER ADJUSTMENT

Group	Percent Level of Confidence at Which Difference Was Significant			Total Percent
	1	5	10	
Cardiac	20.0%	12.0%	4.0%	36.0%
Total Handicapped	17.8%	0.0%	14.3%	32.1%

The first sentence in this group was "When there is a quarrel in my family, I . . .". The category which included the largest percentage of responses of both the cardiac and control groups was the one which indicated a withdrawal from participation in family quarrels. This followed fairly closely the pattern of response found for the total handicapped group. The only difference which was significant among responses to this sentence was found in the response of disliking quarrels, where the non-handicapped group indicated a greater dislike than the cardiac group. It was interesting to note that there was a significant difference in ambivalent liking and disliking of quarrels in the total handicapped group with the handicapped group giving more such responses. The previously found general trend of more ambivalence on the part of handicapped children did not follow for the cardiac children as a group. There were no responses of ambivalence found in their protocols with regard to this question.

The second sentence in this area was "When I am at home with my family . . .". Approximately 75% of the children of both groups indicated that they enjoyed these contacts. However, only the cardiac children indicated that they disliked being at home with their families and this dislike was statistically significant. Contradictory to that which was mentioned above with regard to ambivalence, the cardiac children gave more responses of ambivalence. In terms of response to the third sentence, "When my family gets together, I . . .", about the same percentage of each group gave positive responses as did to the second sentence.

Generally, then, with respect to family relations, it would seem that similarity between the two groups rather than difference between them was the outstanding factor. Both groups showed rather healthy family adjust-

TABLE 5

ADJUSTMENT TO FAMILY

Response	Cardiac	Non-Handicapped	Level of Significance
When there is a quarrel in my family, I . . .			
stay out of it	45.2	42.8	.76
am involved in it	10.9	14.2	.55
like it	1.3	0.0	.27
dislike it	6.8	15.5	.08***
there are no quarrels	2.5	2.5	—
try to solve it	26.0	18.1	.25
am to blame	2.7	5.1	.48
get the worst of it	1.2	1.2	—
unclassified	2.7	0.0	.17
When I am at home with my family . . .			
I enjoy it	73.2	76.0	.68
I don't enjoy it	7.0	0.0	.018**
ambivalence	5.6	0.0	.04**
omission	4.2	4.2	—
my family doesn't get together	1.4	0.0	.25
I behave myself	2.8	4.2	.65
I study	4.2	4.2	—
unclassified	1.4	9.8	.02**
I help around the house	0.0	1.4	.25
When my family gets together, I . . .			
enjoy it	74.6	70.4	.58
don't enjoy it	5.6	2.8	.42
ambivalence	5.6	8.4	.51
omission	8.4	2.8	.13
do things alone	5.6	2.8	.42
unclassified	0.0	12.6	.001*

Column header: Percent of Subjects Who Produced Response

Level of Confidence: * 1%; ** 5%; *** 10%.

ment. Particularly encouraging were the facts that (a) it was difficult to discern many major differences between the cardiac and the non-handicapped children in responses to this test of family adjustment, and (b) those differences which did appear did not lend themselves easily to an interpretation which placed the etiology for the difference in relation to the cardiac disability. This would place greater stress on basic personality differences as the basis for differences between the groups in responses to this test.

The generally better adjustment of cardiac children than handicapped children taken as a whole in the area of family adjustment was substantiated by the data in Table 6.

CONCLUSIONS

The detailed data presented above lends itself to the following conclusions:

(a) Both the cardiac children and the control children showed good adjustment to the father. The cardiac children showed a poorer adjustment to the mother than the control children.

(b) The cardiac children demonstrated better adjustment to the father than to the mother. The reverse was true for the non-handicapped children.

(c) The difficulty in adjustment to the mother by the cardiac children was one of the few differences between the experimental and control groups which could be assumed to be attributable to the cardiac handicap. It probably arose from the mother's role of having to inhibit the activity of the cardiac child and constantly remind him of his handicap.

(d) The cardiac group was more similar to its control group than the whole handicapped group was to its control group. Such earlier findings as more ambivalence and inability to evaluate interpersonal relations on the part of the handicapped child did not hold for the cardiac child in evaluating his parental and family adjustment.

TABLE 6

COMPARISON OF PERCENT OF TOTAL NUMBER OF CATEGORIES
WHICH WERE SIGNIFICANTLY DIFFERENT FOR CARDIAC CHILDREN
AND TOTAL HANDICAPPED GROUP IN AREA OF FAMILY ADJUSTMENT

Group	Percent Level of Confidence at Which Difference Was Significant			Total Percent
	1	5	10	
Cardiac	4.1%	12.5%	4.1%	20.8%
Total Handicapped	9.3%	9.3%	9.3%	28.9%

The position is not held that the similarities and differences summarized and discussed here will follow throughout the responses to other areas of the Projective Sentence Completion Test to be reported subsequently. It will be interesting to note, however, if the adjustment evidenced for the cardiac children in the area of family adjustment is one which characterizes their adjustment in other areas or is a function of the interrelationships within the family.

BIBLIOGRAPHY

1. Cruickshank, William M., and Dolphin, Jane E., "The Emotional Needs of Crippled and Non-crippled Children," *J. Exceptional Children* 16: 33, 1949.

2. _____, "A Study of the Relation of Physical Disability to Social Adjustment," *Amer. J. Occupat. Therapy* 6 (1951):100–109.

3. _____, "The Effect of Physical Disability on Personal Aspiration," *Quart. J. Child Behav.,* 3: 3, 1951.

4. _____, The Relation of Physical Disability to Fear and Guilt Feelings. *Child Dev.,* 22: 4, 1951.

5. Edgerton, H. A., and Paterson, O. G., "Table of Standard Errors and Probable Errors of Percentages for Varying Numbers of Cases," *J. App. Psych.,* 10: 378, 1926.

6. Fisher, R. A., and Yates, F., *Statistical Tables for Biological, Agricultural, and Medical Research* (Edinburgh: Oliver and Boyd, Ltd., 1943), p. 29.

21

GROUP THERAPY WITH
PHYSICALLY HANDICAPPED CHILDREN

I. Report of Study

(*with Emory L. Cowen*)

INTRODUCTION

STUDIES[8,2] ARE REPORTED in which group play therapeutic techniques, essentially non-directive in nature, are utilized following the principles established by Rogers[12] and Axline.[2] Generally these techniques have been used with children who, while presenting emotional problem, are nevertheless physically normal, and mentally are within normal to superior intelligence levels. Axline, however, notes that the handicapped child "benefits by a therapeutic experience if the handicap is a source of conflict and anxiety and emotional disturbance." She reports cases wherein non-directive therapeutic techniques were employed with handicapped children. She also reports the progress made by one child who had a serious visual impairment and who had benefited from a group therapy experience as one child among several physically normal children. The present writers are unaware of any other research studies to supplement Axline's reports of therapy in which a non-directive approach through group play has been applied to physically handicapped children, although Rubenstein[13] has used a 'therapeutic' approach with groups of orthopedically handicapped adolescents.

For some time, as study after study has reported the greater presence of emotional needs and personality maladjustments among the physically handicapped as compared with groups of physically normal individuals,[15,9] the need for the development of counseling and therapy methods for the handicapped has been recognized. Barker[4] has pointed out the somato-

Reprinted from *The Journal of Educational Psychology* 39 (April 1948): 193–215, by permission.

psychological significance of the relationship between physical abnormality and personality growth and development and has stressed the importance of a normal physique in considering the dynamics of good personal adjustment. Although basic differences in philosophy are apparent, Levy,[10] Allen and Pearson,[1] Bender,[5] Schilder,[14] and others have each emphasized the susceptibility of physically atypical individuals to emotional disorders as a sole or partial result of the impact of the imperfect physique upon the individual's potential for adjustment. Preliminary results of a study of the emotional needs of crippled children[7] indicate that there is an increasing feeling of guilt in such children between the years corresponding to the fourth and twelfth grades; that this situation is accompanied by a general trend of increasing fears; and that neither trends are offset by an expressed feeling of acceptance and of security which the crippled child experiences in the home and school. It is apparent that the usual counseling and guidance services available to handicapped children in school are not sufficient to insure adequate personal adjustment. It is also evident that the need is a general characteristic of the group, not specific to particular individuals, and that, therefore, handicapped children must be insured adequate opportunities for emotional release and therapy.

In order to determine whether or not non-directive group therapy techniques were applicable to physically handicapped children a therapy situation, purely experimental and exploratory in nature, was projected. It was hoped that through such an approach it would be possible to develop therapy techniques suitable to the handicapped or to determine what modifications if any to the principles of non-directive group play as established by Axline would be necessary to make the technique applicable to special needs of the handicapped.

METHOD

The study took place in a public day school for physically handicapped children. Five children, all of whom were referred by the school authorities because they presented one or more emotional problems in the school situation, were included in the group. Originally it was planned that the group would include six children, but since one of the children was absent for the first five meetings he was excluded from the group and no replacement was made. The final group consisted of four boys and one girl as shown in Table 1. Two children were handicapped by cardiac conditions; one, handicapped by hemophilia; one, a post-poliomyelitis case; and one, a post-encephalitis case.

TABLE 1

STATUS OF CHILDREN INCLUDED IN GROUP THERAPY MEETINGS

Name	CA in Years and Months	IQ	Handicap	Problem As Stated by School	School Grade	Sessions Missed
Ernest	8-3	63	Post-encephalitis with spasticity of left upper and lower extremity.	Immaturity, inability to grasp classwork or to settle down.	First	Nos. 7, 8
Daniel	9-0	103	Post-poliomyelitis with subsequent underweight and anemia.	Inability to adjust to group and get on in class. Withdrawal behavior; prefers to be alone.	Third	Nos. 1, 7, 9, 10
Janet	8-10	90	Cardiac, acute regurgitation with recent acute exacerbation.	Failure in work, inability to concentrate or sit still. Nervous and flighty. Immaturity.	Third	Nos. 4, 5, 6
George	8-5	101	Severe cardiac and chorea.	Failing in all subjects, refuses to try. Disobedience and negativism to teacher; bully.	Second	Nos. 4, 5, 8, 10, 11, 12
Peter	7-3	107	Hemophilia	Fights, bully, always wants to lead. Shows off, steals, lying, stubborn.	Second	None

The entire experiment took place in the course of about seven weeks during which time the group met twice weekly for fifty-minute periods. There was a total of thirteen meetings which the children could have attended. Table I indicates that certain sessions were missed by several of the children. The question of absence will be discussed elsewhere.[6]

The first nine meetings of the group took place in a vacant kindergarten room in the school. The room contained materials which were designed for children in a kindergarten class and not particularly for play therapy groups. It was a rather large room, measuring approximately forty by twenty feet, and containing a piano, desk, and several small chairs and tables for the children. There were numerous toys available to the group including games, puzzles, paste, crayons, blocks of all sizes, boxes and boards for building, blankets, balls, doll carriages, cabinets, beads, and other items. During the course of the therapy sessions a large three-dimensional doll house was added to the room. This was available to the children to play with, but there were no dolls which could be used with it. Finger paints were also made available to the children when they were requested. The tenth meeting of the group was held in a local psychological clinic therapy room in order to provide the children with materials somewhat more conducive to working out personal problems, but for both the eleventh and the twelfth meetings the children were returned to the original location. The thirteenth meeting was a Christmas party which was suggested to the children. All were wholeheartedly in favor of the party, and it took place in a different room from that used for the group play several afternoons after the last therapy session.

At the beginning of the program the teachers filled out an essay type report stating the main problems presented by the children. The parents filled out a similar report, although in some of the cases the children offered slight problems in the home situation. After the last meeting similar reports were filled out by teachers and parents who commented on observed progress made by the child during the period of time covered by the therapy sessions. None of the children had previous knowledge of the nature or purpose of the therapy program. Their first knowledge of the group came to them when the therapist (hereafter referred to as *C*) structured the situation at the beginning of the first meeting. He said:

> "We're here to have fun and a good time. This group is different from your classes. Here you may do anything that you would like to do. The only things which you may not do are to break any of the things in the room or to hit anybody."

Later, from time to time, it was necessary to establish other limitations in terms of requests made by the school administration. Some of the new limitations prescribed were the following: The teacher's desk and wardrobe were declared off-limits, cautions concerning use of the doll house were established, jumping off the piano was prohibited. An example of the technique used in presenting additional limitations to the group can be seen from an excerpt taken from the protocol of the third meeting:

"I have been told that these closets have things in them which belong to the children and the teacher who are usually in this classroom. Also,
these blankets on the shelf belong to the children in this class. So from now
on we won't be able to go into the closets or to use these blankets. Mr. X will
send up some other blankets and we can play on those. One other thing that
I want to tell you is that when we paint, we must use the oilcloth so that we
won't get any paint on the floor."

A verbatim report of conversations and activities in which the children engaged was made in a form as exact as possible. This record was kept
by the therapist in order to reduce the number of adults in the therapy situation.

ANALYSIS OF GROUP THERAPY

It is the fundamental thesis of many volumes on the handicapped child that
he is, first, a child who is subject to the same emotions as the so-called physically normal child. Baker[3] begins his book as follows: "The principal theme
of this book is that exceptional children are fundamentally similar to normal
children." It follows, therefore, that if a group play therapy program can in
general provide a situation which will help children to work out their problems and achieve a happier life and better adjustment, this contribution will
also be present where such therapy is applied to handicapped children. We
have found this to be the case in the present study. The group therapy situation seems to provide for handicapped children two opportunities: (1) A
situation in which the child can work out personal problems which are not
related to the handicap and which might have been present had the child
been of normal physique. (2) An opportunity to express and understand
problems which are basically the result of the handicap. In the present report
the therapy situations will be considered in the light of the above-mentioned
division.

The first two meetings of the group were largely spent by the children in exploring the limitations of the situation and trying to see how real
the apparent freedom was. The following illustrative excerpts are from the
first and second sessions:

George: (In the middle of the first session, George started shouting and
banging things around, enjoying himself, but apparently expecting to be
curbed any second.) Gee, I never knew I could make all this noise in a
room.

C.: You like to make noise, but you usually can't!
George: Yeah, I'm making a lot of noise and having a lot of fun.
    In the next or second meeting, Janet went to the piano and with a sudden swift move crashed down on it with her hand. She looked up at C. apprehensively.
C.: You're wondering if it's all right to do that!
Janet: Yes.
C.: It's all right. That's something which you may do.
    A little later Peter knocked down some flowers with a ball. He guiltily looked at C.
C.: You're wondering if it was all right to do that!
Peter: (Relieved) It's all right. (Continued playing)

It was interesting to watch the behavior of Daniel, a boy referred to the group because of his withdrawal behavior. He was at first completely withdrawn from the group and regarded the group from a distance. In a short time he began to feel the genuineness of the permissiveness, and, in a succession of violent moves, he smashed the piano, dashed a stick to the ground, and threw some blocks across the room.
    By the end of the session there was considerable feeling of regret expressed by the children that there was no more time.

C.: I guess our time is up so I'm afraid we'll have to stop now.
Peter: Aw! (Closed self in closet)
C.: You're sorry that we have to stop so soon!
Peter: Yes.
C.: I'm sorry, too, but our time is up. We'll be able to play again on Friday.

The other group member, Ernest, a mentally-retarded, post-encephalitic boy, was content to remain apart from the others, and to have contact only with C. He sat next to C. contentedly.

C.: You'd rather be with me than play with the others!
Ernest: Yes (pause). I could kiss you. (Kisses C.)
C.: You like me very much.
Ernest: Yes, I like you. I like you; do you like me?
C.: You like me and you're wondering if I like you.
Ernest: Yes, I don't like people who slap me. I like you.

The first part of the third meeting was marked by considerable instability which was possibly due to the unforeseen presence of another adult.

The children settled down toward the latter part of the session and got together in their first group activity, finger painting. All except Ernest shared the facilities and painted together harmoniously for the latter portion of the meeting. They enjoyed themselves very much so that to bring the meeting to an end was a rather difficult process.

> Peter: Is it almost time to go?
> C.: Yes.
> Peter: How much more time?
> C.: Three minutes.
> Janet: Aw, gee. (Messed paints violently with both hands and looked at them.) Gee . . . I wish they'd stay like this.
> C.: It's nice to have your hands all messy.
> Janet: Mmmm. (Laughed) I wish I didn't have to wash them.
> Peter: Aw, gee . . . It always has to end when we're having so much fun.
> C.: You're sorry that our time is up . . . etc.

The fifth meeting found Daniel and Peter finger-painting. Daniel tired of this after a while and went off to play with some building boxes. Peter smeared paint over him and Daniel became very frustrated. His behavior became more and more aggressive as he smashed the piano, knocked objects over and threw blocks around. When Daniel heard that time was almost up, he went on a rampage, turning over tables and chairs.

> Daniel: Time's nearly up. We've got other things to do. (Pounded piano, whirled chair around) Whee!
> C.: It's really fun to toss the chair around like that.
> Daniel: Yeah, it sure is.
> Peter: C'mon, Dan, let's put these blocks away.
> Daniel: Not me, I'm having too much fun with this chair.

Daniel continued his aggressive behavior. It seemed impossible to believe that the boy could be of a withdrawing nature in any situation. He was at a peak of aggressiveness and enjoying the whole thing thoroughly. Eventually the others joined in, though not so zestfully. Even Ernest got into the swing, and pushed desks and chairs all over the place.

> Daniel: Aren't we devils?
> C.: Sometimes it's fun to be a little devil.
> Daniel: Yah, and how.

Peter: We moved all the furniture—boy, is this fun!

C.: I know you're all having a good time, but our time is up now and we have to go. (Peter and Ernest calmed down but this announcement spurred Daniel on to even more frenzied activity. He went around the room throwing and scattering the few things that he had missed up to that point.)

Daniel: Are we little devils! Is this fun!

C.: Dan is having such fun that he doesn't want to leave, but our time is up and we have to go now.

Peter: Hey! We can't go with the place looking like this.

C.: I know you want to help straighten the place out but our time is up, and we have to go now. (Daniel still was tossing things about. Peter and Ernest left with C. Daniel caught up, breathless and excited, and still talking about what devils "*we*" are," notwithstanding the fact that *he* has done nearly ninety-five percent of the 'damage.' He kept repeating how much fun it was, expressed concern over who would clean up the room, but concluded that he had had such a fine time that he was going to do the same thing again at the next meeting.)

This session was a complete catharsis of Daniel's pent-up feelings—feelings which were unleashed with a volcanic fury in a setting which permitted him to do so.

As the following meeting, the sixth, got underway Daniel decided to again engage in the aggressive behavior of the fifth meeting.

Daniel: Let's move all the furniture again. (Afterthought to C.) It's all right, isn't it?

C.: You want to make sure that it's all right to move the furniture again? It's all right. (Daniel started in, and George, who was absent for the last meeting, looked up in amazement.)

George: No . . . Don't do that.

Peter: Oh, you weren't here last time. It's all right.

(Daniel started violently at first. C. continued recognizing the feeling behind his action and accepting him completely. In about ten or fifteen minutes Daniel stopped, having made relatively little mess in the process. Again a period of equilibrium was present with Daniel, Peter and George building together. Daniel made no further attempt to upset the room.)

The next meeting, the seventh, found Janet back in the group after having missed three sessions. She saw a doll house (which had been added during the fourth session) for the first time, admired and played with it. The children acted out a spontaneous fantasy during this session (which will be discussed below). They expressed their feelings of enjoyment with this game, and left evidencing satisfaction.

At the next meeting, the eighth, an incident took place in which Daniel and Peter both wanted a piece of chalk. Daniel, originally shy and withdrawing, now used physical force in an attempt to pry away the desired object.

Toward the middle of the meeting, Peter removed his shoes and enjoyed it very much. Janet followed suit and started a fantasy involving a family situation with Daniel as her mate. Peter joined the play.

> Peter: Why don't you take your shoes off, too, Dan?
> Daniel: Leave 'em on. (Peter, with Janet's help, took off Daniel's shoes. They also tried to take his socks off.) Leave those socks alone, you. I've got a cold in my feet already and my mother said for me to be careful.

Here is to be seen the introduction of a family situation which represented a problem for Daniel.

The ninth meeting found Peter and George again partially undressing. In this regard they seemed to enjoy the opportunity to utilize the permissiveness which the therapy situation offered. Again, they acted out a fantasy using Ernest, who was not accepted as an equal by the other members, as the scapegoat. Later they settled down and simulated a camping and sleeping outdoors experience.

Before the eleventh meeting got underway, C. was informed that due to the severity of his heart condition George would no longer be able to participate in the group. C. called for the other group members in their rooms. When Peter saw him, he called C. over.

> Peter: (Pointed to a package) This is a present I brought for Johnny. (Smiled shyly) I'm going to bring you a Christmas present. Are you married?
> C.: Yes.
> Peter: O.K., then I'll bring your wife a present, too.
>   (Then the group started for the playroom. Peter, who usually ran ahead, stayed behind and held C's hand.)
> Ernest: Aren't you going to run ahead today?
> Peter: Oh, no. I'm going to hold his hand today. (Rested his cheek on C's hand and shyly kissed it.)

Upon arriving at the other class, Daniel's teacher was uncertain whether or not Daniel should join the group because of a hand injury sustained the week previously, and she asked C. to resolve the issue. He, in turn, passed the decision on to Daniel.

>C.: Would you like to come up and play with us today, Dan?
>Daniel: (Came running over and smiled) Y-e-s-s.

C. broached the possibility of a party and all the children accepted eagerly. They inquired about George and were told he wouldn't be with the group any longer. Janet seemed very enamoured of Daniel and didn't hesitate to say so. In the middle of a game she attempted to go into the wardrobe which was out of bounds. C. cited the limitation to her, but in stressing the limitation did not fully accept her. She was quite frustrated, and entered into markedly aggressive activity by upsetting everything in her path. Daniel helped Janet with his one free hand, while Peter and Ernest unsuccessfully tried to stop them. After the room had been upset Janet and Daniel played a game acting as husband and wife. It was interesting to note in this connection that Janet, who several times started games of this type, is without a father.

>Janet: I kissed Dan on the head.
>C.: It was nice kissing Dan.
>Peter: (Observing nonchalantly) That's one thing we can do, isn't it?
>C.: Yes.
>Janet: (Sighs) Ooh . . . my husband!
>(Janet and Daniel went off to build their own house and have a little privacy. Peter and Ernest picked up a small portion of the felled items, but before the meeting was over Janet threw them over again. This session was quite a catharsis, although probably incomplete, for her. It undoubtedly was magnified by C's failure to simultaneously enforce the limitation and to accept her earlier in the meeting.)

The final meeting is presented as fully as C. was able to record, both to provide some idea of the technique of the on-the-spot evaluation and to give the reader some idea of the status of the group at its conclusion.

C. called for Janet and Daniel first and both were present. Daniel had his arm in a sling once again. Janet threw her arms around C. and exclaimed that she thought that he would never get there. She said to Daniel, "Let's mess the place up like we did last time, Dan," but Daniel didn't answer. C. said, "You had so much fun last time that you would like to do it again." We then called for Peter and Ernest both of whom were present and all five started out for the playroom. Nobody ran ahead, which was quite unlike any of our previous meetings. All walked up slowly and leisurely discussing Christmas parties, things being made for them and so forth. When we got to the playroom, the children all crowded around the Christmas tree which was decorated. Various remarks were made as to how nice it was and about the decorations, and they then headed for the tree itself which had been indicated by Mrs. X as out of bounds.

C.: I know you would like to play with the ornaments, but this tree belongs to the children in the kindergarten, and so we may not touch it.

Janet: (Turns away) Let's throw everything around. That's lots of fun. Let's get the room all messed up. C'mon! (She ran over to the block cabinet and was about to tip it over with its entire contents.)

Daniel: No, don't do that, Janet. (Janet tipped the cabinet anyway and blocks scattered all over the floor. She picked up a carton and was about to throw it down, too.)

Peter: Stop it, Janet. Lookit what you did already. Stop throwing everything around.

Janet: (Undaunted) I won't. I'm going to upset everything. (She scattered and kicked things all over the room.)

Peter: (To Janet) Will you stop already? (Janet wouldn't) (To C.) Make her stop doing that. She's getting the room all wrecked.

C.: I know that you'd very much like me to make Janet stop, but messing the room is one thing that we can do. (By this time only about five minutes had passed but the room was a shamble entirely through the work of Janet.)

Janet: Whee! (Scattered more blocks) (Laughed and smiled)

C.: It's nice to be able to mess the room. (By this time the contagion of Janet's escapade had caught hold. Peter and Daniel joined. They turned over all the tables and threw boxes and chairs all over the room.)

Daniel: Boy, aren't we little devils?

C.: Sometimes it's fun to be a little devil.

Daniel: Yeah, it sure is. (He stopped. Peter stopped, too, and surveyed the damage in horror.)

Peter: Aw, c'mon, let stop this. If you stop it I'll let you all have some of my candy. (All stopped and Peter pulled out a little bag of candy which he distributed to all.) (To C.) You want a piece, too?

C.: Would you want me to have one, or would you rather keep it?

Peter: I want to give you some. (Gave C. some which C. ate.)

Peter: (Looks down at some of the blocks and spots an oblong block.) Hey, you know what? This here block looks just like a quarter of a pound of butter that we have at home.

C.: (Laughs) It sure does. (He glanced around the room and noted that Janet had continued her wrecking party, and that off in a corner Daniel was struggling with one arm to pick up one of the upturned tables.)

Daniel: Will you help me pick this up?

C.: You'd like me to give you a hand, because you can't manage with one hand. (He did. Daniel started picking up the chairs and setting them around the table.) You want to help straighten out the place.

Daniel: Uh huh! (He went about picking up everything that Janet had turned over working slowly because his arm was in a sling, but at the same time conscientiously. Pete, too, picked up a few things here and there. He came over to C. and tapped him.)

Peter: How about a horseback ride?

Janet: (Who wasn't messing the room anymore, but toying with the blocks in the center of the floor.) I want one, too.

Peter: I was here first, don't give her a ride.

Janet: Give me a ride.

C.: Peter and Janet want a piggy-back ride and both can have it, only we'll have to take turns. (They did. After finishing the ride, Janet ambled over to the doll house. Ernest was sitting on the one standing table taking in everything, while Daniel continued to use his one free arm in an attempt to straighten the room. Peter surveyed the room and shook his head.)

Peter: (Went over to Janet.) Boy, oh, boy! Look what you did — cabinets all over, blocks all over the place, chairs you threw down! The room is a mess. What do you think you're doing?

Janet: (Who had opened the wardrobe door.) So what if I did? I can do it if I want to here.

Peter: Yeah, but you're not 'a-posed' (supposed) to. Besides, one thing you can't do here is to go in the wardrobe.

(Janet went off to the center of the floor and continued to build some things with some of the blocks which she had scattered. Daniel and Peter, particularly Daniel, worked rather feverishly in putting the room in order again.)

Peter: Could I have another ride? (C. took Peter for a ride again, and it turned out to be a rather lengthy one with C. none the better for the wear.)

Ernest: (Recognized C's feeling.) S-a-ay . . . you're hot.

C.: (Put Peter down.) I'm pretty hot, all right. (Peter went to toilet and C. sat down next to Ernest. Both watched Daniel continuing to put things away.)

Ernest: (Pointing to Daniel's arm.) He has to use one arm.

C.: Daniel can only use one arm to put things away.

Ernest: Yes. Why are you writing in that book?

C.: You want to know why I'm writing. I'm writing about what we do so that I can read about it when I go home.

Ernest: Do you have a home?

C.: Yes.

Daniel: Say, how much time do we have left?

C.: Twenty-five minutes.

Daniel: Boy! We'll have to hurry if we want to get this placed straightened out in time.

Peter: No we don't. Twenty-five minutes is lots of time. (Daniel worked even faster.)

Ernest: (Screamed. Then Peter, Janet, Daniel all took turns screaming at the very top of their lungs, each trying to outdo the other.)

C.: It's nice to be able to scream as loud as you want to. (Various remarks of agreement.) (C. looked around and noted that Peter is taking a swat at Janet.)

Janet: Go away from me, Peter! Stop hitting me! Stop! (Peter didn't stop. He slapped her angrily.)

C.: I know you're angry, Peter, but one thing which we can't do is hit.

    (By this time Janet was crying, more in frustration than in pain.)

Janet: He hit me for no good reason. (Sobbed.)

C.: It just doesn't seem fair at all that Peter hit you.

Janet: No. (Slackened her crying but Peter came over and hit again. This time Janet really burst into tears.) Whaaaa. Stop it, Peter. I don't want to stay here any more. I'm going to go downstairs. I'm going back to the class. Why does Peter keep hitting me?

C.: Peter has hit you so much that you don't want to stay here anymore.

Janet: (Continued sobbing.) Yeah. I'm going. I'll go to the 'basement.'

    (She left the room sobbing. Peter saw that Janet was really leaving and was sorry.)

Peter: Don't go, Janet. (Janet left.) Aw, gee, I didn't mean nothing.

Daniel: (To Peter) Oh-oh. Now it's curtains for you, Peter.

Peter: What do you mean, "it's curtains for me"?

Daniel: I mean you made Janet go and you're all finished now. You're all washed up.

Peter: (Getting back at Daniel.) Dan loves J-a-n-e-t.

Daniel: No I don't. She loves me.

    (In a few moments, Janet came back feeling a lot better and smiling. Peter went past Ernest and jostled him.)

Ernest: Leave me alone, you stinker.

C.: Peter is angry at Ernest, too, but we may not hit here.

Peter: Well, he hit me with a board last time, and now I've got a black and blue mark all over my leg. (Showed C.)

Ernest: (Who had forgotten the episode.) No I didn't.

C.: I can see that you would be angry, Peter, but one of the things we may not do here is to hit.

Peter: Yeah. I'm sorry I hit you, Janet and Ernest. I won't do it anymore.

(Daniel had been putting the things away all this time. Ernest helped putting some blocks away. Peter gave a hand and between the three they had the entire mess, which Janet had made, cleared away. Janet looked at the goldfish. She didn't help put things away but she didn't upset anything. Peter worked like a little demon. Suddenly he looked at C. with a very puzzled expression.)

Peter: Gee! I want to be sure that we get everything put away, but I'm getting very tired. (Scratched his head and looked up at C.) Would you mind very much putting the rest of these things away after we go?

C.: I'll bet you're really tired of doing that. Sure, I'd be glad to put them away later.

Peter: Could I have a ride again, horsey?

Janet: I want a ride, too.

C.: Well, I'd be glad to give you both rides, but you'll have to take turns.

Both: Me first!

C.: Well, I can't take you both at the same time so one will have to wait. (Went to take Peter.) Since you asked first, I'll take you first, Pete. How's that, Janet?

Janet: All right, but hurry.

Peter: You could go first if you really want to, Janet. (Janet did, and C. took them both for a ride.)

Ernest: You know what? My father painted my room.

C.: Your father painted your room.

Ernest: Yes. Could I have a piece of paper?

C.: Sure. (Gave Ernest a piece from his pad.)

Ernest: I could write my name. (Did)

C.: You're quite a fellow to be able to write your name.

Peter: Our time is almost up, isn't it?

C.: Yes. (Peter starts putting the shade up and down. Daniel, who has done a workmanlike job of straightening out the room, went over to the Christmas tree and redecorated the tree in a spot where a few of the trimmings had fallen off.)

C.: It's really fun to fix the trimmings.

Daniel: Mmmmmmmmm. Yes.

Janet: (Found a couple of cans which she put on her feet.) Look! I've got high heels!

C.: You've got yourself a pair of high heels to walk around in. Well—I guess our time is up now.

Peter: (Screamed) Oh no!

C.: You're sorry to see it end.

This was the last session and it contained several interesting developments or signs of growth. It was interesting to note that for the first time there was a block of group members who actively opposed upsetting the room. Three of the boys pleaded with Janet not to throw furnishings around, but she did so anyway. It is the opinion of C. that her aggression might well have been a carry-over from the hostility which she showed in the eleventh meeting. However, the other members of the group did not partake in the destruction. Daniel failed to stop Janet by plea, but Peter succeeded in doing so by using candy as a bribe. From that point on the trend of the group was toward restoration of the room with Daniel and Peter contributing materially to the job. Ernest helped a little more slowly. All of this activity was voluntary and without presssure of any kind. Towards the end of the session, Peter very humanly expressed his tiredness and asked C. if he would mind completing the job. While this attitude which was expressed by the children may be something which will meet situational reverses, it does represent a definite improvement in attitude and behavior from that shown in earlier meetings insofar as Daniel and Peter and Ernest are concerned. With respect to Janet, it is the writers' opinion that this was a very critical meeting for her. She was definitely frustrated and aggressive. She was alone in opposing the wishes of the others. The aggressive behavior typical of Daniel in earlier therapy sessions was replaced by an expressed desire to keep the room in order and to have the children conform in a socially acceptable way. His earlier withdrawal behavior had been substituted by wholesome group participation and overt expressions of responsibility.

The thirteenth and last meeting of the group was not therapeutic in the usual sense. It was a Christmas party for the children as they had planned it during the eleventh session. Several of the children expressed considerable sorrow that they could not have the group any more. Peter asked if "we couldn't possibly meet on Saturday," and Janet expressed the hope that the meetings would never end and said that she didn't want to leave the group. The children asked if they would see C. again. He explained that there would be no more regular meetings, but that he would come to school from time to time and would stop and see them if they so desired. The children urged him to do so, and the session ended with everyone in good spirit.

We have thus far summarized in skeletal form the progress of group therapy in an attempt to establish the point that the normal course and contribution of such a program in the case of physically normal children with emotional problems is to be found in this therapy group for physically handicapped children. The writers do not wish to stress the artificial dichotomy which has been created by their division between therapy for physically normal and handicapped children. In essence the group therapy situation has the same value for a physically handicapped and normal child with the exception that, other things being equal, the handicapped child may bring to the therapeutic setting a wider range of problems than the normal child due to the impact which the handicap exerts on the former child's ability to adjust. With this in mind the writers wish to discuss the second major contribution of the group therapy situation to the handicapped, i.e., the provision of a permissive atmosphere in which socioemotional problems related directly to the handicap may be resolved.

Reference has been made at several points to some of the spontaneous fantasies which took place during the therapy sessions. Two of these fantasies will be presented in detail now concretely to illustrate the point that the experimental nondirective play group provided an opportunity for physically handicapped children to work out emotional concomitants of their physical disability. The following is quoted from the protocol of the seventh meeting:

> George climbed on the piano and leaped off simulating a parachute jump. He jumped from a standing position atop the piano. Janet was impressed. She, too, climbed up and when she reached the top was a little scared by the height.
>
> Janet: Oooooh, boy! (To George) I'm coming down in my parachute, too. (She jumped down from a sitting position, but George was looking elsewhere.) I jumped in my parachute, too. (George climbed up and jumped and started to roll across the floor. Janet followed and they rolled together.)
>
> George: (Kept rolling.) I'm sinking into the ocean. You save me, Peter. (Desperately Peter pulled him by the arm.) Pull my other arm, Janet (Janet grabbed his other arm and they both pulled him across the floor.) I'm in the hospital now. Cover me with the blanket. (They did.)
>
> Janet: I must get the medicine.
>
> Peter: No, I must.
>
> George: I'm not in the hospital—I'm on a boat.
>
> Peter: Yeah, but you're sick. It's a hospital boat.
>
> Janet: The patient is moving. He's getting up.
>
> George: I'm better. I'm going to the airport. (He climbed up on the piano and made believe he was in a plane.) I'm shot. I've got to bail out. (He jumped.) (Peter was standing off to the side.)
>
> Peter: George is on the ground.
>
> George: (Spied Peter.) Let's make believe you're a German. (He jumped on Peter and wrestled him to the ground.) I've got you covered. (He used a stick for a gun; Janet helped.) Don't try any tricks, you dirty schwein! I've got you covered with my trusty luger, and I'll shoot you dead.
>
> Peter: I must be one of your friends, now. (All three climbed on the piano again as if in a plane.)
>
> George: Shoot the house down. That must be a German house.

Peter: I'll go down and get some bombs and guns. (He climbed down and
got some cylinders to use for hand grenades. All three made believe they
were shooting at an imaginary plane in the air and threw sticks (bombs)
on houses.)
George: I'm shot! (Clutched heart.) Jump for your life!
Janet: (Jumped after George, leaving Peter alone on the piano.) Peter,
you're shot, too.
Peter: (Not keen on the prospect of jumping.) No. I'll get down and look at
the houses that we bombed. (He climbed down.)
George: (Still on the ground.) You find out that I am half-dead.
Janet: Half-dead? He's half-dead. Cover him with the blanket. I'll get some
ice cubes.
Peter: I'll get some medicine and I'll see if there are any Germans around.
        (Janet brought over a bottle of enamel chips, ice cubes, but George
kicked them over.)
Peter: Now why did ya hafta go and do that?
George: Those aren't O.K. for me.
Peter: There's a German hiding over there. I see him but he doesn't see me.
George: I must think that you are a German by mistake. (Jumped on Peter
and threw him down.)
Peter: No. I'm your friend.
George: O.K. (Let him go.) There goes a Jap. He got me. I'm shot. Get
him, Peter. (Peter shot him with his tommy gun. Peter half carried
George across the floor. George staggered because of his 'wound.' They
decided to make believe that Janet was a prisoner. They questioned her
and made her tell when the commander of the enemies was coming back.
They laid in ambush under the table until he did return. Then they opened
up with a furious barrage and shot at this nebulous enemy.)
George: They got me. (Fell.)
Peter: No. You always get shot.
George: You must get shot with me this time.

It is interesting to note that George played the rôle of one who was
shot, who must be rescued, and who even used the term 'half-dead' in connection with his condition in the fantasy. In the real life situation, George
was a boy who, because of the seriousness of his cardiac condition, had
spent the best part of the last four years in hospitals. It is small wonder that
he now conceived of himself as incapacitated, and 'half-dead' even in his
play activity. So consistently did he adopt the rôle of the wounded one, or
the rôle of the person who must be cared for by the others, that even Peter
noticed it. On one occasion Peter exclaimed, "No—you always get shot,"
and challenged George's right to that rôle. The rôle which George habitually
assumed is an interesting illustration of his self-concept which evolved due
to his experience of continued hospitalization.

An equally effective and possibly more dramatic illustration of the importance of group therapy to the expressions of emotional problems resulting from physical disability appears in the protocol of the ninth session. In a spontaneous fantasy acted out by Peter during the ninth meeting and using C. as an aid, the following activity took place:

> Peter: (To George and Janet) Do you want to play cowboy and crook? (No response.) (To C.) Would you be the robber?
> C.: You'd like me to play the robber. I'll be anything you'd like for me to be.
> Peter: Okay. You must sit down here. (C. sat down on the piano chair and Peter tied him up very flimsily.) Now I must cut your finger off. (Peter took a pair of scissors and went through the motion of cutting off a finger.)
> C.: You're going to cut off a finger. (Peter cut it off.)
> Peter: (Very realistically.) Ooooooh — it's bleeding!
> C.: You cut off my finger and now it's bleeding.
> Peter: I'll cut off all your fingers now. (Went through the motions.) They are all bleeding. You're losing all your blood. Maybe you'll bleed to death.
> C.: You think I may bleed to death.
> Peter: We'll have to save the blood. (Runs and gets two jars and puts C's right hand in one jar and the left hand into the other.) All your blood is dripping into the jars. (He filled up the two jars which he had.) It hasn't stopped, you're still bleeding to death. I must get some more jars. (He got some more jars and filled them up with the blood from C's fingers.)
> Peter: Now look at all the blood we have. (To the others) Look, we've got all these jars full of blood. We've got all this blood in case anyone gets hurt and needs blood. (Suddenly he realized C. was bleeding to death.) We must get some medicine to stop the bleeding. (He poured some grains on C's hand.) Leave them there, it hasn't stopped bleeding yet. (After several minutes he shook the grains off into a box.) It's better now. It looks like it's going to stop. I'll untie you now. (Untied C.) Could I go for a ride? (C. took him for a ride.)

Peter, a child who was handicapped by hemophilia, here enacted a fantasy graphically illustrating the impact of the problem for him. Insofar as C. was able to observe, Peter was completely unaware at a conscious level of any relation between his fantasy and his handicap. It developed quite spontaneously, yet there seemed to be little doubt of the presence of such a relation. This was particularly true since Peter went out of his way to "cut off the bandit's fingers," an extremely purposeful and unique move. His actions during the entire scene were dramatic, painstaking and realistic. He collected blood, in the jars as if the cut hands really were dripping blood. He created a

240 SELECTED WRITINGS

threat of death for the bleeding victim, indicating the possible seriousness of the problem in terms of his own meanings, and suggesting a possible diagnostic contribution of the group.[11] However, at the end of the fantasy the victim was saved by means of medication. Peter, who evidenced sincere fright during the fantasy, appeared relieved and emotionally unburdened when it was over. Quite possibly it was coincidental, but it nevertheless was interesting to note the following interchange between Peter and C. as the session closed several minutes later.

> Peter: Gee, we really had a nice game today.
> C.: It really was fun today.
> Peter: There just isn't anybody in the whole school as lucky as us kids.
> C.: Today sure was lots of fun.
> Peter: More than any other time.

It would seem from the examples noted above that the non-directive play-group offers an ideal setting for the self-solution of a particular type of emotional problem; namely, those stemming from the specific disability of the physically handicapped child. More generally, it helps the handicapped child to come to a more satisfactory adjustment as a child, which is the chief contribution which the group play technique offers to physically normal children.

BIBLIOGRAPHY

1. Allen, F. H. and Pearson, G. H. J., "The Emotional Problems of the Physically Handicapped Child," *British Journal of Medical Psychology* 8:212, 1928.
2. Axline, V. M., *Play Therapy.* Boston: Houghton Mifflin Co., 1947.
3. Baker, H., *Introduction to Exceptional Children,* New York: Macmillan, 1945.
4. Barker, R., *et al., Adjustment to Physical Handicap and Illness,* Social Science Research Council, Bulletin 55, 1946.
5. Bender, L., "Psychoses Associated with Somatic Disease that Distort the Body Structure, *Archives of Neurology and Psychiatry* 32:1000, 1934.
6. Cowen, E. L., and Cruickshank, W. M., "Group Therapy with Physically Handicapped Children. II: Evaluation," *Journal of Educational Psychology.* 39 (1948):281-97.
7. Cruickshank, W. M., and Dolphin, J. E., "A Study of Emotional Needs of Crippled Children" 45 (1949):295-305.

8. Fleming, L., and Snyder, W. U., "Social and Personal Changes following Non-Directive Group Play Therapy," *American Journal of Orthopsychiatry* 17: 101, 1947.

9. Kanner, L., and Lachman, S. E., "The Contribution of Physical Illness to the Development of Behavior Disorders in Children," *Mental Hygiene* 17:615, 1933.

10. Levy, D. M., "Body Interest in Children and Hypochondriasis," *American Journal of Psychiatry,* 12:295, 1932.

11. Redl, F., "Diagnostic Group Work," *American Journal of Orthopsychiatry* 14: 1944.

12. Rogers, C., *Counselling and Psychotherapy.* Boston: Houghton Mifflin Co., 1942.

13. Rubenstein, Benjamin, "Therapeutic Use of Groups in an Orthopedic Hospital School," *American Journal of Orthopsychiatry* 15:662, 1945.

14. Schilder, P. F., *The Image and Appearance of the Human Body.* London: Kegan Paul, 1935.

15. Seidenfeld, M. A., "Behavior of Post-polio School Children on the California Test of Personality, Abstract, *American Psychologist* 2:274, 1947.

22

GROUP THERAPY WITH
PHYSICALLY HANDICAPPED CHILDREN

II. Evaluation

(*with Emory L. Cowen*)

*A*XLINE[1] AND CRUICKSHANK AND COWEN[2] have reported the results of group therapy with physically handicapped children who presented emotional disturbances. The latter writers studied an experimental group therapy situation and reported the resulting emotional growth and development of five children—one, a post-encephalitic; one, a post-poliomyelitis case; one, a hemophilia case, and two cardiacs—who were between the chronological ages of seven and nine. The exploratory nature of the experimental situation prompts the writers to evaluate the course of therapy and certain problems pertaining to the therapy in greater detail than might otherwise have been necessitated.

The analysis which follows will include an attempt (1) to trace the effect of the group situation on each of the children and to comment on general problems which result from the participation of the handicapped child in the group, and (2) to evaluate general problems of group therapy and specific problems which have grown out of the investigation. Modifications in technique which would appear to be important in therapy with the handicapped child will also be noted.

We should like first briefly to evaluate the observable results of the therapy experience for each of the group members. Table 1 presents in digest form the comments which parents and teachers made in their reports on therapy.

Ernest, the post-encephalitic, mentally defective child, had very little to do with the other children in the group situation. Sometimes he preferred to remain with C., but most often he constituted a group of one, was

Reprinted from *The Journal of Educational Psychology* 39 (May 1948): 281-97, by permission.

content to play by himself, and paid attention to the others only when they disturbed him. Occasionally he was used as a target for some of the other members of the group in their games, and on infrequent occasions he joined the others when they were involved in a generally aggressive activity. Ernest's relations with C. tended to be somewhat sporadic and dissociated. However, contrary to his reported inability to settle down in class, he seemed

TABLE 1

PARENT AND TEACHER REPORTS OF THERAPY

Parent Report	Teacher Report
Ernest	
Behavior: No observed changes. Attitude to group: Looked forward to meetings. Comment: Group is a splendid idea and should be continued.	Behavior: Some change in that he tends to help others, and does not disrupt the class in any way. Attitude: No change in work: still beyond him, gets noisy for nothing at all. Attitude to group: Always very eager to go to group. Came back excited.
Daniel	
Behavior: Great improvement in evenness of his disposition; his thoughts seem to reflect this improvement. Attitude: Plays games better; doesn't mind being loser any more; no longer accuses others of cheating. Attitude to group: Possible fear of notetaking and enjoying of freedom of therapy situation. Comment: Group is very much worth while. Possibility of making notebook less obvious.	Unsolicited Report: Ninth session—great improvement in general attitude. Attitude: Tremendous changes in terms of increased group activity, participation in and enjoyment of class activities; emergence from his shell. Attitude to group: Enjoyed it after first few weeks; liked doing things with others; never thought until this experience that it was fun to play with group. Evaluation: Group has helped him find self. He listens and plays with others which he has never done before. Emerged from his sheltered standing. Situation has been remedied.
Janet	
Behavior: Appearance of several undesirable behavior symptoms. Attitude: Still unsatisfactory terms of not minding. Attitude to group: Enjoyed every minute of it.	Behavior: No apparent change in behavior. Attitude: No apparent improvement in classroom attitude or attitude toward work. Attitude to group: Loved play therapy "because she could do anything she wanted to."

TABLE 1 *continued*

Parent Report	Teacher Report
George	
Unsolicited phone call: (After second session. (George looks forward to meetings all week. His general behavior is improved. Gets along better with friends.	Behavior: A new willingness to share things with others.
Unsolicited call: (Tenth session.) Stating George must leave group. Mother is extremely sorry. George enjoyed group and looked forward to it immensely. His attitude to play therapy made him want to go to school. Enjoyed not being told what to do or scolded for doing things wrong.	Attitude: Improvement in class work. Disappearance of former unwillingness and negativism to his work. For first time he is completing his work and getting satisfactory marks. Fewer outbursts in class.
Behavior: Improved greatly; also a greater willingness to do his work.	Attitude to group: Thoroughly enjoyed group experience and spoke of it enthusiastically.
Attitude: Felt bad on leaving group, and was hard to reason with.	
Attitude to group: Loved group and expressed longing for it all week.	
Comment: Group experience has increased his self-confidence; as a result of George's improvement, I have felt better personally.	
Peter	
Behavior: His behavior has improved a great deal, though it may be due to changes at home.	Behavior: Disappearance of attitude of "always wanting to be the leader." No longer tries to be the one to start all the games.
Attitude: Improved considerably. He is less rebellious.	Attitude: His marks which always have been good are even better since he began group work.
Attitude to group: Not mentioned.	Attitude to group: Always very eager to go to the group.

always to be at ease in the therapy situation, although it would be difficult to say whether this was the result of the atmosphere of the therapy room or of his own self-segregation.

It is rather difficult to evaluate the therapy experience for this child. While there are some slight improvements reported in Ernest's behavior in terms of somewhat increased helpfulness in class and being more at ease, the predominant tone of these reports indicates little or no behavioral change. It should be borne in mind, however, that Ernest is being compared to his chronological age peers and judged on their standards. Were he to be compared with children similar in mental age to himself, he might appear better adjusted. Whatever the reason which is basic to Ernest's failure to relate himself to others in the group, it does not necessarily mean that the group therapy approach is inapplicable to the mentally retarded child. Rather it emphasizes the importance of experimentation in group therapy with a homogeneous group of children of retarded mental development who have emotional problems. The findings of a preliminary study by Cruickshank and Medve[3] note that physically handicapped children tend to group themselves in self-structured social groups on the basis of intellectual similarities. This phenomenon may have significance in considering the effectiveness of group therapy with retarded children.

With regard to *Daniel,* the post-polio child, reports indicate that the group experience seems to have been of great value. Both parent and teacher reports agree on the tremendous changes which were observed in Daniel. In the school situation Daniel has "come out of his shell." He now joins the others in their activity and enjoys it very much. This is termed in the school report as "having found himself," being willing now to listen, coöperate, and partake in the class program. The parent report indicates changes in Daniel's behavior along similar lines. This is called "a greater evenness of disposition and seeming so much happier." His attitude in play also changed and he no longer resented being the loser in games or accused others of cheating.

Here is a youngster who was suddenly stricken with polio. After the initial attack he was subjected to maternal oversolicitude during the convalescing stage. As is the case with many polio victims, Daniel tended to withdraw more and more from group contacts. In the permissive atmosphere of the play group he was at first still very much withdrawn and cautious. He was content to observe from a distance. He was in no way pushed by the therapist. Gradually he came to realize the genuineness of the situation. He moved slowly from the extreme periphery to the very heart of the group situation. His withdrawing behavior gave way first to slight participation, then to moderate expression of feeling, and finally to a violent catharsis of feeling. He was then able to deal with problems posed by his past over-protected experience both in reference to the home situation and the school situation. He felt more secure in his relations with others as a result of this non- (or at least minimally-) threatening group situation. The vicious circle of his withdrawing behavior was broken. He proceeded to an improved adjustment and to a less threatened existence in all situations.

Janet. On the basis of the therapy protocols and the reports, there is no indication of any improvement in Janet's behavior as a result of the therapy program. While a later follow-up might possibly indicate some change in the direction of improvement, other things being the same, we must consider that the therapy exerience was a failure insofar as Janet is concerned. There are several hypotheses which might be considered as explanations of the inadequacy of the group situation for her. She was the only girl in the group among four boys which may have made the situation threatening for her inherently. Secondly, Fleming and Snyder,[4] in summarizing their study in non-directive group therapy, noted that around the age of ten (Janet was nine years old) there seemed to be an adjustment problem for children to opposite sexed adults. It is conceivable that this factor was operating to inhibit therapeutic progress. The therapist, however, is inclined to accept these hypotheses as partial explanations of the failure of therapy for Janet at the very most and as things which the non-directive situation, if it is adequate, should be able to overcome. In trying to explain why therapy was not adequate in this case it should be noted that Janet was absent for three consecutive therapy sessions: the fourth, fifth, and sixth. This was at a relatively early period in the program. When Janet returned to therapy after her three-week absence she had to 'start again' from the beginning, so to speak. Thus it was not until the tenth and eleventh meetings (the fourth and fifth after her return) that she began to express some of her feelings in her play, a point which other group members had reached by the fifth and sixth meeting. The twelfth and last therapy meeting was a particularly crucial one for her as she completed her wave of aggression and was beginning to settle down once again. C. indicated in his comment after the eleventh meeting that Janet seemed to be passing through a stage which Daniel had gone through six meetings earlier. In evaluating the twelfth meeting, C. noted that Janet's aggression seemed to have been spent and that therapy was ending at a particularly bad time for her. It was C's feeling that despite the possible adverse factors mentioned Janet might well have shown some improvements had therapy lasted several more meetings. This, however, must remain a moot point.

George was with the therapy group for only nine meetings and was absent for two of these. Yet in the short space of time he was a member of the group, there is agreement from all available sources that therapy was a profitable experience for him. George is a youngster who had been pushed around pretty much all his life. He had been going from hospital to hospital with people constantly directing him in terms of institution routines. In the face of such a program he had become negativistic in school, was failing in his work, and was obtaining satisfaction by beating up the other children in his class. In the therapy situation George started by displaying the same type of aggressive behavior which had typified his classroom manner. He was surprised not to be curbed. It was hard for him to accept his freedom at first, but he eventually did and found it very gratifying.

We are particularly fortunate, as noted in Table 1, in having a detailed record of George's feelings as a result of a series of voluntary phone calls from his mother. He told his mother that he enjoyed the group very much, that he was happy to be able to do what he wanted to without being yelled at for doing things wrong, and to have found someone who was nice to him. His fondness for the therapy situation, said his mother, changed his negativistic attitude towards school and his teacher. As a result, George's school work improved considerably. George also worked out several problems in connection with his physical condition. It was interesting to note that at no time during therapy was there any indication of the chorea which George reputedly had.

In his mother's report, it was indicated that, because George found understanding and freedom of expression in the group situation, he became much more self-confident. His behavior at home and his relation with his playmates showed improvement as a result. It is of interest, also, to note that George's mother reported that she felt she had been helped personally as a result of her son's improvement.

It is evident that there was considerable progress for George when he left the group situation after nine sessions following an examination by the cardiologist. He left the group abruptly. This fact probably prevented even greater progress in the direction of a better adjustment, but nevertheless it seems safe to assume that the group experience was in many ways a very valuable one for him.

Peter was a markedly aggressive youngster who came from a 'broken home.' His aggression was a consequence of being shifted around a great deal and a desire to achieve status and gain attention resulted. A very bright youngster, Peter had sought always to be the leader in the class situation. At home he had been argumentative and rebellious.

In the early stages of therapy he was extremely aggressive and constantly tested the limitations. In the group situation his aggression was not limited. Not being squelched or threatened, he gradually came to modify his aggression considerably and behave in a more socially approved manner.

The final parent report regarding Peter indicated many improvements in behavior although some, it was noted, might be due to changes which had taken place in the home situation. His rebelliousness disappeared at home and his desire to be the leader in the school setting became less evident. An honor student already, Peter's grades went still higher during the therapy program. We have already cited an indication of how Peter dealt with the problem resulting from his handicap in the group situation.[2] Such behavior was typical of him throughout therapy.

As a general commentary, it should not be forgotten that the entire evaluation of therapeutic progress has been made from the point of view of observed improvements in social adjustment in two situations—home and school. On that basis it would seem that following the group-play experience, three of these children showed considerable improvement in behavior in home and in school, one showed some slight evidences of gain, while the fifth gave no indication whatsoever of any improvement.

It should be borne in mind that such a review of results takes into account only one dimension—social adjustment. It is difficult to say how many of these youngsters felt personally unhappy when they entered this program, and what changes, if any, in their feelings resulted from their experience. With regard to this latter question, one can only piece together occasional remarks by the children. All expressed a liking for the group. All seemed genuinely sorry to see it end. All five follow-up reports by the teachers indicated an expressed liking for the program by the children, while four of the five parent reports (Peter's excluded) reported the same feeling expressed in the home situation. It would seem reasonable to conclude, apart from the question of whether or not the situation made happier children, that at least the children were happy in the situation.

This study which was described elsewhere has tended to support the thesis that the non-directive group therapeutic approach is applicable to the orthopedically handicapped child. However, there are several departures in technique which should be briefly considered.

THE QUESTION OF LIMITATIONS

Axline states: "The therapist establishes only those limitations which are necessary to anchor therapy in the world of reality and to make the child aware of his responsibility in the relationship." In the case of group therapy with the handicapped such is also the case, but there must be additional limitations in terms of the specific handicap of the particular child (his reality). Whereas ball-playing and strenuous physical activity may have a prominent place in the therapy group of physically normal children, it would not be desirable for the severe cardiac, for example, to partake in any such activity. Thus, the nondirective group must operate within a matrix of limitations which protect the child from physical injury resulting from his handicap. This raises an important point insofar as structuring is concerned, i.e., whatever limitations are set must be set for all members of the group alike in the interests of consistency. It would be an extremely unhealthy situation, if not out and out threatening, to have a group made up of three children who could play ball and two who could not. A natural corollary of this point of view and a hypothesis for further experimental investigation would be that a more homogeneous group of children in terms of physical handicap (or more specifically in terms of physical limitations as to what they could do in the therapy situation) would be more conducive to therapeutic progress.

Axline, in discussing the problem of the presentation of limitations to the group, advocates a policy of holding off as long as possible in the establishment of additional limitations. Once again, while this seems sound for the physically normal child, the therapist working with the handicapped child may not always have as much leeway. For example, if there should happen to be a hemophilia patient in the group, the therapist could not afford to take the chance of having the child hit even once by another child because of very drastic possible consequences. In some emergency situations the therapist might well be forced to resort to physical means to forestall possible serious injury to such a child. The general point connected with this example is that the therapist, while dealing with some handicapped children may not be able to allow any delay whatsoever in citing and enforcing the limitations, and may even be forced to run the risk of anticipating the child in citing such limitations when the child puts himself or another child in jeopardy as a result of his actions.

Certain groups of physically handicapped children are so much more prone to serious injury than is the physically normal child that a real problem is presented to the therapist who works with them. In this relatively more rigid enforcement of limitations, it is doubly important that the therapist be keen in reflecting the feelings of the child and insuring that he carries away the feeling that he is fully accepted.

ABSENCE

Because his mobility is in many cases impaired by his disability, the physically handicapped child, particularly the orthopedic, is apt to have poorer attendance at a day school than would the physically normal child. This raises several points of interest for the therapist. If the average physically handicapped child is subject to more absence than the normal child, his therapy experience insofar as attendence is concerned is shorter than would be the same amount of calendar time for the normal child. Other things being equal, it would seem that the therapy experience for the handicapped would have to be planned to be slightly longer than for the normal child to compensate for more frequent absence. This does not consider the possible retarding influence of an absence insofar as the child's therapeutic progress is concerned or the fact that because of the frequent absences the group composition is different at almost every session. These factors too might tend to lengthen the time of therapy, although such a statement is largely speculative.

The additional problem of multiple consecutive absence warrants consideration. In the group here considered one child was absent for three consecutive meetings in the early stages of therapy, and, as previously noted, she practically had to start over again when she returned to the group. While variations will occur depending on the particular child, the situation, and the stage of therapy, it may be found that to return to the group is perhaps of little value to the child who misses three or four consecutive meetings.

As a general measure to deal with the question of frequent absence, it seems safe to recommend a slightly larger group to allow for absence than is customary with normal children. It is recognized that questions of absence may be pertinent to some therapy groups with the physically normal child, but, since the handicapped child is far more 'absent-prone,' the problem is in sharper focus in this context.

SUGGESTIONS FOR FURTHER RESEARCH

It has been stated that this study was of an exploratory nature. Its basic purpose has been to determine whether or not the methods of non-directive group therapy are applicable to physically handicapped children or what modifications are necessary. It has been conducted at a very gross level, and the results must therefore be taken as suggestive. Having established in broad terms the applicability of the method to the handicapped child, it would seem that some suggestions are in order for a more careful research program, designed to study the question more accurately and precisely and to avoid some of the pitfalls of the present investigation.

The need for a better recording system

In the present study, the therapist served as a recorder of the therapy sessions. The net result of this was that the protocols which were obtained were frequently incomplete. More important, the therapist was not able to work with the children as adequately as he might have been able to do had he not been concerned with recording. It is the feeling of the therapist that the taking of notes detracted in some measure from the effectiveness of the therapy. While the approach may have been justified in this particular study in terms of the importance of having some record of the proceedings, it is apparent that the system which was used is inadequate for a carefully controlled research program. Ideally, the best method for recording the therapy sessions would be a combined motion picture and electric recording device. Where such facilities are lacking, observers stationed behind a one-way screen to keep as detailed and accurate a record of the proceedings as possible would be satisfactory. In any event, two problems should be avoided: first, the therapist should not be burdened with any recording duties and thus be completely free to devote his entire attention to the children; and, secondly, there should be no one else in the therapy room besides the therapist. Any observer or recorder, no matter how aloof he may seek to remain, becomes an integral part of the situation so long as he is in the therapy room.

The need for an adequate evaluation program

Under this general heading of evaluation there are several points of considerable importance which should be noted. The first of these is objectification. The meagre evaluative information obtained in this study has been qualitative in nature. A comprehensive group experimental program should include a complete set of tests to be administered before therapy begins, at its conclusion, and one or more times thereafter after the passage of a period of time. Such a battery of tests might well include an intelligence test, objective personality test, projective test such as the Rorschach or the TAT, and some sociometric device. It would seem important in this connection for the testing program to be structured as apart from the therapy program, and for a person or persons other than the therapist to administer the tests. School grades are another source of objective data which might bear some investigation over a period of time.

A second problem of evaluation concerns itself with consideration of more carefully planned qualitative data. In the present study the qualitative data consists of an essay type report by teacher and parent before and after therapy. In a more adequate program, such static reports might well be augmented by actual interviews designed to get at the more dynamic aspects of the behavior problems of the children. A further possibility is that of actually interviewing the group members with regard to their experience at some time after the program has been concluded. If the facilities are available it would seem best to record all such interviews electrically.

A third consideration is that of the general need for follow-up. While this point has been hinted at indirectly in the above paragraphs, it is important enough to merit separate mention. In the present study we have compared the status of the children before the therapy program got underway and at its conclusion. Such a procedure overlooks several important possibilities. First, it is conceivable that any 'gains' observed in the group situations are highly cyclical or temporary in nature. On the other hand, it is equally possible that the group experience may have succeeded in reversing the direction of the child's behavior, but in such a small amount that the change is not apparent after the relatively short period of time which has elapsed at the end of the program. It may be that only after the passage of a period of time that the real improvements may be observed. In consideration of the fact that the ultimate validation of a (group) therapy program lies in time, a careful and exhaustive follow-up program seems essential.

Lastly, an evaluation program in group therapy should not overlook the possibility of the use of the control group method for purposes of clearly demonstrating the fact that it is the therapy situation which is the critical factor responsible for any observed changes in adjustment and behavior. Using such a technique and matching the groups in terms of such factors as age, sex, IQ, physical handicap and emotional problem, would demonstrate more convincingly whatever generalizations can be made concerning the effects of therapy as opposed to such possible considerations as the mellowing influence of time, the excellent teacher care given to handicapped children and other related factors. The control group technique might be used in many ways; i.e., matched handicapped children who have not had therapy, matched physically normal children who are exposed to group therapy.

Since only a relatively few children can be dealt with in any single therapy group, there is need for experimentation on a larger scale, with all types of handicapped—mentally retarded, visually handicapped, hearing loss children, and other types of orthopedic children.

SOME LIMITATIONS OF GROUP THERAPY

While the non-directive group therapy method may well represent a tremendous contribution to the treatment of emotional problems in both the normal and the handicapped child, the greatness of the contribution should not obscure the immensity of the task. It should be recognized that in many respects the child may not be able to derive as intense therapeutic value from the group situation as he might from an individual play therapy situation, and that certain children may not be suited to a group play situation (in terms of physical handicaps and/or personality make-up). There should be considerable exploration into the question of how best to complement the group experience if needed with such other services as individual counseling or play therapy. There should be some sensitivity to problems of grouping and adequate materials. The question of intelligence as a factor in amenability to therapy and in grouping also warrants consideration. All these have been suggestions for a more comprehensive research program in non-directive group play in general, with particular reference to the handicapped child. Some of the criticisms more specific to the study which has been described are to be considered.

More careful selection of materials for the play situation

While it is the feeling of the present authors that the most important contribution of the therapy experience is the provision of a situation in which the children are fully accepted as they are and one which is devoid of threat for them, there would appear to be certain materials and equipment which will be more conducive to good therapy than some others. In the present study the play-room was a regular kindergarten room which lacked many such items including expressive materials, water facilities, doll-play facilities, sand and considerable other equipment which might be valuable to the children in working out their problems. While there is no dogma on the question of what materials would be best for the play situation, certainly a list such as that presented by Axline would seem to be a better starting point than a normally equipped kindergarten room.

Shifting the scene of the meetings

It does not seem possible accurately to measure the effects of having moved the scene of therapy for one session (tenth), but there is some room for speculation as to the general theoretical implications of this move. Moving the locus of therapy was originally justified on the basis that the new room would provide some materials not available in the regular therapy room which were more conducive to working out personal problems. The new meeting place necessitated that the therapist abandon to some extent the permissiveness of the therapy situation in order to maintain the children's safety while traveling. It put the group in a strange new situation and they were far more concerned with questions about the University and Clinic than anything else. It brought up to some extent insecurity and uncertainty as to future meetings in the minds of the children and in general offered very little to compensate for these debit factors. In terms of the number of new variables and the confusion added to the general situation, it is felt that moving to a different therapy room for the one meeting contributed nothing, and was if anything a retarding influence in the over-all program.

General administrative problems

Several other issues developed as a result of administrative requests during the course of the therapy session. Since the equipment of the therapy room was definitely not expendable, it was necessary to increase the limitations from time to time in terms of making sure that nothing got seriously damaged. The school administration was not aware of the importance of presenting limitations during the course of the therapy program and abiding by them; thus it was necessary on a few occasions to modify more and more the things which could be done and increase the areas which were out of bounds. While the absolute value of the number of limitations in the room is relatively unimportant, it is important to establish those limitations at the very beginning and adhere to them closely. To continually change limitations and add to them (which was done as the therapy threatened the school situation) tends only to breed insecurity and confusion in the children.

A more general problem is suggested herein, i.e., the question of conducting a therapy program subordinate to a school structure. We have already pointed out some of the difficulties in this connection. There are several others. In one of the parent reports following therapy it was pointed out that one of the children was afraid to really 'cut loose' because he thought that either his teacher or principal might see or hear about some of the things he was doing. Another youngster (Peter) constantly asked C. to say goodbye about ten yards away from the classroom door following each therapy session. He was clearly striving to define C. as apart from the school, to maintain the integrity of the therapy situation. This may well be damaged in the eyes of the children by so simple a perception as a cordial interchange of greetings by teacher and therapist, particularly so if the child is on bad terms with the teacher. Despite all structuring to the contrary, the child may well be operating under the threat that his actions in the group situation will be revealed to enemy sources. Still another potential problem in this respect is the question of drastically changing adjustment demands on the child as he leaves the permissive therapy group and returns to the relatively authoritarian classroom discipline where the activities of the therapy situation is intolerable.

While we are by no means trying to prove that therapy is impossible within a school structure, we do hope to suggest some possible pitfalls of having the therapy group subordinate to the school routine, and to suggest, other things being the same, that there may be advantage in having therapy take place on more neutral grounds when this is a practical possibility.

A few of the more obvious outgrowths of this preliminary investigation have been cited. On the basis of this exploratory study we have found the non-directive group play therapy approach to be applicable with certain modifications in dealing with the emotional problems of orthopedically handicapped children. Our investigation has raised many issues and left many questions unanswered. The field of the handicapped child is a particularly fruitful one for the utilization of therapeutic techniques. It is hoped that there will be energetic future research in therapy designed toward helping maladjusted handicapped children to a happier life experience.

BIBLIOGRAPHY

1. Axline, Virginia, *Play Therapy* (Boston: Houghton-Mifflin: 1947).
2. Cruickshank, W. M., and Cowen, E. L., "Group Therapy with Physically Handicapped Children, I: Report of Study," *Journal of Educational Psychology* (April 1948):193–215.
3. Cruickshank, W. M., and Medve, J., "Social Relationships of Physically Handicapped Children," *Journal of Exceptional Children* 14 (January 1948):100.
4. Fleming, L., and Snyder, W. U., "Social and Personal Changes Following Nondirective Group Play Therapy," *American Journal of Orthopsychiatry* 17 (1947):101.

23

REALISTIC EDUCATIONAL PROGRAMS
FOR MOST CEREBRAL PALSY CHILDREN

*A*LTHOUGH NOT AS DRAMATIC as the recent attention given to polio and the Salk vaccine, it is nevertheless seldom that we see as remarkable a national mobilization of interest in behalf of a specific segment of society as that observed in relation to cerebral palsy individuals over the past ten years. The history of special education in the United States as it pertains to all groups of exceptional children has been that of waiting until progress has been made in medicine, in psychology, in electronics, and related fields. The educational planning for most groups of exceptional children is dependent upon developments and understanding in the progressional fields mentioned, and, although educators are willing to undertake educational programs, they are cognizant that their efforts must often times be characterized by treading water until the findings of related professions are made clear.

This has certainly been the situation in considering cerebral palsy. Although it is dangerous to generalize, it can quite accurately be said that the last ten years have been characterized primarily by medical and psychological research which today is at the point of providing educators with the knowledge they need for their effective program. The next ten years should see a refinement of medical and psychological understanding and a remarkable advance in realistic educational programs for cerebral palsy children. Such is not to say that there are no educational programs for cerebral palsy children at the present time. Community after community, in response to parental appeals, have established special schools, school clinics, special classes, and some have tried a program of integration when appropriate, all of which have been concerned with the education of cerebral palsy children.

Reprinted from *The Crippled Child* 37 (February 1958): 6–7, 22.

Educators, however, realize that these programs are in large measure simply expedient measures to satisfy a need, but that in most instances an effective meeting by educational methodology and curriculum of the peculiar needs of cerebral palsy children is yet to be accomplished. Without question, however, of the two professional fields, psychology and education, the field of psychology has made the greatest strides over the past ten years.

It would be remiss not to mention the splendid contributions of several important organizations which as a part of their total programs have done much to stimulate interest in the education of cerebral palsy children. The ten-year record of the National Society for Crippled Children and Adults and many of its state and local organizations is certainly outstanding. The professional programs of United Cerebral Palsy must likewise be credited with much significant effort. The work of the International Council for Exceptional Children and that of a legion of other professional organizations whose primary concern overlaps into the field of cerebral palsy has stimulated important educational developments throughout the world.

In ten years what have been the important educational and psychological developments pertaining to cerebral palsy?

Probably the first and most important development was the recognization that the cerebral palsy child did exist. For this important development, all professions recognize the significant leadership of Dr. Winthrop M. Phelps. Had it not been for the unceasing pressure which Dr. Phelps exerted on every related professional group and the support which he gave to intelligent parent efforts, little knowledge would have been accrued in this ten-year period. Our understanding would certainly have been delayed for an uncertain period of time.

When diverse professional groups move simultaneously to learn about a common problem, a period of confusion always exists. Normally this period of confusion has little effect on practical programming, but in the case of cerebral palsy, it did. The lay community is usually not actively interested in the laboratory research of professional people. Parents, however, by the thousands have been watching professional activity with cerebral palsy with a very large magnifying glass. The most insignificant finding has, for this reason, been implemented into an active program immediately and often times without the data first being corroborated or adequately tested. This leads to a second point regarding major psychological developments.

Cerebral palsy was first looked upon solely as a physical problem. As such, the possibility that cerebral palsy could produce other problems such as retarded mental development escaped many for a long period of time. The intellectual normalcy of cerebral palsy children was an assumed fact. More than a dozen significant studies, independently initiated and executed, executed by competent professional men and women, have appeared in the past five or six years to point up the high incidence of mental retardation in any population of cerebral palsy children. The findings of Bice,[1] Miller,[2] Asher,[3] Parsons,[4] Holeran,[5] their co-workers, and others have been resisted because of earlier attitudes of lay people regarding cerebral palsy and the intelligence factor.

Currently, however, as time slowly passes, a much more realistic appraisal is being given to the intelligence by these same groups and individuals. This information has significant meaning to education which to date has not been able to utilize it fully. If a large percentage of cerebral palsy children are characterized by retarded mental development, then the type of educational program conceived for such a group must be radically different than that conceived for cerebral palsy children as a clinical entity some ten years ago. Since mentality is the controlling factor in the response of the cerebral palsy child to all learning situations, in the classroom, on the treatment table, in the speech situation, with the occupational therapist, or in any other situation, the importance of these studies cannot be over-estimated. We still hear some state that the findings of the studies which have been mentioned are erroneous, that it is impossible to measure the mentality of some cerebral palsy children, that psychological tests are inadequate.

We would agree with these statements in part. It is true that some cerebral palsy children present very difficult diagnostic problems to psychologists. It is true that psychological tests still need refinement. However, such statements as have been made are less accurate than they are more accurate. Competent psychologists can and daily do accurately provide appraisals of the psychological characteristics of most seriously disabled cerebral palsy children. The fact that they cannot or will not specify an intelligence quotient to the parent or school in every instance, perpetuates the belief that intelligence cannot be measured. Actually what is happening, however, is that psychologists have come to realize that the intelligence quotient *per se* is pretty meaningless and that the sooner we begin to think in terms other than I.Q., the more rapidly will we begin to understand the child and his problems and be able to conceive of a program which will be geared to his specific needs. I.Q. implies that we think of children in groups, classify them according to a common figure, and plan for them educationally as a group. There is no such thing as a group of cerebral palsy children from the point of view of educational or psychological planning. The recent data collected about intelligence and cerebral palsy is significant and important.

Thirdly, beginning before 1946, but receiving marked attention during the last ten year period is a vast amount of psychological research dealing with problems of psychopathology and neurological disorders. Although others had been concerned with this problem for some time, much credit for stimulating professional thought in this field is appropriately credited to Dr. Heinz Werner, late of Clarke University, and his co-worker, the late Dr. Alfred A. Strauss. These two gentlemen, combining psychological and neurological interests in studying the psychopathological characteristics of exogenous, non-motor handicapped, mentally retarded children stimulated many psychologists to research in this and related fields.

In this matter the Syracuse University group has been most active. The investigations of Di Carlo and his associates into the psychological characteristics of deaf children stemmed from research in psychopathology which we mention. The studies of Dolphin[6] with cerebral palsy, Shaw[7] with idiopathic epileptic children and endogenous mentally retarded children, of Trippe,[8] Qualtere,[9] and Norris[10] with cerebral palsy children have been related to the broad topic of psychopathology. The recently concluded study of Cruickshank, Bice, and Wallen,[11] supported for three years by the Association for the Aid of Crippled Children, lends further information on the problem of psychopathology in cerebral palsy. Further studies are in progress by promising young investigators such as Roger Alling[12] and James Neely[13] whose findings will plug additional holes in our fabric of understanding.

Comparable work has, of course, been going on in other institutions of higher education throughout the country. Syracuse University is used only as an example of broader interest. The literature pertaining to perception in individuals with brain injury is so great at the present time as to be a real problem for review. More than two hundred published reports have recently been collected for study by the writer. All of these bear directly or indirectly on perception in cerebral palsy.

This important research has brought the realization that, in addition to the complexities of the physical component of cerebral palsy and variations in treatment and educational programs dictated by intelligence of the child, there are significant variations in the psychological status of the patient as regards to figure-background relationship, to visuo-motor perception, tactuo-motor perception, and probably to audio-motor perception. The fact that cerebral palsy children differ in these matters all along a scale of from that which would be considered normal to that which is definitely psychopathological and that such differences are not related to intelligence or to medical classification—although somewhat related to chronological age—complicates educational planning and treatment of these children a great deal.

We now have a good understanding of the psychopathological components of cerebral palsy, although, of course, additional study is necessary.

Such an understanding dictates that different educational approaches be used with cerebral palsy children who show different psychological characteristics. The place where the greatest amount of research and study is needed at the present time is in the area of the next step, i.e., what constitutes an adequate education setting and methodology for cerebral palsy children who show characteristics of psychopathology? Herein we currently have only clinical data. A further fact of significant importance has been brought out in these studies, i.e.; that similarities rather than differences characterize the psychological make-up of cerebral palsy children, epileptic children, exogenous mentally retarded children, aphasic children, and other classifications of children with central nervous systems disorders. Without question, this observation will have great impact on the nature of treatment centers and educational centers and their programs in the next decade or two.

Another point which needs to be highlighted in looking back over a ten-year period, is the activity on the part of psychologists and statisticians to develop psychological instruments which will at one and the same time measure psychological function and take into consideration the limitations of the physical condition of the patient. Through a grant made initially by the New York State Association for Crippled Children, Irving Lorge, Burgemeister and Blum have developed the "Columbia Test of Mental Maturity." The "Ammons Picture Story Test" and "Raven's Progressive Matrices," among others, have all been developed for providing tests which take the limitations of physical movement into consideration. Much additional research is needed in this sphere before we have the adequate tools for which we search. In our own research, we have recently come to recognize that a tachistoscopic test used by Strauss and Werner perfected and modified as the "Syracuse Visual Figure Background Test" may have significant importance in psychological diagnosis. However, much standardization and modification is yet to be done before the tachistoscopic method can be used with any reliability in appraising perception in cerebral palsy children or adults.

Recently the author of a test not mentioned in a published paper complained regarding the omission, pointing out that his test was considered the "best test" for cerebral palsy children. There is no best test. All tests need improvement. The important point is that within the ten year period, strides have been made in development of tests geared to meet peculiar needs. In this respect, beginning in 1933 we have seen in psychology as a result of the immigration into the United States from Germany of outstanding professional people, a blending of quantitative American psychology and the qualitative introspective psychology of the Continent. This has resulted in important new insights regarding the psychological measurement of children with neurological diseases. Such has stimulated us to move away from curiosity about the I.Q. to interest in the pattern of psychological characteristics presented by the patient and to concern for the meaning of these characteristics to the educational and treatment program.

A fifth point is of some interest, although of lesser importance than some previously mentioned factors. There appear in the literature, statements which relate specific medical diagnosis in cerebral palsy to more or less specific personality types. For example, athetoid and spastic types of cerebral palsy have been related to such specific psychological characteristics as extroversion and introversion. Some authors have carried this to greater lengths than others. Two important points should be made in this respect. Typology insofar as personality is concerned is pretty much a thing of the past. Research has not related personality to body-type nor has it delineated succinctly personality types which can be grouped together. Secondly, recent research of Block[14] and more recent and yet unpublished data of Trippe,[15] has specifically concerned itself with personality characteristics of groups of cerebral palsy individuals. In neither of these two studies has there been shown to be any relation between personality type and medical classification. The need for individual psychological appraisal of the patient and of studying him in terms of his own physical and psychological characteristics is reinforced by these studies.

A final — and sixth — factor should be mentioned, namely the multi-handicapped child. The presence of mental retardation in cerebral palsy is certainly one important, if not the most important, aspect of the multi-handicapping problem. This decade has brought the multi-handicapped child to the attention of professional people, but to date this group represents the point where least knowledge is available and where least amount of research and practical programming is under way. Awareness of the problem is important, however, and certainly precludes the next growths mentioned here. The blind cerebral palsy child, the deaf or hard of hearing cerebral palsy child, the cerebral palsy child who also has seizures — these are yet educational and psychological challenges. The situation can be confounded many times. Each time a multiplication takes place we find our understanding less and less. We do not yet know how to educate the cerebral palsy child who is mentally retarded, blind, who has seizures and shows psychopathology in perception. We do not know how to educate him, but we are at a point where professional people and groups of professional people have begun to evidence interest and to stimulate research. The next decade should see us moving in many new directions in this aspect.

These factors among others have typified the progress of psychology in the past decade. Other trends could be mentioned, but these are without question the most important. In the development of the team concept, the integration of the psychologist and the educator into the team within the clinic or school is, of course, important, but no more so than the inclusion of many other professional representatives. It has been stated that education has lagged behind other professions. Perhaps it would be better to state that clinical educational programs relating specifically to psychopathology in cerebral palsy have lagged. These, as a matter of fact, are almost non-existent in the United States at the present time. For children who do not present problems of psychopathology, few modifications in educational methodology are required with cerebral palsy. Educational goals need modification often times, but methodology can with modifications in techniques remain much the same as for all children. Numerous programs exist; many of which have been developed in recent years. To mention any will be dangerous because some are bound to be omitted. Suffice it to say that from coast to coast public schools are rising to the challenge of the cerebral palsy child. The past decade has for education been one of mustering forces, understanding the problem from sister professional groups, and beginning to implement this understanding with action programs. The next decade without question will see a refinement of program and an extension of program to cerebral palsy children who, by reason of their peculiar characteristics, are unable to learn with profit through the same method and procedure as has generally been found appropriate with the great mass of children.

BIBLIOGRAPHY

1. Bice, H. V., in "Evaluation of Intelligence," H. V. Bice and W. M. Cruickshank, Chapter III in *Cerebral Palsy: Its Individual and Community Problems,* eds. W. M. Cruickshank and G. M. Raus, Syracuse: Syracuse University Press, 1955.

2. Miller, E., and Rosefeld, G., "The Psychological Evaluation of Children with Cerebral Palsy and Its Implications in Treatment," *Journal of Pediatrics* 41 (1952): 613–621.

3. Asher, P., and Schonnel, F. E., "A Survey of 400 Cases of Cerebral Palsy in Childhood," *Archives of Diseases of Children* 25 (1950): 360–379.

4. See Cruickshank, W. M., "Psychological Considerations of Crippled Children," in *Psychology of Exceptional Children and Youth,* ed. W. M. Cruickshank, Englewood Cliffs, N.J.; Prentice-Hall, Inc., 1955, p. 320.

5. Ibid.

6. Dolphin, J. E., "A Study of Certain Aspects of Psychopathology in Children with Cerebral Palsy," unpublished doctoral dissertation, Syracuse University, 1950.

7. Shaw, M. E., "A Study of Certain Aspects of Perception and Conceptual Thinking in Idiopathic Epileptic Children," unpublished doctoral dissertation, Syracuse University, 1955.

8. Trippe, M. J., "A Study of the Relationship Between Visual Perceptual Ability and Selected Personality Variables in a Group of Cerebral Palsy Children," unpublished doctoral dissertation, Syracuse University, 1957.

9. Qualtere, T. J., "An Investigation of the Relationship Between Figure Background Disturbance and Performance on the Raven's Progressive Matrices," unpublished doctoral dissertation, Syracuse University, 1957.

10. Norris, H., "An Exploration of the Relation of Certain Theoretical Constructs to a Behavioral Syndrome on Brain Pathology," unpublished doctoral dissertation, Syracuse University, 1958.

11. Cruickshank, W. M., Bice, H. V., and Wallen, N. E., *Perception and Cerebral Palsy: A Study of the Figure Background Relationship,* Syracuse: Syracuse University Press, 1957.

12. Alling, Roger, "A Study of the Level of Aspiration in Children with Cerebral Palsy," doctoral dissertation, Syracuse University, in progress.

13. Neely, James, "A Study of the Relationship Between School Achievement and Perceptual Disorders," doctoral dissertation, Syracuse University, in progress.

14. Block, W. E., "A Study of Somatopsychological Relationships in Cerebral Palsied Children," *Exceptional Children* 22 (1955).

15. Trippe, op. cit.

PART III

PIONEER STUDIES IN THE
FIELD OF LEARNING DISABILITIES

*A*FTER THE VERY EARLY STUDIES (1935–50) by Drs. Heinz Werner and Alfred A. Strauss, studies done at Syracuse University by me and some of my students were historically the next to appear among those antedating the present field of learning diabilities. Some of these studies, e.g., that of Dr. Howard Norris, never appeared in print as articles but remain in the Library of Syracuse University as unpublished doctoral dissertations. This is also the fate of studies by Elizabeth MacKay, Donald Y. Miller, and numerous other scholars.

In 1948 Jane E. Dolphin approached the author and asked for suggestions regarding a future doctoral dissertation. I recommended that she replicate much of what Strauss and Werner had done, but that she complete her work with a population of children known to be both neurologically handicapped and intellectually normal. She did this and her work with a heterogeneous group of cerebral palsy children led later to the extensive study *Perception and Cerebral Palsy: A Study of the Figure-Background Relationship* (2nd edition, Syracuse University Press, 1965), by Cruickshank, H. V. Bice, N. E. Wallen, and K. S. Lynch. Since the work of Werner and Strauss up to that time had all been with mentally retarded youths, intellectual normalcy was insisted upon with Dolphin's group of cerebral palsied children. Indeed, it is likely that Dolphin's study was a key factor in the long-term concept held by parents and included in both federal and state definitions that learning disabled children must be defined as intellectually normal. That this is not so is attested to by the work of Strauss and Werner which preceded the Dolphin-Cruickshank studies. It is for this latter reason that the aforementioned studies have been included in this selection of papers along with some of those by Shaw and Cruickshank which, while not as

266

clear cut as the Dolphin series, do emphasize the intellectual normalcy of an undifferentiated group of children with epilepsy. More than thirty years of argument regarding learning disabilities and intellectual normalcy started with these sets of publications, and has continued until 1980 when state after state, through the impetus of PL 94-142, started to drop the intelligence quotient as a factor in the definition of learning disabilities. The reader will note in the studies included here that the term "learning disabilities" appears infrequently. Many other terms, including "brain-injury," were used prior to 1963, and these terms flood the literature which historically predate the term "learning disabilities".

24

ALFRED A. STRAUSS:
PIONEER IN LEARNING DISABILITIES

(with Daniel P. Hallahan)

*A*PPROXIMATELY 40 YEARS AGO, in the midst of the developing holocaust that was the Germany of that decade, two eminent Jewish scholars began making their ways by separate routes to the United States. Alfred A. Strauss, M.D., and Heinz Werner, Ph.D., ultimately came together at the Wayne County Training School, Northville, Michigan, in 1937 and there began a professional collaboration for several years, laying the cornerstone for what today is known as the field of learning disabilities. While other persons, both antedating and contemporary to Strauss and Werner, had made significant contributions to the early history of this field (Hallahan & Cruickshank, 1973), these two men were instrumental in propelling it forward as none had done previously. At the close of World War II, Werner and Strauss left the Training School and went separate ways: Werner to Brooklyn College and later to Clark University and Strauss to become the founder and cofounder, respectively, of the Cove Schools in Racine, Wisconsin, and Evanston, Illinois.

Following Werner's death in 1964, the complete bibliography of his works was published (Witkin, 1965). Until now no similar publication of the complete written works of Strauss has been published. The year 1973 marks the tenth anniversary of the founding of the National Association for Children with Learning Disabilities. While this event postdated Strauss' death by 6 years, his search to understand these children and to educate them was a vital factor in the ultimate recognition by thousands of parents that the problems of their children were complicated and required highly specialized educational methodology. The anniversary of the parent association, as well as

Reprinted from *Exceptional Children* 39 (January 1973): 321–27, by permission.

the continuing and renewed interest in the work of Werner and Strauss, prompt us in the short space of this article to bring together the highlights of Strauss' professional life and to provide the student a full and, we believe, complete list of his writings. In combination, the aforementioned bibliography of Werner and that contained here for Strauss can provide the student with a complete reference for the contributions of these two great men.

BIOGRAPHICAL SKETCH

After four years at the University of Heidelberg, Alfred Strauss, born May 29, 1897, in Karlsruhe, obtained his medical degree in 1922. In the same year he passed the state examinations in medicine. For the next five years, he received special training in psychiatry and neurology as an assistant at the University Polyclinic for Internal Medicine (Professor Fleiner) and as a voluntary assistant in the Psychiatric Clinic (Professor Wilmanns), both in the University of Heidelberg. In 1924 he was assistant in the Neurological Institute at the University of Frankfort under Professor Kurt Goldstein, while in the winter of 1925 he served as assistant at the City Hospital in Ludwigshafen (Dr. Kaufmann) and in the Psychiatric University Polyclinic in Heidelberg (Professor Homburger). From 1927 to 1930 he maintained a private practice in neuropsychiatry in Mannheim and served as a research associate at the University of Heidelberg. From 1930 until 1933 Strauss held the prestigious position of head of the Neuropsychiatric Polyclinic at the University of Heidelberg as a successor to August Homburger. During those years, Strauss also served as the medical director of the Municipal Home for Abnormal Children in Heidelberg, director of the Child Guidance Department of the University Children's Hospital, and psychiatric consultant to Heidelberg's Board of Social Welfare, Board of Education, and Juvenile Court.

Beginning of work in mental retardation

Sometime during and after May 1932, Strauss had an experience which drew him closer to the area of mental retardation. He became interested in the area of habilitation and prepared a work, "Uber Erkennung und Klinik der Schwersten Schwachs innsformen" ("How to Recognize and Treat the Severest Forms of Mental Deficiency"). A lecture is also reported during this period in the field of habilitation, "über optische Agnosienim Kindesalter, und Hëilpadagogik und Klinik." In a letter dated July 1933 from Professor Hans W. Gruhle to the director of the Neuropsychiatric Clinic at Heidelberg, Gruhle stated,

> Dr. Alfred Strauss, Privatdocent for Psychiatry and Neurology, . . . has contributed and closely followed all the scientific work of the Institute, and in particular has participated with profound interest in the exercises of the Psychological Seminar. In the Histopathological Laboratory of Professor Steiner, he devoted himself to research of the brain of idiots. . . . He has been independently in charge of this whole domain of the personal and social welfare of abnormal children.

Gruhle concluded his statement by saying, "we are grateful to him for his long, zealous and successful collaboration, and appreciate his high qualities as a colleague."

Recognizing his impending departure from Germany, Professor Carl Wilmanns, writing in September of 1933, said, "I regret in the interest of maintaining the highest tradition of the [Psychiatric] clinic [of Heidelberg] that we must lose Dr. Strauss' most valuable service."

Wars and dislocation

The beginning of the young German scientist's promising career in neuropsychiatry was interrupted when Hitler's rise to power prompted Strauss to leave for Spain. Here, while serving as a guest professor at the University of Barcelona, he cofounded for the Catalonian government Spain's first governmental and private child guidance centers. The latter was a joint effort with Mira y Lopez, head of the Department of Psychiatry at the University of Barcelona, and Jeronimo de Moragas. Another major conflict, the Spanish Civil War, forced him to leave Spain. In 1936 the Child Guidance Clinic was seized by the anarchists, and Strauss refused to collaborate further. He requested and obtained an immediate leave from the Psychotechnical Institute in Barcelona to study in Switzerland. The year 1937 found him engaged in a research collaboration with Penrose and in the preparation of a report to the Privy Council in London, England.

Move to US and final years

He accepted an invitation in 1937 from R. H. Haskell, Superintendent of the Wayne County Training School in Northville, Michigan, to take

the position of research psychiatrist in the Training School's research department, which was then directed by T. G. Hegge. He and his family arrived at
the Training School in January, 1937. One month following his naturaliza-
tion as a US citizen in September of 1943, Strauss became the director of
Child Care at the Training School, where he served until ill health made him
resign in 1946. In the final years before his death in Chicago on October 27,
1957, he contributed significantly as special lecturer at Wayne State University and Milwaukee State Teachers College, as well as founder of the Cove
Schools in Racine, Wisconsin, and cofounder of the Cove School in Evanston, Illinois.

STRAUSS'S ACCOMPLISHMENTS

In light of the fact that the active professional career of Strauss was interrupted by two major wars, illness, and an early death, his accomplishments
in the field of special education were indeed extraordinary. The year 1942
saw Strauss serving on the Advisory Committee for Special Education in the
Michigan Department of Education. It must be remembered, too, that while
hardly an inappropriate preparation, his original training as a neuropsychia-
trist did not immediately lead him into the more behavioral aspects of psychology and education. Although he was a renowned figure within the field
of neurology, his frustrations with the paucity of its contributions to the
study of mental retardation (Strauss, 1941) may have served as an impetus
for his endeavors in psychology and education.

    Moreover, the chain of events resulting from World War II and
even from certain incidents connected with World War I profoundly affected his life and work. Hitler's reign, for example, precipitated the emigra-
tion of the German scholar and scientist, Heinz Werner, to the Wayne
County Training School. While Strauss was notably influenced by the ideas
of August Homburger, Ernst Monro, Kurt Goldstein, Alfred Binet, Edward
Segin, and Jean Piaget (having had a great deal of personal contact with the
latter), in retrospect it is clear that the arrival of Werner at the Training
School was the single most significant event in the professional life of
Strauss. During their close professional relationship at the Training School,
they coauthored 17 published articles, the first published within a year of
their arrival at the School.

    Collaboration with Werner and function as a member of a team of
investigators was not difficult for Strauss. He had had much experience in
this type of professional production. In 1932 a teamwork effort by German

psychiatrists of international repute (including in addition to Strauss, the names of Homburger, Neager, Gross, Beringer, Wilmanns, Gruhle, Wetzel, and Steiner) resulted in a significant volume on schizophrenia which was published in Bumke's *Handbook of Psychiatry*. Here was a "group of scientists, independent in their opinion, free in their expression, invited by a common enthusiasm, stimulated by their controversies, but cooperative in their work [E. Straus, 1946, p. 102]." This statement could just as easily have been written about the relationship of Strauss and Werner and those who clustered around them at the Training School. The roles of theoretician, "idea man," conceptualist, implementor, and writer were shared, and these roles passed easily from one to another. The second floor of the School's research building was indeed an active place with ideas constantly being verbalized and integrated into the theory which drove the two men forward.

Werner, with his quiet, dry humor, was Sinclair Lewis' Arrowsmith and Dr. Gottlieb combined. Strauss was more open, jovial, and allocentric in his relation to people and world in general. Each man possessed a dynamism which stimulated the other and those around him. Strauss was direct and forceful and sometimes a little impetuous, yet always intensely concerned for those he studied and for the ways in which his ideas were carried out. Werner, more introspective and reticent, performed a significant balance in the life of the egregious Strauss.

A third man, Hegge, who was mentioned before as director of research, played a significant role for both men. He gave them full reign in their endeavors. He provided latitude for thought and action as well as the freedom to challenge and to try. Simultaneously, his stoic Norwegian deliberateness, if not his physical stature, provided the pause to think and to rethink which was important to their individual and joint success.

Work with brain injured

The post-World War I research of both Head and Goldstein with brain injured soldiers also influenced the establishment of collaborative endeavors by Strauss and Werner. In his work with "traumatic dements," Kurt Goldstein had noted psychological characteristics of figure-background confusion, forced responsiveness to stimuli, meticulosity, perseveration, concrete behavior, and catastrophic behavior. From their first years of working together in the late 1930's through the decade of the 1940's, Strauss and Werner designed ingenious investigations to determine if brain injured, mentally retarded children manifested the same psychological behaviors as Goldstein's adult patients. Using as a basis for their research the writings of

Goldstein and an early paper written by Strauss prior to his departure from Germany, Strauss and Werner found evidence of all the above characteristics in their brain injured children. In particular, the predominance of hyperactivity and distractibility promptly became the major focus of their studies. The impact of these pioneering efforts on the field is evidenced today by frequent reference to the Strauss Syndrome in descriptions of the hyperactive and distractible child.

It would be deceiving to overlook the fact that this early work by Strauss and Werner attracted cogent and vehement criticism (Sarason, 1949). Diagnosis of a child as exogenous (brain injured) rather than endogenous (non brain injured) on the basis of behavioral manifestations led Strauss and Werner into a circular argument when they asserted that the same behaviors were the result of brain damage. Nevertheless, regardless of the true etiological classification of their exogenous group, the important consequence of Strauss and Werner's research was that it demonstrated the existence of a subgroup of mentally retarded children, many of whose behaviors were not within the repertoire of the majority of mentally retarded children.

Concept of individual differences and prescriptive instruction

At the time, this evidence of individual differences in the ability and mode of processing incoming stimuli among mentally retarded children was revolutionary in nature. From this regard for individual differences evolved one of the most significant strands supporting the present day field of learning disabilities (Hallahan & Cruickshank, 1973). In a paper published in 1939, Werner and Strauss advanced the approach of functional analysis for the education and psychology of mentally retarded children. This approach, closely akin to that advocated today, particularly within the field of learning disabilities, stressed the importance of determining the manner of a child's approach to individual test items rather than his total score. Each child was to be examined in terms of his own particular composite of abilities and disabilities.

In addition to establishing his conceptual framework for consideration of the exceptional child, Strauss also advanced numerous educational innovations later to be adopted by many learning disabilities theoreticians and practitioners. Having discovered the Wayne County Training School's positive influence on the measured IQ of children identified as endogenous and its concomitant negative effect on those classified as exogenous, Strauss (1939) concluded that a different educational program was required for exogenous children. The subsequent description by Strauss of his educational approach to the hyperactive and distractible (i.e., exogenous) child was recognized by the editor of *Journal of Exceptional Children* in 1943 as "one of the outstanding educational contributions of the year."

Fully expanded delineations of his techniques for perceptual-motor training and his concept of a structured program within a stimuli reduced environment later appeared in the classic volumes coauthored with Laura Lehtinen and Newell Kephart (Strauss & Lehtinen, 1947; Strauss & Kephart, 1955). Finally, the associations with Strauss at Wayne County Training School by such people as Kephart and Lehtinen, as a graduate student by William Cruickshank, and elsewhere later by Ray Barsch resulted in the adoption of his educational procedures, first with brain injured children of normal intelligence and then with children identified as learning disabled. From time to time, among many others who had association at the School with Strauss and his equally famous colleague were Sidney Bijou, Betty Martinson, Charlotte Philleo, Bluma Weiner, Samuel A. Kirk, Maurice Fouracre, and Boyd McCandless.

Other contributions

Although Strauss should be most remembered for his bequest to the concept of individual abilities and disabilities within the fields of mental retardation and learning disabilities and for his advocacy of prescriptive educational methods based on these characteristics, he made still other significant contributions in his life and work. Among his early endeavors, for example, was the first systematic investigation of finger agnosia in children. From that work arose the discovery of a relationship between arithmetic disability in mentally retarded subjects and deficiencies in the ability to indicate on request, to name, or to choose with open eyes the individual fingers on one's own hand or on that of another (Strauss & Werner, 1938, 1939).

Strauss also engaged in pioneer research into the effects of medication on the psychological functioning of the mentally retarded (Cutler, Little, & Strauss, 1940). His study of the qualitative differences between nonretarded and retarded children's responses on the Stanford-Binet was on the cutting edge in presenting and popularizing the notion that more than IQ scores differentiated the two groups (Martinson & Strauss, 1941; Strauss & Werner, 1940). In addition, he was among the first of the professionals to discredit the then current belief that the capabilities of brain damaged children could not improve through training (Strauss, 1939). While his greatest research thrust was within the perceptual sphere of psychological development, Strauss, toward the end of his career, also began to turn his attention to the investigation of aphasia in children (Strauss, 1954, 1958).

CONCLUDING COMMENTS

While a brief biography such as this one could not possibly touch or do credit to many other contributions made by Strauss to special education and psychology, hopefully it will provide the student and professional special educator with an appreciation of the impact of this man's ideas and work. Those who are inclined to caution against positing single causes may argue that, in time, certain concepts within mental retardation and learning disabilities would have evolved anyway. Nevertheless, the fact remains that because of the potent influence of his innovative procedures, provocative findings, and sound recommendations, Alfred Strauss was a pioneer investigator in mental retardation and one of the forefathers of the current learning disabilities movement. The more than 70 articles and books which he authored and coauthored during his life constitute a major benchmark in understanding the learning problems of children.

A BIBLIOGRAPHY OF THE WRITINGS OF ALFRED A. STRAUSS

1922-1929

Strauss, A. A. Über eine Neue Methode der Spirochäfärbung im Gerfierschnitt. Unpublished doctoral dissertation, University of Heidelberg, 1922.

Kino, F., & Strauss, A. A. Tabes und Muskelatrophie.*D.Z.f. Nervenh.* 1925.

Strauss, A. A. Über das Vorkommen von Ganglienzellen ausserhal der grauen Substanz des Ruckenmarks. Lecture given at the Vereinigung Frankfurter Neurologen und Psychiater, 1925.

Buerger, H., & Strauss, A. Mototische Untersuchungen bei Progressiver Paralyse. *Arch. f. Psych.,* 1925, 85, 404.

Strauss, A. A. Ein Fall von Angeborenem Völligen Fehlen Beider Oberextremitäten. (histopath. unters.) *J. f. Psych. Neur.,* 1926, 36, 75.

Bueger, H., & Strauss, A. Motorisch-amnestische Aphasie, *Arch. f. Psych.,* 1929, 88, 828.

1930–1934

Strauss, A. Fortschritte der Arzneimitteltherapie. *Der Nervenarzt,* 1930, 3, 173.

Buerger, H., Strauss, A., & Kaila, M. Experimenteller Beitrag zum Problem der Lagereflexe des Menschen. *Arch f. Psych.,* 1930, 92, 334.

Korsch, L., & Strauss, A. Das bild der Chenoposanvergiftung bei einem 6-jährigen Kinde. *Der Nervenarzt,* 1931, 4, 545.

Strauss, A. Gibt es Nervoese Folgeerscheinungen bei Kriegsteilnehmern, die an Malaria Erkrankt Waren? *Der Nervenarzt,* 1931, 4, 273.

Strauss, A. Nekrolog August Homburger. *Allg. Z. f. Psychiat.,* 1931, p. 465.

Strauss, A. Pseudoparalytisches Syndrom bei Beirmer'scher Anaemie und Endocarditis Lenta. *Der Nervenarzt,* 1931, 5, 350.

Strauss, A. Zur Psychiatrisch-neurologischen Filmtechnik. *D. Med. Wochenschr.,* 1932.

Bumke, O. *Handbuch der Geisteskrankheiten.* Vol. 9, Part 5: Schizophrenie (Spezieller teil). 1932.

Steiner, G., & Strauss, A. A. *Die Korperlichen Erscheinungen.* Berlin-Verlag, Julius Springer, 1932.

Strauss, A. Beitraege zur Einteilung, Entstehung und Klinik der Schwersten Schwachsinnsformen. *Arch. f. Psych.,* 1933, 99, 693.

Strauss, A. A. Heilpaedagogik und Klinik. *Z. F. Kinderforschung,* 1933, 41, 445–454.

Strauss, A. A. Algunas Modernas Teorias Sobre la Localizacion Cerebral. *Rev. Med. Barcelona,* 1934, 21, 356–363.

1935–1939

Strauss, A. A. Encephalitis lethargica. *Aeratl. Mitt. f. Baden,* 1935, p. 435.

Strauss, A. A., & Moragas, J. Diagnostic cinematografic d'une lesio cerebral. *Bul. Soc. Catalana de Pediatria,* 1935, 8, 111–118.

Strauss, A. A. Pedogogia terapeutica, Editorial, Labor Publishers, S.A., Barcelona, Madrid, Buenos Aires, Rio De Janeiro, 1936.

Werner, H., & Strauss, A. Approaches to a functional analysis of mentally handicapped problem children with illustration in the field of arithmetic disability. *Proc. Am. Assoc. Ment. Def.,* 1938, 43, 105.

Strauss, A. A., & Werner, H. Deficiency in the finger schema in relation to arithmetic disability. *Am. J. Orthopsych.,* 1938, 8, 719–724.

Strauss, A. A. Effects of exogenous factors in the organism as a whole in mentally deficient children. Paper presented at biennial meeting of the Society for Research in Child Development, November 12, 1938.

Strauss, A., & Werner, H.   Deficiency in finger schema (finger agnosia and acalculia). *The Psychological Cinema Register,* Nov. 27, 1939.

Strauss, A., & Werner, H.   Finger agnosia in children. *Am. J. Psychiat.,* 1939, 95, 1215-1225.

Strauss, A., & Werner, H.   Problems and methods of functional analysis in mentally deficient children. *J. Abn. Soc. Psychol.,* 1939, 34, 37-62.

Strauss, A., & Werner, H.   Types of visuo-motor activity in their relation to low and high performance ages. *Proc. Am. Assoc. Ment. Def.,* 1939, 44, 163.

Strauss, A. A., & Kephart, N. C.   Rate of mental growth in a constant environment among higher grade moron and borderline children. *Proc. Am. Assoc. Ment. Def.,* 1939, 44, 137-142.

Strauss, A. A.   Typology in mental deficiency. *Proc. Am. Assoc. Ment. Def.,* 1939, 44, 85-90.

1940-44

Strauss, A. A., & Kephart, N. C.   Behavior differences in mentally retarded children measured by a new behavior rating scale. *Am. J. Psychiat.,* 1940, 96, 1117-1123.

Werner, H., & Strauss, A. A.   Causal factors in low performance. *Am. J. Ment. Def.,* 1940, 45, 213-218.

Strauss, A. A., & Kephart, N. C.   A clinical factor influencing variations in IQ. *Am. J. Orthopsychiat.,* 1940, 10, 343-350.

Martinson, B., & Strauss, A. A.   Education and treatment of an imbecile boy of the exogenous type. *Am. J. Mental Def.,* 1940, 45, 274-280.

Cutler, M., Little, J. W., & Strauss, A. A.   The effect of benzedrine on mentally deficient children. *Am. J. Ment. Def.,* 1940, 45, 59-65.

Strauss, A. A.   The incidence of central nervous system involvement in higher grade moron children. Paper presented at the meeting of the American Association on Mental Deficiency, 1940.

Strauss, A. A., & Werner, H.   The mental organization of the brain-injured mentally defective child. (The mentally crippled child). Paper presented at the meeting of the American Psychiatric Association, 1940.

Strauss, A. A.   Enriching the analysis of the Stanford-Binet test. *J. Except. Child.,* 1940, 7, 260-274.

Martinson, B., & Strauss, A. A.   A method of clinical interpretation of the Stanford-Binet Test. Paper presented at the meeting of the American Psychiatric Association, 1940.

Strauss, A. A.   The nervous child in the dental office. *J. Amer. Dent. Hygiene Assoc.,* 1940, 14, 76.

Strauss, A. A., & Werner, H.   Qualitative analysis of the Binet Test. *Am. J. Ment. Def.,* 1940, 45, 50–55.

Strauss, A. A., Rahm, W. E., Jr., & Barrera, S. E.   Studies on a group of children with psychiatric disorders. I. Electroencephalographic studies, *Psychosom. Med.,* 1940, 2, 34–42.

Strauss, A. A.   The incidence of central nervous system involvement in higher grade moron children. *Am. J. Ment. Def.,* 1941, 45, 548–554.

Strauss, A. A., & Werner, H.   The mental organization of the brain-injured mentally defective child. *Am. J. Psychiat.,* 1941, 97, 1194–1202.

Martinson B., & Strauss, A. A.   A method of clinical evaluation of the responses to the Stanford-Binet Intelligence Test. *Am. J. Ment. Def.,* 1941, 46, 72–83.

Strauss, A. A.   Neurology in mental deficiency. (Editorial) *Am. J. Ment. Def.,* 1941, 46, 192–194.

Werner, H., & Strauss, A. A.   Pathology of figure-background relationship in the child. *J. Ab. Soc. Psychology,* 1941, 36, 236–248.

Werner, H., & Strauss, A. A.   Disorders of conceptual thinking in the brain-injured child. *J. Nerv. and Ment. Dis.,* 1942, 96, 153.

Strauss, A. A., & Werner, H.   Experimental analysis of the clinical symptom "perseveration" in mentally retarded children. *Am. J. Ment. Def.,* 1942, 47, 185–187.

Strauss, A. A., & Werner, H.   Disorders of conceptual thinking in the brain-injured child. *J. Nerv. Ment. Dis.,* 1942, 96, 153–176.

Strauss, A. A.   Principles of the education of brain-injured mentally defective children. *Bull. Forest Sanatorium,* 1942, 1, 54–60.

Strauss, A. A., & Werner, H.   Comparative psychopathology of the brain-injured child and the traumatic brain-injured adult. *Am. J. Psychiat.,* 1943, 99, 835–838.

Strauss, A. A.   Diagnosis and education of the cripple-brained deficient child. *J. Except. Children,* 1943, 9, 163–168.

Strauss, A. A., & Werner, H.   Impairment in thought processes of brain-injured children. *Am. J. Ment. Def.,* 1943, 47, 291–295.

McCandless, B. R., & Strauss, A. A.   Objective criteria diagnostic of deviant personality: An exploratory study. *Am. J. Ment. Def.,* 1943, 47, 445–449.

Haskell, R. H., & Strauss, A. A.   One hundred institutionalized mental defectives in the armed forces. *Am. J. Ment. Def.,* 1943, 48, 67–71.

Strauss, A. A., & Watson, E. H.   Studies in hormone therapy. I. The evaluation of growth hormone treatment. *J. Pediat.,* 1943, 23, 421.

Lehtinen, L. E., & Strauss, A. A.   Arithmetic fundamentals for the brain-crippled child. *Am. J. Ment. Def.,* 1944, 49, 149–154.

Lehtinen, L. E., & Strauss, A. A.   A new approach in educational methods for brain-crippled deficient children. *Am. J. Ment. Def.,* 1944, 48, 283-288.

Strauss, A. A.   Ways of thinking in brain-crippled deficient children. *Am. J. Psychiat.,* 1944, 100, 639-647.

1945-1949

Rossettie, T. M., & Strauss, A. A.   Disciplinary procedures as conceived by boys in a self-determining group. *Am. J. Ment. Def.,* 1945, 49, 307-315.

Strauss, A. A.   Therapeutic pedagogy, a neuro-psychiatric approach to special education. *Am. J. Psychiat.,* 1947, 104, 60-63.

Strauss, A. A., & Lehtinen, L. E.   *Psychopathology and education of the brain-injured child.* Vol 1. New York: Grune & Stratton, 1947.

Strauss, A. A., & Werner, H.   Qualitative analysis of the Binet Test. *Am. J. Ment. Def.,* 1949, 45, 50-55.

1950-1954

Strauss, A. A.   Aphasia in children. *Am. J. Phys. Med.,* 1954, 33, 93-99.

Strauss, A. A.   The education of the brain-injured child. *Am. J. Ment. Def.,* 1951, 56, 712-718.

Lewis, R. S.(with Strauss, A. A., & Lehtinen, L. E.)   *The other child, the brain-injured child.* New York: Grune & Stratton, 1951.

1955-1960

Strauss, A. A., & Kephart, N. C.   *Psychopathology and education of the brain-injured child.* Vol. 2. *Progress in theory and clinic.* New York: Grune & Stratton, 1955.

Strauss, A. A., & Lehtinen, L. E.   Paper presented to Conference on Brain Injury, Department of Special Education and Vocational Rehabilitation, Wayne State University, College of Education, Detroit, Michigan, May 11-12, 1956.

Strauss, A. A., & McCarus, E. N.   A linguist looks at aphasia in children. *J. Spch. Hear. Disorders,* 1958, 23, 54-58.

Lewis, R. S., Strauss, A. A., & Lehtinen, L. E.   *The other child: A book for parents and laymen.* (2nd rev. ed.) New York: Grune & Stratton, 1960.

BIBLIOGRAPHY

Cutler, M., Little, J. W., & Strauss, A. A., The effects of Benzedrine on mentally deficient children. *American Journal of Mental Deficiency* 1940, 45, 59–65.

Hallahan, D. P., & Cruickshank, W. M., *Psychoeducational foundations of learning disabilities.* Englewood Cliffs, N.J.: Prentice-Hall, 1973.

Martinson, B., & Strauss, A. A., A method of clinical evaluation of the responses to the Stanford-Binet Intelligence Test. *American Journal of Mental Deficiency,* 1941, 46, 73–83.

Sarason, S. B., *Psychological problems in mental deficiency.* New York: Harper, 1949.

Straus, E., The life and work of Karl Wilmanns. *American Journal of Psychiatry,* 1946, 102, 688–691.

Strauss, A. A., Typology in mental deficiency. *Proceedings from the American Association on Mental Deficiency* 1939, 44, 85–90.

Strauss, A. A., Neurology in mental deficiency. *American Journal of Mental Deficiency* 1941, 46, 192–194.

Strauss, A. A., Diagnosis and education of the cripple-brained, deficient child. *Journal of Exceptional Children* 1943, 9, 163–168.

Strauss, A. A., Aphasia in children. *American Journal of Physical Medicine* 1954, 33, 93–99.

Strauss, A. A., & Kephart, N. C., *Psychopathology and education of the brain-injured child.* Vol. 2. *Progress in theory and clinic.* New York: Grune & Stratton, 1955.

Strauss, A. A., & Lehtinen, L. E., *Psychopathology and education of the brain-injured child.* New York: Grune & Stratton, 1947.

Strauss, A. A., & McCarus, E. N., A linguist looks at aphasia in children. *Journal of Speech and Hearing Disorders* 1958, 23, 54–58.

Strauss, A. A., & Werner, H., Deficiency in the finger schema in relation to arithmetic disability (finger agnosia and acalculia). *The American Journal of Orthopsychiatry* 1938, 8, 719–724.

Strauss, A. A., & Werner, H., Finger agnosia in children. *American Journal of Psychiatry* 1939, 95, 1215–1225.

Strauss, A. A., & Werner, H., Qualitative analysis of the Binet test. *American Journal of Mental Deficiency* 1940, 45, 50–55.

Werner, H., & Strauss, A. A., Problems and methods of functional analysis in mentally deficient children. *The Journal of Abnormal and Social Psychology* 1939, 34, 37–62.

Witkin, H. A., Heinz Werner, 1890–1964. *Child Development* 1965, 30, 307–328.

25

VISUO-MOTOR PERCEPTION IN CHILDREN WITH CEREBRAL PALSY

(with Jane E. Dolphin)

𝒯HIS PAPER, ONE OF A SERIES being prepared by these writers on various aspects of perception among a group of cerebral palsied children, deals with visuo-motor activity in perception. It is known that one of the chief functions basic to successful performance test achievement is that of visuo-motor ability. Likewise, much of the success of children in the area of academic achievement is in marked degree dependent upon this function. Werner and Strauss,[8] using a group of exogenous mentally retarded children and a group of endogenous mentally retarded children, found that the latter attacked problems involving the construction of abstract forms on a marble board from what the authors termed a *global* and coherent approach. In contradistinction to the endogenous children, the performance of the exogenous children was characterized by incoherence, unrelated, and disconnected moves. The authors concluded that an impairment in visuo-motor skills was present insofar as the exogenous children were concerned which was sufficiently important to account in part for difficulties which these children presented in learning and in adjustment. Klapper and Werner,[3] studying three cerebral palsied children in three sets of identical twins, arrived at a somewhat similar conclusion.

METHOD

The present authors, with some modification of the Strauss and Werner materials, have investigated the visuo-motor function with two groups of chil-

Reprinted from *The Quarterly Journal of Child Behavior* 3, no. 2 (April 1951): 198–209.

dren: one, a group of thirty cerebral palsied children; the other, a group of physically normal children matched with the former on the basis of sex, chronological age, and mental age. The investigation was undertaken as a part of a larger study[1] to determine whether or not differences in perception existed between cerebral palsied children and normal children in the same manner as Strauss and Werner found them existing between non-motor handicapped exogenous mentally retarded and endogenous mentally retarded children. The thirty cerebral palsied children had a mean C.A. of 10.026 years, a mean M.A. of 9.5 years, and a mean regressed intelligence quotient[5] of 93.46; the physically normal children, a mean C.A. of 10.173 years, a mean M.A. of 9.5 years, and a mean intelligence quotient of 93.66. There were sixteen boys and fourteen girls in each group, a total of sixty children. All the cerebral palsied children had been diagnosed as such by competent medical personnel. The range of intelligence quotients was from 78 to 129 inclusive, sixteen children in each group having intelligence quotients above 90; fourteen, between 78 and 89. With respect to the group of cerebral palsied children there was no attempt this time to examine the data in terms of the sub-types of the condition. Spastic, athetoid, ataxic, tremor and rigidity types of cerebral palsy were to be found within the group. Children predominantly characterized by spasticity and athetosis accounted for the majority of the cases. All of the children had relatively little impairment of the upper extremities and all had speech which was at least intelligible. These two facts were considered in selecting the subjects because of the need to have children with some muscular control of the upper extremities during the experimental test and because verbal responses were necessary in certain parts of the test.

Two marble board tests were administered individually to each of the subjects in each group. Marble Board Test I consisted of six patterns made with dark solid colored marbles on a solid grey board as depicted in Fig. 1. In addition to the design therein illustrated, five other patterns involving interlocking squares, interlocking triangles, and other abstract geometrical figures were used. Marble Board Test II consisted of five patterns superimposed on a board which itself was a composite of many small geometrical figures as shown in Fig. 2. Test II was administered some days following Test I. The board with a pattern on it was placed on a table before the child. A second board identical to the first was placed along side of the first on which the child was instructed to "Make one like it." The child was afterwards asked to make a drawing of the design which he had structured. The examiner, on a printed facsimile of the marble boards, recorded by number and position every marble which the child placed on his board and noted

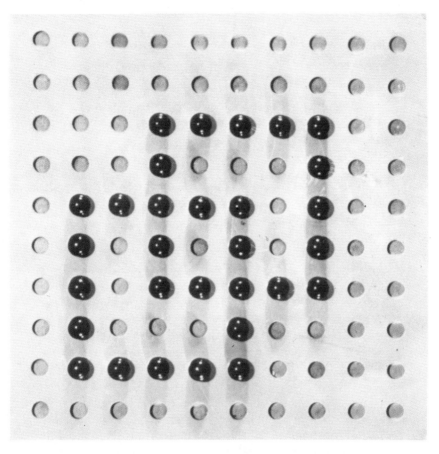

Fig. 25.1. Marbleboard used in Test I together with one of the six patterns.

every marble change or correction which was made. Thus later a careful analysis of the development of each pattern could be made.

In order to determine the type of procedure used by each subject in his reproductions, five judges were used. Each judge, using the examiner's record sheet, selected the method which best suited the type of procedure used by the subject. The judge had been given instructions regarding the characteristics of the various categories and examples of each. The judges were requested to classify, if possible, the reproductions into one of three of

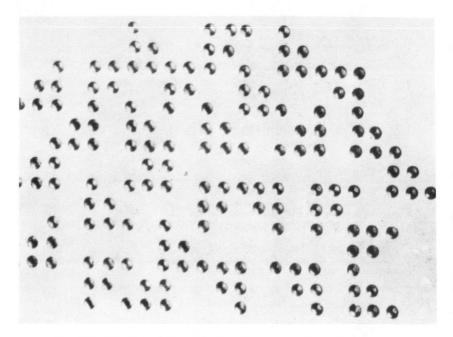

Fig. 25.2. Marbleboard used in Test II with one of the five patterns.

the major classifications which had been observed by Strauss and Werner, namely, *constructive,* in which the subject reproduced the pattern through a series of sub-forms; *global,* in which the pattern was reproduced through continuous lines which were guided by the form itself; and *incoherent,* in which the pattern was reproduced through an unsystematic procedure whose single moves were unrelated. A high degree of consistency in the ratings of the judges was obtained.

RESULTS

Marble Board Test I

Table 1 gives a comparison between the methods used by the cerebral palsy and normal groups in their reproduction of the 6 mosaic patterns of the Marble Board I test. Significant differences below the 5 percent level occurred in 4 instances. There was a statistically significant difference be-

TABLE 1

COMPARISON OF FREQUENCY SCORES OF CEREBRAL PALSY AND NORMAL GROUPS
FOR THE SIX MOSAIC PATTTERNS OF THE MARBLE BOARD I TEST

Marble Board I Test	Cerebral Palsy Group Frequency Scores						Normal Group Frequency Scores					
Pattern	I	II	III	IV	V	VI	I	II	III	IV	V	VI
Procedure (1)	(2)	(3)	(4)	(5)	(6)	(7)	(8)	(9)	(10)	(11)	(12)	(13)
Constructive	18	18	14	13	23	11	15	22	21	11	24	12
Global	6	5	4	5	3	3	14	4	4	13	3	7
Incoherent	2	3	9	5	2	6	0	0	0	0	1	2

tween the two groups in the use of the constructive method for Pattern III of the Marble Board I test. The cerebral palsy group has a frequency score of 14; the control group, 21. The chi square between the two frequencies is 5.1749 which is significant at the 2 percent level. In the use of the global method for the reconstruction of Pattern I, the cerebral palsy group has a frequency score of 6; the normal group, 14, which is significant at better than the 5 percent level. In the use of the global method for the reconstruction of Pattern IV, the cerebral palsy group has a frequency score of 5, the normal group, 13, giving a better than 2 percent level of significance. There is a significant difference in the use of the incoherent method in the reconstruction of Pattern III. The cerebral palsy group has a frequency score of 9; the normal group, 0, giving a better than 1 percent level of significance.

Table 1 also shows that in a comparison of the use of the constructive method by the groups on all other patterns no significant differences exist. The highest level of confidence in a comparison between the frequency scores of the two groups in the use of this method is at the 20 percent level.

In a comparison of the use of the global method by the cerebral palsy and normal groups on Patterns II, III, and IV, the highest level of confidence was at the 20 percent level which is not considered to be significant. Because of the low number of frequencies in the use of the global method by either of the groups on Pattern V, no chi square was attempted because confidence could not be placed in the results.

In a comparison of the use of the incoherent method, although there were no chi squares attempted except for Pattern III because of the low number of frequencies, a glance at the frequency scores indicates that this method was used more frequently by the cerebral palsy group. On the six patterns the cerebral palsy group used this method a total of 27 times as compared with the normal group who used it 3 times.

On the record blank, on which was recorded each move of the subject in reproducing a pattern, the examiner recorded each time the subject made any changes. Table 2 gives a comparison between the number of changes made by the cerebral palsy group and by the normal group. It may be seen that the replacements were made more frequently by the cerebral palsy subjects although the difference is not significant below the 10 percent. The cerebral palsy group made a total of 411 changes or replacements in the reconstruction of the 6 mosaic patterns as compared with 239 for the normal group. Only on Pattern VI did the normal group make more changes. This fact might be accounted for in the fact that this last pattern was the most abstract of the 6 mosaic patterns, and in their inability to cope with this situation in terms of reality the cerebral palsy group abandoned their efforts to complete the reproduction.

Clinical differences

A comparison of the gross results of the methods used by the cerebral palsy and normal groups in the reconstruction of patterns on Marble Board I test has produced a few statistically significant differences. Although some quantitative differences are apparent in the methods used by the two groups of subjects, certain qualitative differences are quite evident and important.

Clinical differences were noted between the cerebral palsy and normal groups in the locations of the pattern on the marble board. Three of the 30 cerebral palsy subjects placed the marbles along the side of the board in their reproduction of the pattern. Machover[4] found that adults with organic pathology were observed to reproduce figures close to the border of the table on which they were working. According to Machover, this was indicative of insecurity in a situation on the part of the subject. None of the normal group subjects did this. Five cerebral palsy children reversed the patterns 90 degrees in their reproductions. Goldstein[2] found that brain injured adults often suffered from what he termed "spacial displacement." According to Goldstein, the subject did not recognize the pattern in the position it had been placed. He could not come to terms with a meaningless pattern and so ignored the spacial relationship to bring the pattern to the concrete level within his grasp. None of the normal group did this.

Three handicapped children consistently used the holes along the edge of the board in their reproduction no matter where the pattern ap-

TABLE 2

COMPARISON OF THE NUMBER OF CHANGES MADE BY CEREBRAL PALSY
AND NORMAL GROUPS IN REPRODUCING MOSAIC PATTERNS OF MARBLE BOARD I TEST
WITH RESULTING T Scores

Mosaic Pattern	Cerebral Palsy Group	Normal Group
	Number of Changes	Number of Changes
I	86	14
II	91	82
III	79	33
IV	40	25
V	89	41
VI	26	44
Total	411	239
Mean	68.5	39.83
Standard Deviation	25.7	21.3
t score		1.9239
Percent of level of significance		10

peared on the examiner's board. Again Machover found that brain injured patients were observed to reproduce drawings on the edge of the paper on which they were working. According to Machover, this was indicative of the insecurity the patients felt in their present situation.

It will be recalled that the subject was requested to draw the design after he had reproduced it on the marble board. In the examiner's analysis of these drawings the same types of behavior that were found in the reconstruction of the pattern on the marble board were observable in the drawings. Three of the 30 cerebral palsy subjects were unable to clearly differentiate the figure from the background and so in their drawings reproduced both. Werner and Strauss[7] found this same behavior in the exogenous mentally retarded children.

Others of the cerebral palsy group resorted to counting as an aid in overcoming the interference of the background. The child counted the number of marbles in each row and placed that number in the row on his board. He not only counted in reconstructing the figure on the board but also in drawing the design. In both cases distorted figures resulted because the background still interfered with his spacial relationships.

Three children of the cerebral palsy group personalized the abstract figures which were given to them to be reproduced. On Pattern I, Case Number 5 called it a *house;* Case Number 15, a *bow;* Case Number 23, a *flag.* Goldstein observed that subjects with an organic pathology could not reproduce abstract concepts of things. According to Goldstein, the only way such a person could handle the situation was to resolve the pattern to the place where they were concrete "things" and as such the organic patient could deal with them.

Summary

From the statistical and clinical evidence it may be observed that the cerebral palsy children differ from the normal children in their method of approach to a problem. The normal group subjects were able to differentiate the figure from the ground and to use the constructive or global methods to reproduce the pattern. However, the background so interfered with the cerebral palsy group's perception of the total configuration that often an incoherent method of approach resulted.

Clinical evidence also showed a difference between the 2 groups. The cerebral palsy group (1) made more changes in the reconstruction of the patterns than the normal group although this difference is not significant, (2) relocated the patterns in their reproductions, (3) displaced the patterns spacially by turning them in their reconstruction, (4) personalized the abstract figures, and (5) used a counting procedure as a method of overcoming background interference to reconstruct the pattern.

Marble Board Test II

Although some quantitative differences which were significant were observed in the results of Test I, certain similarities in procedure were marked. Comment has been made with respect to the impact of the background on visuo-motor function. Marble Board Test II serves to draw attention to this fact further.

Table 3 gives a comparison of the method used by the cerebral palsy and normal groups in their reproduction of the 5 mosaic patterns of the Marble Board II Test. There is a significant difference between the cerebral palsy and normal groups in the use of the constructive method in the reconstruction of Patterns II, III, and V of the test. The cerebral palsy group on Pattern II has a frequency score of 17; the normal group, 27. The resulting chi square is 9.6212 which is significant at the .1 percent level. For Pattern

TABLE 3

COMPARISON OF FREQUENCY SCORES OF CEREBRAL PALSY AND NORMAL GROUPS
FOR THE FIVE MOSAIC PATTTERNS OF THE MARBLE BOARD II TEST

Marble Board II Test	Cerebral Palsy Group Frequency Scores					Normal Group Frequency Scores				
Pattern	I	II	III	IV	V	I	II	III	IV	V
Procedure										
Constructive	18	17	13	15	12	22	27	24	15	25
Global	1	1	1	3	3	2	1	0	7	1
Incoherent	3	9	8	7	7	0	0	1	0	0

III, the cerebral palsy group has a frequency score of 13; the normal group, 2, resulting in a chi square of 9.4298 which is also significant at the .1 percent level. For the reproduction of Pattern V by the constructive method the cerebral palsy group has a frequency score of 12; the normal group, 25, resulting in a chi square of 12.9268 which is significant at the .1 percent level. On Patterns I and IV there was no significant difference between the two groups. The highest level of significance in a comparison between the frequency scores of the two groups in the use of the constructive method of reproduction is the 30 percent level.

Because of the limited number of subjects who used the global method in the reproduction of the patterns, only one chi square of the difference between the frequencies was attempted since no confidence could be placed in the results. There was no significant difference between the two groups in the use of the global method. For Pattern IV, the cerebral palsy group has a frequency score of 3; the normal group, 7, resulting in a chi square of 2,6978 which is significant at the 10 percent level.

There is a significant difference between the groups in the use of the incoherent method in the reproduction of the mosaic patterns. On Pattern II, the cerebral palsy group has a frequency score of 9; the normal group, 0, resulting in a chi square of 11.2494 which is significant at the 1 percent level. On Pattern III, the cerebral palsy group has a frequency score of 8; the normal group, 1. The resulting chi square is 7.9723 which is significant at the 1 percent level. Although the expected frequencies would be too small to do a chi square for Patterns I, IV, and V with any degree of confidence, a glance at Table 3 shows that on these 3 patterns, the cerebral palsy group has a frequency score of 17 as compared with 0 for the normal group.

On the record blank on which each move of the subject was recorded in reproducing the patterns, the examiner also recorded each time the subject made any changes. Table 4 gives a comparison between the number of changes made by the cerebral palsy and the normal groups. It may be seen that these replacements were made more frequently by the cerebral palsy group. This difference is significant at the 2 percent level. The cerebral palsy group made a total of 431 changes in the reconstruction of the 5 mosaic patterns as compared with 248 for the normal group. The resulting t score is 3.1633 which is significant at the 2 percent level. On all patterns the cerebral palsy group made more replacements than the normal group. These changes might be considered as an attempt on the part of brain injured children to withstand the influence of the background which constantly interfered in the reproduction of the patterns by the children. The stimuli that was offered by the highly structured background tended to become the predominate factor in the child's perception and thus changes were necessary in his attempt to produce the pattern in terms of reality.

Clinical differences

It was apparent in the statistical analysis that differences existed in the method of approach to a problem between the two groups. The results of the Marble Board I test showed differences in the method of approach be-

TABLE 4

COMPARISON OF THE NUMBER OF CHANGES MADE BY CEREBRAL PALSY
AND NORMAL GROUPS IN REPRODUCING MOSAIC PATTERNS OF MARBLE BOARD II TEST
WITH RESULTING T Scores

Mosaic Pattern	Cerebral Palsy Group	Normal Group
	Number of Changes	Number of Changes
I	119	61
II	73	38
III	83	34
IV	90	71
V	66	44
Total	431	248
Mean	86.2	49.6
Standard Deviation	18.34	14.12
t score		3.1633
Percent of level of significance		.02

tween the cerebral palsy and normal children. Analysis of the individual records of Marble Board II test gave further evidence of differences between the two groups.

Clinical differences were noted between the two groups in the locations of the patterns on the marble board. The cerebral palsy group subjects compressed their patterns into particular locations on the marble board. Not only was positioning important but the brain injured children reduced the overall size of the pattern. Two of the 30 cerebral palsy children compressed all the patterns and replaced them in the center of the board regardless of their location on the examiner's board. Three of the 30 cerebral palsy subjects, compressed their patterns and replaced them to the left side of the board while one child compressed and replaced his to the right. In the control group none of the subjects were observed to do this.

In order to avoid the background interference which confused their approach to the problem, five of the 30 cerebral palsy children counted the number of marbles in each line and then put that number of marbles in each line and then put that number of marbles into the row on the marble board. In spite of the utilization of this crutch distorted patterns often resulted because the background continued to interfere with the subject's perception of spacial relations. This counting approach was also noted by Werner and Strauss[6] in their work with the exogenous mentally retarded children.

One child was so confused with all the background that the pattern was not followed at all except for the placement of the first 3 marbles. After that all the holes in the background were filled with marbles. In this case the background was so prominent in the field that no figure could be perceived at all by the child. A similar report is given by Werner and Strauss.

Four subjects in the cerebral palsy group broke the patterns into distinct units and built each unit in a separate section of the marble board. In this case the subject was unable to grasp the essential of the given whole and as a result had to break the whole into parts and isolate these parts in order to ultimately synthesize them. This performance is also shown by Goldstein in his work with brain injured adults.

The reader will recall that following the construction of the design, the subjects were asked to draw the designs on a piece of paper. The analysis of these drawings of both groups by the examiner showed that same differences as previously discussed here existed. The normal group children usually used the full sheet of paper that was provided to reproduce the drawing of the pattern. But the experimental group of children showed the same disturbance of placement and size of designs which were clear in the reproduction of the pattern. Two of the experimental group were unable to differentiate the figure from the background clearly and so reproduced both in their drawings. Those who followed the counting procedure in the reconstruction of a pattern on the marble board followed the same procedure in drawing the pattern on paper. The result was that there was no pattern drawn on the paper because again the background interference prevented the child from recognizing spatial relationships.

The normal pupils in reproducing the patterns tended to simplify them and leave out parts, but no major distortion was observed. This is the same result that Werner and Strauss found with the endogenous mentally retarded children.

Summary

It is evident from the statistical and clinical evidence that the background was a distracting element and constantly interfered with the construction of the mosaic patterns by the cerebral palsy children. The subjects of the control group were able to differentiate the figure from the background and used the constructive method in reproducing it. However, the highly structured background so interfered with the perception of the cerebral palsy children that they were unable to differentiate the figure from the background adequately and an incoherent method of approach resulted. The differences between the two groups in the methods used were significant at the 1 percent level. There was also a significant difference at the 2 percent level between the number of changes or displacements made by the two groups. The cerebral palsy children made a significantly greater number of changes.

Clinical evidence also showed differences between the two groups. The cerebral palsy children showed compressions and relocations of patterns; separation of the patterns into isolated units and enclosement of the patterns in the reproductions. Counting procedures were used to overcome the stimulus that the background afforded, but confused and disintegrated patterns resulted. Some of the experimental group were so distracted by the background element that the pattern could not be reproduced in any recognized form and the background was reconstructed. Errors of the control group were solely those tending toward simplification of the design.

BIBLIOGRAPHY

1. Dolphin, J. E., "A Study of Certain Aspects of the Psychopathology of Cerebral Palsy Children." Unpublished doctoral dissertation, Syracuse University, New York, 1950.

2. Goldstein, K., and Sheerer, M., "Abstract and Concrete Behavior: An Experimental Study with Special Tests," *Psychological Monographs,* 53, 1941.

3. Klapper, Z., and Werner, H., "Developmental Deviations in Brain-Injured (Cerebral-palsied) Members of Pairs of Identical Twins", *The Quar. J. Child Behavior,* 2: 3, 1950.

4. Machover, K., *Personality Projection in the Drawing of the Human Figure.* Springfield, Ill.: C. C. Thomas, 1949.

5. Rulon, P. J., Problems of Regression, *Harvard Educational Review,* XI: 1941.

6. Strauss, A. A., and Lehtinen, L., *Psychopathology and Education of the Brain-Injured Child.* New York: Grune and Stratton, 1947.

7. Werner, H., and Strauss, A. A., "Causal Factors in Low Performance", *American Journal of Mental Deficiency,* 45: 2, 1940.

8. Werner, H., and Strauss, A. A., "Types of Visuo-Motor Activity in Their Relation to Low and High Performance Ages", *Proceedings, American Association on Mental Deficiency,* 44: 1, 1939.

26

PATHOLOGY OF CONCEPT FORMATION
IN CHILDREN WITH CEREBRAL PALSY

(with Jane E. Dolphin)

*R*EPORTS OF INVESTIGATIONS by the present writers have heretofore demonstrated marked differences in performance of a group of cerebral palsy children when compared with physically normal children in visuo-motor activity,[2] in tactual motor activity,[3] and, in particular, in the discrimination of figure from background.[4] The cerebral palsy children were observed to function in respect to these psychological functions in a manner similar to the mentally retarded exogenous children without gross motor handicaps which Werner and Strauss included in their earlier important studies. As might have been expected, the cerebral palsy children included in the aforementioned reports showed in their performance and behavior many of the characteristics which are typically ascribed to adults with organic cerebral involvement, to epileptics, and to individuals with post-encephalitis. Psychological processes investigated and earlier reported have for the most part been of a highly concrete nature and in general have involved a good deal of motor function. Because of the close similarity of the cerebral palsy children to exogenous mentally retarded children studied by Strauss and Werner and their associates, it might be concluded that both groups would function similarly on tests of abstract concept formation. It was, however, felt that the cerebral palsy children should be exposed to further study in the area of concept formation in order to obviate argument to the contrary. Thus a test of concept formation similar to that devised by Strauss and Werner[7] and based on earlier studies of Cotton[1] and Halstead[6] was developed for use with the present group.

Reprinted from *American Journal of Mental Deficiency* 56 (1951): 386–92, by permission.

Cotton, using two groups of 26 children matched in sex, chronological age, and estimated mental age (estimated for cerebral palsy children only), studied cerebral palsy and normal children in sorting test situation, on a memory test, and a completion test. In general, she found that the cerebral palsy children differed from the normal group in three respects, namely, a wider range of individual differences of the type of response within a test situation, a greater tendency toward concrete types of response with less ability to shift to the more abstract forms of behavior, and a greater tendency toward stereotyped responses. The experiments of Halstead, Strauss and Werner served to elaborate more fully the findings of Cotton, although they were performed on different populations and with individuals having different mental and chronological ages. In general, these authors have found their subjects to be typified by an adherence to concrete thought processes, by bizarrity of response, by the insertion of fantasy into the thought process, by perseveration, disinhibition, and motor dissociation. Corroboration and further substantiation of certain of these conclusions is seen in the present study.

METHOD

Two groups of children were studied, one, a group of cerebral palsy children; the other, a group of physically normal children. Thirty children were included in each group, 16 boys and 14 girls. The cerebral palsy children had a mean chronological age of 10.026 years, a mean mental age of 9.5 years, and a mean regressed intelligence quotient of 93.46. The normal children had a mean chronological age of 10.173 years, a mean mental age of 9.5 years, and a mean intelligence quotient of 93.66. The range of intelligence quotients was from 78 to 129 inclusive with 16 children in each group having quotients above 90. To these 60 children a grouping test was individually administered. The test involved determining relationships between life situations as represented in pictures and a miscellaneous assortment of small objects. Two pictures were enlarged and pasted on pieces of white cardboard, and these in turn were mounted on wooden blocks. Thus they stood upright on the table in front of the child. Picture I represented individuals running from a large wave which was breaking over a boardwalk. Picture II showed a large building which was on fire during the night. One hundred two small objects were arranged in random order to the left on the top of the table. The pictures were placed facing the child at the rear of the table top. The following objects were used for the study:

glass bottle
colored cube
sunglasses
wax crayon
pink candleholder for cakes
glass stopper
cylindrical wooden piece
colored picture of a rooster
metal jar lid
electric light bulb
paint brush
cork
hairpin
metal whistle
book of matches
metal pulley
house key
blue poker chip
padlock
red poker chip
small metal key
playing card
thin round stick
red paper stock
father doll
mother doll
brother doll
sister doll
baby doll
lipstick
ping-pong ball
rubber covered wire
metal fork
metal spoon

colored picture of a ball
electric socket
pipe bowl
small round red button
paper clip
pink yarn
toy metal knife
small wax candle
picture of a key
piece of red wool cloth
card labelled "ball"
piece of cord
card labelled "pipe"
cancelled foreign postage stamp
thick round stick
metal thimble
rubber band
card labelled "hairpin"
coarse sandpaper
colored picture of a doll
colored picture of a rabbit
scissors
bracelet
black cube
round paper box lid
doll's shoe
doll dishes
toy hammer
toy saw
toy augur
toy wrench
toy screwdriver
bed
cotton

chess pawn
soap
round paper box
bus
fire chief car
police car
oil truck
red coupe
red sedan
fire engine
wire
rubber hose
swab
nails
screws
rubber grommet
yellow yarn
burned matches
earring
metal puzzle
pipe bowl
brown glass bottle
medium size stick
chair
chest of drawers
table
clock
stove
wash stand
typewriter eraser
bathtub
flashlight bulb
small metal spring
plastic bottle top

The objects were chosen to duplicate as closely as possible those in-cluded in the studies of Halstead, Strauss, and Werner. The instructions to the child were as follows:

Do you see this picture? It is a picture of these children who are running from this wave which might drown them. Now this picture shows a building on fire. Do you see the smoke and the flames coming from the house? There you see a number of objects. Put before the picture of the children running from the water those things which go with that picture. Those things which go before the building on fire put over here, and those things which you are sure do not belong to either picture put over here.

The test was finished when the child had taken all the objects from the left side of the table and had placed them in front of one of the pictures or had discarded them in a pile to the right of the scenes. After the child had completed the task, he was asked to state his reasons for the placement of each of the objects. The child's verbatim responses were recorded.

RESULTS

Table 1 gives a comparison between the number of objects which were selected by the cerebral palsy group and those of the normal group. It may be

TABLE 1

COMPARISON OF NUMBER OF OBJECTS USED BY THE CEREBRAL PALSY
AND NORMAL GROUPS WITH THE RESULTING *t* Scores for the Picture Object Test

Cerebral Palsy Group				Normal Group			
Number of Objects Used				Number of Objects Used			
Case Number (1)	Picture I (2)	Picture II (3)	Total (4)	Case Number (5)	Picture I (6)	Picture II (7)	Total (8)
1	1	5	6	31	7	12	19
2	7	35	42	32	5	22	27
3	4	62	66	33	4	19	23
4	3	28	31	34	0	7	7
5	6	10	16	35	4	5	9
6	6	4	10	36	2	7	9
7	6	19	25	37	3	1	4
8	7	20	27	38	3	7	10
9	16	32	48	39	5	35	40
10	3	5	8	40	3	4	7
11	8	23	31	41	4	4	8
12	24	34	58	42	6	5	11
13	50	51	101	43	0	4	4
14	23	40	63	44	1	2	3
15	68	62	130	45	4	36	40

298   SELECTED WRITINGS

TABLE 1 *continued*

	Cerebral Palsy Group				Normal Group		
	Number of Objects Used				Number of Objects Used		
Case Number (1)	Picture I (2)	Picture II (3)	Total (4)	Case Number (5)	Picture I (6)	Picture II (7)	Total (8)
16	1	11	12	46	7	25	32
17	5	33	38	47	5	11	16
18	4	5	9	48	0	5	5
19	5	4	9	49	4	11	15
20	6	27	33	50	3	11	14
21	0	17	17	51	6	4	10
22	9	54	63	52	5	35	40
23	6	10	16	53	5	3	8
24	4	49	53	54	4	14	18
25	4	11	15	55	1	17	18
26	15	71	86	56	4	9	13
27	4	7	11	57	7	6	13
28	4	52	56	58	3	2	5
29	0	38	38	59	1	44	45
30	9	10	19	60	15	33	48
Mean	8.26	27.633	35.9		4.03	13.33	17.36
Standard Deviation	6.571	20.260	26.260		2.851	11.50	14.12

t score between:
Columns 2 and 6   2.2741
Columns 3 and 7   3.3255
Columns 4 and 8   3.5381

Percent of level of significance of t:
Columns 2 and 6   2
Columns 3 and 7   1
Columns 4 and 8   1

seen that the cerebral palsied select more objects than the normal subjects. In the number of objects which were related to Picture I, the drowning scene, the cerebral palsy group has a mean score of 8.26 objects; the normal group, 4.03. The t score of the difference between the means is 2.2741 which is significant at the 2 percent level. In the number of objects which were selected as being related to Picture II, the fire scene, the cerebral palsy group has a mean score of 27.633; the normal group, 13.33. The t score of the difference between the means is 3.3255 which is significant at the 1 percent level. In the total number of objects selected as being related to either picture, the cerebral palsy group has a mean score of 35.9; the normal group, 17.36, resulting in a t score of 3.5381 which is significant at the 1 percent level.

Clinical difference

It was apparent from the statistical analysis that the cerebral palsy group used a larger number of objects than the normal group. From a clinical viewpoint this difference might be attributable to a forced responsiveness to stimuli and motor dissociation which Werner and Strauss[8,9] found in their studies with exogenous and endogenous mentally retarded children. Confronted with the large number of stimuli inherent in the 102 objects which have been placed before them these cerebral palsy children feeling that they must react to them to do so by choosing a larger number of objects for placement before the pictures.

However, analysis of the individual records yields even further evidences of differences between the two groups. There is little difference between the two groups in the choice of the *common objects*. Both groups chose the fire engine, fire chief car, police car, burned match, and matches for the fire scene. For the drowning scene the common choices were the 5 dolls, representing the father, mother, sister, brother, and baby. There is difference, however, in the number of *uncommon objects* selected.

In the variety of the choices a difference between the two groups appeared. Out of a choice of 102 objects the cerebral palsy group selected 79 different objects for placement before the drowning scene; the normal group, 35. For Picture II, the cerebral palsy group chose 97 different objects; the normal group, 81. In their study of the exogenous and endogenous mentally retarded children, Strauss and Werner[7] also found that the brain injured mentally retarded children selected a larger variety of objects. Again this phenomenon can be related to the responsiveness of brain injured children to extraneous stimuli. Some of the *uncommon choices* made by the cerebral palsy group for the drowning scene were the washstand, bathtub, flashlight bulb, bed, chair, scissors, and thimble. None of these objects were selected by the normal control subjects.

Many of the objects which were chosen by the cerebral palsy group were selected on the basis of their secondary characteristics. Twenty-six of the 30 cerebral palsy subjects made 124 selections based on the secondary qualities of an object. The normal group made only 10 such choices and these were made by 4 subjects. Below is a verbatim report of the reasons which were given by some of the cerebral palsy group for their choices:

> Case Number 13: "I put this (soap) before the picture (Picture I) because these waves looked like soap suds."
>
> Case Number 22: "These are platters (poker chips) to bring hot stuff into the dining room from the kitchen. I put them here because mother always had them in the kitchen so they belonged in the house before it burned."
>
> Case Number 22: "This (red paper) is an ink blotter because it is red."
>
> Case Number 24: "This (wrench) is a wrench and I put it in front of the water because it reminds me of water. We use it in the sink to close off the water."
>
> Case Number 25: "This is an ambulance (oil truck) because the back end opens."
>
> Case Number 26: "This (a burned match) is a toothpick because it has a sharp end on it."
>
> Case Number 27: "I put the red paper here because it is the color of the flames."
>
> Case Number 27: "This is a plate (poker chip) because it is round and flat."

The selection of objects for their secondary qualities was noted by Strauss and Werner as being characteristic of the brain injured mentally retarded children and by Halstead as being characteristic of the brain injured adult. From this study it also appeared to be characteristic of the cerebral palsied children.

Strauss and Werner also found that it was characteristic of the exogenous mentally retarded children to extend a picture into time and space in the selection of the objects and in the reasons given for the choice of objects. Eighteen of the cerebral palsy children extended the static picture into a three dimensional reality to include the past, present, and future in their reasons for the choice of the objects. Subject Number 12 chose a bed for the drowning scene because after the girl had been saved from the water, she could lie down on it. Sandpaper was selected by Subject Number 11 for the fire scene, because after the fire it would be needed to clean up the furniture. Dishes, silverware, and furniture were selected because they belonged in the house before the fire took place. This behavior was observed in only 5 of the control subjects.

Some of the cerebral palsy group children also dramatized the scenes by employing fantasy. Subject Number 7 said:

"The family was eating supper when the fire occurred. Father grabbed the baby and ran out. He ran back in and saved the furniture. The mother and children ran out. The ambulance was there to give first aid."

Eighteen of the cerebral palsy group subjects dramatized their selections so that a picture was created and not just a choice based on facts as presented at the time. This is related to the findings of Strauss and Werner in their experiments with brain injured children. They found that the exogenous children dramatized the scene and related the character to themselves. This might also be related to Goldstein's[5] findings and his work on abstract and concrete behavior where the brain injured adult in order to make a selection was found to need a concrete reason for it. Here the cerebral palsy children in order to make a selection must dramatize the scene so that they have a concrete basis on which to make their selection.

Rejections of choices were also noted among a significant number of injured children. Once an object was selected, the child was asked his reason for his choice. Fifteen rejections of the objects following selection and placement before the pictures were noted. Strauss and Werner noted this phenomenon in the brain injured mentally retarded children. In the normal group there were only two such rejections noted.

Three of the cerebral palsy group made their selections for the pictures by placing before the pictures those individual items which were found in the pictures themselves. Such behavior was observed by Goldstein in his discussion of abstract and concrete behavior wherein he noted that the brain injured adult was able only to enumerate the items in the picture and could not grasp the abstract which the picture involved. Goldstein points out that this was based on the inability of the subject to synthesize the whole, and such would appear to be shown to be true in the present study.

SUMMARY

The Picture Object test was presented to the cerebral palsy and normal subjects to observe the conceptual behavior of these children. This test was designed to determine differences in thinking, reasoning, and concept formations of the cerebral palsy children as compared with the normal children. It was evident that differences did exist. Table 1 shows that a significant difference exists between the two groups in the number of items chosen for placement before the pictures. The cerebral palsy group selected a significantly greater number of objects. However, there were also qualitative differences between the two groups. The cerebral palsy group (1) made more selections of objects based on secondary qualities of the objects, (2) chose a larger number of uncommon objects, (3) dramatized the pictures in their selection of objects, (4) extended the pictures into time and space, (5) frequently rejected an object after having initially selected it, and (6) in some cases were unable to organize the picture into a meaningful whole.

BIBLIOGRAPHY

1. Cotton, C. A., "A Study of the Reactions of Spastic Children to Certain Test Situations." *Journal of Genetic Psychology* 57 (1941), 27.

2. Dolphin, J. E., and Cruickshank, W. M., "Visuo-Motor Perception in Children with Cerebral Palsy." *Quarterly Journal of Child Behavior* 3 (1951):198–209.

3. Dolphin, J. E., and Cruickshank, W. M., "Tactual Motor Perception in Children with Cerebral Palsy." *Journal of Personality* 20 (1952):466–71.

4. Dolphin, J. E., and Cruickshank, W. M., "The Figure-Background Relationship in Children with Cerebral Palsy." *Journal of Clinical Psychology* 7 (July, 1951), 228–231.

5. Goldstein, K., and Sheerer, M., "Abstract and Concrete Behavior: An Experimental Study with Special Tests." *Psychological Monographs* 53 (1941), 1–151.

6. Halstead, W. C., "Preliminary Analysis of Grouping Behavior of Patients with Cerebral Injury by the Method of Equivalent and Non-Equivalent Stimuli. *American Journal of Psychiatry* 96 (1940), 1263.

7. Strauss, A. A., and Werner, H., "Disorders of Conceptual Thinking in the Brain Injured Child." *Journal of Nervous and Mental Diseases* 96 (August, 1942), 153.

8. Werner, H., and Strauss, A. A., "Causal Factors in Low Performance." *American Journal of Mental Deficiency* 45 (1940), 213.

9. Werner, H., and Strauss, A. A., "Pathology of the Figure-Background Relation in the Child." *Journal of Abnormal and Social Psychology* 36 (1941), 236.

27

THE FIGURE-BACKGROUND RELATIONSHIP IN CHILDREN WITH CEREBRAL PALSY

(with Jane E. Dolphin)

INTRODUCTION

*S*TUDIES HAVE BEEN UNDERTAKEN and reported in which attempts were made to substantiate the findings of the studies by Werner and Strauss and also to determine whether or not characteristics of the perceptual disturbances which they noted among exogenous mentally retarded children would be observed in the performance of children with cerebral palsy.[2,3] Throughout the research of Werner and Strauss, exogenous children (in contradistinction to endogenous mentally retarded children) were observed to have difficulty in determining the appropriate figure-background relationship in certain test situations to which they were exposed.[8,9] Similarly, the present writers have observed that the performance of children who have cerebral palsy is significantly impaired on visual motor and tactual motor tasks due in part to the interference of the background structure. Because the accurate perception of the figure-background relationship is so important to the learning process, further examination of this factor was undertaken.

METHOD

Since the original purpose of the study had been to corroborate the general findings of other authors by using a population of cerebral palsied children,

Reprinted from *Journal of Clinical Psychology* 7 (1951): 228–31, by permission.

close adherence to earlier methodology was maintained.[10] In the present investigation two groups of thirty children were used as subjects, sixteen boys and fourteen girls in each group. The first group were children who represented all classifications of cerebral palsy and who had a mean chronological age of 10.03 years, a mean mental age of 9.5 years, and a mean regressed intelligence quotient[6] of 93.5. The second group consisted of physically normal children whose mean chronological age was 10.17 years, mean mental age, 9.5 years, and whose mean intelligence quotient was 93.7. To these two groups of children two tests involving the differentiation of the figure-background relationship were administered. Both tests were presented in somewhat modified form to that used by the earlier investigators.

The first test, *a picture test,* consisted of a series of nine cards on which were depicted black and white line drawings of objects, including a hat, a milk bottle and a cup, a knife, a boat, a chicken, an iron, a basket, and a hand holding a stick. These pictures were embedded, as shown in Fig. 1, in clearly structured backgrounds consisting of jagged and waving lines, squares, crosses, and other abstract forms. The pictures were individually tachistoscopically exposed for one-fifth of a second twice in succession. The child was requested to "Tell me what you see." The responses of the children were recorded verbatim.

The second test, *a multiple choice test,* like the picture test, was used to test the hypothesis that disturbances in figure-background relationship exist in the cerebral palsy children. In this test a geometrical figure, modified after Strauss and Werner[7] and constructed of heavy circular dots embedded in a configuration of small dots, was presented to the child for one-half second. Immediately after the presentation the child was shown a series of three cards. One of these cards contained only the background of the original card, the second showed the original background with a different geometrical figure embedded in it, and the third showed the original figure embedded in a different background. The child was asked to choose the card which seemed to him most like the test card as follows: "Pick out the one most like the one you just saw." The responses of the subjects were again recorded verbatim.

RESULTS

The Picture Test

The responses of the two groups of children to the picture test adapt themselves to five categories: (1) the correct figure response in which the

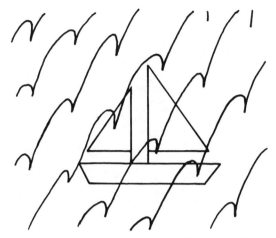

Fig. 27.1. One of the nine cards presented tachistoscopically to the subjects.

child correctly names the figure with no mention of the background, (2) the incorrect figure response in which the child recognizes and names a figure which is similar in shape to the correct one, e.g., a bowl for a cup, (3) background with correct figure in which the subject correctly names the figure and also describes the background. (4) background with vague figure in which the subject correctly describes the background but only recognizes the figure as a vague shape, such as, a circle or a square, and (5) pure background responses in which the subject describes only the background with no mention of the figure.

Table 1 compares the responses of the cerebral palsy and normal groups in the ability to differentiate figure from background. It is seen that the cerebral palsy children are inferior to the physically normal group in differentiating the figure from the background in all but one area and that these differences are significant. In the ability to distinguish the figure from the background and give only the correct figure response, there is a better than .001 percent level of significance between the two groups. The cerebral palsy group has a frequency score for the *correct figure response* of 16; the normal group, 74.

There is a significant difference between the responses of the cerebral palsy and normal groups on the *incorrect figure responses*. The chi square between the two frequencies of 8 for the cerebral palsy group and 56 for the normal group is 40.84 giving a better than .001 percent level of significance.

TABLE 1

COMPARISON OF FREQUENCY SCORES OF CEREBRAL PALSY AND NORMAL GROUPS
FOR THE PICTURE TEST

Picture Test	Cerebral Palsy Group Frequency	Normal Group Frequency	Chi	Level of
Type of Response	Scores	Scores	Squares	Significance
Correct figure	16	74	44.86	.001
Incorrect figure	8	56	40.84	.001
Background with correct figure	55	53	.0378	.90
Background with incorrect figure	97	60	12.36	.001
Background	94	27	47.8126	.001

The difference between the groups on the *background with correct figure response* is negligible. Here a 90 percent level of significance is derived from a chi square of .0378. The great similarity in the frequency of the two groups of subjects in this type of response might be expected because of the inability of the two groups to clearly define both fields and give one the preference over the other.

Other striking differences between the cerebral palsy and normal groups are in the *background with incorrect or vague figure* and *background* types of response. There is a significant difference at the .001 percent level between the responses of the cerebral palsy and normal groups on the *background with vague figure* type of response. The chi square between the two frequencies of 97 for the cerebral palsy group and 60 for the normal group is 12.36, giving a better than .001 percent level of significance between the groups. In the pure *background* type of response there is again evident a significant difference between the two groups with the chi square between the two frequencies of 94 for the cerebral palsy group and 27 for the normal group being 47.8126 and significant at better than the .001 percent level of significance.

The Multiple Choice Test

The responses that the two groups made to this test adapt themselves to three different categories: (1) the pure background response in which the subject selected the card with only the original background; (2) the original background with different geometrical figure response, and (3) the different background with original figure response.

Table 2 gives a comparison between the responses of the cerebral palsy group and those of the normal group in the ability to differentiate the figure from the background. It is seen that the cerebral palsy children are inferior to the physically normal children in differentiating figure from background although this difference is not significant except in one area. In the ability to select the original figure regardless of the background there is a better than 1 percent level of significance between the two groups, the cerebral palsy group having a frequency response of 2; the normal group, 10. There is no significant difference between the responses of the cerebral palsy and normal group in the type of response involving the selection of the original background with different figure. The chi square between the frequency scores of 18 for the cerebral palsy group and 15 for the normal group is .6058 giving a better than 50 percent level of significance.

The difference between the responses of the groups in the selection of the background only with no figure recognition is not significant. The chi square between the frequency scores of 10 for the cerebral palsy group and 5 for the normal group is 2.2219 which is significant at the 10 percent level. However, the selection of the background only type of response more frequently by the cerebral palsy group is consistent with the results of the picture test which showed a figure background disturbance in the cerebral palsy children.

TABLE 2

COMPARISON OF FREQUENCY SCORES OF CEREBRAL PALSY AND NORMAL GROUPS
FOR THE MULTIPLE CHOICE TEST

Multiple Choice Test Type of Response	Cerebral Palsy Group Frequency Scores	Normal Group Frequency Scores	Chi Square	Level of Significance
Background	10	5	2.2219	.10
Original background with different figure	18	15	.6058	.50
Different background with original figure	2	10	6.6640	.01

SUMMARY

The statistical differences in the responses of the cerebral palsy and normal groups to both the nine situations involving figure-background relationships and to the items of the multiple choice test showed that the cerebral palsy children were inferior to normal children in distinguishing the figure from the background. Werner and Strauss[10] reported such disturbances as characteristic of the perception of the exogenous mentally retarded children. Halstead,[4] Cotton,[1] and Machover,[5] in connection with research on other populations, have made somewhat similar observations. In part this difference might be due to the phenomena of forced responsiveness to extraneous stimuli which has been found characteristic of organic pathology. Further the presence of meticulosity also characteristic of individuals with cortical damage may account for the fact that when the cerebral palsy children were able to differentiate the figure they also felt compelled to include the background in their descriptions. The pathology of the figure-background relation in the cerebral palsy child has significant implications for educators and for educational methodology. Such will be discussed in detail in a later paper being prepared by the present writers.

BIBLIOGRAPHY

1. Cotton, C. A., A study of the reactions of spastic children to certain test situations. *J. genet. Psychol.,* 1941, 52, 27.

2. Dolphin, J. E. and Cruickshank, W. M., Visuo-motor perception in children with cerebral palsy. *Quarterly Journal of Child Behavior* 3 (1951):198–209.

3. Dolphin, J. E. and Cruickshank, W. M., Tactual motor perception in children with cerebral palsy. *Journal of Personality* 20 (1952):466–71.

4. Halstead, W. C., and Settlage, P. H., Grouping behavior of normal persons and of persons with lesions of the brain. *Arch. Neurol. Psychiat.,* 1943, 49, 489.

5. Machover, K., *Personality projection in the drawing of the human figure.* Springfield, Ill.: C. C. Thomas, 1949.

6. Rolon, P. J., Problems of regression. *Harvard Educ. Rev.,* 1941, 11, 213.

7. Strauss, A. A. and Lehtinen, L., *Psychopathology and education of the brain injured child.* New York: Grune & Stratton, 1947.

8. Werner, H., Rorschach method applied to two groups of mental defectives. *Amer. J. Ment. Def.,* 1945, 49, 304.

9. Werner, H. and Strauss. A. A., Causal factors in low performance. *Amer. J. Ment. Def.,* 1940, 45, 213.

10. Werner H. and Strauss, A. A., Pathology of figure-background relation in the child. *J. abn. soc. Psychol.,* 1941, 36, 236.

28

TACTUAL MOTOR PERCEPTION
OF CHILDREN WITH CEREBRAL PALSY

(with Jane E. Dolphin)

$\mathcal{T}$HE SIGNIFICANT RESEARCH of Heinz Werner and Alfred Strauss with exogenous mentally retarded children has prompted serious consideration on the part of other investigators concerning the applicability of the findings to other groups of brain-injured children. The research of the former has dealt with brain-injured children whose intelligence quotients were for the most part below eighty and who had no gross motor handicaps. The authors found important differences in perception between exogenous and endogenous mentally retarded children.[6,7,8] A logical question follows such research. Do these findings apply in equal measure to children of normal intelligence who have brain injury? The present writers were concerned to know whether or not children with gross motor handicaps who had been diagnosed as having cerebral palsy would also be typified by the psychopathology described by Werner and Strauss. Should such be the case, implications for radical educational readjustments for the cerebral palsied child would be in order in terms of what is typically provided for them at present. It has previously been pointed out that cerebral palsied children when compared to physically normal children of similar age and mental ability do demonstrate marked differences in visuo-motor activity and perception.[2] As a part of a larger study[1] further examination of the characteristics of cerebral palsied children was undertaken in an investigation of tactual motor perception.

METHOD

For the purpose of the present experiment two groups of children were used. One, a group of cerebral palsied children, had a mean CA of 10.026 years, a mean MA of 9.5 years, and a mean regressed intelligence quotient of 93.46; the other, a group of physically normal children, had a mean CA of 10.173 years, a mean MA of 9.5 years, and a mean intelligence quotient of 93.66. There were thirty children in each group; sixteen boys and fourteen girls. All the cerebral palsied children had been diagnosed as such by competent medical personnel and all were at the time of the study enrolled as pupils in schools or clinics in five centers in New York State. The cerebral palsied children were characterized as spastic, athetoid, ataxic, tremor, and rigidity types, the majority of the children falling in the former two categories. No attempt was made to analyze the present data according to specific diagnosis. The range of intelligence quotients was from 78 to 129 inclusive, sixteen children in each group having quotients above 90, the remaining fourteen between 78 and 89.

The tactual motor test was used to determine experimentally whether or not disturbances in tactual motor perception existed in cerebral palsy children. The test used was a modification of that reported by Werner and Strauss in which the child was requested to perceive tactually three figures, a square, an oval, and a triangle.

The three figures were presented on two sets of boards. On the first set the background was flat and smooth; the figure was a raised wooden solid. On the second the background was composed of rows of flat enamelled thumbtacks; the figure was formed by semispherical rubber tacks measuring the same diameter but rising above the structured background. Each board of each set was presented individually to the child and during the presentation was shielded from view by a screen. The screen had a small opening through which the child could reach. He was asked to explore the surface with his hands until he could draw what he felt was there. When the child indicated that he was through with his tactual explorations the board was removed, and he was asked to make a drawing on a sheet of paper of what he had perceived. There was no time limit imposed for the completion of the task.

RESULTS

The results of the tactual motor test adapt themselves to five descriptive categories: (1) the correct figure response in which the child draws only the fig-

SELECTED WRITINGS

ure with no background present; (2) the incorrect figure response in which the subject draws a figure which is somewhat similar to the presented one but not accurate—in which, for example, a crescent takes the place of a triangle; (3) the background with correct figure in which the subject not only draws the figure correctly but also indicates the background; (4) the background with incorrect figure response in which the subject indicates the background and draws the figure incorrectly; and (5) the background response in which the child indicates only the background.

Table 1 shows that on Part I of the tactual motor test, the part requiring the subject merely to distinguish the figure with no structured background present, there were two areas in which significant differences between the cerebral palsy and normal groups were present. In the correct-figure response the cerebral palsy group had a frequency score of 52; the normal group, 69. The resulting Chi square is 7.286, which gives a greater than 1 percent level of significance between the two groups. A 2 percent level of significance appeared between the frequency scores of the cerebral palsy and normal groups on the background-with-correct-figure response. Here a frequency score of 26 for the cerebral palsy group and 13 for the normal group resulted in a Chi square of 5.53, which is significant, as stated before, at the 2 percent level.

Table 1 also shows that on the background-with-incorrect-figure response and on the incorrect-figure response there was no significant difference above the 20 percent level between the two groups. On the background-with-incorrect-figure response, the cerebral palsy group had a frequency score of 7; the normal group, 3. The resulting Chi square is 1.694, which is significant at the 20 percent level. On the incorrect-figure response, the cerebral palsy group had a frequency score of 5; the normal group, 5. The resulting Chi square is 0.000, which is significant at the 99 percent level. There were no background responses given by either group to Part I.

TABLE 1

COMPARISON OF FREQUENCY SCORES OF CEREBRAL PALSY AND NORMAL GROUPS
FOR THE TACTUAL MOTOR TEST PART I

Type of Response	Cerebral Palsy Group Frequency Scores	Normal Group Frequency Scores
Correct figure	52	69
Incorrect figure	5	5
Background with correct figure	26	13
Background with incorrect figure	7	3

Table 2 shows that on Part II of the tactual motor test, the part requiring the subject to distinguish the figure with a highly structured background present, there are three areas in which significant differences between the cerebral palsy and normal groups were present. In the correct-figure response the cerebral palsy group had a frequency score of 15; the normal group, 41. The resulting Chi square is 16.52, which gives a greater than .1 percent level of significance between the two groups. In the correct-figure response the cerebral palsy group had a frequency score of 8; the normal group, 21. The resulting Chi square is 6.944, which gives a better than 1 percent level of significance between the two groups. In the pure background response the cerebral palsy group had a frequency score of 55; the normal group, 19. The resulting Chi square is 29.720, which gives a better than .001 percent level of significance between the two groups.

Table 2 also shows that on the background-with-correct-figure response there is no significant difference between the two groups. On this response the cerebral palsy group had a frequency score of 8; the normal group, 7. The resulting Chi square is .075, which is significant at the 80 percent level. Since the frequency scores on the background-with-incorrect-figure were so few, it was impractical to do Chi squares for them because no confidence could be placed in the results.

Clinical differences

It was apparent from the statistical analysis that the presence of a highly structured background in the tactual motor situation caused a disturbance in the tactual motor perception of the cerebral palsy children. Analy-

TABLE 2

COMPARISON OF FREQUENCY SCORES OF CEREBRAL PALSY AND NORMAL GROUPS
FOR THE TACTUAL MOTOR TEST PART II

Type of Response (1)	Cerebral Palsy Group Frequency Scores (2)	Normal Group Frequency Scores (3)
Correct figure	15	41
Incorrect figure	8	21
Background with correct figure	8	7
Background with incorrect figure	4	2
Background	55	19

sis of the performance from the individual records of the two groups gave further evidence of the nature of this difference.

On Part I of the tactual motor test the figure was a raised wooden solid on another square wooden solid. There was no structured background present which might interfere with the perception of the figure. However, 10 of the 30 cerebral palsy subjects in their drawings of the figure also included the back board in their drawings. Only 4 of the normal children did this. This phenomenon might be related to the forced responsiveness to stimuli which Werner and Strauss[8] observed in their study of the brain-injured mentally retarded children. Even though there was no prominent background present one-third of the cerebral palsy children responded to these almost negligible stimuli.

In 14 of the cerebral palsy group's background drawings the children were extremely meticulous in their presentations. The drawings of the background were exact in the presentation of the rows of tacks. In the 5 cases in the normal group where the background was drawn, a random procedure with no care given as to the neatness and straightness of the rows was used. This meticulosity has been frequently observed also in the drawings and performance of brain-injured adults. Halstead[3] noted this fact in his work with brain-injured adults; Strauss and Werner[5] noted it in their work with the brain-injured mentally retarded children; and Machover[4] also commented on this behavior in the brain-injured organism.

Meticulosity was also noted in the drawings of the figures on Part II of the tactural motor test. In this part of the test it will be remembered that the figure was made with rubber tacks which rose above the structured background of enamelled tacks. Six of the 30 cerebral palsy children drew the figure using circular dots which represented the tacks of which the figure was composed. The normal group drew straight line drawings.

SUMMARY

It was evident from the statistical and observational data that the cerebral palsy children were not as adept as the normal children in differentiating the figure from the background. Evidence also was presented that the normal children were more successful than the cerebral palsy children in distinguishing the figure freed from background interference. The difference in the responses of the two groups in differentiating figure from background was much greater when highly structured background was present than when the background interference was structurally insignificant. This finding is consistent with the other findings by these writers.[4] Two clinical differences between the two groups, (1) meticulosity, and (2) forced responsiveness to stimuli, were shown in the drawings that were made by the experimental group.

BIBLIOGRAPHY

1. Dolphin, J. E., "A Study of Certain Aspects of the Psychopathology of Children with Cerebral Palsy." Unpublished dissertation, Syracuse Univ., 1950.

2. Dolphin, J. E., and Cruickshank, W. M., "Visuo-motor perception in children with cerebral palsy." *Quarterly Journal of Child Behavior* 3 (1951):198–209.

3. Halstead, W., "Preliminary analysis of the grouping behavior of patients with cerebral injury by the method of equivalent and non-equivalent stimuli." *Amer. J. Psychiat.* 96 (1940):1263.

4. Machover, K., *Personality Projection in the Drawing of the Human Figure.* Springfield, Ill.: Thomas, 1949.

5. Strauss, A. A., and Lehtinen, L., *Psychopathology and Education of the Brain-Injured Child.* New York: Grune and Stratton, 1947.

6. Werner, H., and Strauss, A. A., "Types of Visuo-Motor Activity in Their Relation to Low and High Performance Ages." *Proc. Amer. Ass. Stud. Ment. Def.* 44 (1939):163.

7. Werner, H., and Strauss, A. A., "Causal Factors in Low Performance." *Amer. J. Ment. Def.* 45 (1940):213.

8. Werner, H., and Strauss, A. A., "Pathology of Figure-Background Relation in the Child." *J. Abnorm. Soc. Psychol.* 36 (1941):236.

29

THE EDUCATIONAL IMPLICATIONS OF PSYCHOLOGICAL STUDIES OF CEREBRAL PALSIED CHILDREN

(with Jane E. Dolphin)

*D*URING THE PAST 20 YEARS considerable psychological research has been completed dealing with groups of individuals diagnosed with different types of cerebro-cortical damage. Heinz Werner, Alfred Strauss, and their associates have extensively examined the psychopathology of exogenous mentally retarded children[12,14,16,17] Strauss and Lehtinen,[13] on the basis of such research have made specific suggestions regarding the education of children with brain injury. Halstead[8] has intensively investigated the psychological functions of adults with brain pathology. Similarly, Machover,[11] Cotton,[1] Goldstein,[7] and more recently, Dolphin and Cruickshank,[3,4,5,6] have contributed to further analysis of this problem. The latter authors have been concerned specifically with the psychological characteristics of children with various types of cerebral palsy.

The education of the child with cerebral palsy is particularly important. At the present time increasing interest is being shown toward this group of children throughout the country, and in many communities educational and treatment centers are being established. Both in the new centers which are developing and in the older and longer established centers, the education of children with cerebral palsy is considered in much the same light as is education for physically normal children. Teachers and supervisors typically employ the same technics for developing communicative arts and number concepts used with children who do not have basic neuro-physical disorders. In effect, no discrimination in educational methodology has been made between those children who have cerebral palsy and those not so handicapped. In the light of the research which has been completed, this situation places

Reprinted from *Exceptional Children* 17 (1951): 3–11, by permission.

many cerebral-palsied children at a great disadvantage. Actually, it is here being suggested that many of the methods, materials, and technics used in the education of normal children may operate to hinder the learning process in a large proportion of children with cerebral palsy. To fully understand the learning process of the child with cerebral palsy it is necessary first to examine certain of his psychological characteristics. Five major factors must be kept in mind, altho all may not operate with equal importance in the learning process as it is being considered here, that is in terms of abstract learning involved in those aspects of school instruction typically considered of an academic nature and including the three Rs. These factors include the characteristics of (a) forced responsiveness to stimuli, (b) perseveration, (c) dissociation, (d) disinhibition, and (e) disturbances of the figure-background relationship.

Children and adults with brain injuries function in a manner which can best be described as hyperactive. The basis of this behavior is the inability of the child to refrain from reacting to stimuli in the environment. Such reactions are referred to by Werner and Strauss as forced responsiveness to stimuli and Goldstein[7] likewise used this term. Dolphin and Cruickshank have observed that many children with cerebral palsy are characterized by forced responsiveness to the stimuli which are presented them in certain test situations. Cotton, altho not referring to unusual responsiveness to stimuli, does comment on the fact that the cerebral-palsied children in her study used many different approaches in a sorting test.

In the studies reported by Dolphin and Cruickshank many cerebral-palsied children were observed to be inferior in a number of basic perceptive functions when compared with physically normal children with whom they had been matched. It was noted that both on a visual[3] and on a tactual[4] basis, perception of form was impaired. The cerebral-palsied children could not duplicate forms on a marble-board which had been presented to them visually. When they were asked to draw simple geometric figures which they had felt with their hands while the figures were hidden from view, many cerebral-palsied children were not able to perform satisfactorily. They made incorrect figures and drew in the background more frequently than the figure. The inability of these cerebral-palsied children to function satisfactorily on the two tests was due to two factors: first, inclusion in the tests of many background stimuli in the form of holes in the marble-boards and tacks in the tactual form boards, and second, responsiveness of the cerebral-palsied children and their inability to withstand these background stimuli. The two factors operating simultaneously resulted either in only partial perception of the situation, or in erroneous perception of the required tasks. These two tests consisted of relatively concrete situations. On more abstract tests which were more closely related to life situations[5] the cerebral-palsied children behaved in a similar manner. This has also been observed by Strauss and Werner and others in earlier experiments involving sorting and grouping of objects. It is thus concluded that many cerebral-palsied children are characterized by forced responsiveness to stimuli and that this characteristic operates to their detriment in any situation in which the behavior required of the child calls for attention or concentration.

PERSEVERATION

A second characteristic of brain-injured individuals which has long been recognized is that of *perseveration*. The presence of this factor is immediately recognized by any clinician who has administered such tests as the Rorschach or Vigotsky to adults with organic brain pathology. As Strauss and Werner[15] observe, perseveration involves two distinct phenomena, one external in nature, the other internal. Perseveration or abnormal fixation, as discussed by Goldstein, is closely related to the forced responsiveness to stimuli upon which we have commented. The prolonged after effect of stimuli observed in the behavior of brain-injured individuals is similar to that seen in the behavior of young children who have returned to a classroom after a fire drill. The intensity of the stimulus of the fire bell and the activity connected with it make it difficult for the children to return to the quiet and concentration of activity which preceded the bell. An after effect of intense stimulation is observed. A somewhat similar effect has been observed among children and adults with cerebral injury when they react to any stimulus.

The second aspect of perseveration involves the inability of the subject to move spontaneously from one activity to another. This seems to be related to selfimposed inertia within the organism. This has been observed by many investigators such as Werner,[16] Cotton, and Dolphin,[2] particularly in relation to the present topic. In Dolphin's study cerebral-palsied children were frequently observed to continue the same behavior and approach through a series of tasks which differed in their essential elements.

DISSOCIATION AND DISINHIBITION

A third characteristic is that of *dissociation*. Dissociation, or inability to synthesize aspects of a situation into a meaningful Gestalt, has been observed among many different groups of brain-injured individuals. Research with exogenous mentally retarded boys has demonstrated this on numerous occasions. The writings of clinicians who have used the Rorschach test with persons known to have brain pathology have illustrated this tendency to such an extent that it has become a recognized clinical sign in psychological differential diagnosis. Brain-injured children and adults who are asked to participate in such tests as those involving the Kohs Block Design, the Bender-Gestalt cards, or the Goldstein-Sheerer Stick Test, are observed frequently to be unable to copy patterns with blocks, or to construct connecting abstract geometrical forms from designs provided them. Dolphin and Cruickshank observed similar behavior among many members of a group of cerebral-palsied children.[3,4] These children were frequently unable to reproduce figures involving interlocking squares or triangles, but formed them as completely separate abstracts. Psychologically, they performed the tasks required of them in a dissociated unintegrated, and incoherent manner. They were often unable to synthesize separate elements into integrated and meaningful wholes. In part, this is due to the presence of extraneous stimuli inherent in the tests themselves which the cerebral-palsied children were unable to reject because of the operation of perseverative tendencies. In part, it also stands as an independent psychological phenomenon which operates to hinder accurate perception by cerebral-palsied children.

Disinhibition of a motor variety has been observed in brain-injured individuals so frequently as to need little mention here. Werner, Strauss, Kahn and Cohn,[9] Kasinan,[10] and many others have treated this topic under a variety of headings. Aspects of disinhibition, as discussed by these authors, include exaggerated attention, hyperactivity, restlessness, inability to avoid the manipulation of objects which serve as stimuli for motor activity, and the like. Suffice it to say that cerebral-palsied children in a grouping test[5] were observed to place more than twice as many objects before their appropriate pictures than normal children. This was probaby due in large part to the operation of what Kahn and Cohn consider a characteristic of the brain-stem syndrome, i.e., motor disinhibition, which prompts the cerebral-palsied child to attend to more objects than does the normal child of the same sex, chronological age, and mental age.

Finally, the *pathology of the figure-background relationship* in the child with cerebral involvement must be seriously considered. Werner and Strauss[18] observed a profound difference between exogenous and endogenous mentally retarded boys in this connection, Dolphin and Cruickshank[6] have found identical results in two groups of children with whom they worked, one, a group of cerebral-palsied children; the other, a group of physically normal children. Werner[16] has observed that, in the administration of the Rorschach test to exogenous children, there is a frequent reversal of field in the perceptions which are produced. On tachistoscopic experiments all four of these authors have found that the inability of brain-injured children to differentiate background from figure was an important aspect of their psychopathology. Although the exogenous-endogenous groups of Werner and Strauss are not specifically comparable to the cerebral-palsied-normal groups of Dolphin and Cruickshank, the handicapped children of the latter study showed the tendency to reversal of field even more frequently than those of the former experiment. The impact of the background on the perception of cerebral-palsied children was observed in visuo-motor and tactual-motor tasks as well as in more abstract test situations.

Psychologically, the individual with brain pathology behaves quite differently from the individual with normal brain structure. In general, cerebral-palsied children have been observed to perceive in the same manner as do individuals with other forms of central nervous system injuries. (A study is currently under way to evaluate the perception of children with epilepsy.) The perceptive process of the child with cerebral palsy is now known to be characterized by (a) inability to withstand the impact of stimuli, (b) difficulty in discriminating background from foreground stimuli, (c) perseveration, (d) dissociation, and (e) motor disinhibition.

The presence of these pathological perceptive processes in the cerebral-palsied child demands a careful evaluation of the learning situation and the development of technics of teaching and methods of education which are specific to such pathology and which exploit the child's deficiencies to his own advantage. This means that many of the methods and procedures currently accepted and proven satisfactory in general education with normal children must be replaced by others which are specific to the needs of the child with cerebral palsy. Two aspects of this problem must be considered, first, the general situation in which learning takes place; that is, the school building and the classroom; and, second, the educational materials themselves.

THE CLASSROOM AND SCHOOL BUILDING

Since many children with cerebral palsy find it difficult, if not impossible, to withstand the impact of stimuli, it follows that such stimuli must be reduced to a minimum for optimum educational adjustment and academic achievement. The typical modern classroom and school building are characterized by a multiplicity of colors in rooms and halls, by bulletin boards filled with pictures, by windows so placed as to display beautiful views, by blackboards covered with seasonal projects developed by the children, and by other media through which children may be stimulated to learn. The teacher arouses the interest of the normal child in learning through the addition of stimuli and the simultaneous operation of many sensory fields.

Such a schoolroom disregards the basic perceptive processes of many cerebral-palsied children and operates to their disadvantage as they attempt to learn and adjust. The prime objective of the teacher of the cerebral-palsied child must be to reduce stimulation of a psychological nature to the point where extraneous stimuli inherent in the background of the classroom or building cease to interfere actively with the learning process. Such a situation must continue until the child has acquired basic knowledge and skills or until he has learned to attend to specific situations and to withstand the impact of his surroundings. When he has reached this stage, background stimuli may be gradually added to the classroom, care being taken never to exceed the child's threshold of tolerance. What does this mean in terms of specific classroom organizations or in terms of building construction?

If we were in a position to build a school building for cerebral-palsied children or to recondition a single classroom for their use, we would be concerned with a number of important features. The prime goal would be that of stimulus reduction. Hence, classrooms would be windowless or windows would be so placed as to prevent the children from being forced to observe out-of-doors activities. Opaque rather than transparent window glass would be appropriate. The use of glass brick to admit light would in some ways be more acceptable in a classroom for cerebral-palsied children than the use of transparent window glass, but in other ways it might prove harmful. The geometric patterns formed by the bricks in a wall space would operate as background stimuli, but would probably be less stimulating than the direct view of moving trees, clouds, airplanes, or children playing on a playground.

Walls, ceiling, floor, woodwork, and doors should probably be painted the same color to avoid the distraction which opposing colors or change in color produces. The difference in color between woodwork and wall constitutes an extraneous stimulus to many children with cerebral palsy. Ceiling lights should be as inconspicuous as possible and flush with the ceiling itself. The room should be devoid of wall brackets, border decorations, or other features which would interrupt the smoothness of the wall itself. The room need not be painted in a dull color to reduce stimuli. Any pastel color could probably be used satisfactorily. The prime factor to be considered is that the color selected to be used throughout the room on walls, ceiling, woodwork, cupboards, and the like. The presence of blackboards constitutes a problem; they are needed for instructional work. However, if left in a room in the usual position, they constitute further stimulation for the child. It is suggested that blackboards be so constructed that they may be concealed by hinged or sliding wooden shields when not needed for actual teaching. These shields should be painted the same color as the walls. The desks also should be of a similar color in order to be as inconspicuous as possible. Ten to 15 desks in a classroom of cerebral-palsied children constitute a marked stimulus factor.

Although the background stimuli may be reduced, certain children will still be distracted by the presence of other children and the teacher in the classroom. It is, of course, impossible and impractical to provide separate classrooms for each child, but it is not impossible to isolate such highly distractible children from the rest of the group for short intervals by the use of screens or the construction of temporary boothlike arrangements within the classroom. Thus, during the time when the attention of the child is demanded on number experiences, language arts, or other forms of educational activity of an individual nature, he can work by himself and his attention will not be interrupted by the movement of other children, the teacher, or by the various colors in the clothing of other persons in the schoolroom. It is possible to imagine a class functioning at certain times during the day with all the children thus isolated one from the other. Such an arrangement would be in accord with the results of accepted research.

Mental health considerations are important to the learning process of the child with cerebral palsy. If the needs of the child require his isolation from the group for numerous periods throughout the school day, he should understand the reason for such treatment. He must continue to feel that he is accepted by his teacher and his peers. One of the present authors has had occasion to make such recommendations for temporary isolation as these, and has observed that improvements take place in the achievement level and adjustment of certain children. Experiments with groups following the suggestions given here have not yet been undertaken, although they are to begin in the near future.

TEACHING MATERIALS

Though an attempt should be made to reduce the amount of distractibility for the cerebral-palsied child in classroom surroundings and in the school building, the stimulus value of specific teaching materials must be increased. Strauss and Lehtinen[13] have made a most significant contribution in this respect so that the present writers will attempt to focus their methodology only on cerebral-palsied children as a group. It is known that these children react with greater frequency and intensity to stimuli than do normal children. Experiments have shown the impact of such stimuli on the performance of the cerebral-palsied child. Can this fact not be used to help the child?

Let us consider reading, for example. The usual reader provided in the elementary schools is filled with pictures, but it has only one kind, size, and intensity of print. Theoretically the best reading book for the cerebral-palsied child would probably be one in which pictures were deleted or significantly reduced in stimulation value, and in which there would be a multiplicity of colors of print used for letters and words; variation within the words of size, shape, and type of print, and possibly variations in the positioning of words and sentences on the printed page. In using what may, at first glance, seem to be bizarre materials, the teacher is actually employing the maximum stimulation value in an activity and during a time when she wants the full attention of the child. If the cerebral-palsied child is hyper-responsive to stimuli, then it follows that he will best attend to educational materials if such materials are highly stimulating. This does not mean the addition of pictures. It means that the printed word itself and the letters which compose words and sentences must have their stimulation value increased materially. Experience with individual children has proven that once the concept of reading from left to right has been achieved through such materials, once the value of the printed letter, word, or phrase is appreciated, gradual transference to less stimulating material and ultimate adjustment to the usual reader can be made. A period of months or years may intervene before this point is reached by some cerebral-palsied children.

Penmanship paper with lines of different colors rather than the same color of line throughout may help the cerebral-palsied child to recognize that the line is important in the horizontal positioning of his written work. Strauss and Lehtinen have commented fully on a number of technics employing variations in design, color, shape, and depth which may be used in helping the child to an appreciation of number concepts. All of these technics, and others which may be developed, must employ the principle of increase in stimulation value.

One further point needs to be made in connection with the response to stimuli and with the perseveration phenomenon. With children who are psychologically as hyperactive as are cerebral-palsied children, learning and school adjustment will be advanced by frequent changes in intellectual activities. Periods requiring attention and concentration should probably be shorter than those usually considered appropriate for normal children. Activities which constitute rather radical changes one from another should be employed in succession. We have already noted that perseveration interferes with the flexibility of thought processes in the cerebral-palsied child. Frequent changes in activity not only will help to reduce distractibility, but, if there are marked differences in the nature of the succeeding activities, the impact of perseveration on the child will be somewhat reduced.

The pathology of the figure-background relationship in the child is a factor of which teachers of cerebral-palsied children must be continually aware as they consider developing educational materials. It is probably impossible to prevent reversal of field entirely. However, care in developing teaching technics can help to minimize the effect of this barrier to good learning and adjustment. Ideally, to circumvent the tendency to reversal of field, the figure should be presented to the child without any background at all. The importance of motion pictures, slides, and filmstrips in the learning process immediately becomes obvious. Such materials can be presented and discussed in a completely darkened room in which the background stimuli are almost entirely absent. The projected view of the slide or motion picture constitutes the figure to which the child is asked to attend. It is viewed without any background, except the blackness of the darkened room.

Such an approach is not possible in all aspects of the day's work. Other technics which can approximate the dark-room-and-motion-picture setting contribute greatly to achievement. Cardboards with small rectangular openings, which can be placed over a page of arithmetic problems and thus expose only one at a time, reduce the background interference contained in other problems or other printed material on the same page. A similar cardboard can be used in reading to permit only one or two lines to be exposed at a time. The teacher may prepare arithmetic lessons for the child by placing only one problem on each page or paper. This problem may be emphasized for the child by enclosing it in a square made with colored crayon. For children who are highly distractible, the use of the screen for purposes of isolation again becomes important. For such a child all the activities of other children in the room cause background stimuli. These, because of the child's distractibility, frequently can become more stimulating than the activities on the desk before him. The effect of such background factors can be reduced by setting up a screen around the child.

Motor disinhibition and the factor of dissociation are further aspects of the psychopathology of cerebral-palsied children which teachers must consider in planning teaching materials. Number concepts can be developed through the use of the abacus. The manipulation of the beads uses the child's tendency to motor activity to his own advantage. Peg boards, boards into which nails or screws can be fixed in keeping with predetermined number concepts, and line-guides the child can move during the reading lesson involve motor activity. In expending motor activity in such fruitful operations rather than in random movement, the child himself facilitates his learning and progress.

Cerebral-palsied children need practice and training in overcoming the dissociative characteristics which so frequently typify them. The inability of the child to synthesize is an important barrier to good learning. The use of increasingly difficult puzzle situations starting early in the child's training help him to synthesize and involve him in purposeful motor activity. Letters and numbers, words, and other forms of abstract material can be cut in halves or quarters and the child motivated to reconstruct the whole. Placing heavy borders around problems, around pictures, and under important reading materials often may help cerebral-palsied children to recognize the material so marked as a meaningful unity. Games which force the child to compare figures, to evaluate abstract shapes, to judge weights, or to integrate varied elements will also assist him in overcoming this inherent psychological barrier to successful achievement.

The education of the cerebral-palsied child is not a simple task. Appropriate materials are rarely found among currently available commercial items. Most of the materials will have to be made by the teacher herself to meet the needs of the individual children in her group. However, when serious thought is given to the peculiar psychology of many cerebral-palsied children and their inherent traits, it becomes obvious that the educational methodology used for the so-called normal child is, in large measure, inappropriate for this group of exceptional children.

BIBLIOGRAPHY

1. Cotton, C. B., "A Study of the Reactions of Spastic Children to Certain Test Situations," *J. of Genetic Psychology* 42 (March 1941):27.

2. Dolphin, J. E., "A Study of Certain Aspects of the Psychopathology of Children with Cerebral Palsy." Unpublished doctoral dissertation. Syracuse University, 1950.

3. Dolphin, J. E. and Cruickshank, W. M., "Visuo-Motor Perception in Children with Cerebral Palsy." *Quarterly J. of Child Behavior* 3 (1951):198–209.

4. Dolphin, J. E., and Cruickshank, W. M., "Tactual Motor Perception in Children with Cerebral Palsy," *J. of Personality* 20 (1952):466–71.

5. Dolphin, J. E. and Cruickshank, W. M., "Pathology of Concept Formation in Children with Cerebral Palsy." *Am. J. of Mental Deficiency* 56 (1951):308–12.

6. Dolphin, J. E. and Cruickshank, W. M., "Figure-Background Relationship in Children with Cerebral Palsy." *J. of Clinical Psychology* 7 (July 1951):228.

7. Goldstein, K., *The Organism.* New York: American Book Co., 1939.

8. Halstead, W. C., *Brain and Intelligence.* Chicago: University of Chicago Press, 1947.

9. Kahn, E., and Cohn, L. H., "Organic Driveness, a Brain-Stem Syndrome, and an Experience," *New England J. of Medicine* 210, no. 14 (April 1934):748.

10. Kasanin, J., "Personality Changes in Children Following Cerebral Injury." *J. of Nervous and Mental Diseases* 69 (1929): 385.

11. Machover, K., *Personality Projection in the Drawing of the Human Figure.* Springfield, Illinois: Thomas, 1949.

12. Strauss, A. A., "Ways of Thinking in Brain Crippled Deficient Children." *Am. J. of Psychiatry* 100, no. 5 (March 1944):639.

13. Strauss, A. A., and Lehtinen, L., *Psychopathology and Education of the Brain-Injured Child.* New York: Grune and Stratton, 1947.

14. Strauss, A. A., and Werner, H., "Comparative Psychology of the Brain-Injured Child and the Traumatic Brain-Injured Adult." *Am. J. of Psychiatry* 99 (1943):835.

15. Strauss, A. A., and Werner, H., "Disorders of Conceptual Thinking in the Brain-Injured Child." *J. of Nervous and Mental Diseases* 96, no. 1 (July 1942):153.

16. Werner, H., "Perceptual Behavior of Brain-Injured Mentally Defective Children: An Experimental Study by Means of the Rorschach Technique." *Genetic Psychology Monographs* 31, no. 2 (May 1945):51.

17. Werner, H., and Strauss, A. A., "Causal Factors in Low Performance." *Am. J. of Mental Deficiency* 45, no. 2 (Oct. 1940):213.

18. Werner, H., and Strauss, A. A. "Pathology of the Figure Background Relation in the Child." *J. of Abnormal and Social Psychology* 36, no. 2 (April 1941): 236.

30

THE MULTIPLY HANDICAPPED
CEREBRAL PALSIED CHILD

*S*YSTEMS OF CLASSIFICATION do not solve problems. On the other hand, a classification system frequently makes a problem clearer so that one can see the essential elements of a complicated situation and thus take steps towards its partial or complete solution. There are few conditions found in human beings which are more complicated than that of cerebral palsy. The classification system developed in this paper attempts to give a fuller understanding of an already complicated problem, the implications of certain types of handicap in the multiply handicapped cerebral palsied child.

The staggering proportions of this problem for rehabilitation and education appear when one considers the multiplicity of variables which are possible in cerebral palsied children. This writer, realizing that there are other factors such as emotional development or maldevelopment, has considered three variables in the present classification. These are (a) the presence in the cerebral palsied child of other physical defects of whatsoever kind or degree, (b) the presence in the cerebral palsied child of retarded mental development, and (c) the presence in the cerebral palsied child of psychopathological characteristics of preception which are independent of mental retardation.

Before discussing each of these three variables, it must be pointed out that cerebral palsy itself, without the presence of any of the three, has many variables which complicate therapeutic and educational programs. These often make it difficult to work with cerebral palsied children in groups. Cerebral palsy itself, whether athetoid, ataxic, spastic, or other, produces problems and necessitates variation in method and procedure of

Reprinted from *Exceptional Children* 20 (October 1953): 16–22, by permission.

both therapy and education. The extent of the lesion and the location of the lesion appear to complicate the broad adjustment and learning problems of the child. These are factors inherent in the condition of cerebral palsy as a clinical entity. The principle of individual differences in groups of cerebral palsied children is accentuated over that in normal children because of the extreme variations in the manifestations of the clinical characteristics themselves.

When secondary physical conditions are observed in a child with cerebral palsy, the problems of planning, care, and treatment are magnified. All types of physical disabilities are possible in cerebral palsied children just as they are in any child or in any group of children. That the incidence of such factors is greater in this group of children than in non-cerebral palsied children has been recognized for some time.

Perlstein[12] found that, of 212 cerebral palsied children, 46 percent had epileptic seizures. Spasticity, which indicates involvement of the cerebral hemispheres, was associated with convulsions in 60 percent of the children in contrast to athetosis which showed an incidence of seizures in 17 percent of the subjects. Blindness and impaired vision, impaired hearing, congenital defects of varying types, and physical defects due to accident, disease, or injury are to be found in many cerebral palsied children. Such conditions may be the result of the same factors which caused the cerebral palsy, or they may be the result of totally independent causative agents.

The second factor mentioned above was that of retarded mental development. This condition, as with physically normal children and with children who have other types of physical disorders, may also occur with cerebral palsy. The results of numerous studies differ insofar as the percentage of incidence of mental retardation in cerebral palsy is concerned. However, clinical observation and an increasing number of carefully developed research projects seem to point to a higher incidence of mental retardation than was formerly recognized in cerebral palsied children. It is accepted that, when lesions in the cortex of the brain or in other portions of the cranial structures are to be found, psychological problems frequently accompany neurological complications. The brain does not function as a segmented organ, but in large measure as a totality whose parts are closely interrelated. Thus, when injuries take place, they often create multiple problems. Among such problems will be that of mental retardation. Early statements by Phelps[13] indicated that approximately 70 percent of the total group of cerebral palsied children have intelligence quotients which are above 70. Studies by Heilman,[10] and by Asher[1] indicate that the percentage of mental retardation in cerebral palsied children is much higher than Phelps states. Asher, in a careful study of children with cerebral palsy, found that 72 percent of the children have intelligence quotients below 89. In a normal population such should occur in approximately 22 percent of the cases. This data has been independently corroborated in a study completed at the Children's Hospital, Buffalo, N.Y., with a group of 261 cerebral palsied children.[11] (See also a report on Bice's unpublished data which appeared in "Education of Children with Mental Retardation Accompanied by Cerebral Palsy," by M. H. Fouracre and E. A. Thiel, *A. J. of Mental Deficiency,* Jan. 1953, 57: 402). Taibl,[16] using Raven's Progressive Matrices, has reported somewhat conflicting data which are of such importance as to indicate the need for further research in this area to determine the reason for the disparity between his results using the Matrices and those of other authors employing other instruments. The close relationship between the results of studies by Heilman, Bice, Miller, and Asher must be seriously considered pending further study of Raven's tests.

Studies such as these place in bold relief a significant problem for educators, therapists, and medical personnel. The course of therapy and education is in large measure a matter of the rapidity with which the child can form insights and cooperate with professional personnel who work with him in various capacities. Learning is also dependent on the ability of the child to generalize from one situation to another and thus facilitate achievement. The ability to abstract, the ability to generalize, and the ability to profit through transfer of training — all essential to the physical improvement and to the academic achievement of cerebral palsied children — are significantly restricted as the mental capacity of the child is reduced. The lower the innate capacity of the child, the more limited are the outcomes of the therapeutic and educational program.

The third variable frequently noted in cerebral palsied children defects in perception, concerns aspects of the learning process about which we are not yet fully informed. Cotton,[3] Halstead,[9] Strauss and Werner,[15] Dolphin and Cruickshank,[4] among others, have contributed to a further understanding of the perceptive problems of the cerebral palsied child. Dolphin and Cruickshank in a series of exploratory reports involving 30 cerebral palsied children[5,6,7,8] have demonstrated that such children have impairments in visuo-motor and tactual-motor perception. Further, these authors have demonstrated that numerous cerebral palsied children in their group are handicapped in their performance through an inability to differentiate between figure and background. Finally, it has been noted that many of these children show the same phenomena of dissociation, motor disinhibition, and perseveration characteristic of other groups of individuals with organic pathology which have long been recognized in psychology as important features of the behavior of such groups. While much further information is needed in this regard, there is no question but that these pathological features of perception retard learning and psychological growth in marked degree in those children wherein such are found if the learning situation does not take cognizance of them.

In combination, these three variables produce seven distinct clinical problems. Arbitrary groupings such as these always result in oversimplification. This writer is fully cognizant that clinically "pure" cases are rare, and that such matters as the degree of impairment, level of intelligence, extent of physical disability, auditory acuity, visual acuity, and so forth will each vary between individuals and complicate any classification including that outlined below. However, the following discussion may well point up a problem in a somewhat logical fashion and thus make it possible for professional workers to attack the many unsolved issues in a rational and profitable manner. Table 1 will serve to demonstrate the combinations of difficulties which may be observed in considering the three variables which we have mentioned.

Type 1. This type simply involves the basic form of the disability, i.e., cerebral palsy of whatsoever variety with no other physical or psychological deviations.

Type 2. This group of children includes those with cerebral palsy who also show defects of perception, but in whom there is no evidence of mental retardation or other type of physical disability. Type 2 in our classification of multiply handicapped cerebral palsied children constitutes a group about which we admittedly know relatively little at the present time. The va-

TABLE 1

MAJOR VARIATIONS OF MULTIPLY HANDICAPPED CEREBRAL PALSIED CHILDREN

Type	Presence of Cerebral Palsy	Presence of Other Physical Defect	Presence of Retarded Mental Development	Presence of Perceptive Pathology
1	Yes	No	No	No
2	Yes	No	No	Yes
3	Yes	No	Yes	No
4	Yes	Yes	No	No
5	Yes	No	Yes	Yes
6	Yes	Yes	Yes	No
7	Yes	Yes	No	Yes
8	Yes	Yes	Yes	Yes

lidity of this clinical type is assured, however, in the opinion of this writer. Strauss and Werner briefly report findings which are subjective, but which were nevertheless gathered from the responses of a small group of children of normal intelligence and who demonstrated perceptive defects.[15] In the group of children studied by Dolphin and Cruickshank there were 14 children whose intelligence quotients were above 95. Within this group numerous children showed defects of perception which significantly differentiated them from their control subjects who were physically normal. Cotton similarly reports perceptive difficulties in a number of children whom she studied, some of whom were intellectually normal and without other physical handicap. The prognosis for this type of multiply handicapped child is good educationally and psychologically provided the child received his educational experiences in an environment which recognizes his basic learning problems,[4] and in the degree to which he can profit from a total program of physical reconstruction.

   Type 3. This group includes those cerebral palsied children who show no physical handicap other than the basic one and who are free of perceptive disabilities but whose intelligence is retarded significantly. Psychologically these children appear like the endogenous mentally retarded children as defined by Strauss.[14] Many of these children show the classical symptoms of primary mental retardation, indicating that mental retardation might have existed even had cerebral palsy not been present. Such children, in addition to the physical characteristics of cerebral palsy (which are assumed throughout the remaining discussion of each type), exhibit lack of ability to form insight, poor comprehension, restricted memory functions, poor judgment, faulty reasoning, and limited problem-solving ability. These factors are those, among others, which characterize all primary forms of mental retardation. In general, each of the above factors will, of course, be accentuated in direct proportion to the degree of mental impairment. Both the rate of growth and the ultimate level of achievement, physical as well as mental, will be governed primarily by the innate mental ability of the child. While no adjustments are required in the learning environment, such as are suggested in connection with Type 2, the same sort of adjustments in curriculum and teaching materials are necessary as for endogenous mentally retarded children. Prognosis — educationally, psychologically, and to a somewhat lesser degree, physically — depends directly upon the intelligence level and the adequacy of the educational program. At best, the level of achievement is significantly limited.

   Type 4. This group of cerebral palsied children includes numerous problems of great seriousness. These are children who possess secondary physical disabilities other than cerebral palsy but whose intelligence is determined to be within normal limits and who do not show characteristics of perceptive difficulties. The frequency with which visual and auditory impairments accompany cerebral palsy is well known. Epilepsy, as we have stated, is common among children with cerebral palsy. As a matter of fact, there is no physical disability which might not also occur in conjunction with cerebral palsy. The degree of visual or auditory defect may, of course, vary from mild impairments to those of a profound nature. Epilepsy may take the form of petit mal or grand mal seizures.

Children who present this variety of multiple disorder constitute one of the most difficult educational and psychological problems of any to be mentioned. Teachers, psychologists, and medical personnel may well be confused with respect to the appropriate methods of education and physical training for these children. Secondary physical defects of mild degree may not constitute a serious block to the learning or to the adjustment of cerebral palsied patients. More involved physical defects, however, may seriously retard learning. Prognosis with Type 4 children is undetermined. Outcome is based primarily on the degree of severity of the secondary handicap and on the adequacy of the educational and therapeutic programs to cope with both primary and secondary disabilities. Educational methodology and therapy requisite to the secondary defect must, of course, be available to the child in order to insure even the most moderate psychological growth and educational achievement.

Type 5. With Types 5, 6, 7, and 8 the problem of multiple handicaps becomes more complicated. Cerebral palsied children in Type 5 category are those who have no secondary physical defects, but who demonstrate both retarded mental development and psychopathological perceptive functions. This group insofar as psychological development is concerned corresponds to the mixed category in the classification of mental deficiency as described by Strauss.[14] These children will demonstrate the psychological characteristics of both the exogenous and endogenous types of retarded children. Insofar as educational and therapeutic programs are concerned, this writer feels that the perceptive problems of exogeny will demand major consideration in program planning, in learning or therapy situations, and in teaching materials. On the other hand, the professional worker will also have to keep in mind those psychological characteristics briefly mentioned in connection with Type 3 which are typical endogeny. Prognosis — educationally and psychologically — will depend directly on the level of innate intellectual ability and the extent of the cranial damage which has caused both the manifestations of cerebral palsy and those of exogeny.

Type 6. These cerebral palsied children are those who are characterized by secondary physical defects of a nature described in Type 4 who also show retarded mental development, but who do not have perceptive malfunction. It must be pointed out that to measure the intelligence of such children with accuracy is a most difficult operation since satisfactory instruments for the assessment of multiply handicapped children, and in particular those with cerebral palsy, are not yet available. Some important steps are being taken in this direction, notably the research of Blum, Burgameister, and Lorge,[2] and the encouraging reports of studies wherein the Progressive Matrices have been used.[16,17] But when cerebral palsy, secondary physical disturbances, and mental retardation are found in combination, extreme caution must be exercised and careful periodic re-assessments be made before a final decision is reached regarding the mental level of the child. Even then accuracy in establishing a mental age may be impossible. If mental retardation is a bona fide diagnosis, then the prognosis of the child will depend upon the level of mental ability. At best, the outcomes, educationally and psychologically, may be significantly restricted.

Type 7. Type 7 includes those cerebral palsied children who have secondary physical disabilities and who also demonstrate the peculiarities of perception which have been commented upon above, but who are of normal intelligence. Prognosis here is better than in Type 6 because of the better intellectual ability of the child, although it, of course, depends upon the severity of the secondary physical disabilities. Experience has shown that some cerebral palsied children will superficially demonstrate auditory and visual impairments, but that in reality these may be manifestations of the perceptive difficulties and not actual sensory disorders. Such findings and observations would warrant careful and cautious psychological, audiological, and/ or ophthalmological evaluations of cerebral palsied children to ascertain the exact etiology of the secondary physical manifestations.

Type 8. This final group of cerebral palsied children is one in whom are observed secondary physical disabilities, accurately diagnosed mental retardation, and the psychopathological perceptive characteristics. This group will constitute the most serious educational, social, and therapeutic problem. Prognosis will be exceedingly poor, and the possibility of any independent adult experiences will be significantly limited. Comments which have been made above in connection with other appropriate groups of children will, in combination, all apply in this instance.

A classification of eight distinct types of multiple handicapped cerebral palsied children has been made. This classification is based upon the type of physical and psychological problem which the child demonstrates. It is a functional classification. Research of an educational and psychological nature is necessary with each type to determine the most adequate procedures which can be used to facilitate learning, social adjustment, and physical growth and development.

BIBLIOGRAPHY

1. Asher, P. and Schonell, F. E., "A Survey of 400 Cases of Cerebral Palsy in Childhood." *Archives of Diseases of Children.* 1950. 360–369.
2. Blum, L. H., Burgameister, B. B., and Lorge, I., "Trends in Estimating the Mental Maturity of the Cerebral Palsied Child." *J. of Exceptional Children.* 1951. 17:174–178.
3. Cotton, C. B., "A Study of the Reactions of Spastic Children to Certain Test Situations." *J. of Genetic Psychology.* 1941. 58:27–44.
4. Cruickshank, W. M. and Dolphin, J. E., "The Educational Implications of Psychological Studies of Cerebral Palsied Children." *Exceptional Children.* 1951. 18:1–8.
5. Dolphin, J. E. and Cruickshank, W. M., "The Figure-Background Relationship in Children with Cerebral Palsy." *J. of Clinical Psychology.* 1951. 7:228–231.
6. Dolphin, J. E. and Cruickshank, W. M., "Pathology of Concept Formation in Children with Cerebral Palsy." *A. J. of Mental Deficiency.* 1951. 56:386–392.
7. Dolphin, J. E. and Cruickshank, W. M., "Visuo-Motor Perception in Children with Cerebral Palsy." *Q. J. of Child Behavior.* 1951. 3:198–209.
8. Dolphin, J. E. and Cruickshank, W. M., "Tactuo-Motor Perception in Children with Cerebral Palsy." *J. of Personality.* 1952. 20:466–471.
9. Halstead, W. C., "Preliminary Analysis of Grouping Behavior in Patients with Cerebral Injury by the Method of Equivalent and Non-Equivalent Stimuli." *A. J. of Psychiatry.* 1940. 96:1263.
10. Heilman, A. E., "Appraisal of Abilities of the Cerebral Palsied Child." *A. J. of Mental Deficiency.* Apr. 1949. 53:606–09.
11. Miller, E. and Rosenfield, G. B., "Psychological Evaluation of Children with Cerebral Palsy." *A. J. of Diseases of Children.* Oct. 1952. 84:504–5, also *J. of Pediatrics.* Nov. 1952. 41:613–621.
12. Perlstein, M. A., Gibbs, E. L., and Gibbs, F. A., *The Electroencephalogram in Infantile Cerebral Palsy, Epilepsy.* 1947. Williams and Wilkins, Baltimore, Md. p. 377.
13. Phelps, W. M. and Turner, T. A., *The Farthest Corner.* 1944. National Society for Crippled Children and Adults, Inc., Chicago, Ill.

14. Strauss, A. A., "Typology in Mental Deficiency." *Proceedings A. Assn on Mental Deficiency.* 1939. 44:85–90.

15. Strauss. A. A. and Werner, H., "Disorders of Conceptual Thinking in the Brain-Injured Child." *J. of Nervous and Mental Diseases.* Aug. 1942. 96:153–172.

16. Taibl, R. M. *An Investigation of Raven's "Progressive Matrices" as a Tool for the Psychological Evaluation of Cerebral Palsied Children.* Unpublished Dissertation, University of Nebraska, Lincoln, Nebr. July 1951.

17. Tracht, V. S. "Preliminary Findings on Testing the Cerebral Palsied with Raven's Progressive Matrices." *J. of Exceptional Children.* Dec. 1948. 15:77.

31

THE USE OF THE MARBLEBOARD TEST
TO MEASURE PSYCHOPATHOLOGY
IN EPILEPTICS

(*with Merville C. Shaw*)

*I*N RECENT YEARS several studies have been done which have made use of the marbleboard test developed by Werner and Strauss.[3] They developed two types of this test. The first type consisted of two boards with holes drilled partially through them. The holes were arranged in triangular groupings and were painted a different color than the rest of the board. The examiner constructed a design on his board and the subject was instructed to copy it. The second type of marbleboard test developed by these investigators also consisted of two boards with holes drilled partially through them, but the holes were arranged in ten rows of ten holes each. Instructions to the subject were essentially similar to those for the other test.

Werner and Strauss made use of the marbleboard test primarily on groups of retarded children of both the exogenous and endogenous type. They reported that they were able to distinguish three basic types of performance: (1) a global performance in which the subject tended to follow the outline of the figure in copying it, (2) an incoherent type of performance in which the individual's performance is erratic and seems to follow no particular pattern, although he may eventually get the design correctly copied, and (3) the constructive type of performance, in which subforms of the design were built to make the completed design. They felt that the performance of the exogenous group was characterized chiefly by the incoherent type of performance, while the performance of the endogenous group was characterized by a global type of performance. The third type, the constructive, was

Reprinted from *American Journal of Mental Deficiency* 60, no. 4 (April 1956): 813–17, by permission.

found only among the endogenous group, and then was not common. They indicate that it is the highest type of performance on this test.

Dolphin,[1] in a study of the psychopathology of cerebral palsy children, also made use of the marbleboard tests. She used somewhat more refined methods than Werner and Strauss, but came to essentially the same conclusions that they did. She found that her cerebral palsy group performed in essentially the same way as the exogenous mentally retarded group of Werner and Strauss.

METHOD

In the present study a group of twenty-five idiopathic epileptic children was individually matched with a group of twenty-five non-convulsive children on the basis of age, sex and intelligence. The final experimental and control groups were very closely matched. The mean mental age of the experimental group was 10 years 10 months; of the control group, 10 years 11 months. The mean chronological age of the experimental group was 14 years 2 months; of the control group, 14 years 3 months. No children were included in either group who had motor defects or uncorrectable sensory difficulties.

Only the marbleboard test consisting of two boards with ten rows of ten holes each was used. The boards and patterns used were as nearly identical with those used by Strauss and Werner as their good description would permit. The boards were the identical ones used by Dolphin in her study. The method of administration was also as near like that of previous investigators as possible. The only difference between present procedure, and that of previous investigators is that clear marbles were used in the construction of the first three patterns and blue marbles were used in the construction of the last three. The moves made by subjects were recorded on mimeographed grids identical to the pattern of the marbleboards.

The resulting records were then shuffled, and all identifying marks removed so that it was impossible to tell whether the record was that of a member of the control group or of the experimental group. The three hundred records were then submitted to a panel of five professional level judges (four Ph.D.'s in psychology, one A.B.). The judges were given detailed written instructions, including examples, and asked to classify each record as being of the global, constructive, or incoherent type.

In analyzing the results, both the reliability of judging and the extent of differences between the experimental and control groups were checked through the use of Chi square techniques.

338 SELECTED WRITINGS

RESULTS

Analysis of the reliability of judging revealed that on three of the six patterns the amount of disagreement was enough so that no reliance could be placed in results obtained from an analysis of these patterns. These results are summarized in Table 1. In an effort to determine whether or not any particular judges contributed excessively to the unreliability of judging, analysis was made to determine the degree to which each judge was consistent with every other judge. The results revealed that every judge except one shows at least one significant variation from his fellow judges. Even if we were to arbitrarily leave out the most inconsistent judge the three unreliably judged patterns would still show a significant lack of reliability.

Bearing in mind that three of the six patterns were unreliably judged, an analysis of the differences between experimental and control groups on the three different types of responses, using all six patterns, was carried out. They indicate significant differences between the two groups on the constructive and global types of response. Table 2 summarizes these findings.

The same procedure was carried out using only the three reliably judged patterns. In this case no significant differences were found between the two groups on any of the three possible types of response.

An analysis of the individual patterns was carried out on all eighteen possible comparisons, but the validity of these results is to be doubted in eleven of the eighteen cases because the expected frequencies in these cases are less than five.* Another reason for using caution in the interpretation of

TABLE 1

ANALYSIS OF THE CONSISTENCY OF JUDGES IN CATEGORIZING RESPONSES
TO THE MARBLEBOARD TEST

Pattern Number	X^2	Level of Significance	Degrees of Freedom
1	11.4406	10–20%	8
2	4.5881	20–30%	8
3	9.8867	5–10%	8
4	13.4018	1%*	8
5	13.9404	1%*	8
6	14.1712	1%*	8

*Indicates marked disagreement among judges in categorizing responses to these patterns.

*Quinn McNemar says on this point, "We have already pointed out that since the sam-

TABLE 2

ANALYSIS OF ALL SIX MARBLEBOARD PATTERNS COMBINED,
ACCORDING TO TYPE OF RESPONSE

| Type of Response | X^2 | Level of Significance | Degrees of Freedom | Frequencies | |
				Experimental Group	Control Group
Constructive	7.3993	1⅛	1	123	106
Global	11.1852	1%	1	8	29
Incoherent	.2169	50–70%	1	13	12

these results is a fact previously mentioned, namely the lack of reliability of judging on three of the six patterns. The three unreliably judged patterns are numbers four, five and six. With these cautions in mind it can be reported that in only two cases, figure four in the constructive response and figure four in the global response, was there any significant difference between the two groups. Results of the analysis of individual patterns are summarized in Tables 3, 4, and 5.

TABLE 3

RESULTS OF ANALYSIS OF EACH INDIVIDUAL MARBLEBOARD PATTERN:
CONSTRUCTIVE TYPE OF RESPONSE

| Pattern Number | X^2 | Level of Significance | Degrees of Freedom | Frequencies | |
				Experimental Group	Control Group
1	.0470	80–90%	1	19	19
2	.5148	30–50%	1	15	19
3	1.5361	20–30%	1	17	15
4	6.7833	1%	1	22	12
5	.2718	50–70%	1	24	22
6	2.6578	10–20%	1	24	19

pling distribution of Chi square is continuous, the use of Chi square where any one E is less than 5 is questionable." (*Psychological Statistics,* New York: John Wiley and Sons, Inc., 1949, 207.)

TABLE 4

RESULTS OF ANALYSIS OF EACH INDIVIDUAL MARBLEBOARD PATTERN: GLOBAL TYPE OF RESPONSE

Pattern Number	X^2	Level of Significance	Degrees of Freedom	Frequencies Experimental Group	Control Group
1*	.0957	70–80%	1	3	5
2*	.1221	70–80%	1	3	3
3*	.7227	30–50%	1	1	4
4	9.3453	1%	1	1	11
5*	.4806	30–50%	1	0	2
6*	2.4456	10–20%	1	0	4

*In all of these cases expected frequencies were less than five.

TABLE 5

RESULTS OF ANALYSIS OF EACH INDIVIDUAL MARBLEBOARD PATTERN: INCOHERENT TYPE OF RESPONSE

Pattern Number	X^2	Level of Significance	Degrees of Freedom	Frequencies Experimental Group	Control Group
1*	.0612	80–90%	1	2	1
2*	.8130	30–50%	1	5	2
3*	.0964	70–80%	1	3	5
4*	.0612	80–90%	1	2	1
5*	.0004	98–99%	1	0	1
6*	.0612	80–90%	1	1	2

*In all of these cases expected frequencies were less than five.

DISCUSSION

In spite of what appear to be essentially negative results there are two reasons why the current study is of interest. First, on three of the six marbleboard patterns the judges failed to agree on the categorization of a given pattern to such an extent that no faith can be placed in the results obtained. This disagreement was not due to one judge being off in his judgments as compared to other judges, but rather was due to the combined disagreement of most of the judges. The present authors doubt that this disagreement can be attributed either to the competence of the judges or to faulty instruction. In the present instance the nature of the material being judged appears to be the critical factor in provoking such marked disagreement. The second reason for interest in the results of this study is that on the patterns which were reliably judged there were no significant differences between the experimental and control groups. These two findings tend to disagree with the findings of other studies wherein this technique has been used.[1,3] Werner and Strauss make no mention of the use of judges, while Dolphin reports satisfactory reliability of judging, although she does not indicate that the material was randomized nor that the group to which the subjects belong was unknown to the judges. Either of these factors, failure to use judges and failure to disguise the identity of the subjects, could bias the results.

The fact that the unreliably judged patterns were all patterns which made use of blue marbles in their construction is an interesting phenomena. Prior to the determination of these results it would have been suspected that the patterns making use of clear marbles might be more unreliably judged because they would blend in more with the background. The result obtained in the current study seems to substantiate further the hypothesis previously advanced by one of the present authors[2] that it is not a confusion of figure with ground, in itself, which leads to faulty perception but may possibly be the outgrowth of disorganized thought processes resulting in the appearance of perceptual disturbances.

SUMMARY

Using the results of this study as criteria, it must be concluded that there is no difference in the visuo-motor performance of idiopathic epileptic and non-epileptic subjects, insofar as the marbleboard test is capable of measuring it, and further, that the reliability of scoring this technique is of such a degree that its usefulness for diagnostic purposes is to be questioned.

BIBLIOGRAPHY

1. Dolphin, J., "A Study of Certain Aspects of the Psychopathology of Cerebral Palsied Children." Unpublished Doctoral dissertation, Syracuse University, 1950.

2. Shaw, M., "A Study of Some Aspects of Perception and Conceptual Thinking in Idiopathic Epileptic Children." Unpublished Doctoral dissertation, Syracuse University, 1955.

3. Werner, H., and Strauss, H., "Types of Visuo-Motor Activity in Relation to High and Low Performance Ages," *Proceedings of the American Association of Mental Deficiency* 44 (1939):163–169.

32

THE RORSCHACH PERFORMANCE OF EPILEPTIC CHILDREN

(*with Merville C. Shaw*)

A NUMBER OF STUDIES involving the Rorschach performance of epileptics have been reported. In general, these studies report certain major differences between epileptic and nonepileptic patients. Rorschach himself[6] stated that epileptics show more *S* responses, color naming, *C* responses, *M* responses, and total number of responses. Piotrowski[5] compiled a list of ten signs which he feels are indicative of cortical involvement, although his study did not deal specifically with epileptic subjects. They include: color naming, response total less than 15, average time per response less than one minute, not more than one *M* response, *F* % less than 70, *P* % less than 25, perseveration, impotence, perplexity, and automatic phrases. Presence of any five of these signs in one record was felt to be indicative of the existence of brain damage.

Altable[1] reported the Rorschach performances of thirty epileptics of widely varying ages and with many different types and degrees of epilepsy. He stated that 70–75% of interpretations were based on *F,* that there was an excess of detail percepts, a scarcity of *W,* an excess of white space percepts, and excessive *D* in relation to *W*. A study by Arluck[2] on sixteen idiopathic epileptics also reported certain differences. His subjects were characterized by a *D-Dd* approach, longer reaction time, decreased number of responses and a sum of *CF* and *C* which exceeded *FC*.

Other studies, including those of Guirdham[3] and Martin,[4] have reported differences between epileptic and nonepileptic subjects on the Rorschach test, although the differences found by various authors have sometimes been in contradiction to one another.

Reprinted from *Journal of Consulting Psychology* 21, no. 5 (1957): 422–24, by permission.

METHOD

A number of factors may possibly account for the sometimes contradictory results obtained in studies of this sort: (*a*) failure to use control groups, (*b*) use of epileptic subjects of varying severity and type, and (*c*) inadequate statistical treatment of the data. The current study was designed to overcome, insofar as possible, these shortcomings. Twenty-five institutionalized idiopathic epileptic children classed as grand mal were individually matched with 25 nonepileptic children from other institutional populations on the basis of age, sex, and intelligence. Children were not included in either group if motor defects, uncorrectable sensory defects, or any history which might conceivably indicate brain damage were present.

The mean chronological age of the subjects in the control group was 14 years 3 months, and in the experimental group, 14 years 2 months. The mean IQ of control subjects in the control group was 81.52; of experimental subjects, 81.16. The 1937 revision of the Stanford-Binet was used as the measure of intelligence.

The Rorschach was then administered to all fifty children. The protocols were scored three times by the senior author. The first scoring came almost immediately after the administration of the test, the second after an interval of approximately a month, and the third after the interval of another month. On the final scoring only three changes of any kind were made. The *t* test for matched groups was used to compare the scores of the experimental and control groups on the various Rorschach scoring categories.

RESULTS

Analysis of the location of percepts by use of the *t* test indicated that there were no significant differences between the two groups on any of the three variables involved. These results are summarized in Table 1.

Analysis of the differences between the two groups with regard to determinants was carried out in those cases where the frequencies were high enough to make it a valid procedure. In a number of cases it was not possible to do so because of the low frequencies. In four cases, the means of the two groups were identical, or nearly so, and no computations were carried out. This was true in the case of *CF, M,* Sum *C,* and *FT.* In the case of the *CF* and *M* determinants, the means were the same for both groups. For the sum of *C,* the means were 1.92 for the experimental group and 2.00 for the control group. For the *FT* determinant, the mean was .80 for the experimental group and .72 for the control group.

TABLE 1

SIGNIFICANCE OF DIFFERENCES BETWEEN EPILEPTIC AND CONTROL GROUPS
IN RORSCHACH LOCATION, DETERMINANT, AND CONTENT SCORES

Score	Epileptic Means	Control Means	Difference Between Means	t	P
Location					
W	3.24	4.10	.86	1.21	n.s.
D	16.84	13.36	3.48	1.51	n.s.
Dd	2.36	1.28	1.08	1.29	n.s.
Determinant					
F	10.12	8.16	1.96	1.41	n.s.
F−	5.04	3.68	1.36	1.86	.10
FC	1.32	1.48	.16	.48	n.s.
C	.32	.16	.16	.88	n.s.
FV	.72	.32	.40	2.38	.05
FY	1.00	1.32	.32	1.09	n.s.
S	1.08	.52	.56	.85	n.s.
Content					
No. different types of content	8.04	6.00	2.04	2.05	.05
No. different types of secondary content	.92	1.20	.28	.97	n.s.
P	3.32	4.08	.76	1.79	.10
A	9.84	10.24	.40	.28	n.s.
Ad	1.48	1.00	.48	1.88	.10
H	1.88	1.96	.08	.07	n.s.
Hd	2.04	1.04	1.00	1.73	.10
Z score	27.58	28.56	.98	.22	n.s.

In the case of determinants where a plus or minus scoring is possible the signs were disregarded. It was felt that the nature of the determinant, rather than its quality, was the important factor. The procedure was also desirable from the statistical point of view, to increase the number of frequencies of some of the scorings. The determinants for which t was computed include *FV, FC, FY, C, F, F−,* and *S.* In only one case, the *FV* determinant, was there a significant difference between the two groups, at the .05 level. The results are summarized in Table 1.

Statistical tests were applied to the various types of content responses. The *t* test indicated only one difference at the .05 level on any of the

TABLE 2

THE AVERAGE RORSCHACH OF THE EPILEPTIC GROUP
COMPARED TO THE AVERAGE RORSCHACH OF THE CONTROL GROUP

Type of Response	Average Number of Responses	
	Epileptic Group	Control Group
Response Total	22	19
W	3	4
D	17	14
Dd	2	1
F	10	8
$F-$	5	4
M	1	1
C	0	0
CF	0	0
FC	1	1
Y	0	0
YF	0	0
FY	1	1
V	0	0
VF	0	0
FV	1	0
T	0	0
FT	1	1
Content	8 types	6 types
H	2	2
Hd	2	1
A	10	10
Ad	1	1
Z score	29	29
Total time	9′32″	12′35″
Time per response	1′16″	57″
Time/1R	10.61″	16.74″
Time/1 color R	12.24″	13.86″
Time/1 black R	9.79″	17.76″
Rejections	1	1
Exp/Bal	½	½
Approach	W:D:Dd	W:D:Dd
Expected Approach	4/16/2	3/14/2
Popular	3	4
Secondary content	1	1
S	1	1
Sum of C	2	2

variables tested. This was found on the number of different types of content. Differences significant at the .10 level were found on the *P, Ad,* and *Hd* variables.

A summary of the differences found between the two groups on the content responses may be found in Table 1.

The various time scores kept throughout the Rorschach test were analyzed. There were no significant differences between the two groups on the time of first response, time of first color response, or total time. The number of rejections was not significantly different in the two groups, nor was the response total of each group significantly different from the other.

It is interesting to see what the pattern of the average Rorschach of the epileptic group looks like, compared to that of the control group. The comparison is presented in Table 2. Fractions have been rounded to the nearest whole number. It is perhaps important to note that without the application of proper statistical tests, differences other than those pointed up by the statistical results would be easily inferred.

SUMMARY

The results of the present study fail to confirm most of the alleged Rorschach indicators of epilepsy. The results may possibly be accounted for in several ways. First, the present study seems to be one of the first in which a rigorous system of matching experimental subjects with control subjects has been used. In previous studies the experimental groups have, for the most part, been compared only with the so-called normal Rorschach pattern. Second, the current study made use of statistical tests of significance, rather than subjective comparisons. Finally, this study was confined to one particular diagnostic category of epilepsy of homogeneous severity, while other studies have tended to lump together all types of epileptic patients without regard to etiology. On the basis of the present study, the Rorschach does not appear to be a useful clinic tool for the differential diagnosis of idiopathic epilepsy.

REFERENCES

1. Altable, J. P., Rorschach diagnosis in a group of epileptic children. *Nerv. Child,* 1947, 6, 23–33.

2. Arluck, E. W., A study of some personality differences between epileptics and normals. *Rorschach Res. Exch.,* 1940, 4, 154–156.

3. Guirdham, A., The Rorschach test in epileptics. *J. ment. Sci.,* 1935, 81, 870–893.

4. Martin, A., Rorschach pattern of nondeteriorated epileptics. Unpublished doctor's dissertation, Univer. of Texas, 1947.

5. Piotrowski, Z., On the Rorschach method and its application in organic disturbances of the central nervous system. *Rorschach Res. Exch.,* 1936, 1, 23–39.

6. Rorschach, H., *Psychodiagnostics.* Berne, Switzerland: Hans Huber, 1942.

33

THE USE OF THE BENDER-GESTALT TEST WITH EPILEPTIC CHILDREN

(with Merville C. Shaw)

PROBLEM

*T*HE BENDER-GESTALT TEST has often been used as a means of diagnosing the existence of cortical involvement. Until the development of more objective scoring criteria by Pascal and Suttell,[2] however, the evaluation of such protocols has depended solely upon the skill of the clinician. From a research point of view it is still a question as to what types and degrees of cortical involvement are detectable through the use of this instrument. The present study is intended to give a partial answer to this question.

METHOD

A group of twenty-five institutionalized idiopathic epileptic children was matched with a group of twenty-five institutionalized non-convulsive children on the basis of age, sex and intelligence. Individual matching techniques were used, and the groups are highly similar in chronological age and in intelligence as measured by the 1937 Revision of the Binet Scale. No children were included in either group who suffered from uncorrectable sensory or motor defects. No children were included in the control group whose case histories indicated any evidence of possible brain damage.

The Bender-Gestalt Test was administered to the fifty children according to standard procedure. Immediately following the administration of

Reprinted from *Journal of Clinical Psychology* 12, 3 (April, 1956): 192–93, by permission.

the test the protocols were scored by the examiner according to the criteria set up by Pascal and Suttell. The tests were rescored after an interval of one to two months. The *t* test was then applied to the total scores of the two groups and also to the configuration score.

RESULTS

Analysis of the total scores of the Bender-Gestalt Test through use of the *t* test indicates that there is no significant difference between mean scores of the two groups dealt with in this study. This would indicate that the Bender-Gestalt Test does not differentiate between the two groups on the basis of total score. In addition to the analysis of the total score, a separate study of the configuration score was made. Results of the *t* test indicate that a difference between the two groups significant at the 2% level of confidence exists. With this result in mind, it would seem that a real difference exists between the epileptic and control subjects in the placement, size, and order of the designs on the paper. Table 1 summarizes the results of the Bender-Gestalt Test.

These results are essentially different from the results obtained on this instrument by other groups of brain damaged persons. Basing a prediction upon past research we would have expected to find significant differences between these two groups. The answer may lie in the statement by Pascal and Suttell[2] to the effect that, "Performance on the B-G test then, is not always able to suggest damage to the cortex, but when it does, it seems to indicate damage of a serious nature". We can probably assume that when they speak of damage of a serious nature, they refer more to the extent and severity of the actual lesion than to the symptoms produced by it. In idio-

TABLE 1

SUMMARY OF RESULTS OF THE BENDER-GESTALT TEST

Criterion	*t*	Level of Significance of *t*	Degrees of Freedom	Means Experimental Group	Control Group
Total Bender-Gestalt Score	1.1968	20–30%	24	68.36	55.07
Configuration Score Only	2.4095	2%	24	8.00	4.52

pathic epilepsy the damage to the cortex is not of a gross nature, even though the effects are serious, hence the Bender-Gestalt does not reveal the existence of damage of this sort.

Bender[1] has little to say about the performance of epileptics on this test. She cites one case of epilepsy, but the record was obtained during a post-epileptoid confusional state, and in the present study every attempt was made to see that patients had not suffered a convulsive attack for twenty-four hours prior to the administration of any tests, so the results are not comparable. At another point in the same reference she states, "Confusional difficulties with disorientation, with essential difficulties in spatial orientation of configuration on the background may occur with epilepsy or other conditions." No absolute comparison of the present groups on this specific criterion could be made, but the configuration scores of Pascal and Suttell seem roughly similar and present results would seem to bear out Bender's conclusion. Whether or not this is a differential diagnostic sign indicating the presence of epilepsy is as yet undetermined.

SUMMARY

The overall results of this study would seem to indicate that while the epileptic subjects experienced no more difficulty than the control subjects in drawing the figures, they did have a more difficult time in placing the figures on the paper, in spacing them, and in making them the proper size. This might suggest that the epileptic subjects can adequately perform a simple visual-motor task, but that they find it difficult to integrate the subparts in a harmonious fashion. This difficulty cannot be said to be due to the fact that the background causes confusion since the original background is only a blank piece of paper. Some authors have concluded that it is the presence of a confusing background, per se, which results in the perceptual difficulties found in brain damaged persons.[3] From the present results we might infer that it is not the confusing background which results in misperception, but an inability to organize thought processes in what might be considered an orderly fashion.

BIBLIOGRAPHY

1. Bender, L., *A Visual Motor Test and Its Clinical Use.* New York: American Orthopsychiatric Association, 1938, 96.

2. Pascal, G., and Suttell, B., *The Bender-Gestalt Test*. New York: Grune & Stratton, 1951.

3. Werner, H., and Strauss, A., Pathology of Figure Background Relation in the Child. *J. abnorm. soc. Psychol.*, 194, 36, 236.

34

EDUCATIONAL IMPLICATIONS
OF PSYCHOPATHOLOGY
IN BRAIN-INJURED CHILDREN

*N*OT ALL CHILDREN who are called brain-injured are hyperactive, but hyperactive children constitute a significant percentage of the total group of brain-injured children. Hyperactive children by reason of their concomitant learning and management problems constitute one of the most perplexing issues to teachers and administrators and indeed to emotionally normal children within the school. Teachers as a group have long been known for their willingness and ability to serve children often far beyond the call of duty. As one talks with teachers one observes that the point at which they find it difficult to incorporate a child within their purview is when that child by reason of learning behavior, which is too often not understood, fails to respond on any basis to instruction or when his physical failure *per se* daily brings him and his classmates to the brink of catastrophe. Failure by the child to respond to a teacher's instruction and his failure to adjust within the limitations established by the teacher for group behavior constitutes a challenge to the teacher by the child which pits one against another. In this paper I shall try to analyze this educational and behavioral impasse and to make certain suggestions for its amelioration. I shall examine, first, the issue of hyperactivity. Secondly, I shall consider the essential needs of hyperactive children. Thirdly, I shall examine what the educational setting and curriculum considerations must be for children with these needs.

Hyperactivity in this writer's opinion consists of two major aspects, which are interrelated and organically based. The concept of the organic nature of hyperactivity is admittedly to a large extent theoretical at our present

Reprinted from *Educational Implications of Psychopathology in Brain-Injured Children,* Graduate School of Education, Leslie College, 1967.

state of knowledge. Although very little has been done about the problem insofar as education is concerned, the brain-injured child as a clinical entity has been known to medicine, psychology and to a lesser extent to education for three or four decades now. The term 'brain-injured' here does not refer to the grossly involved child with cerebral palsy, although many of these children do come within its scope, or to children with epilepsy, although these are all children with neurological problems and many of them fall into this group. The term refers to brain-injured children who by reason of prenatal, perinatal, or postnatal etiology show an exceedingly interesting syndrome of psychological characteristics. As a result they often fail to respond to learning situations with appropriate achievement. They fail to adjust as a child to a child's society within the expectancies of the adult society.

In speaking of the brain-injured child we enter a semantic jungle out of which the profession has yet to find its way. In the current literature one can quickly develop a list of more than forty terms all used frequently and all referring to the same child. Little wonder that parents are confused; the professions are more than confused. These children may be spoken of as dyslexic, or as children with language disorders, with cognitive defects, with maturational lag, with minimal brain dysfunction, with neurophysiological immaturity, or with chronic brain dysfunction. They may be called hyperkinetic children or children with specific or special learning disorders. I call them brain-injured children which is what in reality they probably are, although we do not have the diagnostic instrumentation sufficiently sensitive or sophisticated as yet to make this diagnosis definitive every time. When that day arrives we shall undoubtedly see that most if not all hyperactive children have a specific neurological basis to their behavior.

We do, however, know enough about the learning characteristics and behavior characteristics of brain-injured children to be able to make educational generalizations about them which are accurate and helpful in planning for their growth and adjustment. We also know that there are many children without a specific diagnosis of neurological disorder who demonstrate the same characteristics of learning and adjustment as do those children on whom definitive diagnosis can be obtained. These are often emotionally disturbed hyperactive children. To exclude these children from our consideration simply because they have been born two or three decades earlier than professional maturity would like, is absurd.

As was stated earlier, hyperactivity has two interrelated aspects. The first of these is sensory hyperactivity; the second, motor hyperactivity. Either of these aspects, if they are present in a child, brings the child into direct conflict with the educational program. In the case of sensory hyperactivity school achievement is directly impaired; in the case of motor hyperactivity, school achievement is also involved but in addition adjustment in the classroom and in the home becomes most difficult.

SENSORY HYPERACTIVITY

One of the chief characteristics of this is *distractibility*. As a result of what is assumed to be a lack of cortical control, the child is unable to attend to a given stimulus or group of stimuli for a sufficient period of time to be able to make an appropriate intellectual reaction. Normal people adapt negatively to the inessential, they can ignore irrelevant stimuli and attent to the task in hand. Hyperactive children, however, are unable to react negatively to extraneous stimuli in their environment. They tend to react to the inessential. They seem almost to have a compulsion to react to every stimulus within their sensory field. The problem involves all the sensory systems: auditory, tactual, thermal, and to a lesser extent taste and smell. The hyperactive child is unable to attend to the primary stimulus in his sensory field because of the multitude of inessential stimuli in his environment to which he is forced to attend. Any color, noise, or movement, irrespective of its appropriateness to the task at hand, may distract his attention and cause him to respond. In thus responding he fails to react as the adult would wish him to react to a specific learning assignment.

Sensory hyperactivity is manifest in a number of serious ways. As a result of the child's constant need to react, he characteristically has an exceedingly short attention span. I have many times seen children whose attention span was at best no more than a minute or two. When a child has a two-minute attention span under optimal conditions, what is the teacher-pupil problem when the reading lesson is planned for a twenty-minute period? The last eighteen minutes becomes a disciplinary hassle instead of an instructional experience.

The difficulties are increased by the nature of the reading material. A typical page out of a child's reading book may contain, say, 150 words the average length of which would be approximately five letters. Hence there may be on the page a minimum of 750 letters. Each letter and word has a space between it and the next. Thus there is in addition a minimum of 750 spaces. Each letter forms an angle in relationship to another letter or to several letters. Hence, there is an unlimited number of possible angles and relationships of a visual nature. There may be a picture on the page which includes numerous details, colors, and relationships. Thus on this single page there are hundreds of stimuli. The words are stimuli; the letters are stimuli, the spaces and angles and colors are stimuli. In this highly stimulating situation, which constitutes no problem for the normal child because of his ability to adapt negatively, a hyperactive child is asked by his teacher to 'Begin reading today on the first word of the first line of the second paragraph.' That first word is the *figure*. Insofar as the child can attend and not be distracted he may focus on the first word. If he is distracted by the inessential stimuli on the printed page, stimuli which for normal children form the *background,* he will be unable to attend to the essential word, the figure, long enough to make an appropriate response. Reading specialists and psychologists tell us that these children are characterized by a figure-ground reversal problem—a *figure-background pathology*—which is indeed true. More basic than this, however, is the inability of the child to refrain from reacting to inessential stimuli. This results in a figure-ground problem. The end result of this situation is the child's inability to respond orally in spite of the fact that he may know the meaning of most of the words on the printed page.

Another child is asked by his teacher or by a psychologist to assemble a block design. There may be from six to twelve blocks—six to twelve stimuli. Often these are of multicolored materials. Because of the multiplicity of stimuli, the child may not be able to conceptualize the design he is asked to copy. The child's inability to assemble the blocks appropriately is called *dissociation,* but in reality this psychological problem is another manifestation of sensory hyperactivity. Dissociation, the inability to conceptualize things as a whole, is a serious deterrent to good learning.

Similar problems arise in teaching arithmetic. Let us assume that the child is given a piece of paper containing twelve three-digit problems arranged in three rows of four problems each. On the paper are 36 numerals, 12 addition symbols, and 12 straight lines under the 12 problems. Angles, spaces and other visual factors constitute additional stimuli. The child is likely to obtain the correct answer to problem Number One, because its location on the page brings it into relationship with two edges of the paper and a corner. This provides sufficient structure for the child to allow him to attend. Furthermore, on two sides of the arithmetic problem there is space only and no distracting stimuli. From that point on, however, as he moves to problem two, three, or four, the chances are that he will solve few problems correctly. Extraneous visual stimuli surrounding the problems on the paper, coupled by a third factor, the child's insecurity *in space*, constitute a major series of hurdles to successful achievement.

Often a child's attachment to a single stimulus and the pervading influence of this stimulus will also cause failure to learn. We speak of this as *perseveration.* The prolonged aftereffect of a stimulus will interfere with the reception and coding of new stimuli to the end that learning fails to take place.

I have used examples of sensory hyperactivity which are essentially visual in nature, but the same problems may occur in other sensory modalities. Figure-background problems appear as the child attempts to sort out auditory stimuli. Localization and identification of gustatory stimuli is similarly affected. Auditory perseveration and dissociation are not unusual in hyperactive or brain-injured children. Sensory hyperactivity, then, is an essential element in the failure of the child to respond appropriately to learning situations. Furthermore, this situation quickly becomes compounded, for in the failure of the child to respond appropriately on a sensory basis, ego concepts are immediately involved. The ego concept of the teacher is also involved, for the child does not respond to her experience or wisdom in the same way as do other children. This is a threat to the adult. The child's inability to have the reward of a 'success experience' causes frustration and a lessening of his tolerance level to additional frustrations. There shortly appears a significant emotional overlay to what originally was a neurophysiological problem. As a matter of fact, the term 'hyperactive child' is often used synonymously with the term 'emotionally disturbed child'. The latter issue clouds the former completely. This clouding of what in reality is the basic problem results, I believe, in much mismanagement of these children from an educational and psychological point of view.

MOTOR HYPERACTIVITY

This is more accurately called *motor disinhibition,* and is the inability of the child to refrain from reacting to a stimulus which produces a motor response. Anything which can be pulled, turned, pushed, twisted, bent, torn, wiggled, scratched, or otherwise manipulated will be so handled. These are the children who cannot sit still, who fall out of their chairs, who in a line are always pushing or pulling others around them. (Some similar corporal behaviour is seen in the normal adjustment of the preadolescent, and careful discrimination must be made at that age between what is normative behavior and what is pathological.) These hyperactive children over-react motorically to certain stimuli, for example, the ringing of a fire drill bell. They seem to 'fall apart' behavioristically in the face of any tension-producing social situation. A birthday party can result in tragedy for these children — the tragedy of never being invited again. The diffuse and uncontrolled *space* of the playground, the auditorium, the school cafeteria, or the school hallways constitutes a stimulus the nature of which the child and often the adult fails to understand, but which violates the child's being and may preclude any possibility of his appropriate adjustment. Tensions – which are physical – which result from these experiences and situations in turn produce motor reactions in the hyperactive child. The combination of motor disinhibition and sensory distractibility constitute a barrier to good learning which is often unprecedented in the experience of the individual teacher and more so in the experience of the child's parents.

The degree of psychopathology in the child's behavior can be measured and described by careful psychological assessment. It is the responsibility of the psychologists to ascertain the essential elements of the child's intellectual response pattern. Without this psychological blueprint, the educator cannot conveniently, if at all, develop an educational program.

THE NEEDS OF THE CHILD

The basic need of hyperactive children is for success – success in something in which adults and adult society genuinely believe. All children have this need, but most children have had their share of success. They have found ways of appealing to the ego needs of their parents and other adults. They smile cutely. They parrot words and then are reported to 'talk'. The whole family, including all the in-laws, are formally notified when the child takes his first step. Children have success experiences, and through them parents have success experiences. This prompts parents to set more situations in which the child can prove himself, and when he does the basis for strong parent-child relationships is present. The hyperactive child does not have this built-in insurance. More and more his behavior propels him outside the circle of acceptance in family, in neighborhood, in school, and in the community generally.

Hyperactive children have had a remarkable experience with failure, but a poor experience with success. They have found few bases on which they are able to satisfy adults or to meet the standards of adjustment and behavior expected of them by adults.

Because of neurological disturbance, the child may be unable to perform appropriately fine motor movements involved in sucking. Nursing then can become a failure experience from the first instance. The failure to suck or swallow efficiently is extended to delayed sitting, to delayed walking, talking, running, learning to balance, and to most other skills which are learned by normal children in the daily activities of childhood without extensive formal teaching. The child soon comes to conceptualize himself as 'I am one who cannot' instead of the normal child's approach to himself of 'I am one who can.'

Since reading and writing also involve fine motor movements, these skills, like sucking from a bottle or swallowing, are also defective. A child who dissociates will have extreme difficulty in learning manuscript writing, yet how infrequently are these children taught cursive writing when they are beginning to write! This is a time when success is uniquely important, but the child's first attempts at writing are met with failure because the method of manuscript writing itself produces failure in that it inherently involves those very concepts of association and dissociation which in the hyperactive child are characterized by pathology. The early success experience he needs is supplanted by another failure experience, of which he has already had more than his share.

In practically every psychologist's file there are many records of children which contain drawings of persons. These drawings are oftentimes fragmentary and incoherent translations of what the child conceptualized the human form to be. When one's own fingers fail to perform satisfactorily, one cannot for long claim ownership of the offending digits. When fingers fail to tie shoes, to button boots, to 'zip' zippers, to pick up a glass, or to do the many other things without accidents which are required of them each day, they tend to become divorced psychologically from the body of which they are an inherent part. When legs won't kick a ball, or arms appropriately swing a bat, or when arms together cannot manipulate a knife and fork to the end that appropriate eating behavior is experienced, then faulty notions develop of what the human form really is. Negative self-concepts and poor concepts of body image are almost universally found in hyperactive children.

EDUCATIONAL IMPLICATIONS

The implications for education of what has been said can only briefly be discussed, for in detail the issue is a complicated one. There are some essentials, however, which must be kept in mind at all times in dealing with the hyperactive child, whether in a teacher-child relationship or parent-child relationship.

First, it is necessary for the adult to find a level of achievement at which the child has already experienced success on which to base whatever educational program is possible. Secondly, the educational program for a given child must directly reflect the psychopathology which is inherent in the child. Thirdly, the educational program must always be presented to the child in a learning situation and within a time span which permits conditioning to take place. Fourthly, the teaching should be carried out with the child within arm's reach of the teacher. Finally, the program for the child must be structured environmentally and methodologically. Let us look at these five elements in turn.

1. *It is necessary for the adult to find a level of achievement at which the child has already experienced success.* One of the great misunderstandings which educators perpetuate is that of remedial education. Remediation implies that something has taken place, something has been learned, which if modified in some form, can bring better achievement to the individual. In the case of the hyperactive child there is little to remedy. In contrast, new learning is required, initial concepts must be established. The education of hyperactive children is not a matter for the remedial reading teacher. It is something else entirely.

It is essential then, for the teacher to assess the skills of the child in all aspects of his learning and to find a level of competence so primitive that success is possible, not on a chance basis, but continuously. On this primitive level other learnings are then based. Since, unfortunately, most of these children are 'discovered' for the first time officially about the time they are in the third or fourth grade, this may mean that the teacher will have to retreat with the child to pre-academic levels.

2. *The educational program must directly reflect the psychopathology inherent in the child.* There is little value in providing a child who is characterized by figure-background pathology with the typical reading lesson which was described earlier. If figure-ground relationship is a problem reading material must be provided which reduce figure-ground problems to a minimum. Instead of reading a book with many words on a single page, the reading material for this child may utilize many pages of paper with only one word at a time per page. Now there are no background stimuli for the child to confuse with the foreground figure. The figure alone is presented on the page. Twelve arithmetic problems would never be presented to the child at one time. Instead one problem per page will be given him to work, and one page at a time may be in his hand.

The child we speak about is probably dissociating. He cannot see the whole because of the individual parts, which have great attraction for him. This child must be taught to write using cursive methods from the beginning. He will not be taught manuscript writing at all. One method minimizes his pathology; the other accentuates it. Some children who dissociate may need additional help; when in arithmetic the teacher places one problem alone on a piece of paper, he may then enclose the single problem within heavy black lines in order that the child conceptualizes more easily the two or three digits to be added, the addition sign, and the line under it all as all being part of the same concept.

The child's hyper-responsiveness to stimuli may also sometimes be exploited by the teacher to the child's advantage. However, in an appropriate learning environment, it is possible to increase the stimulus value of the thing the teacher desires the child to see. The child may then be attracted to a given visual presentation long enough for positive conditioning to take place. For example, in handwriting, instead of using a white paper with faint blue lines, the teacher may use a brilliant colored paper with many different colored lines. This increases the stimulus value of the line, the element he is anxious for the child to perceive. The brilliant colored paper delineates the visual field within which the child is to write. This is using the disability to the child's advantage.

A final example of this approach pertains to the problem of perseveration. Normally a teacher's instructional plan will be to accentuate similarities. Spelling may grow out of reading. Reading may grow out of social studies. With the hyperactive child who is perseverating, this is not the most appropriate procedure. Dissimilarities are stressed in order that one element not be perseverated into the next and thus confuse the child's perception of the second fact by the first. For example, reading might be followed by parquetry activities. These might be followed by motor training. Motor training might be followed by spelling. No two experiences are sufficiently similar to permit perseveration to be a significant issue.

3. *The education program must always be presented in a situation and within a time span which permits conditioning to take place.* If a child is hyperactive to extraneous stimuli, such stimuli must be reduced in the learning environment if an optimal learning situation is to be created for him. The best classroom in an elementary school, bright and gay and filled with things which are intended to motivate children, is the worst classroom possible for the hyperactive child. There are too many stimuli which he cannot avoid. These become, for him, deterrents to his education.

The classroom for hyperactive children should be as free of distractions as possible. In an ideal classroom, in my opinion, walls, furniture, woodwork and floor covering would all be the same color. Windows would have opaque glass to reduce stimuli outside the building. The ceiling would be sound treated, and the floor would have wall-to-wall carpeting. Shelves would be behind wooden doors. Every effort would be made to have the environment surrounding the learner as stimulus-free as possible.

Another aspect of stimuli reduction pertains to the matter of space. Hyperactive children experience increased tension in space over which they feel no psychological control. As space increases so stimuli increase; the converse is also true. Thus, the classroom for hyperactive children will be smaller than the traditional one and it has been found helpful to provide within the classroom small cubicles for each child. Within the small area the child finds a spatial arrangement of which he can feel that he is the master. If necessary he can actually reach out and touch the three walls of his cubicle, as one child told the writer, 'to remind myself where I am'. When the child is oriented in space, he can begin to organize himself in relation to his environment. Although the environmental area is small, his feeling of satisfaction within it serves as a springboard from which he can begin to have other types of success experience with abstract as well as concrete achievements.

4. *The teaching should be carried out with the child within arm's reach of the teacher.* Although this is not always possible, it is essential that as close a personal relationship as possible be established between the adult and the child. The hyperactive child, because of his tendency to dissociate and to reverse field, often has a very confused understanding of what the adult is like. His perception of the adult may be as inappropriate as are his perception of numerals, letters, or other symbols. The child is insecure in his relationship to his environment and to the things in it. If the teacher can always carry on the instruction with his hand on the child's arm or shoulder, the child experiences a definite and physical structure between himself and the adult.

5. *Finally the program for the child must be structured environmentally and methodologically.* We have already mentioned the environmental structure through the utilization of stimuli reduction and the cubicle. Similarly, everything which goes on within the classroom must be structured. This is not a place for permissiveness, for the child cannot make adequate choices within a permissive framework if he has never had a success experience when choice has been possible. In seeking to find the primitive level on which to start learning experiences, as mentioned earlier, the teacher is in effect seeking a base upon which he can provide an adequate conditioning experience. As success responses are developed, as security in learning begins to be experienced, as confidence builds up, then choice can be provided. Whenever choice is provided, the child must also always have an escape valve available to him, a feeling of permission to retreat again to a level of performance on which he knows he can succeed. When this is not understood the child may hesitate a long while before he tries something new, and to remain too long on a behavioural plateau is itself not conducive to learning.

Structure permeates the entire teaching concept. We speak of relationship structure between the teacher and the child. We speak of program structure in the conceptualisation of the school day and program. We have seen the significance of environmental structure. We help the teacher to devise structured teaching materials in keeping with the psychopathological needs of the child. For a child whose whole life to date has been one of lack of structure and failure, the externally imposed structure provides him with a concrete fabric on which to rest his life. As Rappaport so accurately states in another situation, the environment and all its components must serve as an 'ego-bank' to the child, who has in the beginning nothing to invest, from which he must withdraw his total life structure. As conditioning takes place positively and as the child begins to see himself accurately in relationship to his social order, the need for the external structuring may become less and less until the child is able to re-establish himself as a member of the normal school group.

Hyperactive children are multihandicapped children in the truest sense of the word. They present the most complex teaching problem of any in the entire spectrum of exceptional children, and it occurs to me that in the approach which is being suggested here, which has been tried sufficiently to convince this writer and many others of its efficacy, some solution to the education of multihandicapped children may exist. No two hyperactive children are the same in any respect. Neither the degree of distractibility nor the relationship between characteristics of psychopathology is ever identical in these children. In one child the problem may be chiefly visuo-motor; in a second, predominately audio-motor; in a third, hyperkinesis and tactuo-motor. The concept of a *group* of hyperactive children is a figment of someone's imagination, for groups of children with sufficiently homogeneous characteristics to be considered comparable for educational purposes do not exist. Small collections of from six to eight children with relatively similar problems can be organized, but within this social structure the teacher of hyperactive children soon understands that she must constantly deal with six or eight individuals as individuals. It will be many months before she is able to bring them together for even small group activities involving two or three children at one time. These educators are forced by the nature of the children to think in terms of individual needs.

The concept of individualization of instruction and the concept of a teacher meeting the needs of a child are old. In educational history they are first discussed by Froebel, Pestalozzi, and Herbert. They became the banner and cry of the progressive educators of the 1930's. These concepts were fundamental in the thinking of Dewey and practically every great educator of the western world in modern times. But how infrequently do we see them implemented in the classroom? In practical educational situations the concept of meeting the needs of children is nothing more than a hollow cliche. It is an empty symbol of something which should be an aggressive concept.

   With the hyperactive child these concepts must take on immediate meaning. The education of the hyperactive child cannot be successfully consummated unless his individual needs are identified, thoroughly understood, and become so well known by the adults who work with him that they are a constant and vital part of every educational decision which is made on the child's behalf. As a teacher I cannot work successfully with the hyperactive child if all I know is his diagnosis and his intelligence quotient and perhaps his mental age. As a teacher I cannot meet this child's needs if all I possess is a feeling that he like all children should be considered as an individual. I do not know from this which handle to grasp first to meet his needs. I don't know what his needs are. As a teacher, I have the right to expect that the diagnosticians who assess this child will provide me with a detailed description of how this child functions mentally, of what his psychological strengths are and what is the nature of his disabilities. I must know what the length of his attention span is. If I don't, I shall violate his being a dozen times a day by exceeding it. I must know when his attention span begins to increase as a result of the success experiences which I am able to provide for him. If I don't, I shall undersell him educationally. I must know if he dissociates. If I don't, I shall violate him psychologically by not providing him with the visual cues to reduce the impact of his disability. I must know if he reverses field. If I don't, I shall perpetuate his problem by providing him with inappropriate educational materials. I must know if he is a psychologically damaged child, damaged to the extent that he has little or no feeling of personal worth, for if I don't, I shall fail to provide him with those learning experiences which may give him the solidity he needs for a positive self concept to develop.

   Those who work with the hyperactive child—his teachers and his parents for the most part, for they have him for more hours than anyone else —must have information about the child in such minute detail that they can relate the child, his characteristics, and their teaching method and materials so perfectly together that the outcome is logical and can be predicted. The educational material, the education technique, the education setting for the hyperactive child must reflect in a one-to-one relationship the psychopathology and the needs of the child. When this is done it can then truly be said that we have provided an educational milieu for the hyperactive child, and have met his needs.

   This seeming utopia can be achieved. We cannot do it now sufficiently often to be able to serve even a fraction of the children who need it. The status quo too often prevents sound educational programs from being activated. Professional educators are still too comfortable with what they do to try to do it differently. We still teach all children by the manuscript method. Too few administrators understand this problem to permit the too few teachers who are prepared to practise their learning on behalf of these children to do so. College professors to prepare these teachers are almost non-existent today. The situation will change in the years ahead, for the very nature of the children requires that it change. We have seen radical changes in our *understanding* of these children since 1940. There is little question in my mind, but that in a comparable period of time in the future we shall see the understanding translated into action programs and the needs of these children more universally met.

BIBLIOGRAPHY

1. Dolphin, J. E. and Cruickshank, W. M., (1951) Visuo-Motor Perception in Children with Cerebral Palsy. *Quarterly Journal of Child Behavior,* 3, 198.

2. Dolphin, J. E., and Cruickshank, W. M., (1951) "The Figure-Background Relationship in Children with Cerebral Palsy." *J. clin. Psychol.,* 7, 228–231.

3. Dolphin, J. E., and Cruickshank, W. M., (1951) "Pathology of Concept Formation in Children with Cerebral Palsy." *Amer. J. Ment. Def.,* 56, 386–392.

4. Dolphin, J. E. and Cruickshank, W. M., (1952) 'Tactual Motor Perception of Children with Cerebral Palsy.' *Journal of Personality,* 20, 446–471.

5. Cruickshank, W. M., Frances A. Bentzen, Frederick H. Ratzeburg, and Mirian T. Tannhauser, (1961) A Teaching Method for Brain-Injured and Hyperactive Children. Syracuse: Syracuse University Press.

6. Cruickshank, W. M., Harry V. Bice, Norman E. Wallen, and Karen S. Lynch, (1965) Perception and Cerebral Palsy: Studies in Figure Background Relationship. Syracuse University Press, 2nd edition.

7. Cruickshank, W. M. (ed.), (1966) The Teacher of Brain-Injured Children: A Discussion of the Bases for Competency. Syracuse: Syracuse University Press.

8. Cruickshank, W. M. (ed.), (1966) Cerebral Palsy: Its Individual and Community Problems. Syracuse: Syracuse University Press, 2nd edition, with special note to chapter IV, 'Personality Characteristics' (by W. M. Cruickshank and H. V. Bice) and chapter X, 'Educational Planning for the Cerebral Palsied' (by W. M. Cruickshank).

9. Cruickshank, W. M., (1967) 'The Education of the Child with Brain-Injury,' chapter 6 in Education of Exceptional Children and Youth, eds: W. M. Cruickshank and G. O. Johnson, Englewood Cliffs, N. J.: Prentice-Hall, Inc., 2nd revision pp. 238–284.

10. Cruickshank, W. M., (1967) The Brain-Injured Child in Home, School and Community. Syracuse: Syracuse University Press.

BIBLIOGRAPHY, 1946–65

William M. Cruickshank

1. Cruickshank, W. M. "Arithmetic Vocabulary of Mentally Retarded Boys." *Journal of Exceptional Children* 13 (1946): 65–69.

2. _____. "Mental Hygiene Approach to the Handicapped Child." *American Journal of Occupational Therapy* 1 (1947): 215–21.

3. _____. "Qualitative Analysis of Intelligence Test Responses." *Journal of Clinical Psychology* 3 (1947): 381–86.

4. _____. "New York State Planning Conference for the Exceptional." *School and Society* 67 (1948): 13–14.

5. _____ and J. Medve. "Social Relationships of Physically Handicapped Children." *Journal of Exceptional Children* 14 (1948): 100–106.

6. Cruickshank, W. M. "Arithmetic Work Habits of Mentally Retarded Boys." *American Journal of Mental Deficiency* 51 (1948): 318–30.

7. _____ and E. L. Cowen. "Group Therapy with Physically Handicapped Children. I. Report of Study." *Journal of Educational Psychology* 39 (1948): 193–215.

8. _____ and E. L. Cowen. "Group Therapy with Physically Handicapped Children. II. Evaluation." *Journal of Educational Psychology* 39 (1948): 281–97.

9. Cruickshank, W. M. "Arithmetic Ability of Mentally Retarded Children. I. Ability to Differentiate Extraneous Materials from Needed Arithmetical Facts." *Journal of Educational Research* 42 (1948): 161–70.

10. _____. "Arithmetic Ability of Mentally Retarded Children. II. Understanding Arithmetic Processes." *Journal of Educational Research* 42 (1948): 279–88.

11. _____ and E. Sprague. "A Survey of Exceptional Children in Three School Districts of Onondaga County, Including a Study of Exemption Status of Children Reported Not in School." Syracuse University, 1948, 1–51.

12. Cruickshank, W. M. "The Impact of Physical Disability on Social Adjustment." *Journal of Social Issues* 4 (1948): 78-83.

13. _____ and J. E. Dolphin. "A Study of the Emotional Needs of Crippled Children." *Journal of Educational Psychology* 45 (1949): 295-305.

14. _____ and Dolphin. "The Emotional Needs of Crippled and Non-Crippled Children." *Journal of Exceptional Children* 16 (1949): 33-40.

15. _____ and T. J. Qualtere. "The Use of Intelligence Tests with Children of Retarded Mental Development. I. Comparison of 1916 and 1937 Revisions of the Stanford-Binet Intelligence Scale." *American Journal of Mental Deficiency* 54 (1950): 361-69.

16. _____ and T. J. Qualtere. "The Use of Intelligence Tests with Children of Retarded Mental Development. II. Clinical Considerations." *American Journal of Mental Deficiency* 54 (1950): 370-81.

17. Cruickshank, W. M. "Syracuse University Laboratory for the Handicapped." *Journal of Exceptional Children* 16 (1950): 115.

18. _____ and W. D. Peacher. "Special Education for the Epileptic, the Tubercular, and Children with Glandular Disorders." Chapter XII, 49th Yearbook, National Society for the Study of Education. *The Education of Exceptional Children* (1950): 218-36.

19. _____, D. Broida, and C. Izard. "Thematic Apperception Reactions of Crippled Children." *Journal of Clinical Psychology* 6 (1950): 243-48.

20. Cruickshank, W. M. "Growth in Quality of Local Services to Exceptional Children." *Journal of Exceptional Children* 17 (1951): 233-36.

21. _____. "Six Ways to Aid Exceptional Children." *Journal of Education* 134 (1951): 124-26.

22. Dolphin, J. E. and W. M. Cruickshank. "Visuo-Motor Perception of Children with Cerebral Palsy." *The Quarterly Journal of Child Behavior* 3 (1951): 198-209.

23. Dolphin, J. E., and W. M. Cruickshank. "The Figure-Background Relationship in Children with Cerebral Palsy." *Journal of Clinical Psychology* 7 (1951): 228-31.

24. Dolphin, J. E., and W. M. Cruickshank. "Pathology of Concept Formation in Children with Cerebral Palsy." *American Journal of Mental Deficiency* 56 (1951): 386-92.

25. Cruickshank, W. M., and J. E. Dolphin. "The Educational Implications of Psychological Studies of Cerebral Palsied Children." *Exceptional Children* 17 (1951): 3-11.

26. Cruickshank, W. M. "Research in the Education of Children with Retarded Mental Development." *American Journal of Mental Deficiency* 56 (1951): 308-12.

27. _____. "Relation of Physical Disability to Fear and Guilt Feelings." *Child Developent* 22 (1951): 292–98.

28. _____. "Relation of Physical Disability to Fear and Guilt Feelings." *Cerebral Palsy Review* 13 (1952): 9–13, 15.

29. _____. "The Effect of Physical Disability on Personal Aspiration." *The Quarterly Journal of Child Behavior* 3 (1951): 323–33.

30. _____. "Who is the Exceptional Child?" *New York Parent-Teacher* 30 (1952): 14–15.

31. _____. "A Study of the Relation of Physical Disability to Social Adjustment." *American Journal of Occupational Therapy* 6 (1952): 100–109.

32. Dolphin, J. E., and W. M. Cruickshank. "Tactual Motor Perception of Children with Cerebral Palsy." *Journal of Personality* 20 (1952): 466–71.

33. Cruickshank, W. M., and L. M. DiCarlo. "The Role of the University in the Preparation of Personnel for the Education of Children with Impairments of Hearing and Speech." *Exceptional Children* 18 (1952): 168–73; reprinted in *The Newsletter of the Council of Day School Teachers of the Deaf and Hard of Hearing* (January 1952).

34. Cruickshank, W. M. "The Challenge of the Exceptional Child." *Music Educators Journal* 38 (1952): 18–20.

35. _____. "Team Action with Exceptional Children." *Exceptional Children* 18 (1952): 242–44.

36. Smock, C., and W. M. Cruickshank. "Responses of Handicapped and Normal Children to the Rosenzweig P-F Study." *The Quarterly Journal of Child Behavior* 4 (1952): 156–64.

37. Cruickshank, W. M. "The Exceptional Child in Contemporary Education." The J. Richard Street Lecture. Syracuse: Syracuse University Press, 1952; revised, 1957.

38. _____, M. Greenbaum, T. Qualtere, and B. Carruth. "Evaluation of a Modification of the Thematic Apperception Test for Use with Physically Handicapped Children." *Journal of Clinical Psychology* 9 (1953): 40–44.

39. _____ and E. X. Freed. "The Effect of Cardiac Disability on Adjustment to Parents and Family." *Quarterly Journal of Child Behavior* 4 (1952): 299–309.

40. Cruickshank, W. M. "The Multiple Handicapped Cerebral Palsied Child." *Exceptional Children* 20 (1953): 16–22.

41. _____ and E. X. Freed. "The Relation of Cardiac Disease to Feelings of Fear." *The Journal of Pediatrics* 43 (1953): 483–88.

42. Cruickshank, W. M. "New Horizons in the Education of the Handicapped Child." *American Journal of Public Health* 45 (1955): 306–11.

43. _____ and G. M. Raus, eds. *Cerebral Palsy: Its Individual and Community Problems.* Syracuse: Syracuse University Press, 1955.

44. _____, ed. *Cerebral Palsy: Its Individual and Community Problems,* 2nd ed. Syracuse: Syracuse University Press, 1966.

45. _____ and G. M. Raus. "The Problem and Its Scope. In W. M. Cruickshank and G. M. Raus, eds., *Cerebral Palsy: Its Individual and Community Problems.* Syracuse University Press, 1955; 2nd edition, 1966.

46. Cruickshank, W. M., and H. V. Bice. "Evaluation and Intelligence." In *Cerebral Palsy: Its Individual and Community Problems,* edited by W. M. Cruickshank and G. M. Raus. Syracuse: Syracuse University Press, 1955; 2nd ed., 1966.

47. Cruickshank, W. M., and H. V. Bice. "Personality Characteristics." In *Cerebral Palsy: Its Individual and Community Problems,* edited by W. M. Cruickshank and G. M. Raus. Syracuse: Syracuse University Press, 1955; 2nd ed., 1966.

48. Cruickshank, W. M. "Educational Planning." In *Cerebral Palsy: Its Individual and Community Problems,* edited by W. M. Cruickshank and G. M. Raus. Syracuse: Syracuse University Press, 1955: 2nd ed., 1966.

49. Cruickshank, W. M., and N. G. Haring. "Adjustment of Physically Handicapped Adolescent Youth." *Exceptional Children* 21 (1955): 282–88.

50. Cruickshank, W. M., ed. *Psychology of Exceptional Children and Youth.* Englewood Cliffs, N.J.: Prentice-Hall, 1955. 2nd rev. ed., 1963; 3rd rev. ed. 1971; 4th rev. ed., 1980. *Psicologia de los ninos y jovenes marginales.* Spanish ed. of *Psychology of Exceptional Children and Youth,* trans. by Alfonso Alvarez Villar. Madrid: Editorial Prentice-Hall International, 1973.

51. _____. "Psychological Considerations with Crippled Children." In *Psychology of Exceptional Children and Youth,* edited by W. M. Cruickshank. Englewood Cliffs, N.J.: Prentice-Hall, 1955.

52. _____ and M. C. Shaw. "The Use of the Bender Gestalt Test with Epileptic Children." *Journal of Clinical Psychology* 12 (1956): 192–93.

53. Cruickshank, W. M., "Frontiers in the Education of Exceptional Children in Secondary School." In Syracuse University School of Education, *Frontiers of secondary education I.* Syracuse: Syracuse University Press, 1956.

54. Shaw, M. C., and W. M. Cruickshank. "The Use of the Marbleboard Test to Measure Psychopathology in Epileptics." *American Journal of Mental Deficiency* 60 (1956): 813–17.

55. Cruickshank, W. M. "Preplanning for the Severely Retarded Child." *American Journal of Mental Deficiency* 60 (1956): 3–9.

56. _____. "Total Planning to Meet the Needs of the Handicapped." *Proceedings of the Fifth Year of Nemours Foundation Conferences.* Richmond, Va.: Virginia State Department of Health, 1956.

57. _____. Review of *Studies of Reading and Arithmetic in Mentally Retarded Boys.* Monographs of the Society for Research in Child Development 19 no. 1 (Serial No. 58), 1954. *Exceptional Children* 23 (1956): 120–22.

58. _____. Review of *Special Education for the Exceptional,* edited by M. E. Frampton and E. D. Gall (Boston: Porter Sargent, 1955). *Exceptional Children* 22 (1956): 201, 208, 210.

59. _____; T. E. Newland; and M. R. Barnett. "Some Observations on the Policy Statement of the American Association of Instructors of the Blind." *Exceptional Children* 23 (1957): 320–30.

60. Cruickshank, W. M., and N. G. Haring. *Assistants for Teachers of Exceptional Children: A Demonstration.* Syracuse: Syracuse University Press, 1957.

61. Cruickshank, W. M.; H. V. Bice; and N. E. Wallen. *Perception and Cerebral Palsy: A Study of the Figure-Background Relationship.* Syracuse: Syracuse University Press, 1957.

62. Cruickshank, W. M.; H. V. Bice; N. E. Wallen; and K. S. Lynch. *Perception and Cerebral Palsy: A Study of the Figure-Background Relationship,* 2nd ed. Syracuse: Syracuse University Press, 1965.

63. Cruickshank, W. M. "Services in Special Education." *Education* 77 (1957): 460–63.

64. _____, and M. C. Shaw. "The Rorschach Performance of Epileptic Children. *Journal of Consulting Psychology* 21 (1957): 422–24.

65. Cruickshank, W. M., and K. A. Blake. *A Comparative Study of the Performance of Mentally Handicapped and Intellectually Normal Boys on Selected Tasks Involving Learning and Transfer.* Syracuse: Syracuse University Research Institute, Office of Research in Special Education and Rehabilitation, 1957.

66. Cruickshank, W. M. *Two Stars Take Their Place: A Collection of Poems.* Syracuse: Privately printed, 1957.

67. _____; N. G. Haring; and G. G. Stern. *Attitudes of Educators toward Exceptional Children.* Special Education and Rehabilitation Research Monograph Series No. 3. Syracuse: Syracuse University Press, 1958.

68. Cruickshank, W. M., and G. O. Johnson, eds. *Education of Exceptional Children and Youth.* Englewood Cliffs, N.J.: Prentice-Hall, 1958; 2nd rev. ed., 1966; 3rd rev. ed., 1975.

   A educacao da crianca e do joven excepcional. Portuguese ed. in two volumes of *Education of Exceptional Children and Youth.* Vol. 1 trans. by L. Villandro (1974); Vol. 2 trans. by J. A. Cunha. Englewood Cliffs, N.J.: Prentice-Hall International (1975).

69. Cruickshank, W. M. "The Development of the Principle of Special Education." In *Education of Exceptional Children and Youth,* edited by W. M. Cruickshank and G. O. Johnson. Englewood Cliffs, N.J.: Prentice-Hall, 1958; 2nd rev. ed., 1966; 3rd rev. ed., 1975; Portuguese trans., 1974, 1975.

70. _____. "Current Educational Practices with Exceptional Children." In *Education of Exceptional Children and Youth,* edited by W. M. Cruickshank and G. O. Johnson. Englewood Cliffs, N.J.: Prentice-Hall, 1958; 2nd rev. ed., 1966; 3rd rev. ed., 1975; Portuguese trans., 1974, 1975.

71. Cruickshank, W. M. "Exceptional Children in the Elementary Secondary School. In *Education of Exceptional Children and Youth,* edited by W. M. Cruickshank and G. O. Johnson. Englewood Cliffs, N.J.: Prentice-Hall, 1958; 2nd rev. ed., 1966; 3rd rev. ed., 1975; Portuguese trans., 1974, 1975.

72. _____. "The Education of the Child with Brain Injury." In *Education of Exceptional Children and Youth,* edited by W. M. Cruickshank and G. O. Johnson. Englewood Cliffs, N.J.: Prentice-Hall, 1958; 2nd rev. ed., 1966; 3rd rev. ed., 1975; Portuguese trans., 1974, 1975.

73. _____. "Realistic Educational Programs for Most Cerebral Palsy Children." *The Crippled Child* 37 (1958): 6–7, 22.

74. Goldberg, I. I., and W. M. Cruickshank. "The Trainable but Non-Educable: Whose Responsibility?" *National Educational Association Journal* 47 (1958): 622–23.

75. Cruickshank, W. M., and M. J. Trippe. *Services to Blind Children in New York State.* Syracuse: Syracuse University Press, 1959.

76. Cruickshank, W. M. "Education for All Children in a Democracy." *Rhode Island College Journal* 1 (1969): 43–49.

77. _____. "The Mentally Retarded Child in School." In *Freeing capacity to learn.* Washington, D.C.: Association for Supervision and Curriculum Development, 1960.

78. _____. "The Implications for Education of Psychopathology in Children with Cerebral Palsy." In *The Modern Educational Treatment of Deafness,* edited by A. Ewing. Manchester, England: Manchester University Press, 1960.

79. Cruickshank, W. M.; F. Bentzen; F. Ratzeberg; and M. Tannhauser. *A Teaching Method for Brain-Injured and Hyperactive Children: A Demonstration-Pilot Study.* Prepared with the assistance of U.S. Office of Education, Cooperative Research Branch, Contract No. SAE-6415. Syracuse: Syracuse University Press, 1961. Pratt Library Award for Medical Writing, 1962.

80. "Las Demandas Educativos del Ninos Excepcional." *Nueva Educacion* 30 (1962): 5–10 (published in Peru).

81. "The Multiply-Handicapped Child and Courageous Action." *The International Journal for the Education of the Blind* 13 (1964): 65–75. Also in J. Wolf and R. Anderson, eds., *The Multiply Handicapped Child.* Springfield, Ill.: Charles C. Thomas, 1969.

CONTENTS OF VOLUME 2

CONCEPTS IN SPECIAL EDUCATION

Selected Writings, Volume 1

was composed in 10-point Compugraphic Times Roman and leaded two points
by Metricomp Studios;
with display type in Foundry Lydian and Lydian Cursive by J. M. Bundscho, Inc.;
printed by sheet-fed offset on 50-pound acid-free Warren Antique Cream paper,
Smyth-sewn and bound over 80-point binder's boards in Columbia Bayside Linen,
by Maple-Vail Book Manufacturing Group, Inc.;
and published by

SYRACUSE UNIVERSITY PRESS
Syracuse, New York 13210